Editions SR / 10

EDITIONS SR

Volume 10

Prometheus Rebound

The Irony of Atheism

Joseph C. McLelland

Published for the Canadian Corporation for Studies in
Religion/Corporation Canadienne des Sciences Religieuses
by Wilfrid Laurier University Press

1988

Canadian Cataloguing in Publication Data

McLelland, Joseph C. (Joseph Cumming), 1925-
  Prometheus rebound : the irony of atheism

(Editions SR ; 10)
Includes bibliographical references and index.
ISBN 0-88920-974-X

1. Atheism – History. 2. Theism – History.
3. Death of God theology. I. Canadian Corporation
for Studies in Religion. II. Title. III. Series.

BL2747.3.M35 1988   211'.8   C88-094470-6

88 89 90 91 4 3 2 1

Prometheus Rebound: The Irony of Atheism has been produced from a manuscript supplied in camera-ready form by the author.

Cover design by Michael Baldwin, MSIAD

Order from:
Wilfrid Laurier University Press
Wilfrid Laurier University
Waterloo, Ontario, Canada   N2L 3C5

Prometheus Bound (Rubens, 1611-12)

In Memoriam

WALTER W. BRYDEN

Knox College, Toronto

GERALD B. PHELAN

Pontifical Institute of
Mediaeval Studies, Toronto

*two masters of the narrow way
between belief and unbelief*

Contents

PART II
UNBINDING PROMETHEUS

PART III
END OF ENLIGHTENMENT

PART IV
THE RETURN OF IDOLS

Acknowledgments

This book has been published with the help of a grant from the Canadian Federation for the Humanities, using funds provided by the Social Sciences and Humanities Research Council of Canada.

Rubens's *Prometheus Bound* is reproduced on the Frontispiece courtesy of the Philadelphia Museum of Art: Wilstach Collection (W'50-3-1). Rubens himself noted: "Original by my hand, and the Eagle done by Frans Snyders. Nine feet high by eight feet wide."

Preface

The central subject of philosophy of religion is belief and unbelief, or theism and antitheism, focused for me by early teachers in a dialectical manner, as the dedication suggests. The privilege of teaching graduate students is particularly relevant to this study. Over the years graduate seminars have heard and discussed the material, while my doctoral students have provided stimulation by their own research in related topics. The substance of the work formed the basis of special lectureships, including St. Andrew's College, Saskatoon, the Wilson-Nichols Lectures at Austin College, Sherman, Texas, and Staley Lectures at Rollins College, Winter Park, Florida.

Thanks are due for sponsorship of this book to the Canadian Corporation for the Study of Religion and to the Social Sciences and Humanities Research Council of Canada. The latter also supported a sabbatical when the first draft was prepared. My colleagues deserve gratitude for providing a milieu conducive to research and dialogue, while my wife Audrey is a constant support for my writing endeavours. Three assistants have prepared the work on word-processors: Darlene Fowler for the initial draft, Zayn Kassam for extensive revision, and Samieun Khan for the camera-ready copy. Miss Khan selected the Waterloo Script program, adapted from the University of Waterloo, version 88.1. The font type is "Times," with appropriate point sizes for reduction.

Such an ambitious work necessitates many judgments of selection and interpretation; I trust these are not overly extreme or irritating to the reader. Otherwise the point of the book – to assist in others' reflection on the topic – will be blunted. I hope my readers may come, as I have, to admire Prometheus and his followers by this exploration.

Faced as we are with the complex array of views and data that constitute the contemporary intellectual stage, it may seem strange to recall us to an ancient "scene" set by a playwright whose burden was the problem of evil and the quest for a just society. The story of how Prometheus became archetype of the postulatory atheism so influential for modern thought is not only instructive but intriguing. Both theism and atheism, so it seems to me, are lacking in knowledge of their roots at this point. The present study attempts to outline a major objection to classical theism, one that demands not just consideration but appropriate response. I offer the present work as a small contribution to the awareness and critique required for revision of both theism and antitheism today.

The introductory typology may be left aside by those less inter-
ested in questions of method and classification. In turn, the historical survey may prove of unequal value for readers. For my own
part, the typology represents the way into the subject that took shape
over many years of attention to the myth and its career in Western
thought. The ancient tale cast in dramatic form continues to play our
neighbourhood: that is my thesis.

Montreal, 1988   *Joseph C. McLelland*

INTRODUCTION:
TYPES OF ATHEISM

Introduction: Types of Atheism

The subject of atheism opens on questions of definition. Its literal meaning of godless, or disbelief in the existence of gods or God, misses the complexity and dynamism of this phenomenon. It remains negative, without describing the kind of belief being rejected; one would require a typology of theism to classify the corresponding negations. Such opposition constitutes the theme of our study, as in the famous statement of Goethe: "The real, the deepest, the sole theme of the world and of history, to which all other themes are subordinate, remains the conflict of belief and unbelief."

Typologies fulfil the need for perspective, for a credible categorial scheme. Our own concern with types involves a thesis: that among various kinds of atheism, the dominant modern form is best understood as wilful rebellion on behalf of human freedom. And further, that the figure of Prometheus functions on its behalf as a striking archetype of autonomy. Freedom and independence have gone together since classical times – Pericles noted that "happiness depends on being free, and freedom depends on being courageous." The Platonic ideal of *autarkeia* is on view, that self-reliance that stems from the courage to move beyond mere opinion to rational knowledge. If for Plato this involved The Good or God, modern rationalism makes do with human autonomous reason.[1]

With roots reaching back to Greek mythology, Prometheanism is by definition a substitutionary humanism. That is, it does not deny the existence of God so much as transfer to humanity the attributes traditionally predicated of deity by classical theism. Thus the figure of Prometheus is paradigmatic – it embodies that autonomy of will that is the true archetypical power behind the symbols of rebellion and freedom. In this sense both Prometheus and Zeus are themselves ektypes, since they share the common belief in absolute will that locks them in immortal combat. Either Zeus or Prometheus, but not both: that is the root of the issue.

As a reaction to Christian classical theism, Prometheanism represents "classical atheism." For both share the same definition of

---

"God," both participate in a common metaphor of reality. Noting this phenomenon, Richard Kroner concludes that whereas Greek thought was theological but not Christian, "modern, and especially Kantian, thought, though *not theological*, nevertheless is essentially *Christian*."[2] Thus the "irony" of atheism involves its properly theological dimension, as the rejection of God terminates in an alter Ego.

The irony proceeds even further: the substitution of human for divine regains a god but loses that humanity that formerly coexisted with him in contest or partnership. Thus the new Humanity is but old Divinity writ small. It suffers from the same faults as theology in predicating qualities of its Subject. As a reactionary antitheism it shares the difficulties of projection. In its "rebound" it loses momentum and so opens the way for the return of idols.

The related question of agnosticism is always difficult. Its meaning seems clear as a "suspension of judgment," yet this term, coined in 1869 by T.H. Huxley, suffers by analysis. Paul Edwards argues that it is self-defeating. While agnosticism agrees with fideism that the existence of God cannot be proved by argument, it draws a somewhat arbitrary line between what can be known and what cannot. Why should lack of evidence lead merely to suspension of judgment rather than to disbelief? The atheist position seems logically superior, granted the premise that there is no evidence for the existence of God.[3] As we shall see in examining the classical era, the epistemological problem of grounds for certainty of knowledge has always posed difficulties for sceptics as well as believers. If belief is a mean between scepticism and credulity, to use Aristotelian categories, then agnosticism fails to follow the logic of the sceptical position; it lacks the courage of the extreme. On the other hand, it mounts a significant rebuttal of credulity. In the hot debates of nineteenth-century England, for instance, Leslie Stephen remarked of the "religious agnosticism" of the Hamilton-Mansel-Spencer type, "Call your doubts mysteries and they won't disturb you any longer."[4]

Certain attitudes informing types of atheism may be noted without resorting to faculty psychology. Thus the traditional case against theism founded on the so-called problem of evil shows the weight of emotional protest. It is notorious, for instance, that Ivan Karamazov did not deny God's existence while returning his "entrance ticket." Such protest against ostensible injustice on the part of God often leads to an "ethical atheism" committed to noble causes.[5] Another type of protest is more intellectual, associated today with logical positivism. This is the denial of divine existence on the ground that propositions of which the subject is "God" make no logical sense. Although the axioms for such logic are disputable, particularly the criterion of falsifiability, a sort of "natural atheology" is produced, in Alvin Plantinga's terms. This is usually linked with the protest against evil, so that theodicy must include not only a justification of God but of "God-talk" as well.[6] Bertrand Russell is typical: he rejects the idea of God as "a conception derived from the ancient Oriental despotisms . . . quite unworthy of free men." The basis of religion is fear; though our doom is certain, on this "long march through the night" he calls us to stoic fatalism. One should resist the blind and unconscious forces of this dark cosmos like "a weary but unyielding Atlas."[7] With Atlas, brother of Prometheus, we are in the realm of titanic will.

Certain types of atheism, essentially negative in themselves, may prove both therapeutic on behalf of theism and even positive in their ethical thrust. Prometheanism, however, offers contrast in its particular kind of attack, what Max Scheler called "postulatory atheism."[8] It is an aggressive, even militant type of world-view. As we shall suggest, analysis of its chief protagonists indicates lines to other kinds of antitheism, such as the strategic positivism of modern science or the theogony that informs Marxism. There is also a place for a more psychological approach, to uncover what Ignace Lepp terms "neurotic atheism." He refers to the Prometheus of Marx: "We can understand nothing about the psychology of modern atheism if we forget that its origin lies in man's will." Gabriel Marcel has developed this idea with Sartre in mind: for "authentic philosophical atheism," not only must it be the case that "God is not" but also "that He cannot be." André Malraux has made the point well: "God is dead, *and so* man is born." Marcel also notes that Promethean atheism challenges us to a "rigorous critique" of "the idea of the 'obstacle God' from whom atheistic humanism seeks to liberate man."[9]

It is a commonplace to say that modern philosophy – in principle from Descartes and in practice from Kant – is essentially philosophy of science. The emergence of typically modern science in the seventeenth century entailed a profound shift in epistemology. Theory of knowledge tended to mean a turn to the knowing subject, consistent only with itself and its mastery over its objects: autonomous reason. What seems equally clear, however, is the corollary that such modality of knowing puts the weight on the human will. Modern philosophy is thus philosophy of will – from Kant to Ricoeur, for instance. Classical philosophy understood the will to be a difficult horse for reason to bridle and direct (e.g., Plato's *Phaedrus* 246ff); classical theism agreed that it must be essentially related to rationality; but now it is becoming the very seat of autonomy. We shall suggest that the Cartesian reduction of the cogito and the Kantian confidence in practical reason offer a fateful new theoretical possibility to modernity: the postulate of atheism. This implies a prior concept of a will-in-itself, the construct of mentalist individualism. Such focus on volition, in relative isolation from both cognition and conation, fails the test of "axiological validation" (J.N. Findlay). Thus the naturalistic theory of value of C.I. Lewis and Stephen Pepper must continue to struggle with Kant's problematic, the relation between (aesthetic) judgment and moral evaluation. Brian O'Shaughnessy's analysis of "natural theories of philosophical thought about the will" offers severe criticism of all volitionism and voluntarism deriving from materialist or dualist ideas of desire as a kind of natural force. His own "dual aspect theory" of bodily action attempts to expose the logical and bodily "limits" of willing. His work recalls Iris Murdoch's distinction between heroes "existential" and "mystical." The former is "the new version of the romantic man, the man of power, abandoned by God . . . strong, self-reliant and uncrushable." It embodies "freedom, thought of as will-power." The latter is "the new version of the man of faith, believing in goodness without religious guarantee . . . possessed of genuine intuitions of an authoritative good." Here are hints of the trouble that an uncritical idea of the will attracts by its Cartesian assumption about the ego.[10]

Some kinds of atheism or antitheism are ancillary to our model of wilfulness. Our modern scientific-technological age involves what has been described as "methodological atheism" or "un positivisme de méthode," so that science may be termed "the Christian form of godlessness." Such a necessary method or strategy may be mistaken for substance, for the necessity of nontranscendence in a scientific age. But neither science nor philosophy of science entails materialism. Michael Polanyi has argued that to opt for a "reductive program" – he has Laplace in mind – is to accept a "deceptive substitution" resulting in illusory knowledge: ignorance.[11]

Related to the category-mistake of thinking that science implies materialism is that of seeing secularism as the logical end of secularization. For the historical process documented by Gogarten and others is ethically neutral, even though used by many as a stepping-stone to a secularized world-view. Indeed, some analysts challenge the very notion that secularism is so widespread or influential a force in modern society, including its related notion of the world come of age (*die mündige Welt*), which continues the Enlightenment notion of maturity. This critique of the conventional wisdom of sociology, for instance, argues that the facts imply rather the "persistence of religion," or "unsecular man."[12] Thus the data of our "scientific" age are patient of more than one interpretation. Some sociologists analyze the same data in religious terms: Robert Bellah's category of "civil religion," for example. Indeed, North American scholars are now remarking the rapid growth of "new religions," not to mention contemporary credulity in regard to such phenomena as astrology and the occult. Charles Campbell calls for a "sociology of irreligion" to map the complex terrain and suggests that the range of phenomena from religion to unreligion is probably "closer to a continuum than a dichotomy."[13]

Against such familiar ways of viewing the secular, however, there stands a more profound dichotomy yet: that between the sacred and the profane. For the secular may be neutral in ethical and religious terms, but what counts for a religious world-view is not neutrality but commitment, either for or against the Holy. There may be negative as well as positive manifestations of such power, or sacred and profane ways of being; the neutral, however, is merely superficial. It is this claim that lies behind the idea that no one is *atheos* in the strict sense; one serves either God or idols. Such a functional view is seen in Luther, for whom God is whatever claims our final allegiance. It is reflected in Paul Tillich's category of "ultimate concern," a universal category that replaces godlessness by alienation. No one can escape the dimension of depth, the symbols of transcendence. Despite his qualifications about the negative print, Tillich's idea, like Karl Rahner's category of "anonymous Christian," implies what might be called the illusion of atheism. Although this move safeguards the ontological relatedness of divine and human, it subverts the traditional role of the atheist as authentic denier of divine reality.[14]

One characteristic of modern atheism appears unique when compared with former ages and is taken as a sign of its growing dominance, namely its extension. It is difficult to judge either quality or quantity of faith in former ages. If past belief appears the greater, history suggests the presence of more than enough practical atheists to qualify any theory that mistakes official religion for faith. For example, Matthew Arnold's "Dover Beach" is a notorious example of the romanticizing of medieval Christendom: "The Sea of Faith / Was once, too, at the full." But doing theology in this mode, as Nicholas Lash has noted, has its own ambiguities.[15] It is likely that theocratic or ontocratic societies were little different from the modern secular state in practical terms. Even Jewish prophets mounted a serious critique of their own society. Well aware of the bad faith of nominal believers, they saw things as a simple opposition between sacred and profane modes of being, in both worship and morality.

Wilfred Cantwell Smith has proposed a bold and odd thesis that it is a modern "heresy," shared by insiders and outsiders both, that "believing is religiously significant." That is, both religious and antireligious thinkers hold that "believing is what religious people primarily do;" Robert Bellah accuses sociologists in particular of such an "objectivist fallacy."[16] If this be true, if "faith" is so distinct from belief that it demands analysis in other terms than a/theism, then the unhappy irony outlined below is largely the result of a fundamental error in apprehending the reality denoted "religion;" and even "God." For if the primary data are not things believed, objects of our intellectual assent, how is the philosopher of religion – or sociologist, psychologist, even theologian – to proceed?

Smith's radical thesis may be supported by the witness of the neglected tradition of mystical theology. Masters of the Way contrasted mere *scientia* with that *sapientia* that describes knowledge of God, and posited suffering as necessary to that knowledge: *divina patior*. Only the ascetic way of life allows higher knowledge: a "doing" of the truth. But our Western philosophical tradition turned faith into mere believing, and by developing a congruent theism of rational postulates (the *ens necessarium*) made room for its logical contrary, an atheism of mental constructs. The particular irony here is that what is lost in such mentalism is the very rationality of the knowledge of God. What used to be called the "science of God" has become, in too many cases, an apologia for the irrational. Smith's point seems well taken, that we have seen a "steady and strong movement away from belief's connotation of truth." Since this movement occurred in the very period – roughly since Enlightenment – we emphasize in our present study, Smith's contribution to our subject is far greater than this brief reference suggests.

Another critique of theism may be mentioned in this context. Feminist scholars suggest that traditional theology (like all institutional pursuits) has been male dominated and therefore biased or truncated. A chief voice for this position, herself a striking crafter of words, is that of Mary Daly. (If women are wordspinners, men are wordsmiths, a very Promethean role.) For instance, she has denounced the "blatant misogynism" of the theologians of classical theism on the ground that they are guilty of "the androcentrism of God-language." She feels an imperative to dethrone the "false deities" of this tradition. Her remedy is "the becoming of women," which she regards as "potentially a new and very different *way of eminence.*" Now the (patristic!) tradition of triplex via, with its way of eminence as the appropriate modality of transcendence, might be considered self-critical enough to correct any chauvinism and exclusivism, despite feminist axioms. Notwithstanding, Daly's thesis that "God" represents "the necrophilia of patriarchy" must be attended to, as an aid in our analysis of both theism and antitheism, the Zeus of the one and his partner the Prometheus of the other.[17] In one sense our thesis does concern male chauvinism. For we claim that Prometheanism is a theogony – the new god born of rebellion, with autonomous will as midwife and instrumental reason as nurse, is Man.

One scholar calls for a shift in the very grounds of debate. Antony Flew would opt for what he calls "the presumption of atheism" as a more adequate preliminary axiom. He has in mind a legal context, in which the burden of proof rests on the positive: *Ei incumbit probatio qui dicit, non qui negat.* On the analogy of the presumption of innocence in English law, he promotes Hume's insistence that we must take the universe on its own terms, a version of Stratonician atheism, or "mitigated, consequent scepticism" in Hume's definition. But this presumption is more like begging the question. Both parties dispute the interpretation of reality, so that a polarity of positive and negative is impossible. They are arguing the definition of ultimacy, whether theist or antitheist, how to "name the whirlwind." To assign privileged status to a hypothesis that disclaims God-talk is a false presumption. In a recent essay, Flew proposes a more nuanced meaning, in which "atheist" maintains a neutral rather than a negative sense (the alpha privative) as in "amoral" or "asymmetrical." He introduces two labels, that of "positive atheist" for the positive asserter of the nonexistence of God, and "negative atheist" for "someone who is, simply, just not a theist."[18]

More helpful is analysis of the structure of atheism with special reference to its nature as "closed" or "open." Cornelio Fabro's exhaustive work should be noted in this respect, as well as that of other Catholic scholars such as Henri de Lubac and Etienne Gilson. Martin Marty acknowledges the pluralism of our time, also distinguishing open from closed systems, whether of belief or unbelief. A system whose "integralism" is challenged may simply reinforce its privatism, as with the *integristas* of Franco-Spanish Catholicism on the one hand, or the integral atheism of Jean-Paul Sartre on the other. As we shall see in relation to the Marxist-Christian dialogue, two systems may prove open enough, even if they constitute revisionist forms of theistic or antitheistic positions, to engage in fruitful dialogue, though at risk. In this situation, both systems will be conscious of themselves as born of radical freedom. Placing Marxism in this context of systemic varieties will prove more fruitful than taking it as a form of religion, attractive as this may be.[19]

While those who attempt typologies of atheism opt for structural analysis which includes Marxism, revisionist Marxists themselves make distinctions within it. Vitězslav Gardavsky, for one, rejects two forms of outmoded atheism, Enlightenment antitheism, which turns to irrational cynicism, and the optimistic atheism of early Marxism. He notes five categories of the phenomenon: practical, conformist, anticlerical-antitheist, abstract humanist, and Marxist. His countryman Milan Machoveč agrees, noting that some forms of atheism are "much below the level of religion." A superior type is the "critical atheism" that in fact serves Christian theology – even Marx is thus "a theologian *honoris causa* in the history of theology." As to developed Marxist atheism, he insists that it does not promote a doctrine of the nonexistence of God; rather, "we doubt all these dogmas."[20]

A related question concerns the thorny problem of how to categorize Buddhism. Is this properly "religion"? It is usual to acknowledge non-theistic capabilities in the religions of India, developing into a distinct type of no-soul and nondivine ontology. Whether *atheism* is the right term for such an a-theism remains problematic, inasmuch as categories such as sunyatta and nirvana appear ambiguous to discursive thought. But there are scholars – R.H.L. Slater and Wilfred C. Smith, for example – who argue that while the Buddha and early Buddhism were non-theist, not only is developed Buddhism theistic for many but even the original Dharma may be related positively to theism.[21] A further question is posed by mysticism, at least in its abstract form. Do ecstatic or paranormal experiences constitute evidence for or against the existence of God? Is the "oceanic feeling" of certain mystics akin to the Buddhist experience, or can it be positively joined with more concrete forms of mysticism? These familiar questions were pushed boldly by Karl Barth's description of mysticism as "esoteric atheism." No doubt he had in mind chiefly the abstract or monistic type of mysticism, in relation to the Christian form of theism. Nevertheless, he sharpens the question posed by Theravada Buddhism, a favourite test case. Walter Stace observes that "Atheism is not as such, I believe, inconsistent with introvertive mystical experience." And W.C. Smith reminds us that some Sufi mystics meditate on the "atheism" implied in the first part of the Muslim creed, "There is no God (but God)."[22]

Both belief and unbelief reach conclusions that differ, finally and fundamentally, about the nature and role of reason. It is not the case that one side is rational and the other is not. John Courtney Murray has stated: "Only in virtue of an original act of freedom, the will to atheism as a project, could the atheistic conclusion have appeared. The decision was to make a separation where the tradition had made only a distinction – between faith and reason."[23] Such theological appreciation and critique of atheism should be mentioned as particularly significant for our work. Alisdair MacIntyre and Paul Ricoeur attempted to address the subject with better questions, for as MacIntyre observed, "the God in whom the nineteenth and early twentieth centuries came to disbelieve had been invented only in the seventeenth century." Recognition of this historical variable is noted also by Rudolf Bultmann, Paul Holmer and Johann Figl.[24] This recalls what we might term the "logical parentage" of atheism – the logical Mother's matrix or context providing the possibility of atheism, and the occasion or heuristic drive of the logical Father. The former would include the ambiguity of transcendental presence, the process of secularization; the latter, the dynamics of emergent rationalism and the thrust of postulatory atheism, particularly in Promethean form.

Vatican II produced a text and established a structure in explicit relation to atheism and atheists. The text is *Pastoral Constitution on the Church in the Modern World* (1965), and the structure is the Secretariat for Non-believers. Together they show a new face to the Church of Rome, concerned to make the understanding of atheism and its causes a priority in its new agenda of dialogue. The story of the debates at the Council and the disputed passage of the text has been told and its implications discussed thoroughly. Older concepts of unbelief as merely aberrant or idiosyncratic are being replaced by recognition that unbelief is "a central question of theology itself."[25] The official constitution approaches the subject by distinguishing varieties of atheism, including "an exaggerated idea of man" making this type "more prone, it would seem, to affirm man than to deny God." The more systematic form of modern atheism "so insists on man's desire for autonomy as to object to any dependence on God at all." Both humanist and Marxist ideologies participate in such an understanding of freedom. Thus the theological treatment of atheism today, by both Protestants and Catholics, agrees in locating its leading qualities in autonomy of will and reliance on human power alone.

A final introductory item concerns method or starting-point. Wolfhart Pannenberg, for instance, notes that our modern situation is characterized by "a new atheistic metaphysics" which "is evidently the given premise on which even the question of God is being debated today." He has developed anthropological prolegomena from the idea of dependence to that of freedom. The "structure of human existence" offers data such as "openness to the world" from which to argue toward the existence of God.[26]

Eberhard Jüngel takes a different tack. He considers the new axiom of modernity to be that we "no longer dare to think God." Both atheism and theology "stand equally overshadowed by the dark clouds of the unthinkability of God." He therefore attempts to clear the ground by asserting the "worldly nonnecessity" of God. This formulation breaks with images of God as absolute Lord, as Zeus. It allows categories of grace and love to determine the doctrine of God itself, in essentials. And once God is grasped as not necessary, he can be understood as "more than necessary."[27]

Such debating positions as the ultimate meaning of human being, and the kind of necessity and freedom attributable to human and divine willing, introduce our subject. The human journey constitutes a dramatic encounter of rival and therefore alien wills. This is the burden of our thesis.

The drama – to pursue the metaphor – opens on a stage in ancient Greece. Let it be Athens, at the time of the Dionysian rites. We are seated in the great amphitheatre on the Acropolis slope, awaiting a tragedy by Aeschylus, in the archetypal trilogy of the *Prometheia*. As the smoke from the incense clears, we behold a desolate landscape of "crag-capt rocks" – "the world's end" indeed. Three figures, robed and masked, slowly cross the stage, leading a fourth with chains of iron. Might and Force represent the power of Zeus, while their reluctant ally Hephaistos obeys the divine decree; their captive Prometheus is the play's protagonist. The *Prometheus Bound* is a play of ideas, a "pure ideolyrical drama."[28] Tyranny and freedom, autarchy and rebellion begin their contest. Or: heteronomy and autonomy, the *agōn* of a/theism.

PART I

THE CLASSICAL DILEMMA

1

Loaded Questions: Zeus or Prometheus? God or Freedom?

Prometheus is the classical symbol of rebellion against tyranny. The ancient myth was a powerful tale of Titanic revolt: the theft of fire and the gift of the sacrificial meal; the power and cost of knowledge: suffering and redemption. It was recounted and expanded by poets from Aeschylus to Goethe; it has become the inspiration of dissenters from Voltaire to Sartre. Among this latter group it stands for rejection of the divine will, a Promethean vocation summoning modernity to atheism. In this history a profound shift has taken place. For the classical age the myth was a hypothesis to be tested: *if* the divine takes the form of Zeus, *should* there not be a Prometheus to respond on our behalf? But today it has become a statement of fact: *since* the divine is by definition Tyrant, *therefore* we must choose Promethean rebellion for ourselves.

Gods for All Seasons

The myths and legends of the classical age, particularly those of ancient Greece, mean many things. At school we may have scorned those absurd genealogies while delighting in the earthy tales of cohabitation between gods and mortals. The renewed interest in myth in modern times takes them seriously as symbols of the human condition, our perennial dealings with a mysterious environment. Social scientists explore them through psychological or sociological categories, such as the Oedipus complex of Freud. Even Karl Marx

---

Notes to Chapter 1 appear on page 302.

summed up his developing world-view by promoting Prometheus as chief in philosophy's calendar of saints.

For the student of religion, the gods reflect a reality not simply reducible to terms and categories of school lore or of apparently sophisticated "social sciences." The myth of Prometheus is typical of a profound and enduring theme that gathers to itself the most vital and pressing of human questions. The fact that it has been the happy burden of poets and philosophers and politicians adds weight to our thesis that it is a fitting story about which to weave the peculiar and particular tale of modern atheism.

Flowing from that ancient oral and literary tradition concerning the gods, and especially the case of *Prometheus vs Zeus*, several points are made that prove crucial in investigating atheism. One is that this Titan is a figure of strength and will, raising his protest against authority. He is the prototype of rebel. Another theme concerns the significance of the fire that he stole on our behalf: agent of warmth, of cooking, of ironworking. Thus both culture (the cooked is superior to the raw) and technology (the smiths, the engineers) stem from his gift. Other themes are the creation and temptation of the human race, the stories of Epimetheus and Pandora, the suffering sacrifice of Prometheus himself, his deliverance from Hades through the substitutionary sacrifice of Cheiron, and his gnostic power over Zeus because of the secret that he refused to tell. The blend of such rich themes suggests the sort of power at work in the development of modern atheism.

Zeus was always high and mighty – sky-god or solar deity. His name is linked to the Sanskrit *dyaus* and the Indo-European *djeus*, his symbols are thunder and lightning.[1] Residing in the upper air, he was worshipped on many a hill and crag, until at last Mount Olympus served as official residence for him and his pantheon of gods and goddesses. From Hesiod come the earliest tales, embellished, refined and developed by others, notably Aeschylus. "Let no god, let no goddess attempt to curb my will" is one of the earliest sayings attributed to this young upstart destined to rule as tyrant over divine and human lesser powers. The genealogy of the gods – what Hesiod terms "theogony" – shows how Zeus sprang from Kronos and Rheia, the youngest and only child to be saved from that Titan's savagery. In order to prevent the doom awaiting him from his offspring, he swallowed each newborn infant, until his wife tricked him and saved Zeus. Kronos knew the game, of course, for had he not overthrown his own father? So Zeus becomes the young rebel leading in revolt against that very Kronos who once defied Uranos.

Now beyond Uranos lies only the void, Chaos. Thus we are on the way from chaos to order, to civilization and its highest qualities: justice and mercy. Their dialectical play informed the creative genius of Aeschylus, who took the old myth of Prometheus and lifted it into the classic drama of protest, rebellion and suffering that has inspired and enlightened so many poetic souls in their hymns to freedom. Freedom holds the key to the human condition. The struggle between Zeus and Prometheus is the struggle against tyranny on behalf of liberty. The rule of Zeus is authoritarian, that alien and alienating law termed heteronomy: "with laws . . . lawlessly holds dominion" (*Prom. Bound* 149f).[2] Hera his wife, who well knows his arbitrary judgments and wilful ways, warns her fellow immortals: "Foolish that we are to lose our tempers with Zeus. . . . He sits apart and neither worries nor is disturbed; for he boasts of being incontestably superior to the immortal gods in might and power. So resign yourselves." That might have served as motto for all in heaven and below: Resign Yourselves to the Absolute Will of Zeus. To be sure, there is development and change over the centuries of storytelling as the power of Zeus (or Jupiter) increases until he is the highest god among the Olympians. To challenge his will was the gauntlet that Prometheus took up, not indeed for his own sake but on behalf of the human race, which Zeus was neglecting in his haughty disdain. (The creation of humanity by Prometheus is another and perhaps later form of the myth.) As we shall see, Aeschylus himself participates in the maturation process of Zeus, in the *Oresteia* especially. But in the *Prometheia* the primitive "revengeful tyrant" is on the godwalk: truly a *deus ex machina*.

The relationship between Prometheus and Zeus is subtle, akin to the dialectic to be worked out later on the theme of freedom and fate. In the view of Werner Jaeger, Prometheus is "the first counsellor of the jealous and distrustful young tyrant Zeus," a theme that continues in Aeschylus: "In *Prometheus Bound*, Zeus is a modern tyrant as seen by the contemporaries of Harmodius and Aristogeiton."[3] Thus the dramatist makes the ancient heroes contemporary in his reinterpretation of their situation, one with the Athenian context in which tyranny (for the citizens, at least) was the constant antithesis to freedom. The same kind of relevance is achieved in the next generation when both Protagoras' Prometheus and Sophocles' Antigone reflect the stirring of liberty as a call and challenge. As Hegel saw clearly, the *Antigone* in particular embodies the peculiar logic of tragedy, namely the conflict between two goods.[4]

Revolution of the Heavenly Bodies

Kronos against Uranos, Zeus against Kronos, and at last Prometheus against Zeus: such is the primal setting of Western mythology, the celestial prelude to the human story. Prometheus was the wily ally of Zeus in overthrowing Kronos, and like the latter was himself a Titan, whose brothers include Atlas and Epimetheus. The role of Epimetheus is played out in the second act, as it were, concerning Pandora and human destiny. In this first act Prometheus is the rebel opposing the will of Zeus. It is ironical that the stage is set by an act of reconciliation between Zeus and mortals marked by a sacrificial meal. Prometheus tricks Zeus into accepting the worse share by concealing the bones of the victim inside layers of fat. For Hesiod, the "brilliant and shifty" Prometheus does not fool Zeus: "He spoke deceitfully, but Zeus who knows / Undying plans, was not deceived" (*Theog.* 551f).

Zeus retaliates by refusing fire to the human race, whereupon Prometheus steals fire from the sun (or from the forge of Hephaistos). It is this act that precipitates the wrath of Zeus and its punitive decree: fastened to a crag at the edge of the world, his immortal liver gnawed by an eagle (or griffon-vulture) who returns each day for the replenished feast.

A second source of enmity between Prometheus and Zeus is woven into the story. Prometheus knows a secret that is the doom of Zeus: if he has a son by Thetis the child will overthrow him – she will "bear a son greater than his father." At length he gives up his age-long struggle and confesses the secret. He is released through the mediation of Heracles and Cheiron: the one shoots the eagle and the other takes his place in Hades. The various strands of the myth are unravelled selectively by different authors – an Aeschylus, a Lucian, a Goethe. For the Greek tragedian it is the wilful defiance that is emphasized; for the Roman both defiance and the creation of humanity are important, as they are for Goethe. Lucian's Hermes sums up the charges against Prometheus as he and Hephaistos prepare to "crucify" him on the Caucasus: "But if you admit the distribution of meat in the manner described, the introduction of men, and the theft of fire – then my case is complete, and there is no more to be said" (*Prometheus on Caucasus*).

Aeschylus

In the *Agamemnon* the first choral ode includes the line: "The kindness of the enthroned gods contains an element of force." Thus the struggle between justice and mercy, which is the burden of this great tragedian, is interiorized within divinity. The tension and dialectical play between the two form the backdrop to the human story. The gods have marked out the path by which we may gain wisdom, and its name is suffering.

It seems that *Prometheus Bound* (*Desmōtēs*) is the first of a trilogy, produced about 465 BCE when Aeschylus was sixty years of age. Fragments of the second play, *Prometheus Unbound* (*Luomenos*) – properly "The Unbinding of Prometheus," as Gilbert Murray points out – indicate the telling of the secret and the release from Hades. The third play would be *Prometheus the Firebearer* (*Pyrphoros*). A satyr-play, *Prometheus the Firekindler* (*Pyrkaeus*), completed the cycle. In the last, our hero is restored to dignity, and Zeus establishes a festival in his honour. The very idea of the subject reduced to buffoonery may baffle moderns, but Aeschylus was known as a master of the satyr genre. Indeed, classical dramaturgy provides clues to the history of our myth: the dithyramb, then the tragic trilogy and satyr-play by the same playwright, then comedy. The dithyramb recalls Nietzsche above all; the tragedy bears chief burden of commentary and imitation; of satyrs and comedians there are more examples than perhaps expected. With Attic comedy we are introduced to irony. Aristotle classified the characters in comedy as buffoon, eiron and impostor. The irony in our analysis of Prometheus and his fate as chief saint of atheism would not have surprised the ancients. They appreciated the duality of things, the dialectic play of light and darkness of which all drama is symbol and sign. Northrop Frye has anatomized the types of *mythoi*, with winter drama characterized by irony and satire. The eiron is he who deprecates himself, thus rendering his persona invulnerable, as compared with the impostor or victim. Moreover, whereas in tragedy the hero's fate is inevitable and thus predictable, in irony the arbitrary nature of the plot introduces a note of possibility and freedom. Thus Prometheus himself is hardly a properly "tragic" figure. He recalls the clash of wills, making him the scapegoat (*pharmakos*) of Zeus, but with the open future made possible by his possession of the secret and so the power over his own destiny. In the *Prometheia* and *Oresteia* we see how the master playwright moulds the old myth to his thesis of growth through conflict and its resolution. For him it is

Zeus rather than Prometheus who holds the key to change for the better: "worn out" is the wrath of the "wicked god," and so the human prospect is assured, our freedom to choose our own way ahead. Liberty is always bound up with justice, and both with what is the deepest of all questions, the so-called problem of evil, which for Aeschylus means a positive role ascribed to suffering.[5]

Prometheus is constantly rebuked by chorus and others for his pride, although the *Prometheus Unbound* must have shifted the emphasis so that the scales are in rough balance for Aeschylus. Yet the early theme, the lemma that has hardened and become the stumbling block for scepticism and for atheism down the centuries, is put briefly by Hephaistos as he fulfils his bitter task of fastening the Titan to the rock: "All roles are hard, except to rule in heaven: / none alive is free but Zeus alone." Only Zeus is free: there's the rub, for any other seeking liberty, whether divine or human. Indeed Prometheus can complain that no limit is set "except what he sees fit," despite the larger framework of fate, the vague yet omnipresent form of *Moira*, which sets the limits for all, even for Zeus. Prometheus considers himself to be "Man's great teacher of the arts, his universal boon" so that his punishment is "all because I was a friend too much of man." So we have the bare plot, much as one would expect from a playwright who loves spectacle and is not daunted by the lack of dramatic action in this play of much dialogue in the single setting of a mountain rock.

What constitutes sufficient action for Aeschylus is the passion. Prometheus becomes in his hands a symbol of unconditional humanity, that being which stands firm in its own self-sufficiency, despite and against the gods: "Against these plans none stood save I: I dared." With these words Prometheus enters the stage of history as the pre-eminent One who dares, who is free.

Something more sinister, and more significant, is to come. Prometheus, whose very name means foresight, knows that ultimate deliverance involves fearful reversal, with terrible consequences, of the word of Zeus. Aristotle's categories in his discussion of tragedy in the *Poetics* are clearly on view: reversal, discovery, suffering. The *peripateia* involves our protagonist's downfall; the *anagnorisis* comes in stages through the trilogy, while the *pathos* is supreme in the first. There is also the literal unbinding (*lysis*) of Prometheus as well as the dramatic dénouement of plot. He is fated to descend into Hades – the play ends with the disappearance of Prometheus, still bound to his craggy prison, as he slips downward. In a moving passage from the mouth of Hermes there are words fraught with meaning on more than one level:

> And you may hope for no release
> From such a torment, till some god be found to take
> Your pains upon him, and of his own will descend
> To sunless Hades and the black depths of Tartarus.

(1026-29)

Here is hope, a promise that is fulfilled when the centaur Cheiron, afflicted with an incurable wound in his heel, volunteers to be the substitute deity whose descent purchases the release of Prometheus by satisfying the demand of Hades.

At last Prometheus is free, but at cost. Zeus is recognized as supreme, while the right of humanity to survive is guaranteed. More important is the victory of reason over violence, the point dear to the author, a moot point still in his time, but one he struggles to show in his work. Out of the kinship (through mother Earth) of gods and humans, out of their difference exhibited through conflict of wills, resolution has come. There has been divine suffering for human good. Culture and civilization are assured through the arts and sciences flowing from the master gift of fire. The Olympians, who overthrew the old dynasty of Kronos, are faced with the necessity of justice and mercy as the polarity of their force and capriciousness.

The glory on high is revealed as originally hostile to the human venture: "pitiless god, thy hand alone has guided all." Through the intercession of Prometheus the progress of the venture is assured, while suffering is introduced into divinity itself. Whether the lost *Prometheus Unbound* points toward a deliverance from the tragic, a sort of divine repentance and fresh start, remains unclear. Ugo Bianchi considers the Prometheus myth to symbolize the new *traffica* between gods and humans, born of the sense of guilt: "Una visione olimpica della 'colpa antecedente' nel mondo greco." Thus a soteriological perspective is achieved, a clarification of the tension between Olympian and mystical views of the origins of divine and human culpability.[6]

The Creatures of Prometheus

The revolt of the Titan gave gifts to a race whose lot was cast in an inheritance of dire need, powerless and afflicted. So the Greeks saw things. Pindar's sixth *Nemean Ode* is a good example:

> There is one
> race of men, one race of gods; both have breath
> of life from a single mother. But sundered power
> holds us divided, so that one side is nothing, while
> on the other the brazen sky is established
> a sure citadel forever.[7]

In the oldest form of the myth, accepted by Hesiod and Aeschylus, Prometheus is not the creator but the benefactor of humans. His role enacts his name, "he who knows in advance" (from the archaic Greek stem *mēthē*) – Foresight or Providence – so that the destiny of the race is anticipated by his endowments. In particular the technique of metalworking derives from the gift of fire: the smithy. As Prometheus himself had to wear an iron ring wrought from his chains as symbol of his penitence, so the smiths of the world – our "engineers" – continue to wear the Promethean ring, symbol of titanic rebellion and reward: doubly "ironic." Hesiod uses the Pandora story to account for the origin and the need of work: she is the "price for men to pay for fire" (*Theog.* 571). Before her, human life was free from "sorrow and from painful work" and disease; now her gifts are bitter (*Works and Days* 90ff).

The grip of Necessity fastens on the human race, rendering intelligence helpless before Fate. Etiological myths helped classical people to live with the questions of why work is necessary and hard (because Prometheus deceived Zeus) and why life is both heroic and full of toil (because Pandora was the divine trick on the human).

Thus the mythological origin and explanation for civilization and technology is a tale of Titans and of the rivalry and conflict between two orders of deity. Here is the first Enlightenment, the awakening of reason by Prometheus and the call to "a self-directed *vita humana.*"[8] Whereas Zeus represents a spirit of antagonism and jealousy, Prometheus brings creative inspiration and support for human endeavour and human potential.

The *Prometheus Bound* is a text written in behalf of a better cosmogony: Aeschylus wishes to found a world based on order, justice (*Dikē*). The play opens to display Might (*Kratos*) assisted by Force (*Bia*) dragging Prometheus to his rocky prison. As he is chained by Hephaistos he provides "a sight eyes should not look upon *[theāma dystheāton],*" so that the bittersweet cost of human being is on display, the ransom price of progress, of civilization itself.

The Promethean enlightenment was an awakening of the human spirit in the face of a divine threat to the liberty of expression and development. The Titanic setting of the essential human problem – necessity and freedom – recalls the context for subsequent working out of the theme: human autonomy at any cost. The restless seeking and striving, the ambition and pride associated with the titanic struggles and Olympian story, offer a warning of the destiny awaiting the protégé of the giver of *technē*. "All human skill and science was Prometheus' gift," says our hero himself in boasting that he alone discovered the earth's metals and recognized their promise. "All arts [*pasai technai*]" symbolize the totality of that human life assured by promethean rebellion.

The revolt of the Titans comes at last to rest on the handiwork of the smiths. Now metalworking is akin to magic, as the phenomenon of alchemy suggests. This alternative "science" involves certain ideas associated with the Promethean tradition. The four elements of fire, earth, air and water are sometimes regarded as four stages of fire, *ignis*. They may be related also to the *lapis*, the philosopher's stone, source of alchemical *gnosis*, the *arcanum* of Paracelsus. The importance of the signs of the zodiac is part of the dynamics of light and darkness. For C.G. Jung this is symbolic of the dialectic of selfhood, of conscious and unconscious. The modern "uprooted consciousness" soars above the earth, but may collapse and "like Prometheus [become] chained to the Caucasus of the unconscious."[9] In magic there lies hidden a secret that has ultimate power, masking a striving for mastery in competition with God. The original animosity toward Zeus is inherited by the creatures of Prometheus along with the power to effect a successful rebellion. In a sense the titanic provenance for human progress continues the underground nature of the human enterprise, over against the gods associated with the upper air – as if the earlier, more primitive and powerful gods once relegated (by Hesiod, for one) to the region of Tartarus are now leading a revolt of the powers of darkness against the powers of light. Prometheus suffers in daylight (before he descends into Hades), but it is the suffering of darkness, as the eagle's feasting on his liver symbolizes. The liver was considered by Galen to be the origin of veins and therefore of the dark, venous blood, as well as of the appetitive soul. As the subject of the art of hepatoscopy, it reflects that picture of the world afforded by the night sky.[10] Humanity's benefactor offers gifts of ambiguous consequence: power toward liberty, yet ranged with darkness. The revolt against Zeus is inevitably a questioning of the powers of light, the order of daytime culture.

In one sense, Prometheus represents the rebellion of will rather than of reason. The Titan pits his strength of will over against the tyrant Zeus: his victory stems from defiance rather than logic. Thus it will issue in postulatory atheism, a stance of wilful rebellion, which could be related to the Dionysian consciousness as distinct from Apollonian rationality. The fate of such rebellion is contained within its dynamics, its apriori, which pits divine tyranny against human autonomy. The result is bound to be self-will, the moral burden of universal Good taken over by the human project: the old Prometheus has become the new Zeus.

Consequences

A myth once told begins its own story. The history and development of the Prometheus myth provides a fascinating case study.[11] From Hesiod through Aeschylus and Plato the myth becomes an expression of the human condition and of those transcendent powers that constitute our environment and our destiny. In the Platonic dialogue *Protagoras* (320ff) Socrates uses the myth of Prometheus and Epimetheus to illustrate the disputed question of whether "virtue can be taught." The gods wish to endow all creatures for survival, but the rash Epimetheus bungles the job and exhausts the gifts among the lower animals. Prometheus discovers that "man alone was naked and shoeless, and had neither bed nor arms for defence." Therefore he "stole the mechanical arts of Hephaistos and Athene, and fire with them (they could neither have been acquired nor used without fire) and gave them to man. Thus man had the wisdom necessary to the support of life, but political wisdom he had not; for that was in the keeping of Zeus." In fact, this Zeus is less the tyrant than in Aeschylus. Fearing the extermination of the human venture, he sends Hermes to bring reverence and justice as "the ordering principles of cities and the bonds of friendship and conciliation."

Socrates wishes to communicate (indirectly as ever) a distinction between such arts as are possessed by "the favoured few" and that quality of political virtue that all have in common. In this sense Prometheus is benefactor and patron saint of the élite – an aristocracy of skills and insight that will become a feature of modern Prometheanism, as in Marx or Nietzsche. Here Zeus appears more benign, caring for the human race, and truly "father of gods and men." The Socratic view obscures the primeval contest between tyrant deity and champion of the human. Yet it is the latter feature of the myth that inspires modernity, shaped especially by Goethe in his retelling of the ancient tale. From now on, "Zeus" stands for omnipotence, the despotism of heaven, while "Prometheus" symbolizes noble rebellion on behalf of human freedom.

Before leaving the original dramatic figure to pursue his journey in Western thought, we should attend to the cogent argument of Eric Voegelin on this same phenomenon. Whereas the original was "an episode of the Titanomachia in the Hesiodian sense," the development of "modern" Prometheanism is "in fact a form of Gnosis."[12] The classical myth cast Zeus as *tyrannis* only in the technical sense: he pronounced appropriate punishment "in order to uphold Dikē." A certain harshness obtained, and so gave credence to the charge of heteronomy; but Prometheus was guilty, particularly of the sin of self-will, as Hermes pointed out. Indeed, he was the first Sophist: "You, the *sophistēs*, bitter beyond all bitterness" (I. 944). Thus the primitive struggle involves the backdrop of *Anankē* and *Dikē*, that larger theonomy that pits Zeus and Prometheus as antagonists with much less freedom on either side than the subsequent development of both figures allows. Voegelin advances a sharp thesis:

> The Promethean symbols of Shaftesbury and Goethe, of Shelley and the young Marx, belong to the age of enlightened, human self-reliance, of the titanism of the artist, and of the defiant revolutionary who will take the destiny of mankind into his own hands. All that has nothing to do with Aeschylus, but it has been an additional obstacle to understanding him in our time.[13]

Goethe's Prometheus

> I know of nothing poorer
> Under the sun than you gods.
> Wretchedly
> You feed your majesty
> On imposed sacrifices
> And the breath of prayers.
> You would waste away
> If children and beggars
> Were not hopeful fools.[14]

This verse from the monologue of 1820 casts Zeus as heartless tyrant, unworthy of human honour:

> Did you ever appease the pain
> Of the sufferer?

> Did you ever quench the tears
> Of the fearful?

The concluding stanza sets the tone for every enlightened modern who takes Prometheus as his guide:

> Here I sit, shaping man
> After my image,
> A race that is like me,
> To suffer, to weep,
> To rejoice and be glad,
> And like myself
> To have no regard for you!

Prometheus has become Lord of the earth, the creative spirit in human being. "The fable of Prometheus came alive in me. I cut the old Titan robe to my own size."[15] Goethe created a mythologem to suit his own purposes, to depict humanity as a third dynasty over against both gods and Titans – the primordial orphan. "Goethe's Prometheus is no God, no Titan, no man, but the immortal prototype of man as an antigod, as the Lord of the Earth."[16]

The definitive work of Carl Kerényi on the Prometheus myth suggests that Goethe's recasting created a distinctively modern myth whose effect on the younger generation was later feared by the old master himself. Thus Goethe is "a modern mythologos." The essential feature of the new myth is the heroic and titanic acceptance of the human condition as one of suffering to be borne and overcome through knowledge. In the ancient myth Prometheus accepted the pain decreed on behalf of humanity; the modern promethean is one who tackles the burden of suffering through the power inherent in his skills and who puts his hope in their superiority over mere suffering. He is truly a child of earth, and chooses immanence against transcendence: gifts over Giver.[17]

Prometheus thus links with Faust as expression of Goethe's vision of hope despite his youthful pessimism. Faust laments our fate:

> I am not like the Gods: That truth is felt too deep:
> The worm am I, that in the dust doth creep.
>
> (*Faust* Act I, Scene I)

But before his monologue is over he rises to proclaim a high intention – within this very speech he responds to the offer of the Earth-Spirit with his decision to transcend the bonds of earth:

'Tis time, through deeds this word of truth to thunder:
That with the height of Gods Man's dignity may vie!

Thus does Faust begin his fateful quest in Promethean fashion: "Here I am Man, – dare man to be!" This line (Bk I, Sc 2) matches the cry of Enlightenment, *Sapere aude*, dare to think.

Prometheus and Faust are thus portrayed and related by one who represents the spirit of modernity – eclectic, practical and theoretical both, tasting and testing what is novel, committed to the natural, the human, the reasonable. Goethe bids us follow the lead of that creative spirit within which is the only and the proper transcendence open to humankind.

Playing with Fire

Prometheus's people are inspired to try harder: they are the chosen of the earth to lead the struggle for survival, the rebellion against every alien power, every higher force that pretends to hold the secret of human being. In positive terms this may be called humanism; its usual corollary, on the negative side, is atheism. It is the historical conjunction of these twin phenomena that we wish to explore in this work under the subtitle *The Irony of Atheism*, the ironic fate of the new prometheans. By this is intended the link with the master-image of tragedy, namely playing with fire. In our time the image takes form in firebombing and napalming, in nuclear explosions, in furnaces at death camps.[18] Therefore Prometheus started something with his stolen gifts – mastery over nature, power through technology, independence. It is the last promise that has proved most volatile in Western history, so that the quest for autonomy, liberation from alien wills (heteronomy), remains the benchmark of atheism. It is an instance of "tragic necessity." The quest has been necessary in view of the apparent heteronomy of the transcendent will of God; it has proved tragic because of the ambiguous legacy of the gift of fire.

One could speculate on the universal symbolism of fire with its equivocal nature. Bane and blessing, *probandus* and *benedictio*, one can undergo ordeal by fire, or be tempered by its refinement; it is home to the salamander, and to the phoenix both an end and a beginning, as it was in medieval legend of the Chaldean fire (taking Ur for *urere*, to burn) that occasioned Abraham's deliverance. As with many symbols or archetypes, fire shows itself through a polarity or ambivalence, the key to its elemental significance in the alchemical tradition.[19] In the Rig Veda the ancient tradition of India casts Agni in the multifaceted role of firegiver, firebringer, intermediary. He is hymned for the double edge of fear and deliverance.[20] Vedic lore places his birth on December 25, progeny of the solar Deva and the virgin Maya. The winter solstice is familiar in the West also – Hannukah, Saturnalia, St. Lucia, Christmas – with the return of Sun and his victory over the powers of darkness. Fire and light keep at bay the threatening chaos that lurks in the shadowy places of the world. Space is cleared for order, reason, civilization – the hearth-fire (related to the cult of both Hestia and Hephaistos) must never go out. Yahweh over Chaos, Apollo against Dionysus, the protagonists represent the final ambivalence of life and the hope that we put in the forces of light, the fire of reason. With great insight Gaston Bachelard has observed: "The Prometheus complex is the Oedipus complex of the life of the intellect."[21]

Still another religious tradition offers a doctrine of ambivalent fire. Iranian Islam includes the heritage of Parsee dualism concerning light and darkness, with corresponding good and evil uses of fire. Henry Corbin has written of this, relating the latter ("le feu ahrimanien") to that Promethean audacity that wishes to seize divine light for itself.

> Pour le croyant qui vit au profond de lui-même la conception iranienne de la Lumière, le mythe de Prométhée ne peut apparaître que comme une farouche perversion de la réalité des choses, car Feu et Lumière sont le don sacré fait aux hommes par les Puissances de Lumière.[22]

The gracious fire of Ohrmazd illuminates without consuming, provides that light and fire that allows human being to use the natural as gift and so to function as its steward. But the role of Ahriman, imitated by promethean humans, usurps and perverts the natural order. Here fire is merely incendiary, its effects destructive and evil.

The figure of Prometheus surely reflects such an ambiguity concerning the use and abuse of fire. In the West he has come to stand for the heroic commitment to the costly gain of fire as the basis of arts and sciences, but particularly of technological skills. His descendants are typified by self-reliance, by their assertion of the human will in behalf of human freedom; in short, their struggle for human autonomy. The enemy is heteronomy, and the chief symbol of this threatening tyranny is Zeus.

Zeus or Prometheus? Our initial question has been quickly

transposed into another: divine will or human freedom? Thus the question is a loaded one, and the conclusions beg the question. To serve God, to afford him reality by believing in the possibility of his existence, is to opt for the tyranny of heaven rather than for the freedom of human being; to believe in God is to enter into slavery, to lose your humanity. To think for yourself means to trust only in the human and the worldly, and so to deny God. The atheist postulate is thus implied in the original terms of the problem. It turns on the crucial question of whether divine and human willing may be compatible rather than antithetical. Can God will the human good so that choosing his will is *ipso facto* choosing authentic humanity? That is one way of phrasing the terms of debate, which must remain before us as we trace the story of the development of postulatory atheism.

First we shall look at a strange phenomenon, presenting itself in the earliest days of the Christian era: Prometheus and Christ. This is not merely an alternative to "Prometheus against Christ" but at times becomes the contradictory thesis: Prometheus *as* Christ. It warns us not to begin with loaded questions. It forms a sort of perennial question mark over the adventure of atheism. It suggests the irony of the search for autonomy by denying a heteronomy already assumed and defined.

2

Prometheus and/or Christ

. . . verus Prometheus Deus omnipotens blasphemiis lancinatur.

Tertullian[1]

It was the Voltaire of his time, Lucian of Samosata (*c.* 125-200 CE), who preserved the variant tradition that Prometheus was not bound but crucified. The faith of Aeschylus is now lost, the myth transmuted into an earthly story with no heavenly meaning. (Karl Marx noted that the gods of Greece were wounded tragically in Aeschylus, then "had to re-die a comic death" in Lucian.) The possibility of rebellion, however, is maintained in a renewed way. The two works of Lucian bearing directly on Prometheus – "Prometheus on Caucasus" and the first of the "Dialogues of the Gods" – draw on the tradition of Plato's *Protagoras*.[2] Prometheus is the benefactor who provides example for human life and inspiration for protest against tyranny. Three charges are brought against Prometheus, namely the unjust distribution of meat, the creation of humankind and the theft of fire. The style is comic: "to think that [Zeus] should be so touchy about trifles, as to send off a God of my quality to crucifixion, just because he found a little bit of bones in his share!" Prometheus nevertheless defends all three of his actions and almost tells Hermes and Hephaistos his secret concerning Thetis. In the brief dialogue with Zeus he does tell, and Zeus utters the final speech: "Thetis, farewell: and for this Hephaistos shall set you free."

Apology and Typology

Meanwhile, Christian Fathers could refer to Prometheus as symbol of the Creator and example of poetic reification. Lactantius, for

---

Notes to Chapter 2 appear on page 305.

one: "The poets . . . said that man was made by Prometheus from clay. They were not mistaken in the matter itself, but in the name of the artificer."[3] In another place he draws on the work of Euhemerus to show how the poets developed and aggrandized the legends of the classical heroes until they became divine beings.[4] What seems essential in the tradition is the creation story. Thus Augustine, speculating on "who were kings when Moses was born," refers to Prometheus: "He is reported to have formed men out of clay, because he was esteemed the best teacher of wisdom; yet it does not appear what wise men there were in his days" (*De Civ. Dei* XVIII, 8). Beside this rather phlegmatic utterance, the reminder of the providential nature of the name is reassuring: "Prometheus is foresight (PROMETHEIA), by which all things arose."[5]

There is also the allegorical use of the myth, not surprisingly in the Alexandrian tradition. Clement milks the story: the theft of fire is like philosophy's theft of truth; Prometheus creates man as a figure (appearance) of true creation; Pandora is a female tempter, like Eve.[6] Pandora is always a favourite and sometimes enjoys a good press, being included with the Pleroma or subsumed under the office of saviour (Irenaeus).[7] In both these cases it is the Pandora *Hesiodi* that is on view, with no transition to the Prometheus of Aeschylus. It is Tertullian who rescues the dramatic Titan and forces the issue of Christ and Prometheus.

Earlier scholars tended to see an explicit assimilation of Prometheus to the gospel on the part of the Fathers of the Church; but they could cite only Tertullian, so that modern scholars are more reserved on the point.[8] Yet such references as were noted earlier by others of the patristic era show that his acceptance of Prometheus as a type of Christ is hardly unique. Like Clement of Alexandria, Tertullian promotes the gospel as the truth foreshadowed by myth and legend. He pays homage to poets and playwrights, acknowledging an element of proleptic truth in "the stories of the sacrifices of the Taurians . . . the torments of the Caucasus."[9] What went on in these *cruces Caucasorum*? A kind of suffering, which witnesses to the divine being himself. Against Marcion's dissevering of Old from New Testament, his negation through *ana-lysis* (the same word was used for the tearing asunder of Dionysus), Tertullian laments that "the true Prometheus, Almighty God, is mangled by [Marcion's] blasphemies." God as *verus Prometheus* – the striking identification occurs again in another place: "Here is the true Prometheus who gave order to the World by arranging the seasons and their course" (*Apol.* XVIII, 2).

It is significant that such parallelism or typology of the church fathers is present again in the contemporary dialogue between Christians and Marxists. The new issue turns on the fascinating statement of Karl Marx that Prometheus is "the noblest of saints and martyrs in the calendar of philosophy," as we shall see. And this in turn is interpreted as leaving room for "the readmission of Prometheus to the Christian calendar" as one dialogist, Father Gonzalez Ruiz, puts it.[10] Thus the ancient question "Prometheus or Christ?" continues among us, with special significance for Marxian atheism and its understanding of holy suffering. Yet we must qualify this positive evaluation of a titanic image of the Christ figure on the part of such atheists. For they continue, for the most part, to rely on the concept of projection, often without argument as if this were an assured datum. The history of this concept stretches from Euhemerus to the disciples of Marx and Freud. Since it operates within a reductionist horizon, that is, one in which nothing beyond a naturalistic explanation is allowed, it proceeds as if reality corresponds to its preconceived idea of minimal explanation. Given the dominant philosophy of our age – naturalism or positivism – the key question is how to go "beyond reductionism," as a recent symposium phrases it.[11]

Christian apologists seized on the theory of Euhemerus that the origin of gods lies in human heroes and hero-worship. The polytheism around them was explained on euhemeristic grounds. Isidore of Seville (560-636) illustrates the logical conclusion of this desacralizing process in his *Etymologiae.* One chapter, "De diis gentium," singles out the line of heroes, from Prometheus on, who have been leaders in civilization. Here and elsewhere Prometheus is referred to as the one "believed to have fashioned men out of clay."[12] This process rendered the gods harmless, and open to historical analysis. It is continued in the Renaissance, although new strength is accorded the tradition by the humanist quest for human dignity and for a piety consonant with freedom.

In the patristic era, of course, a curious reversal was in play whereby it was the Christian who was labelled "atheist." A second century statement suggests the state of affairs in which Christian is associated with Epicurean in this regard: "if any godless person either Christian or Epicurean has come to spy on the mysteries, let him depart; let those who believe the god be initiated propitiously."[13] In particular, the lack of visible idols on the part of both Jew and Christian convinced the Graeco-Roman age that some form of denial of the gods was present. On a deeper and more significant level, moreover, were the implications of the patristic doctrine of *creatio ex nihilo*. The church fathers were accused of impiety because they taught that the order of things is not eternal, as the philosophical schools maintained, but contingent, created along with the universe. To call in question the rationality of the eternal forms is a kind of atheism, for it "denied the necessary connection between the rationality immanent in things and its source in Deity."[14] Although the notion of contingent rationality has proved to be one of the requirements for the development of modern science, at the time when the Fathers sought a hearing for Christian theology it had to overthrow the dualism of philosophy as well as the polytheism of religion.

The Christian apologist Athenagoras, philosopher in Athens in the second century CE, gave answer to the three current charges of atheism, incest and cannibalism (the mystery of the Supper). The central point in his "plea regarding Christians" is the case against atheism. A modern commentator writes:

> To deny the traditional gods, to stand in opposition to the syncretic temper of the age, and above all to claim to practice a religion which dispensed with the most essential marks of ancient religion, viz., sacrifice, could not but have provoked the accusation of atheism.[15]

Historically, one type of atheism in the classical world was that of Christianity. Any typology of unbelief must pause before this fact to assess the criteria for theism and its contraries. To deny the dominant religiosity is to be declared atheistic. Thus the relations among theism, antitheism and atheism are before us in this study. Christianity is that religion that is identified with each of the three from time to time.

Despite the scholarly assumption that church fathers were fond of parallelism between Prometheus and Christ, Tertullian's reference to the crucified figure of the Caucasus proves to be the singular hard datum; still, the correspondence is clear on the level of such parallels as benefactor of humanity, gifts from on high, derision from persecutors and physical binding and suffering. It is noteworthy that it is the suffering Prometheus of Aeschylus that comes closer to the figure of the New Testament Passion narratives rather than the ancient myth of Titan rebellion. In turn one might say that it is the latter rather than Aeschylus that gives substance to the heroic atheism of modernity.

Such patristic parallelism was set forth in a modern context by Edgar Quinet in *Préface à Prométhée* (1857). Christian symbolism is explicit in this dramatic poem, which succeeds in presenting a thoroughly Christianized Titan. The archangels Michael and Raphael descend to visit the suffering Prometheus. In a foretaste of redemption Raphael breaks the chains "au nom de notre père" while Michael fells the eagle with an arrow. At last, to a chorus of angels, Prometheus follows the archangelic word: "Où donc m'emportez-vous?" And the converted Titan bows to a converted Zeus: "Au sein de Jéhovah."[16]

The Sin of Pride

After the patristic era there is little evidence for symbolic use of the myth on the part of theology. Not until the Renaissance were the antipathy to "paganism" and the Western forgetfulness of the Greek language overcome. Even then it was more a case of an emerging humanism than a return to classical theism. Thus it was appropriate for the myth to be recovered and applied by Enlightenment mentality. For if the Promethean myth means an assertion of self-will in defiance of authority, its doctrine of human being is at odds with classical and medieval theology. At the heart of this doctrine is the concept of pride. Now in the Greek world-view *hybris* leads to a fall, insofar as *Moira* is transgressed and Necessity challenged; Oedipus remains the archetype here. But there was also a commendable pride, which was not overweening, and which is to be cultivated for the sake of authentic humanity. Thus Aristotle is clear on the virtue of pride. It is a mean between undue humility and vanity, a case of "good in the highest degree" and even "the crown of the virtues."

> The proud man, then, is an extreme in respect of the greatness of his claims, but a mean in respect of the rightness of them; for he claims what is in accordance with his merits, while the others go to excess or fall short.
>
> (*Nic. Eth.* 1123B)

This thesis, that "pride implies greatness," fell before the medieval category of the sin of pride, *in seipsum*. He who seeks the admiration of others in overweening vanity of self-centredness is not autonomous but idolatrous, his heart curved back on his own self as his deity. Perhaps the best way to appreciate the shift is to follow the lead of E.R. Dodds as to the passage "from Shame-culture to Guilt-culture."[17] Dodds underlines the category of human helplessness (*anmēania*) with its religious correlate, "the feeling of divine hostility" as "an overmastering Power and Wisdom" holding us down. The gods themselves are "primarily concerned with their own honour." It is against such a backdrop that the drama of the *Iliad* is enacted, as well as the more developed tragedies of Aeschylus. The shame of losing face before gods and men drives the heroes to their destined fate. The transition to guilt-culture, on the other hand, introduces the dimension of transcendence in a determinate way: "before God" the human drama is played out, with his presence and absence as the correlate to dramatic action and dénouement. This is what Luther implied in his use of the category *coram Deo*, while Kierkegaard expounded the difference between guilt and sin with brilliant finesse.[18]

Robert Payne's *Hubris, a Study of Pride*, considers Prometheus in light of the above ideas, since for him it is the Titans who offer the best mythological clue to "a short history of the European soul as it shows itself in pride."[19] From the emergence of the nymph Hubris in prehistoric Arcadia to the ominous signs of holocaust around him when he wrote originally in 1937, Payne traces the story of Promethean self-will and its symbol of fire. In a chapter devoted to the Titans he notes:

> Michelangelo sketched the Christian Prometheus in two designs: one representing the Titan gnawed by the eagle, the other crucified vertically on the branches of an enormous oak. Somehow, and very gradually over the centuries, there had come about an identification between Christ and the Titan prince. Christ was the tragic hero, who harrowed hell after suffering as Prometheus had suffered; and in the high Renaissance Christianity and paganism found common ground. (216)

Payne's thesis that Prometheus represents a species of pride in human affairs is better served by his survey of "six great poets at the turn of the eighteenth century . . . tormented by the legend of the Titans." Goethe, Hölderlin, Blake, Shelley, Keats and Wordsworth – an impressive talent seized with the issue of human Prometheanism, or Man-God. We treat them in a different order and conjunction from Payne's, while our thesis is roughly the same. Yet the subject of pride in the hands of the poets is a warning: they deal with the Titans time and again, but always in fragments. Except for Shelley: "but there is a sense in which his vision of them is the most fragmentary of all."

In the guilt-culture of medieval Christendom a horizon

obtained that did not allow for Promethean rebellion. God was transcendent and omnipotent, while the catalogue of virtues and vices accounted for human behaviour in an exhaustive and therapeutic way. The *ordo* of clerical and lay society made rebellion itself a prime problem for moralists, a subject to ponder even in the sixteenth century. Indeed, our myth underwent a significant transformation: Prometheus the Firebringer and rebel was lost, while Prometheus as Creator remained to play a part analogous to the God of Genesis. The inconceivability of revolt and the absorption of "all skills and science" within the range of divine gifts for human vocation robbed the Titan of the power so obvious to the Greek mind. "Le Moyen Age ne s'est donc attaché qu'à une déformation du mythe. La pensée mediévale n'a pas pu connaître le *Prométhée* d'Eschyle, mais, l'eut-elle pu, elle ne l'aurait pas compris."[20]

The myth thus deformed concentrated on the creation motif and the role of Pandora. Such preoccupation with "first things" particularly relating to temptation and fall missed the potent imagery of fire and of costly revolt. Constraining human selfhood within the catalogue of the theological virtues and vices, pride and rebellion were condemned in favour of a different kind of wilfulness: the virtue of obedience. Submission to God is the dynamic of losing one's self in order to find it again, in the Christian view of things. But in pride/shame selfhood, such submission is viewed as under an authority that is alien and alienating, the heteronomy that negates the proud and proper self of autonomous humanity.

Satan and Other Heroes

The relation between Christ and Prometheus has been taken by later Christian scholars either to highlight Promethean figures such as Job or to contrast with Satan, the original biblical firebringer: Pyrphoros, Lucifer. Elizabeth Barrett Browning felt called to discourse on the contrast between Satan and Prometheus in the preface to her translation of *Prometheus Bound* (1835): "Satan suffered from his ambition; Prometheus from his humanity: Satan for himself; Prometheus for mankind: Satan dared peril which he had not weighed; Prometheus devoted himself to sorrows which he had foreknown. 'Better to rule in hell', said Satan; 'better to serve this rock', said Prometheus."[21]

As one might expect, Simone Weil can identify Prometheus

explicitly with a "pre-Christian intuition:" "The story of Prometheus is like the refraction into eternity of the Passion of Christ. Prometheus is the Lamb slain from the foundation of the world."[22] More critical is theologian Fritz Buri: while it is true that both Prometheus and Christ have "earth beneath and beauty above" them, the former is characterized essentially by his defiance and only secondarily by his suffering (*der Trotzige, der Dulder*). Christ, on the other hand, accepts and wills his destiny (*Schicksal*) through his dying.[23] A similar working of themes of destiny, sin and salvation is provided recently by Ugo Bianchi in *Prometeo, Orfeo, Adamo*.[24] Prometheus now affords a vision of "antecedent" fault, thus contributing to the moot question of the origin of sin. The Titan is a genuine mediator, whose traffic between gods and men allows for both pity and hope. He also functions as demiurge, indeed one who acts as trickster of Zeus. In Prometheus humanity receives hope against the fatalism of Olympian deity, a promise of renewal through this agony of proto-humanity.

In attempting an advance on this treatment of the theme of Christ and Prometheus, recent Christian thought has advocated a theology of secularity, thus imitating, in William F. Lynch's terms, the "secular project" first begun by Prometheus.

> By secularity and the secular project I mean the march of humankind, in the autonomous light of its own resources, toward the mastery and humanization of the world, in the objective terms of all the arts and sciences as these have taken shape and are still taking shape in history. The great symbol of this project was Prometheus.[25]

This formulation of the human journey suggests a sort of dialectical relationship between the two figures, the Titan and the Christ. It turns, clearly, on the acceptance of a definition of secularity that is different from the traditional opposition between sacred and secular. Since this will be treated again, here we may simply note Lynch's own argument on behalf of the "religious imagination." He believes that classical theism's sacred/secular dualism was destructive of both, since it set in opposition two powers that need one another, as in our thesis concerning Prometheus and Zeus: "One of the prevailing images western man has of himself is of a creature who must live and die unbowed and unsubmissive to the world; it is one of the great stances of Prometheus." The alienated Stranger of our fiction – from Paris bistro to American frontier – goes his way as if the whole world hung on the outcome of his exploits. He is too solemn to be picaresque, too moralistic to be truly liberated. (One thinks of Sartre immediately: his antiheroes talk of nausea and nothingness and a little later of the need to choose on behalf of all humanity.)

Lynch uses Promethean symbolism to describe the passage of the secular project "from a cosmocentric to an anthropocentric structure."[26] The point is not merely to repeat the cliché about "the secularization process" within Western history, but to underline its secularist consequence: "the human simplicism" that narrows the meaning of human. The narrowing has chiefly to do with the emergence of the will to the relative exclusion of the imagination. The secular project is thus a will-ful positing of delimited human being over against "the other." A clash of wills is bound to prove alienating, divisive; it lacks the creative play of imagination, and therefore the possibility of harmony, reconciliation. Accordingly, Lynch commends a strengthening of the human, an all-inclusive being that will be "the best way to handle Prometheanism." He seeks a "common logic" to unite secular and sacred, and so to redeem Prometheus in relation to Christ.

Another Christian writer who emphasizes the role of the Titan is Paul Ricoeur, in his "empirical" section of the philosophy of the will in which he is engaged.[27] In *The Symbolism of Evil* he turns to Prometheus as the crown and completion of "the series of heroic figures on whom transcendent misfortune is poured." His is "the supreme action of a will that says No." Ricoeur distinguishes the "innocent passion" that the Titan symbolizes from "the wrath of man, rising up against the wrath of god." In this double thrust of symbolism he stands fast and fastened: "True, Prometheus is powerless; crucified on his rock, he does nothing; but has the power of the word and the hardness of a will that withholds consent" (224).

This is the "tragic vision of existence," the recognition that the gods share with us the ambiguities of *Moira*, of Necessity, of Pride and of Fault. All we can do is hope, with Sophocles, that through time and the *drōmena* of the human *drama* we can observe at last: "Worn out the wrath." Even for Aeschylus there was a dénouement in which the celestial wrath wanes and we can say: Prometheus delivered.

Ricoeur also refers to another dimension of symbolism for Prometheus: a protestation like that of Job. But there is a material difference: "the Zeus that Prometheus calls in question is not the holy God of the Prophets." The argument of Job participates in a tradition of protest and complaint incompatible with Greek theology. The God of Israel is known as a covenanting deity whose will is so selfless that even his Commandments take the form not of heteronomous or arbitrary dictates but of guidance for the Way of authentic humanity.

In Job we have a figure of protest who stands near the beginning of the tradition, indeed at its fringe so far as emphasis on the covenant with Israel is concerned. He opens the debate well – not the debate *about* God but the debate *with* God – but he is content with a divine reply that stands on the doctrine of Creation and the monstrous shape of being. The Hebrew prophets pursue the quest for understanding into a new dimension. Like Job they too recognize the need for a total commitment and so for an unverifiable faith; like him they acknowledge the nature of evil to be irrational, a surd in the mathematics of creation. But unlike him, they gain a vision of the pain within God, the costly grace that transposes the problem of evil into the mystery of Good.[28]

The relationship of Prometheus to Job is a theme that concerns not only classicists but also existentialists and Marxists: Gilbert Murray, Maurice Friedman and Ernst Bloch to name leading examples. We shall notice Bloch later, in a proper context. Murray takes the problem of Aeschylus to be whether Zeus can learn through suffering, itself a corollary of the power of understanding. Although the issue is clearly resolved only in the *Oresteia*, the *Prometheia* take the measure of the primitive Tyrant whose rule is to mark the transition from "blind forces of nature" to "the new and extraordinary faculty," that of thought. "Where they could only smite and be smitten, Zeus could think. He could therefore learn by suffering, or by experience, and thus he can save the world." Thus does Aeschylus present "speculative answers to the Question of Job." We are reminded of C.G. Jung's attempt – "theoanalysis" would be a good description – to answer Job's appeal with an improved deity, rather than the "amoral" Yahweh who bespeaks only "divine savagery and ruthlessness." Friedman's study of the "problematic rebel" holds that we moderns stand "between Job and Prometheus." But in between something has been lost: modern rebels no longer have "the order that gave the original Prometheus his strength." He sees in Melville's Moby Dick the figure of "Job's Whale," the Leviathan of the Book of Job. Captain Ahab cannot fathom the mystery of his Leviathan – despite the erudite cetology that Melville exhibits in the book – whereas Job contends not with the monster but with its Creator.[29]

Thomas Merton

Thomas Merton, poet-monk, brings great insight into "the behavior of Titans," as he entitles his chief treatment of our myth.[30] Merton is struck by the two differing versions of Hesiod and Aeschylus, producing "two faces of Prometheus." Hesiod approves and promotes the Olympian order with its hegemony of Zeus. Prometheus draws the ancient earth gods, the chthonic powers, into rebellion against the new formalism of the Olympian pantheon with its ordered regimen. Merton also links Herakleitos, philosopher of fire, with the Firebringer in protest against the Olympian way.

The Olympian religion of order and light, symbolized by Zeus and Apollo, contains a darkness at its heart, "this oppressive and guilty view that life and love are somehow a punishment." Merton means here the version of Hesiod in which Prometheus is forced to steal fire so that life may be tolerated, while Pandora is the revenge of Zeus.

> Epimetheus, the brother of Prometheus, receives
> woman as a gift from Zeus and does not wake up
> to the nature of the gift until it is too late. Then he
> remembers what Prometheus had told him: *never*
> *accept any gift from the gods.*[31]

Aeschylus presents an exactly opposite Prometheus to that of Hesiod: "in Aeschylus it is Zeus, not Prometheus, who is the usurper." The hope in *Prometheus Bound* is for deliverance and a turn in the attitude of Zeus: "The struggling gods will be reconciled, and the reconciliation will be the victory of Prometheus but also the victory of Earth, that is to say of mercy, of humanity, of innocence, of trust."[32] Such a hopeful view may also be related to a psychoanalysis of the myth in terms of the maturation process and the quest for identity. In this sense the fire represents Prometheus himself, his identification or acknowledgment by God, as well as his purification or sanctification by God, since his selfhood was obscured by "the terror of having to be someone, of having to be himself." Liberty is a crime against the God who possesses all selfhood, all power, all freedom. Zeus is his alter ego, indeed his true self (projection is in full operation here). Merton sees the symbolism in both fire and theft of fire.

> No one was ever less like Prometheus on Caucasus,
> than Christ on His Cross. For Prometheus thought
> he had to ascend into heaven to steal what God
> had already decreed to give him. But Christ, Who
> had in Himself all the riches of God and all the

> poverty of Prometheus, came down with the fire
> Prometheus needed, hidden in His Heart. And He
> had Himself put to death next to the thief Prome-
> theus in order to show him that in reality God can-
> not seek to keep anything good to Himself alone.[33]

How can one steal that which is already given? On this view, God –
not Zeus the heteronomous but "the Living God" – needs nothing for
himself and thus all that is "His" is intended for sharing with his
creatures. This idea of divine participation will concern us again,
since it is so at odds with the perennial Prometheanism of wilful selfhood, achieved by theft from the Other.

In another place Thomas Merton has spoken of the sort of
litigious and bartering components that constitute "Promethean theology."[34] This is evident in two extremes, Pelagian on the one hand and
predestinarian on the other. Neither can accept the gift of grace:
somehow it must be earned, stolen like fire from on high. Merton
the mystic also scores a kind of "Promethean mysticism" that places
all emphasis on Self, so that there is really no Other. Of the guilt
and frustration of Prometheus he writes:

> He cannot enjoy the gift of God unless he snatches
> it away when God is not looking. This is neces-
> sary, for Prometheus demands that the fire be his
> by right of conquest. Otherwise he will not believe
> it is really his own. And that is the paradox that
> St. Paul saw so clearly: salvation belongs to the
> order of love, of freedom and of giving. It is not
> ours if it is conquered, only if it is freely received,
> as it is freely given.[35]

Christ and Prometheus: sometimes a case of either/or, sometimes both/and. Perhaps a more disquieting logic is advanced by
David Miller, a contemporary analyst who profiles a new polytheism,
the "rebirth of the Gods and Goddesses." He takes the Zeus-Prometheus conflict to be attacking the very definition of being. Zeus
wishes to be all in all, he does not wish to share divinity or its freedom. Therefore: "Prometheus' secret concerning the death of God
is that Zeus will one day die of a disease we call monotheism . . . .
And can anyone doubt that *the doctrine of God is the work of
Zeus*?"[36]

If it is true that the ultimate issue of being, in particular of
freedom-in-being, is met in the conflict between Zeus and the rebel
Titan, then Miller is correct in identifying the problematics of Christianity as the self-defeatism of radical monotheism. For if God is to
be "all in all," how can human being respond except in utter

submission or total defiance? Either Zeus or Prometheus – this is the refrain from ancient lore. Both Christ and Prometheus – this were to introduce a *tertium quid*, a mediating presence who shifts the balance to a three-term logic and so sublates the simplism of the old debate. That this may be the possibility qualifying "monotheism" itself needs further exploration. As we follow the clues of Prometheus's way it may become clearer as to whether we have to do merely with the same old contradiction between God and human freedom, or whether something new is at hand awaiting a better and more realistic understanding.

– 3 –

The Promethean Spirit

The Classical Age

We have noted certain roots of the myth of Prometheus as well as early reactions, in particular that of church fathers. It is not our purpose to concentrate on the fate of this myth as if it alone carries the weight of developing atheism. In a remarkable way it appears to do just that for recent European thought; in earlier ages one can discern at least the spirit of this story of rebellion, this quest for identity as autonomous human being. But strict continuity is lacking, chiefly because the *philosophia perennis* entailed theism, if at times in attenuated and even bizarre forms, as the stance of the intellectual establishment. The alternative to Christian theology was not atheism but other forms of theism – usually heterodox or "heathen." Sometimes these were underground in the hermetic-gnostic tradition recently the subject of considerable scholarly pursuit, and to be noted later in relation to the "Renaissance Magus."[1]

The classical age itself knew about atheism, of course, even if chiefly to refute it (as in Plato) rather than to explore it for commitment (as in Epicurus). One must be careful here; neophyte philosophers are regularly taught that Thales' famous dictum "Water is the material cause of all things" represents a first step in properly "philosophical" reasoning against the older "theological" interpretation of reality. But if one remembers his other saying, "All things are full of gods," and honours the context of Milesian thought, it is less easy to be dogmatic. The Presocratics in general provide analyses adumbrating Aristotle's distinction between *theologi* and *physiologi* (*Meta.* A 983b 20); while the tension between "scientific" and "mystical" schools even at the earliest period warns against unified field laws.[2] Still another, and in our view decisive, distinction is that

---

Notes to Chapter 3 appear on page 308.

45

between philosophy in the Platonist tradition of "optimistic rational-ism" and those elements that constitute the Mysteries with their product, tragic drama.[3]

In any case, the complex story of the classical world contains an element of distinctively atheistic thought. In part this was served by the euhemerism noted in the last chapter, and chiefly by the tradi-tion in which intellectual scepticism and moral striving postulated human autonomy and pragmatic judgment. Several names are rele-vant to our study. The Milesian tradition led to the atomists, Leu-cippus and Democritus, who were rediscovered in modern times by Marx and in a later and different context by Heisenberg. In their own time they taught a "scientific" attitude of geometrical atomism, with Necessity (*anankē, Moira*) in control.

But a caveat is in order here. Perhaps Bruno Snell has put it best, in warning that the "trials for irreligion" of ancient Greece – significantly contained within a generation of fifth century BCE – were not concerned with religion or with "faith"; they were political and social. The capital crime of *asebeia* (transgression against the gods) must be interpreted by the verb *nomizein*, to believe in the gods. The negative could not mean "deny their existence" until the mid-fifth century, when Protagoras advanced the thesis explicitly. Before that it signified a failure to value or respect the established gods. Snell suggests an unconscious shift in the meaning of *nomizein* in Socrates' case, a shift similar to that which led Romans to consider Christians atheistic:

> About the faith of an earlier generation when piety was owned by all, these trials tell us nothing; nor were they concerned with "faith," as the Christian trials of heretics were. Atheists were persecuted only once, during the brief period when the enlight-enment of the philosophers seemed about to destroy the firm structure of human society, and then only in Athens.[4]

What was emerging was a new inspiration for the human *polis*, deriving from a new understanding of human nature as autono-mous being. The traditional reverence for gods of place and function was being questioned, and the critique of superstition, *deisidaimonia*, led through linguistic analysis to negative theology and beyond. It was not the exemplary "atheists" on trial who bear the greatest signif-icance, but the subtle reasoners who raise fundamental questions about knowledge, sometimes on behalf of reason and sometimes against it.

Sophists

Most noteworthy are the group of Sophists and later Sceptics from Pyrrho to Sextus Empiricus. The former are represented best by Protagoras (486/5-4ll BCE) whose treatise *On the Gods* was publicly burnt in Athens. It began: "When it comes to the gods, I am unable to discover whether they are or are not, or even what they are like in form. For there are many things that stand in the way of this knowledge – the obscurity of the problem and the brevity of man's life" (*Antilogiae: Peri Theon* l). Protagoras was brought to trial in 411 and suffered death by shipwreck, either being banished from Athens or in flight to avoid the trial, as his disciple Timon's verses state:

> They chose to reduce his writings to ashes,
> Because he wrote that he neither knew nor could
>   discover concerning the gods
> Who and what they are;
> Yet he showed every caution belonging to virtue.
> This was of no help to him, but he took to flight
> So that we might not thus drink the chill draught of
>   Socrates and descend into Hades.[5]

The example of Protagoras is a key to understanding the phenomenon of atheism and reaction to it. Protagoras's views concerning the gods are rather (in modern terms) agnostic than atheist. This relates to his epistemology, in which our knowledge consists chiefly in opinion (*doxa*), and opinion is inadmissible for knowledge of God. Again, Timon observes that even his care for "virtue" did not save Protagoras; the relationship between faith and ethics continues to plague the modern debate on God. Protagoras was credited with discovering, in line with Zeno's paradoxes, that conceptual thinking involves "two logoi in opposition to each other." Thus theoretical reconciliation proves impossible – the "tragedy" of intellect – and "knowledge" turns toward the practical mastery of things.[6]

Other Sophists follow suit, especially Gorgias (*c.* 485-376 BCE) whose treatise *On Not-being or on Nature* (*Peri mē ontōs*) maintains that nothing exists; or if something exists it is unknowable; or if knowable then incommunicable. The cynical politician Critias taught (in his lost drama *Sisyphus*) that gods were invented as moral authority to prevent lawlessness, a theory akin to euhemerism, firmly established in the Roman Empire (the *pax deorum*) and still useful in antireligious argument today.

Hippias (b. 443? BCE) endeavoured to reconcile the two warring concepts that shaped current politics as well as philosophy: *nomos* and *physis*. His tendentious theory of justice through written law (opposed by Plato) reflects something of the authentic sophist for whom individual virtue and the culture of states remains the goal of *paideia*. He will not divorce rhetoric from grammar and dialectic – the original *trivium* on which higher education would be based. The parody of this school in popular "sophistry" should not blind us to the searching theories of knowledge that lay behind their views on virtue and statecraft.[7]

Sceptics

Pyrrho of Elis (*c*. 365-275 BCE) is named as founder of the Sceptic movement by later members in this line, notably Sextus Empiricus. Although his teaching is known only through others, chiefly his pupil Timon, one can reconstruct its essentials, particularly epistemological. Things are in essence "indifferent" (*adiaphora*) or indeterminate. Therefore neither our sense experiences (*aisthēseis*) nor our beliefs (*doxai*) can be termed true or false. Timon (*c*. 315-225 BCE) reinforces this view, which leads to a suspension of judgment – later definite ways of attaining suspension will develop, such as the Ten Tropes of Epoche attributed to Aenesidemus. The arguments aimed at suspending judgment (*epochē*) by stating conflicting beliefs and experiences. Perception depends on a complex of conditions such that "objects" appear differently from case to case, person to person. This early form of Abelard's *sic et non* method relies on the "empiricist axiom" (Stough) that knowledge has its origin in sensory experience. Reason is unable to apprehend reality apart from sensations, with their inevitable distortion and relativism. Once the seeker has learned the state of the question of truth he will choose to cultivate a state of mind which refuses to answer unanswerable questions: *aphasia*. This leads to the sort of well-being appropriate to sceptical minds: *ataraxia*. Such quiescence matches the concern with practical affairs, with philosophy as way of life, common to Sceptics and Sophists, indeed to most classical thought. Later Sceptics were tempted to concentrate on subtle problems of epistemology but did not lose their empiricist foundation.[8]

Academic Scepticism, associated with Arcesilaus (315-240 BCE) and Carneades (214-129 BCE) in the New Academy of Athens, is an alternative to Pyrrhonism within the general school. It sought to continue the Platonic tradition, with the Socratic maxim in mind: "All I know is that I know nothing." Carneades' search for criteria of truth entails a sort of verification theory, the method of moving from evidence to assertion of fact. Leaning on the distinction between phenomena and "reality," these philosophers find little to doubt in how things appear to us, but refuse to make statements about their real nature.

Sextus Empiricus (*c.* 150-250 CE) sums up the school through his work and influence. He was also a physician, reflecting the connection between Scepticism and that school of "Empirical" medicine long associated with Pyrrhonic philosophy. Accepting the Ten Tropes of Aenesidemus, Sextus agrees that because of such conditioning of sense impressions, we lack criteria by which to differentiate between veridical and nonveridical experience. Hence the distinction noted earlier between appearance and reality. The appearances (*phainomena*) are based on sense data (*aisthēta*), leaving their reality (*hypokeitai*) unproved: "Phenomena merely establish the fact that they appear, but are not able to indicate further that they really exist."[9]

The Charge Against Socrates

The ignorance professed by Socrates (*c.* 470-399 BCE) included a dose of sceptical enquiry concerning the gods, intended to bring forth (in the maieutic fashion adopted by this philosophical midwife) the hidden truth obscured by opinion and illusion. This is evident in such dialogues as the *Euthyphro*, where Socrates attacks the popular feeling about religion as a matter of *do ut des,* a business transaction between gods and men: "Then piety, Euthyphro, is an art which gods and men have of doing business with one another?" But in the *Apology* things have got out of hand, and statements of Socrates are being taken out of context to charge him with a capital offence against the state; as his accuser Meletus puts it: "you are a complete atheist." Socrates' defence, in questioning Meletus, exposes the logical contradiction involved: he stands accused of believing in "spirits and divine agencies" *and* denying the gods' existence. Yet he makes it clear, in his opening speech, why he follows his strange vocation associated with "a certain kind of wisdom which I have." He says, "I will refer you to a witness who is worthy of credit; that witness shall be the God of Delphi."

It was the oracle of the Pythian goddess (no one is wiser than Socrates) that spurred him to explore the so-called wisdom of his day and so discover the sort of *sophia* he apparently possessed. After visiting men of repute – politicians, poets of all kinds – he sought out artisans and found them to make the same mistake: "because they were good workmen they thought that they also knew all sorts of high matters, and this defect in them overshadowed their wisdom." Thus he reached the conclusion that "only God is wise" and that the oracle means "He, O men, is the wisest, who, like Socrates, knows that his wisdom is in truth worth nothing."

The case of Socrates is instructive in illustrating a strand of inquiry that poses alternative theories that may be termed antitheistic rather than atheistic. We shall see such an enquiry throughout Western history, often underground but at certain times surfacing as a serious contender with the civil religion. Plato helped reinforce the Socratic scepticism with his criticism of superstition, particularly those "gods of aversion" promoted by "mendicant quacks" of the Mysteries (*Laws* 854B). In his sketch of the ideal republic, popular religion must serve the state, and private speculation is discouraged. Plato's quarrel with the poets was grounded in his Socratic sense that if "only God is wise," human knowledge is always subject to the severe limitation on which his master had insisted. Plato was conscious of human failings, but maintained that "The maker and father of this universe it is difficult to discover; nor, if he were discovered, could he be declared to all" (*Timaeus* 28C). This has been called "perhaps the most hackneyed quotation from Plato in Hellenistic writers,"[10] since it appears regularly in the arsenal of those who developed a religious and mystical Platonism in subsequent centuries. Despite the complex nature of Plato's own theology, and the difficulty in interpreting the periods of his teaching, particularly the final stage of unwritten doctrine and *Letters*, we may agree with a recent writer that "even at his gloomiest he is never in essentials a sceptic."[11] Indeed, the development of religious Platonism offered to Christian theology a philosophy so compatible with the gospel that to the later eyes of many, it threatened its essential nature with what von Harnack termed "acute Hellenization."

The power of the philosophical theology of hellenism lay in its quest for what is "appropriate to God [*theoprepes*]." The criteria for what is worthy of attribution to deity derived from idealistic logic, according to which the great error was that of anthropomorphism. Xenophanes (b. 570 BCE) is a familiar spokesman for the position:

> Homer and Hesiod have attributed to the Gods
> everything that is a shame and reproach among
> men, theft and adultery and mutual deception . . .
> if oxen had hands and could draw . . . horses

> would draw forms of gods like horses, and oxen
> like oxen, giving them bodies after the fashion of
> their own.
>
> *(Frag.* 11,15)

The demythologization of the Homeric narrative thus functions as the method of interpretation that reveals hidden and eternal truth. With Plato we see the reduction of Homeric mythology to an etiological role, as in the *Protagoras*. Prometheus is no longer hero and champion, but a sort of prelude to the story of Pandora to explain a disputed question. Moreover, to discuss the matter abstractly would have been preferable, but Protagoras chooses the form of "apologue or myth" as an elder addressing a younger, and because "the myth will be more interesting" than "arguing out the question." It is to be noted, however, that such etiological use of myth is secondary to a more sublime use at certain points, where Plato finds that even *logos*, while generally superior to *mythos*, reaches its limits and yields to higher myths to carry the burden of the quest for truth.[12]

Epicurus

The name Epicurean has come to represent a popular caricature of a serious philosophical school. Epicurus (341-270 BCE) himself is known as the father of Western atheism, and his followers were ridiculed even by Horace: a "plump sleek pig from Epicurus' herd," embodying a type of "sensual hedonism combined with a crude atheism."[13] Christian Fathers agreed – Gregory Nazianzen for instance recommended: "Attack the atheism of Epicurus, and his atoms, and his unphilosophic pleasure."[14]

The fact is that this was a smallish sect, unpopular with the dominant schools of Platonism, Aristotelianism and Stoicism and hence an easy victim for propaganda. Philosophy meant a way of life, and for Epicurus this was to be based on reason and fixed on the goal of *ataraxia*. Such tranquillity or imperturbability, more negative than for the Stoics, must be guarded against every perturbation even from divine influence; hence the antipathy to theological speculation about gods or fate or providence. Much of its charm and power is evident from such a work as Walter Pater's *Marius the Epicurean*, particularly the ambiguous relation to Christianity. The young Roman's quest, amid the obvious "tears of the world [*lacrimae rerum*]," discovers in Epicureanism "the special philosophy of the poor." For himself, consolation lies with Christian community and its belief in resurrection. Yet his Epicureanism marks and guides him to the end.

Now for Epicurus the gods themselves represent tranquillity to perfection; hence religious festivals should be attended to remind one of this fact. The practical way of *ataraxia*, however, is governed less by theories of this sort than by the study of natural philosophy, which removes fear of the gods by explaining phenomena in empirical terms. Indeed, the atomic theory applied also to human organisms rules out a nonempirical self for Epicurus. In fact what happened was that Epicurean morality was hardly a systematic guide for ethics. It was bolstered by Stoic principles but, more importantly, opted for a pragmatism that amounted to "a conformist morality" with an eye on mainline standards.[15] The cultivation of those lasting pleasures ("catastematic" against "kinetic") that make for peace of mind attracted a devoted following, and Epicureanism continued for four centuries, spreading also to Italy. It was the Roman writer Lucretius (*c.* 99-55 BCE) whose *De Rerum Natura* assured lasting fame to Epicurus.

Lucretius almost idolized Epicurus: "Therefore, superstition in its turn lies crushed beneath his feet, and we by his triumph are raised to the heavens" (*De Rer. Nat.* 29). For the later Roman, even the vestiges of mythology and state religion, which the master apparently condoned, must go, so corrupt is the institution of religion. *Tantum religio potuit suadere* (Such great evils could religion prompt). If Epicurus remains ambiguous on the gods, Lucretius celebrates the freedom resulting from the end of superstition (still in the sense of fear of the gods, *deisidaimonia*). Clearly, Epicurus is here the hero of Enlightenment, as Karl Marx regarded him in his doctoral thesis, *The Difference Between the Natural Philosophy of Democritus and Epicurus*. It is in this work that Marx declares the Epicurean philosophy to constitute nothing short of a "Promethean" revolt against the divine orders. He understands the ancient Greek to have been the first enlightener, with autonomous self-consciousness as the new divinity, even though his proximate goal is merely *ataraxia* rather than a "Marxist" knowledge of the essence of things in matter and work. Georg Siegmund comments: "For him [Epicurus] philosophy is a kind of hygiene of the soul, an art in which the suffering of the soul is explained as the result of fear – of men's fear of Fate, fear of the gods, fear of death."[16]

To appreciate Lucretius we must see him as more than a

transmitter of Epicurus's thoughts. The latter was himself "heir to a long, at times secret, tradition of the world's de-divinization," while Lucretius "holds the monopoly on materialist atheism."[17] The proper materialist learns from the tradition of desacralization that the elements of this world are sufficient to explain its workings, without recourse to unseen forces behind or ahead of those elements.

> Nature, delivered from every haughty lord
> And forthwith free, is seen to have done all things
> Herself, and through herself, of her own accord
> Rid of all gods. . . .
>
> (*De Rer. Nat.* II.1090ff)

Such was the "ontological materialism" of Leucippus, Democritus and Epicurus. Such was also the theory of the Enlightenment revival of Epicurus and Lucretius, leading Karl Marx to promote the positivistic science of the ancient materialists.

Lucretius's aim is to overthrow Greek theology or metaphysics or both, on behalf of an empirical theory of knowledge and a materialist ontology. Perhaps the most significant aspect of this materialism concerns the question of necessity and free will. It would seem that Lucretius is well on the way to replacing not only outside agency (divine heteronomy) but also inner chance or will, by some form of determinism. In fact he develops Epicurus's famous doctrine of the "swerve" (*parenklisis*, Lat. *clinamen*) of the flow of atoms to argue for freedom of the will – a point that Marx in turn will honour as the key element in distinguishing Epicurus from Democritus. Lucretius had used this moot point of physics in seeking the cause of our "power inborn" as "free act":

> *this* state comes to man
> From that slight swervement of the elements
> In no fixed line of space, in no fixed time.[18]

The *editio princeps* of the *De Rerum Natura* is 1473, by Ferrandus of Brescia. The Renaissance humanists remained ambiguous about this classical poet whom they rediscovered. The dominant Platonism of Florence, as well as the variety of Aristotles available through interpretation, were strong enough to test themselves against Lucretius without yielding the field. Their theories of knowledge were not open to his sensationalism – and, curiously, he had not noticed the role of *prolepsis* in Epicurus's own epistemology. Thus they passed on this pair of classical materialists to the eager hands of Enlightenment scholars whose views were more compatible. Pierre Gassendi made personal use not only of the Epicurean philosophy of life but also of the classical theory of atomism. His view has been described as a "mitigated skepticism and limited Epicureanism" (Richard Popkin) and helped establish the figures of Epicurus and Lucretius as authorities for the *philosophes* as well as for Hobbes and John Locke, the latter at least in respect of the atomic theory of sense knowledge.

Atheism in classical times, therefore, is a fact and a complex one. Certain individuals were even surnamed "the Atheist," notably Diagoras and Theodoros in the fifth century BCE. Moreover, the "materialism" of the atomists Democritus and Leucippus, combined with the empirical tradition, makes for a solid philosophical type of atheism. This was both theoretical as to arguments for the nonexistence of the gods, at least in their mythological and popular form, and practical as a way of human life seeking peace of mind even from disturbance from divine agency. Thomas Molnar distinguishes three motives or elements in Greek humanism, which suggest the variety that converged to form a classical "syncretic humanism."[19] First is the Lucretian materialism, which dispels fear of the gods by reducing everything to impersonal matter and motion. Next is the Pyrrhonian motive, which substitutes philosophy for religion since reason can never attain certitude and therefore is more appropriate for the sceptical world-view. Finally, the Stoic motive insists on the human link with the world-soul; we transcend our materiality (passions) by working for the human society or cosmopolis. One sees here how easily materialism and scepticism attract one another.

It should be noted, however, that such syntheses as appear in the noble works of a Cicero or a Seneca, and which proved influential in later ages such as the Renaissance, in their own time appeared élitist and soon gave way to the religions – often themselves syncretic – that dominated the classical world. Originating in Egypt or the Near East or Greece, the cults or mysteries of Isis, of Adonis and Mithra and of Dionysus-Orpheus thrived and drew the reverence and submission that the philosophical schools continued to brand as mere superstition.

Classical Theism

The establishment of Christendom signified a civil religion enjoying majority rule and privilege throughout the Roman Empire. The fate of atheism during this period, roughly the fifth to the fifteenth centuries CE, was conditioned by the reprisals awaiting deviation from the state-church line, as well as the virtual hegemony of the patristic-scholastic theology developed as Augustinianism in the West and as Conciliar Orthodoxy in the East. In both cases it was a hellenized theology that allowed continuity with the religious philosophy of the classical world, so that Lucretius could be dismissed as a madman and Epicurus singled out as the exception, the atheist among the god-fearing majority of ancient philosophers. Such propaganda obtained until the Renaissance recovered the texts as well as the spirit of classical enquiry.

Meanwhile the medieval debates themselves prepared the way for modern atheism. By this is meant the entrenchment of classical theism, interpreted as projecting such attributes upon transcendence as make the Jewish and Christian God a virtual Zeus. Along with this development went those sterile disputations caricatured in the question about the number of angels dancing on a pinhead. Certainly the *quaestio disputata* is easily parodied, missing the point of its disciplined method and impressive results. Yet it cast reasons for belief in God in the form of logico-deductive arguments which proved unable to withstand the attack of philosophers, Kant in particular. The world-view that constituted the horizon for those famous arguments has passed; the harmony of Platonism and of Aristotelianism (as well as, ironically, the moralism of Kant himself) proves difficult for moderns to appreciate, much less to cultivate. Atheism in its modern dress was made possible in part by the philosophical-theological synthesis of medieval schoolmen.

The metaphysical problem that dominated classical theism derived from Greek philosophy: can human minds *think* God? By this time the heritage involved Plato the theologian and hierophant, the *esotericus* of the *Letters* and the Middle- and Neoplatonic reading. From Parmenides, Plato took the doctrine of the bare One beyond definition except through negation (*Parm.* 137C-142A). This apophatic modality states that God is even "beyond being" (*Rep.* 509B). Thus the *triplex via* began that careful analogical predication that provided the scholastic theo-logic. Yet it could not overcome the essentialism and triumphalism of its inheritance; it produced what Luther aptly styled a "theology of glory." When absoluteness is accepted as entailing metaphysical necessity (*ens necessarium*), the existence of God is rendered ambiguous for both theism and atheism. The one finds itself unable to accept biblical or revelatory data as to God's relatedness, especially his humanization through incarnation; the other regards the absoluteness steadily and concludes that it means Nothing.[20]

The school debates in fact produced conceptual diversity and flexibility – to mention two leading examples: justification by works or by faith? transubstantiation or spiritual presence in the Eucharist? – but they also led to uncertainty about the role of theology and the power of reason. We may applaud the twelfth-century Renaissance, with its revival of systematic and mystical theology; we must remember also the shape of Latin Averroism, with its separation of theology from philosophy and its extreme doctrine of twofold truth – not only the great Anselms of Laon and Canterbury but also Siger of Brabant. The dispute over universals, for instance, involving subtle questions about the relation between faith and reason, while neither so simple nor so scandalous as the Reformers were to think, tended toward a growing fideism.[21]

Part of this development crucial for our thesis was the case of divine and human willing, a perennial problem for discursive thought. Aristotle's *Organon* provided the method for interpreting the logic of categorical statements, and Augustine developed a sophisticated and nuanced model for Western orthodoxy. In our concluding chapter we shall argue that modern philosophy has tended to reduce theism to the oppositions (antitheses) of formal logic. In particular, it commits the crucial category-mistake of confusing omnipotence with all-mightiness, whereas the Aristotelian-Augustinian tradition appreciated the logic of modal relations, especially necessity and possibility (equated with contingency). Medieval books entitled *De Consequentiis* grasped the complexity of "implication" and saved the debates on divine knowledge and power from total reduction.

The problem of harmonizing disparate wills had occupied twelfth-century mystical theologians such as William of St-Thierry and the Cistercians in their exegesis of the Wisdom literature, particularly the Song of Songs. In their search for classical sources on friendship and love, Ovid offered little help, whereas Cicero's *De amicitia* provided a model of disinterested affection allowing consensus of two wills. Thus the issue of one all-powerful will robbing the other of freedom seemed solved in theory. The freedom (*libertas*) bestowed on humans in creation was taken to mean not "independent of God" but loyalty to one's essential being, the good known and attainable within the limits of the created order. Anselm of Canterbury's treatise on freedom of choice (*De Libertate Arbitrii*) thus emphasized "uprightness of will," since *rectitudo* is the goal of free will. His careful distinctions drawn within freedom, willing and necessity indicate the complex argument that informed the school debates. For "Power or powerlessness may be classified in various ways [*Pluribus modis dividi possit potentia vel impotentia*]." The chief point is to deny any coercion (*necessitas coactionis*), preserving what today is termed "negative freedom," freedom from external constraints. As for positive freedom, this is not threatened by divine willing but is established, inasmuch as the divine infallibility involves decisions *ex hypothesi*; that is, connected with human faith and action. Hence the proper corollary of human freedom is not divine will but grace. Anselm's treatise *De Concordia* sees grace and free will as coadjutors. This concord derives from Augustine, although Anselm is more sanguine than his predecessor about the uprightness attained by free choice.[22]

Augustine had argued that while divine omniscience entails foreknowledge of events, this does not preclude human freedom. Prescience is like memory; "before" and "after" do not pertain to the perspective of eternity (e.g., *De Trin.* 5.2). Thus determination in the form of divine determinism is ruled out. Boethius and Aquinas, most notably, reinforced this approach. But an ambiguity haunts classical theism because it begins with a major paradox, namely the coexistence of divine predestination with human freedom. This famous "dialectic" of Augustine's follows the biblical, especially Pauline, insistence on such coexistence without theoretical resolution. For instance, he continued to hold to the "natural" freedom of the will after the Fall, intending by *servum arbitrium* – so important for Luther – the loss of "acquired" freedom to do the morally good. Here is the key distinction between free choice (*liberum arbitrium*) or universal free will, and freedom (*libertas*) or the good will as fruit of divine grace.[23] Subsequent debate, however, shifted the emphasis to divine power in general, preparing different ground for the fateful doctrine of predestination. It would seem that little freedom survived from Augustine, or consolation from Boethius. Once again the stage was prepared for the old drama of confrontation. For if God is cast in the role of Zeus (high and mighty), who will play Prometheus?

The magisterial teaching of Aquinas offers clues to the development of doctrine on this disputed question. We should note the significance of his idea of God for our thesis. Since the divine essence is "to be," this unique One entails identity of essence and existence. Although he rejects the ontological argument, Aquinas agrees with Anselm of Canterbury that "God" is a unique and incomparable Being-itself. God is his own essence; hence "certain philosophers" can say that he has no essence (*ST* I.3f; *SCG* I.21f; *De ente et essentia* 6). It would be equally true to say that God does not exist, since "existence" (*pace* Bertrand Russell and objectors to the Cartesian form of ontological argument) is not a predicate. Paul Tillich has this in mind when he observes: "It is as atheistic to affirm the existence of God as it is to deny it" (*ST* I.237). From such reflection the epistemology of Aquinas follows in its ana-logic. Aquinas's theory of concept – a *simplex apprehensio* producing a *verbum mentale* – reflects his moderate realism. He accepts the dictum of Isaac Israeli, *veritas est adaequatio rei et intellectus* (*ST* I.16.2,2; 21.2). Between simply univocal and purely equivocal religious language lies the golden mean of analogy, honouring the biblical rule of metaphor. It is significant for our purpose that Aquinas opens the greater *Summa* with a concept intended to illustrate "how God is not [*quomodo non sit*]." He is not constructing a doctrine of God through analogical reasoning, but provides introductory language analysis. The tension between the poles of *remotio* and *eminentia* is stronger toward the former, in behalf of a *theologia negativa*. In this Aquinas resembles Maimonides – the "divine science" accords attributes in a negative manner, so that the "attributes of action . . . do not mean that He possesses qualities" (*Guide of the Perplexed* I.54). He also resembles John Calvin, who stresses the "impropriety" of talk about God, and "the great disproportion [*plurimum differre*] of all the similitudes" of the Fathers (*Inst.* I.13.18). The crucial concept of analogy ("proper proportionality") avoids the opposing errors of anthropomorphism and agnosticism.

Between rational knowledge and belief falls the will. Aristotle taught that the will follows the intellect: "both the reasoning must be true and the desire right, if the choice is to be good" (*Nic. Eth.* VI.2). The point proved moot ("choice is either desiderative reason or ratiocinative desire") and bred bitter controversy among Schoolmen. Scotus gave priority to will, Aquinas the reverse. Thomas blended Augustine with Aristotle, following the great Father's position against Pelagian and semi-Pelagian inflation of the role of willing. We do not believe without willing (*nullus credit nisi volens* – Augustine), but the will chooses what the intellect judges good. Among finite goods choice is required, against the standard of sovereign Goodness (*ST* I.1.81,1). The intention of our willing involves deliberation and consent (*consilium, consensus*). The good cannot be desired unless it is known; where practical reason is wrong, the will follows suit.[24] But such harmony of intellect and will was soon to suffer eclipse in the new theology already in the making.

The school called nominalist (or terminist) shows this

development best, especially in its late medieval form, influential for both Reform and Counter-Reform. Followers of the new method (*via moderna*) of interpreting Aristotle, its adherents challenged the Thomist synthesis. Their tendency to separate natural from revealed theology meant the severance of metaphysics from theology, giving unbalanced weight to revelation. For example, the critique of Duns Scotus (1266-1308) by William of Ockham (*c.* 1285-1349) rejected the Scotist "common natures" or essences abstracted from sensory data. With this went the kind of order or structure that Scotus thought to distinguish within deity, his "divine psychology," which allowed God's love to guide his will. Instead, Ockham posited the utter simplicity of God, and in turn absolute divine freedom. His treatment of the test question of future contingencies argues that such propositions can be determinately true by what will be the case, thus assuring human freedom along with divine intuitive cognition. His positive theology, however, involves scepticism about the possibility of reconciling logic with faith. Thus the so-called Ockham's Razor – the rule of parsimony or economy of explanation – could be used for a self-inflicted wound on the body of scholasticism. The critique assumes a harder form in Thomas Bradwardine (*c.* 1290-1349) at Oxford. Although he posits the divine love as source of the divine will, human autonomy is sacrificed to God's complete causality, by which he participates in every worldly event. Such doctrine was an attempt to develop the classical concept of providence, which from Cicero on had been a weapon against fatalism, as an apologetic against the new determinism of Arabic Aristotelianism. But the philosophical theologians found determinism most difficult to avoid.[25]

The scholastic teaching on power remains decisive, as we shall see in examining the contemporary debate on the paradox of omnipotence in our conclusion. Aristotle's analysis of potency (*Meta* V.12ff, IX) had spelled out the formal definition, "that which is not of necessity false" in relation to privation, incapacity and limit. Peter Lombard follows: some things require "impotence" – *posse corrumpi*, for instance – because they derive from imperfection or infirmity. Thus for God to be able to sin "would not be a power but an infirmity [*non potentia sed infirmitas*]" (*Sent.* 1, d.42, ch.2). Thomas and Bonaventure, lecturing on the standard *Libros Sententiarum*, state that God can do not merely what other agents can, but whatever does not involve imperfection. For Aquinas this means that "He can do all things that are possible absolutely" (*ST* I, 25, 3c). Thus *potest omnia* is set within the context of logical possibility: what is absolute or intrinsic. It is this nice bit of linguistic analysis that gets tangled in subsequent mistranslation and debate, as James F. Ross argues. Rather than acknowledging that "God has within his power anything that is intrinsically possible," the *secundum se* becomes "can do anything (he wills)." Moreover, even the circumspect work of Gabriel Biel (d. 1495) on the distinction between divine power absolute and actual or ordained (*potentia absoluta, ordinata*) was unable to avoid the simplism of popular interpretation. For Biel the *ordinata* is decisive, inasmuch as divine will is moved by its own grace: God's *libertas* entails *misericordia*. As Peter Martyr Vermigli will argue against Lutheran teaching on christology and Eucharist, not the *posse* but the *velle* is what counts. Moreover, the divine liberty is matched or mirrored by the freedom of human willing, hence the problematics of preparatory grace and dispositions of the will to which Biel commits himself in working out his theology of freedom.[26]

Now the medieval intent was to hold truth and goodness together, since the intellect guides the will in its choice. Yet later nominalism could be misused as mere "ecclesiastical positivism." Its stress on revelation demanded a turn toward an authoritative (because authoritarian) church for the truth. So its distinctions were taken less seriously than its slogans, and at the cost of subtlety of reasoning another voice was added to the familiar charge that a divine despotism rules human affairs, rendering human free will a charade.

This development of doctrine that, in our view, gave credence to interpreting God as Zeus for Christendom, may be referred to the analysis of Charles Hartshorne, without implying that his process theology provides the best alternative. Hartshorne provides a typology of theistic forms involving five questions as criteria: Is God eternal? Is he temporal? Is he conscious? Does he know the world? Does he include the world?[27] Seeing "a pattern in the history of rational reflection about God," he notes that reason always tends to simplify, a tendency with fateful results in theological reasoning, where simplification destroys the "law of polarity" (Morris Cohen) or complementarity of categories. Thus to oversimplify is to fall into a "monopolar" concept of deity rather than the proper "dipolar" concept. The former characterizes what Hartshorne calls "classical theism" and the latter his preferred view of "panentheism." To compare: classical theism sees God as "Eternal Consciousness, Knowing but not including the world"; panentheism sees "The Supreme as Eternal-Temporal Consciousness, Knowing and including the World."

As shorthand for the mainstream Christian tradition,

"classical theism" describes well the traditional image of Western orthodoxy. It misses, however, the qualifications and nuanced terminology, in both Fathers and Schoolmen. Still, in the popular mind – including its atheistic opponents – this monopolar deity of absolutist qualities continues to hold sway. Indeed it is a curious fact that nonbelievers in argument with believers often insist that such a loaded image of absolutism is the Subject under discussion: they "know" the sort of God they will not believe in. William Hamilton has termed this "the Walter Kaufmann syndrome," which likes its foes to be "as orthodox as possible so they can be rejected as irrelevant."[28]

The point about the description of "classical theism" is that it affects the debate about God usually in its hardened form of scholastic summary. The divine attributes are loosened from their context in systematic theology and lack the discussion of types and definitions (in particular the concept of analogical predication). An extreme parody, echoing the textbook theology of the schools, is found on the lips of Lucky, a character of Samuel Beckett's *Waiting for Godot*. Like his master, James Joyce, Beckett reflects that hardening of religion (whether Catholic or Protestant) where dogma is eternally certain and the chief divine attributes are power and jealousy. The unfortunate Lucky, slave to Pozzo, recites his set speech on command and breaks it off as his strength flags. "Given the existence . . . of a personal God" who is defined (*quaquaquaqua*) by negative attributes such as apathia, athambia and aphasia – such a God "loves us dearly with some exceptions for reasons unknown but time will tell." Here is a brilliant reduction of popular religion to its familiar mixture of tendentious phrases, which only professional theologians understand, and of blind faith in a God who seems cruel but surely must have his own reasons. Moreover, according to Lucky's rendering of Christian faith, humanity (whether Essy or Possy) "wastes and pines . . . what is more for reasons unknown but time will tell fades away." As the speech itself fades we are left with the stark terms: unfinished . . . unfinished . . . the skull the skull . . . unfinished.

If such a parody contains even half the truth about the popular understanding of Christianity, and if it reflects also much of what sceptical academics think, it will be clear that modern atheism may be described more properly as a particular kind of antitheism. Promethean atheism in particular derives its power from a distinct interpretation of Western Christian theology. It sees this as either a formal and abstract speculation or an emotional and irrational fideism. It is such a theism that modernity has in mind, since the Enlightenment in particular, when it rejects Christianity in the name of human freedom, human free will.

Thus from the classical age to the classical theism of medieval Christendom there emerged a particular theology, which cast the Christian God in the role of Zeus – or so it seemed to the popular imagination. The subtleties of scholastic debates were lost on people struggling for livelihood against terrible odds of infant mortality, plague, famine and war. The image of God as wilful Emperor seemed to fit their lot – a "lot" largely in the hands of Dame Fortune, medieval successor to the ancient Three Spinners. Fortune became Fate, and God the Tyrant had the final say.

Charles Hartshorne's "neoclassical metaphysics" attempts to correct this heritage by radical surgery. But modern atheism is so far committed to the theology of classical theism in its counter arguments. Whether process thinking or alternative doctrines of divine being can shift the debating ground remains to be seen. Meanwhile, the Promethean spirit offers a clear choice to its age-old opponent, God as Zeus.

PART II
UNBINDING PROMETHEUS

– 4 –

Rebirth of Will

"Renaissance Man"

The myths of historiography die hard. About that strange and revolutionary phenomenon known as the Renaissance, certain theories continue to haunt scholarly research. One is – following nineteenth-century reckoning – that all was darkness until the fifteenth century; suddenly a great light dawned, heralding the end of Christendom and the beginning of reason and culture. Related to this is the thesis that in the Italian Renaissance (especially its Averroism) we have "a phase in the history of free thought," as P.O. Kristeller sums up the position of Renan he is rejecting.[1] This latter thesis, similarly rooted in nineteenth century interpretation, sees the Italian Renaissance as "a secret atheism or as a new Paganism incompatible with Christianity."[2]

Such views are modified by contemporary scholarship, which grasps the continuity between medieval and Renaissance cultures and thought. Indeed, the Italian Renaissance itself shows a strong religious philosophy at work, in its relation to Reformation and Counter-Reformation themes.[3] Yet there is considerable truth to the idea of novelty in this phenomenon. There was a new way of looking, linked with the development of scientific method with its attention to the world as given to the human eye. The emphasis on the doctrine of human nature displaced the theocentrism of traditional dogma with an anthropocentrism that reconstituted such concepts as freedom of the will in a powerful way.

Prometheus himself is hailed as symbol of the creative spirit, although not explicitly in his role as defier of gods. This continues that older tradition, already noted in Isidore of Seville, whereby gods are explained in terms of hero-worship, so that euhemerism allows

---

Notes to Chapter 4 appear on page 311.

65

them to exist in harmony with strict monotheism. Such heroic stature sat well with Renaissance philosophy. Boccaccio could speak of a "first Prometheus" and a "second Prometheus," the latter symbolizing the new man whose will assures both freedom and dignity. Even earlier, the twelfth-century Alexander Nequam had called himself *novus Prometheus*, but it was the mood and outlook of Boccaccio's generation that gave weight to the implication.[4] The Florentine Academy revived the myth according to Plato's *Protagoras*. Ficino's exegesis shows the promise of technique for the new man: *Prometheus rationalis animal gubernator in hominem trajecit artis industriam*. Along with Pomponazzi, Ficino platonizes the Titan, in that technical promise is subservient to the realm of the Ideas. For Pomponazzi, the true *interpretatio fabulae Promethei* will reveal the philosopher's search for truth (*scire Dei archana*) with its hardship and suffering, its deprivation of the goods of this earth – such constitute the riches of philosophers, their "income."[5]

Erasmus uses the myth in various ways, chiefly as symbol for his view of that *virtù* that is the hope of the human condition. Prometheus is an example for our imitation, that we should endeavour by human craft to strive after what is best and highest. It is noteworthy that we have now passed into the familiar Promethean vocabulary of human striving, human potential, human artifice: *Prometheus est nobis imitandus . . . humano artificio praestari*.[6] Here too, as for the Platonists, the Titan represents wisdom, especially foresight in contrast with Epimetheus. For Erasmus moreover human well-being is a matter of *devotio*, harmonious with the solitary sufferer of the Caucasus – "in all respects is he superior, who acknowledges the teacher of the heavenly Philosophy [*Philosophiae coelestis doctorem*]." For this Christian humanist, humanity is at its best when it serves within its proper limits, guided by the *scopus*, which determines our proper horizon. As a recent Erasmian scholar has argued, this polestar is for Erasmus Christ himself. Rather than Prometheus, Christ is for him a Proteus, fulfilling the concept of *accommodatio* by subserving all things to his own will. Thus the myth of Prometheus is accommodated to the Christian view.[7]

For other Renaissance scholars too Prometheus is symbol of the contemplative life. Lefèvre d'Etaples emphasizes the potential in human being, so that wisdom consists in the process, in disengagement and denial: *Hac enim in parte celebrem illum Prometheum imitatur*. Alciati includes Prometheus in his *Emblematum liber* (1531) to point the moral lesson beloved of the emblematic compilers. Charles de Bouelles followed the Florentine example to depict the Prometheus of the *Protagoras* tradition.[8]

The idea of "Renaissance man" holds a great truth, pointing not merely to the eclectic genius such as da Vinci (close to a proper *uomo universale*) but more generally to the ideal of wisdom cultivated over many generations. The Renaissance as phenomenon, of course, is a mixture of things: a call to return *ad fontes*; a working out of new and better methods for handling texts and data in jurisprudence, medicine, philosophy and theology; a recovery of ideals of human justice, freedom and dignity. It owes much to the classical tradition but much also to the creative spirit of the quattrocento in particular. There remains something uncanny in the sympathetic bond that allowed the leap over a millennium and more so that genuine understanding was established through their hermeneutic. This is true also of the Reformation, which established similar bonds in its recovery of Hebrew as well as Greek and its vivifying exegesis of both Old and New Testaments. Indeed, the Reformation may be termed the Hebraicization of Christianity when one considers the weight of authority that the Old Testament bore for it, whatever one thinks of the typological exegesis involved.[9]

Pico on Dignity

If one Renaissance text suggests itself as exemplary it is surely Pico della Mirandola's *De hominis dignitate*. Pico (1463-94) was attracted to Florentine Platonism but modified its anthropology (humanity is midway in the chain of being between lowest matter and God) to stress human potential and freedom of the will. The oration was prepared as introduction to the nine hundred philosophical-theological propositions that he offered for debate with any takers; no one accepted. He was twenty years old at the time.

Pico agrees that the human is special and exceptional, but not for traditional reasons deriving from philosophy and theology. His voluntarism conflates the "image and likeness" of God into the single aim of human destiny: assimilation to God through achieving the divine point of view. When God the Creator completed his handiwork he wished for someone to "contemplate the nature of so great a work, love its beauty and admire its magnitude." But everywhere the fullness of creation was manifest already. Therefore he decreed that the creature "of indeterminate form" should share in all that others possessed:

> I have given you no fixed abode, no form of your own, no gifts peculiarly yours, O Adam, so that you might have and possess the abode, form and gifts you yourself desire according to your will and judgment. The defined nature of other beings is confined by laws which I have prescribed. You, compelled by no limitations, according to your free choice in whose hands I have placed you, shall prescribe your own limits . . . so that, free of constraint and more honourable as your own moulder and maker, you might give yourself whatever form you prefer.[10]

Such is the free choice, the openness of will, the power to move within creation accorded to "this our chameleon," placed *in mundi meditullio*. Pico asks therefore, "Could anything else be more an object of wonder?" Now the earlier answer would have been: "Yes – God!" For this is truly humanistic, to make the chief wonder of humanity no longer our maker but ourselves. The theme will be taken up and echoed by generations of humanists: "The chief study of mankind is man." Not that Pico is antitheist or atheist, for what is proffered is the glory of that special creature appointed to share the Creator's contemplation of his unique and original work. But a subtle change is taking place, and the heroic venture is again before us, a titanic call to a higher humanity not yet clearly seen nor firmly grasped.

Pico's tract is important for our purposes in showing the stress on human dignity for which freedom is an absolute necessity; and for the fact that although no doubt taken rightly as a classic source of humanism, it is not atheist. When this truly Renaissance man died of fever in Florence at age thirty-one, he was dressed in the robes of a Dominican friar.

The Renaissance was Aristotelian in the sense that theory issues in action, philosophy is practical. The *Politics* and the *Nicomachean Ethics* were favourite texts for humanist and theologian alike. Despite the Italian penchant for high theory, the mood is caught better by the term "moral philosophy" than by "speculation." Perhaps the truth is that the humanism of the high Renaissance, a "Christian" humanism still, paved the way for something different when conditions altered. Its focus on human freedom and dignity and on the practicality of human being made room for a later Promethean stress on wilful autonomy and on technique. But this was owing as much to the consequences of the religious disputes and dogmas as to technical or "scientific" methods or to humanistic doctrines.

Coming of Age

Humanity was coming of age in Europe. Ficino called us from slavery to nature to be its equals, indeed its rivals: *non servi simus naturae sed aemuli*. The ideal of supremacy, of creative endeavour showing who is master, leads beyond Pico's contemplator to the titanism of the geniuses of Tuscany. In Leonardo and Michelangelo we have the prototypical Renaissance man, master of several arts, enlarging the frontiers of knowledge and experimental lore through creative genius, children of their age yet truly universal. Leonardo, the Italian Faust, and Michelangelo reflect the new spirit of heroic endeavour and potential in their various works. If the *David* of Michelangelo symbolizes the libertarian defiance of Florence, then Florence itself can stand as symbol for the spirit of the age. This is particularly clear when we compare the statue to two already on display when Michelangelo completed his in 1504. Donatello and Verrocchio (Leonardo's teacher) had portrayed the adolescent of the biblical story, requiring a miracle to fulfil his promise against Goliath. Michelangelo's *David*, however, is at the peak of physical prowess, embodying that calm force of *terribilità* familiar to the Medici age. Robert Coughlan has written of the *David*: "With the head of a beautiful Apollo and the body of a young Hercules, he is an apotheosis of all the most heroic qualities . . . not the son of Jesse the Bethlehemite but figuratively of Lorenzo the Florentine – and his godfathers were Poliziano, Pico and the rest of that great informal faculty at the Medici Palace where Michelangelo had acquired so much of his education."[11]

Romain Rolland once stated that Michelangelo lived "at the very heart of the Renaissance." In the house of Lorenzo the Magnificent, he audited the classes of Poliziano arranged for the young Medici (including two future popes). These were complemented by the philosophical discourse of Lorenzo and Pico as well as the classical knowledge of Cristofor Landino (the Dante expert) and Gentile Becchi. The eclecticism of Florentine Neoplatonism is suggested best by Raphael's *The School of Athens*. Central are the figures of Plato and Aristotle, the one (holding the *Timaeus*) with finger pointing heavenward while his younger companion (holding his *Ethics*) points earthward. This happy harmony that the Renaissance saw between Platonism and Aristotelianism, issuing in the practical and even pragmatic turn of moral philosophy, suggests further the sort of human heroics that Michelangelo intended, the Renaissance form of Prometheanism.

Charles Trinkaus maintains that the "new" and "heroic" vision includes both sides of the harmony: Christ, to take the most notable example, is both the fragile figure of the *Pietà* and the glorified Man, the Judge of the Sistine Chapel.[12] This is an interesting statement, echoing the liturgical vocabulary of the Church with its balanced and polar accents on the humanity and the divinity, and on the modes of humiliation and exaltation. The subtlety of this polarity, this dialectic of the eternal indwelling the temporal, tends to disappear in subsequent generations, until the Enlightenment dialectic of enmity to heaven erupts in a new and atheistic Prometheanism. With a Michelangelo we are still in continuity with the world of Dante, with the Thomist synthesis of nature and grace. When that topples, a new choice opens out for wilful freedom: atheism.

Such a reading of Renaissance and Reformation seeks to recognize the two sympathies at work in that turbulent age: the nostalgic recovery of the past with its classical formulation of human placing in God's world, and the bold adventure into new possibilities. Yet this kind of study isolates unduly the ideas of the age. Other factors were at work, factors which social science, for instance, would perhaps deem more decisive. These include the growing urbanization of the time, the passage from city-states to nations, the development of capitalism and a money economy, the emergence of scientific method. And the Thirty Years' War. The last is one socioeconomic factor attendant upon the Reformation and Counter-Reformation that bears on the crisis of faith of modernity. From 1618 to 1650 havoc was wrought across Europe – Dresden suffered the loss of over two-thirds of its populace, while Württemberg was reduced from 400,000 to 40,000. Survivors sought refuge in the countryside or in ruins, living like wild animals. There was hardly a "last valley" untouched by the scourge of warfare and brutality. Rubens's canvas *The Horrors of War* comes from this period (*c.* 1638). This experience, combined with the renewed scholasticism, which seemed a reversion to medieval dogmatism, alerted the intelligentsia to the weakness of organized religion and classical theism.

There continues to exist an uneasy tension between traditional "intellectual history" and "sociology of knowledge." This is salutary for both approaches; it would be wrong either to isolate the ideas of Renaissance and Reformation in terms of humanist and scholastic moods or moments, for example, or contrariwise to concentrate on military history and related phenomena. The emergence of Promethean atheism has more than one condition and no overwhelming "cause."

Reformation and Scholasticism

That the Church was deformed constituted the chief premise of Reformation. The "face of the church" was to be revealed in its purity and intrinsic beauty, once stripped of those religious cosmetics applied so lavishly during the previous millennium. Indeed, the late medieval doctrine of ("bloody") sacrifice combined with the beginnings of the Baroque Mass lend weight to this assumption. Luther spoke of cleansing what was "vitiated by most abominable additions" and so allowing "a pious use." Calvin, deeply influenced by the church fathers, wished to restore "the ancient face of the church." His colleague Peter Martyr Vermigli advanced criteria for discriminating among the Fathers and so developing proper models of Church government and worship.[13]

The primitive reforming spirit proved unable to maintain Church unity despite its agreement on Scripture and Fathers as authorities. Soon rival factions vied for territory and for dogmatic supremacy. Moreover, the heady days of enthusiasm gave place to more sober and systematic theory, and soon scholasticism characterized Protestant as well as Catholic teaching. The arid debates over scriptural inerrancy (are the Hebrew vowel points also "inspired" by God, inasmuch as they were added later?) and predestination offered little defence to the new atheism of the seventeenth century. Unfortunately, the "magisterial" Reformers were so preoccupied with ecclesiology that they did not reopen properly theological matters; that is, the doctrine of God of classical theism. (This failure to reform the doctrine of the triunity of God we regard as giving us the unfinished business of Reformation.)

The debate on freedom of the will of the sixteenth century provided groundwork and battlefield. The encounter between Erasmus and Luther is classic. The Reformer accused the humanist of scepticism concerning the Christian rule of faith, whereas *Spiritus sanctus non est Scepticus*. It is this disagreement concerning the role of reason that separates the two. Erasmus stands in the scholastic tradition, for which the human will is a "rational appetite," weak but able to cooperate with divine grace. He finds in this nature/grace dialectic sufficient basis for the school distinction (of modal logic) between necessities of "consequent" and "consequence." The latter avoids compulsion; freedom means self-determination rather than heteronomy. Thus Erasmus musters his arguments on familiar ground and in the technical terms developed over generations of subtle "disputed questions."[14]

Not so Luther. For him, the proper understanding of free will is the key to the doctrine of divine grace. He begins with a view that the will is "extraordinarily depraved," preventing faith and trust. It is captive to sin and requires an objective act of the Holy Spirit to set it free to will and to choose the good. Such "royal freedom" is itself a kind of captivity. "Thus the human will is placed between the two like a beast of burden." Luther identifies the root of the problem as the human desire to be as God: *homo deificatus.* Overcoming this temptation requires a resignation of will (*Gelassenheit*), allowing Christ to form himself within. The will's conformity to God is thus inextricably joined with a mystical union of faith, empowering the believer to imitate Christ.[15] To understand Luther properly, of course, one must acknowledge the biblical insight usually overlooked in the philosophical debate, that "originally," human being lived unto God, willing the good in perfect freedom and innocence. To opt for a knowledge of good and evil, for an "autonomy" caught in the new bondage of sinful choosing, was the demonic temptation.

Thus the ambiguous heritage of Augustine on the question of will continues among his descendants. It becomes hardened in the Calvinist schools, especially where Reformed Aristotelianism flourished. Calvin's own polemical works show a Lutheran decision to approach the freedom of the will strictly in terms of the grace of salvation. He does recognize that this is a "high mystery" to be handled with caution and due respect for the "impropriety" of theological language. But like Luther his zeal in debate carries him beyond this initial insight.[16] And his colleague and successor, Theodore Beza, along with Vermigli's disciple Girolamo Zanchi, may be credited with moving what had been for Calvin a corollary of grace to the position of keystone in the theological arch.[17] When we read the arguments for double predestination, for supralapsarianism, for the bondage of the will, we have entered the Reformation of the "second scholastic." This is no longer offset by a "mystical union" providing the dynamic for both faith and works. The latter was present in Calvin, as in Luther, but tended to become lost in the weight of affairs intellectual as well as ecclesiastical. Peter Martyr Vermigli, who attempted a more central position for this dynamic, received private agreement from both Calvin and Beza without pursuing the matter publicly. And when Vermigli's own theology was cast in the form of Commonplaces of great influence on later Calvinists, particulary the Puritans, the very form obscured his own less scholastic appproach.[18]

The return of scholasticism to both Roman and Reformed Christianity came at the very time when a new militancy and self-confidence characterized the opposition. The general response of the intelligentsia, especially the *philosophes* of the Enlightenment, was a haughty disdain for the theism that based itself on such irrational grounds and that led to such polemic and hatred. The form that classical theism had reached by the seventeenth century was in some ways a degraded and perverted form of a noble theology. Huxley's *The Devils of Loudon* portrays one of the tragic consequences of a theism that operates with a simplistic dualism and a theologized psychology. Similar is the evidence for a fall from grace in Scotland, famous for its developed Calvinism, by such diverse sources as the poets Robert Burns and James Hogg. The latter's novel *The Memoirs and Confessions of a Justified Sinner* (1824) has been seized on by André Gide as prototype for his own *The Immoralist*. A similar witness for the prosecution is John Buchan, who in *Witch Wood* drew back the curtain from the secret religion of hilltop and copse, the alternative to orthodoxy. Such fictionalized accounts are by nature extreme yet remind us of the ambiguous face of religion that theistic theology entailed at this period.

Renaissance Magus

New attention is being given by scholars to a different phenomenon from scholasticism, if complementary and even causally connected with it. The dimension of underground teaching, esoteric lore – the "Renaissance Magus" – is now established as an area of considerable significance for more than a few idiosyncratic intellectuals of the time.[19] It relates to our subject as symptomatic of the recovered Promethean strain of self-confidence and human power, as well as the exploration of alternative forms of theism. The tradition of *prisci theologi* attributed to Orpheus, Zoroaster and especially Hermes Trismegistus was thought to have influenced both Moses and Plato. On this reading, not only is Giordano Bruno (like Roger Bacon) an example of the Magus tradition, but so too is Ficino's reading of Plato, including the *Protagoras*. Pico thus learned his image of the human as *magnum miraculum* from the Corpus Hermeticum (its *Asclepius* in particular). Not only does Pico see human being as singled out for such a role, but himself above all. Frances Yates concludes:

> The profound significance of Pico della Mirandola
> in the history of humanity can hardly be overesti-
> mated. It was he who first boldly formulated a new

position for European man, man as Magus using
both Magia and Cabala to act upon the world, to
control his destiny by science.[20]

Thus the emphasis upon autonomy of the human will, the
godlike ability to choose grandly and effectively, is well grasped by a
time and place in which ancient lore was mined for the clue to such
an autocrator, a Man-God. If such dark studies remain as yet unas-
similated into the mainstream of intellectual history, it cannot be
gainsaid that our traditional academic reading of the history of science, and of politics and philosophy itself, needs considerable
reworking in their light. From one angle it reinforces much of what
C.G. Jung claimed in his work on alchemy; from another, it bids us
look again at the role of magic and the mystical in the development
of romanticism and idealism, and perhaps in our vaunted empirical
philosophies and sciences too. Finally, it impinges on our thesis also
in its support of that fideism that rejected classical theism and scholasticism but was far from opting for atheism.

Fideism and Scepticism

One consequence of the Renaissance revival of classicism was
renewed interest in classical Scepticism. This did not necessarily signify unbelief but rather that doubt about the adequacy and reliability
of the evidence for truth-claims already noted among Sophists and
Sceptics. "By the end of the seventeenth century, the great sceptic,
Pierre Bayle, could look back and see the reintroduction of the arguments of Sextus as the beginning of modern philosophy."[21] The sixteenth century became familiar with the works of Sextus Empiricus,
whose difficulties with the criteria for truth suited well an age struggling over the rule of faith and the peculiarities of theological epistemology. Montaigne held a special reverence for Pyrrho, while
François Sanchez could write *Quod nil scitur* (1581). His method
affords a remarkable anticipation of Descartes. "I turned in upon
myself and put everything to doubt. Hence the thesis which is the
starting-point of my reflections: the more I think, the more I doubt."
Related to Scepticism is fideism, which agrees that belief
cannot be "proved" but seeks such arguments and persuasive definitions as will clarify and commend it. Noted Christian Sceptics were
Pico's nephew Gian Francesco Pico della Mirandola (1470-1533) and
Cornelius Agrippa. The latter's *De vanitate* ("On the uncertainty

and vanity of sciences and arts," 1527) denies the power of reason to achieve truth and repudiates the author's earlier predilection for occult philosophy, geomancy and the Kabbala, returning to the authority of Scripture and Church.[22] In France, Pierre de la Ramée (Peter Ramus) and Omer Talon explored the scepticism about reason of the Academic tradition. They reacted to Aristotelian logic and found themselves in sympathy with fideism. Talon distinguished carefully between human philosophy in which "il faut d'abord connaître avant de croire" and religious questions that surpass intelligence so that "il faut d'abord croire afin d'arriver ensuite à la connaissance."[23]

Behind fideism lie the more extreme statements about the errors of Reason depicted by Luther as whore and by Calvin as decrepit. They appear in a long tradition represented by Tertullian against Origen and later complicated further by the nominalist-realist controversy. Such statements are easily misunderstood when taken out of their polemical context. Still, it is true that the reconstruction of theology involved such frontal attack on the medieval synthesis that nature was divorced from grace, reason from revelation. A great gap was opened between two kinds of knowledge so that further weight is given the fideistic position as interpreted by philosophers. By 1584 Giordano Bruno could deride those *efettici e pirroni* who profess not to be able to know anything. Bruno's own case for a world-soul (*Della causa, principio, ed uno*) may go too far in the direction of a new dogmatism based on questionable argument; yet like his younger contemporary, Francis Bacon, he sees the need for a new basis on which to build knowledge, free from scepticism on the one hand and dogmatism on the other; or from the infirm reason allowed by theologians and their untouchable revelation.

A factor in the shift from that humanism compatible with Christian theism to one avowedly atheistic is the presence of libertines and atheists who troubled the righteous in Italy and Switzerland and who found Paris a friendlier place. Thomas Molnar traces the movement back into the "Italian naturalism" of late medieval universities, notably Padua.[24] Monist and atomist philosophies deriving from classical studies, on this thesis, spread with the disintegration of the medieval synthesis and of papal authority. Oxford and Paris followed the Paduan lead, until by the Renaissance scepticism and libertinism paved the way for subsequent Enlightenment rationalism. "Italian atheists" in particular were prominent in Paris among a collection of "the libertines, the *esprits forts*, the naturalists, the sceptics, the Gassendists" often termed deists but in fact much less.

Molnar's interpretation is based on evidence applicable to many of the philosophers as well as to the freethinkers of the age, if exaggerated. "What French scholars brought back from Padua after 1530, and what Italian humanists brought to the rest of Europe during the sixteenth century was an atheistic ideology, part infatuation with whatever the Ancients did or wrote, part conviction that the Christian religion, opposed to the Ancients' paganism, was an indefensible system of superstitions."[25]

Molnar's view is similar to ours, although in our opinion there is less development of naturalism and less heterodoxy in Italy at this time. The interpretation of Aristotle at Padua, for instance, did not deter the young Vermigli from his Christian faith, although it helped in steering his Thomism toward union with Calvinism. (He spent the years 1518-26 at the university, about the same time as Reginald Pole.) Moreover, there is a tradition according to which Italy is a breeding ground for speculators, sceptics, immoralists, all summed up in the figure of Niccolò Machiavelli – what Antonio D'Andrea has called "the myth of Italy."[26] One encounters something of this myth in observers of the Italian scene, who tend to miss the more significant phenomenon of antitrinitarianism. Flourishing around both Venice (influenced by the writings of Servetus) and Naples (the circle of Juan de Valdés), the liberal spirit produced several offspring including unitarianism. Its most famous exiles were Ochino and the Sozzini, but other Italians feature in the high drama of scholarly debate, church politics, persecution and martyrdom – Gribaldi, Alciati, Gentile, for example. The repressive climate of the times forced the movement to seek sanctuary in Moravia and Poland. Thus the "minor reformed church," an alternative to classical theism, was thwarted, and a not unworthy debating partner for Promethean humanism was denied a hearing.

The Promethean spirit is hardly on view in the dilettante atheism of the libertines, while those humanists who display it conceive themselves not as defying God but as defying the recalcitrant matter over which God has appointed us shapers and lords. The vision is symbolized by those rough-hewn "captives" from the Boboli Gardens, caught struggling out of the marble: Michelangelo's silent testimony to the superhuman, the titanic vocation to which we are called. So well did he express the ideal of the age that at last he was called Michelangelo "the divine." Between Il Magnifico Lorenzo and Il Divino Michelangelo only a few years intervene; but such a leap of humanist logic symbolizes the shape of the future.

– 5 –

Reason and the Lightbearer

verum et hoc paecipue proponitur, quod homo
veluti centrum mundi sit.

(Bacon, *Prometheus*)

Francis Bacon

Francis Bacon (1561-1626) revitalized the myth of Prometheus in his
De sapientia veterum XXVI: *Prometheus, sive status hominis*.[1]
Recounting the story in detail, Bacon notes: "This fable carries in it
many true and grave speculations both on the surface and under-
neath." Chief is the peculiar "state of humanity" as centre of the
world. Prometheus himself "clearly and expressly signifies Providence" and so is creator and provider. Moreover, since the mind or
intellect "is the seat of providence," we find a likeness to Prometheus at the heart of the ability to take the world as given for our
"use and fruit," all its parts indeed working together "in the service
of man." Thus Bacon's magisterial philosophy of human endeavour
and investigation is reinforced by the old tale. This point is served
even better by the variant according to which the gift of fire was ill
received, and complaints mounted against Prometheus himself.
Bacon applauds such scepticism as far preferable to the dogmatism
of Aristotelians, which brooks no such critique. Thus "complaints
against nature and the arts" give entrance into the bounties of discovery and plenty: to be truly Promethean is to accuse Prometheus. We
have now encountered the Titan as *Phosphoros*, Lightbearer.

    The myth, in Bacon's hands, is both etiological and allegori-
cal. The ancient torch race in honour of Prometheus, for instance,
"alludes to arts and sciences," pointing the moral that no single
inquirer may attain "the perfection of the sciences" through his own

---

Notes to Chapter 5 appear on page 314.

swiftness and ability, but only "a succession" of inquirers. The essay concludes:

> The voyage of Hercules especially, sailing in a pitcher to set Prometheus free, seems to present an image of God the Word hastening in the frail vessel of the flesh to redeem the human race. But I purposely refrain myself from all licence of speculation in this kind, lest peradventure I bring strange fire to the altar of the Lord.

Thus is Prometheus promoted as an aid to faith rather than an example of atheism.

Bacon's essay *Of Atheism* contains the famous sentence, "It is true that a little philosophy inclineth man's mind to atheism; but depth in philosophy bringeth men's minds about to religion."[2] His reasoning turns on the chain of second causes, a form of cosmological argument in fact, leading to "Deity and Providence." Even "that school which is most accused of atheism" – Leucippus, Democritus and Epicurus – demonstrates religion: "For it is a thousand times more credible, that four mutable elements, and one immutable fifth essence, duly and eternally placed, need no God, than that an army of infinite small portions or seeds unplaced, should have produced this order and beauty without a divine marshal." After this nod to teleology Bacon suggests that Epicurus's dissembling points to atheism of the lip rather than of the heart. Plato would agree with his words: "there is no profanity in refusing to believe in the gods of the people: the profanity is in believing of the gods what the people believe of them." Bacon seems to think that atheists are very few, seldom "contemplative" and often hypocritical. He also notes the causes of atheism such as divisions in religion, scandal of priests and finally the combination of affluence and learning, which scoffs at that which in trouble and adversity seems a necessity.

The companion essay, *Of Superstition*, begins, "It were better to have no opinion of God at all, than such an opinion as is unworthy of him." For atheism may promote morality and the peace of society, but superstition brings confusion as to proper authority, and so makes way for tyranny. Superstition is the corruption of religion, and so a deformity when compared with the relative innocence of atheism. Bacon is hardly indulging in Aristotelian logic, therefore, as if superstition were excess, and atheism defect, of religion. He sees in superstition a common yielding to self-serving piety and formality due to mixed motivation. Atheism leaves room for the influence of philosophy and law and "natural piety," whereas superstition leads to scorn and irreverence.

The two essays do not sit well with each other, the first speaking harshly of atheism as a denial of God and human nobility, the second allowing it considerable openness to ameliorating law and philosophy, even natural piety. This ambiguity is quite in keeping with Bacon's views on religion: he is probably not enough of an atheist for his admirer Diderot, yet too much for his critic de Maistre. His "great instauration" to restore humanity to mastery over nature found the search for final causes irrelevant: yet he remained a kind of deist or latitudinarian in his benign attitude toward religion.

Bacon's intention was "to lay the foundation," as his preface to the *Great Instauration* puts it, "not of any sect or doctrine, but of human utility and power." He took the old Roman saying "Man is the architect of his fortune" as a kind of programmatic motto. Science will give power over nature, thus restoring the dominion lost through the Fall: our "empire over creation" (*Novum Organum* II.52). His "utopian" vision in *New Atlantis* (1624) has the new Atlantians teaching the European mariners their science that masters nature, inviting them to share it with the whole world. Bacon wishes to "demolish" traditional deductive method with its breed of "idols," preparing for a "sound and fruitful knowledge." The inductive way into the "form" of things, their causality, makes for "human power and dignity" (I.116). Induction is the clue to the labyrinthine mystery of world, a *filum labyrinthi.* In a famous aphorism:

> Knowledge and human power are synonymous, since the ignorance of the cause frustrates the effect; for nature is only subdued by submission, and that which in contemplative philosophy corresponds with the cause in practical science becomes the rule.
>
> (*NO* I, Aph. 3)

The closing words of the second book of this work sound like an Enlightenment manifesto: as guardians of the treasures of nature, we "yield up their fortune to mankind upon the emancipation and majority of their understanding; from which must necessarily follow an improvement of their estate, and an increase of their power over nature" (II.52). Thus was the *Organon* of Aristotle replaced by a new instrument for exploring nature in more utilitarian terms.

If Bacon's inductive method requires correction, his view of this "power over nature" remains ambiguous. Science has moved considerably, toward hypothetico-deductive modelling and a complex method. But debate over his understanding of human "mastery" of nature continues. A popular conclusion is that he is a major contributor to the emerging theory of knowledge as power, with the scientific experimenter cast as controller, even manipulator. His program was especially therapeutic for those "idols of the theatre" that stem from theoretical errors, chiefly confusion between philosophy and theology. Plato's mistake was in his mind when he wrote: "Not only fantastical philosophy but heretical religion springs from an absurd mixture of matters divine and human." Thus the separation of revealed theology from philosophy, according to F.H. Anderson, is "fundamental to Bacon's philosophy of nature, man and God." But T.F. Torrance for one insists on a different reading of the evidence. He notes Bacon's recognition of the distinction between secondary and final causes, such that God keeps the latter "within His own curtain." His new method, *novum organum*, remains inductive in behalf of an instrumental science only, in which the scientist is but "the servant and interpreter of nature" (*NO* Aph. 1). On this view, Bacon's *instauratio magna* is quite compatible with the limitation placed on scientific method by the religious bent of the *virtuosi* in the Royal Academy, for instance. A.C. Crombie agrees that Bacon's mastery has to do with epistemic form rather than human aggrandizement.[3] Certainly his cautious use of natural theology to refute atheism but not to prove divine existence reflects his understanding of "the three philosophies, divine, natural, and human" (I.VI.1). And he states explicitly that we should "give to faith the things that are faith's" (I.66). This echoes a theological tenet familiar in Calvinist circles: there are two books by which God reveals his will to humans, that of nature and that of scripture: "scripture, revealing God's will, and . . . . creatures, revealing God's power." Both Bacon and Thomas Browne (*Religio Medici*) accept such a harmony between the books of God and of Nature, along with a similar method of reading them.

Thus we see at the end of the Renaissance another sort of *renovatio*, a scientific revolution that creates the new age of modernity. That it may be typified by the Promethean figure suggests the sort of hero now on stage. Peter Gay's work on the Enlightenment calls this aspect "the science of freedom," as the *philosophes* interpret the new scientific method and discovery as the way to establish at long last the philosophical goal of liberty. Gay entitles the earlier work of Bacon and Descartes "Prelude to modernity: the recovery of nerve."[4] He has in mind Gilbert Murray's description of the pessimism, guided by asceticism and mysticism, that signalled the end of the optimistic aspirations of the Roman Empire. This "failure of nerve," according to Gay's reading of history, is reversed in the eighteenth century. He sees the "recovery of nerve" in "growing hope for life and trust in effort, [of] commitment to inquiry and criticism," as well as "increasing secularism."

Something new had arrived, to be sure. Even Renaissance man still bowed to Fortune, to a mimetic universe in which heavenly forms impressed themselves willy-nilly on human affairs. It is precisely this will-ye-or-nill-ye attitude that Enlightenment calls in question. It would replace it with the autonomous will of free spirits. No doubt the Renaissance prepared the way. In terms of Prometheus, to take our thematic exemplar, it was during the Renaissance that he was reduced from divinity to manhood, but also exalted to the role of archetypical human. His function as creator – and sufferer the more so – now pales beside that of educator, symbol of progress by human ability and ingenuity – the Baconian "advancement of learning."

René Descartes

It is ironical that Descartes (1596-1650) is known among us as chief doubter, since he considered himself the conqueror of scepticism.[5] The Renaissance revival of classical Scepticism alluded to earlier flourished through *Nouveaux Pyrrhoniens* such as Michel de Montaigne and his disciple Father Pierre Charron. The latter's polemical works against the Calvinists adopted the same fideist position he used against atheists. Again, Descartes's critic Gassendi adopted a "scientific pyrrhonism" under the influence of Sextus Empiricus. Like others of that early scientific period such as Mersenne and Chillingworth, Gassendi maintained a modified realism, which accepts reality as appearance entailing probable truth-claims. This modern view is labelled by Richard Popkin "constructive or mitigated scepticism."

Descartes sought that *certitude philosophique* that should replace both the dogmatism of previous philosophy and theology and the scepticism evident in the *nouveaux pyrrhonistes*. His systematic doubt, summarized and formalized in the phrase *Cogito, ergo sum*, was a method to cast off the layers of speculation and falsehood accruing to human knowledge, and so to aim at indubitable truth. Using analytic method already successful in mathematics, he "found" certain rules such as the superiority of clear and distinct ideas. His attainment of the root certainty is a process of suspension (*epochē*) through doubt similar to classical Scepticism; a sort of intellectual *ascēsis*.

Difficult questions attend any study of Descartes: Is the *cogito* the proper radical for the new beginning he sought? Is his form of the ontological argument for the existence of God true to Anselm and true in itself? Is the *Cogito, ergo sum* an analytic proposition or an existential postulate? Was Descartes a Cartesian?[6]

Another question appears more fruitful for our thesis. William Temple charged the "Cartesian faux pas" with false confidence in the existence of a bare self apart from the existence of others. This may be related to J.G. Hamann's correction: "Not *cogito ergo sum* but the other way round, or even more Hebraic, *est, ergo cogito.*" In this reversal – "I am/he is, therefore I think" (a better translation than "Something is," given Hamann's theological confession) – a similar point to Temple's is being made, the necessity for the analytic of consciousness to recognize the presence of otherness, similar to phenomenology's concept of intentionality. For the Cartesian heritage of dualism, the unhappy divorce between mind and matter, still haunts Western thought: *res cogitans, res extensa.* Nor is the subjectivist circle much affected by Descartes's form of the ontological argument for the existence of God. Two comments from unlike philosophers are apt. Pascal stated that Descartes had God present to give creation the initial *chiquenaude* or flick of the fingers but does not need him further (*Pensées* 77). And Leibniz remarked that Descartes murmured to himself what Spinoza stated aloud – "Descartes pense tout bas ce que Spinoza dit tout haut."[7]

Helmut Thielicke uses "Cartesian" to describe the modern stance in philosophy and theology inasmuch as Descartes "initiated all the movements which find their point of departure in the I as the subject of experience and understanding." Thielicke's estimate of Descartes is echoed by Hans Küng: "For with him begins the priority of the subject over the object, of consciousness over being, of personal freedom over cosmic order, of questioning in immanent rather than transcendent terms."[8] The Cartesian shift provides a new foundation for certainty, namely immediate selfhood, the touchstone for all else. One now begins at the centre in the subjective self and reaches out to others, including other subjects, and finally the Other, God. The certainty (as distinct from certitude) of his existence is guaranteed by the selfhood that originates the search for divinity. Thus "certainty of faith" comes to mean much the same as "certainty of the self." The testament written for modern thought, indissolubly linked with the scientific revolution and its kind of certainty, therefore assists the revival of the Promethean spirit, that journey to the centre that discovers both beast and god in the human self.

Cartesian solipsism is subject to a weighty critique by philosophers as well as theologians. Its prominence in British analytic philosophy especially has provoked sharp debate. Bertrand Russell's logical atomism, as a familiar example, caused D.H. Lawrence (an early colleague in opposition to the Great War) to remark that the idea of "free agent" meant "independent little gods, referred nowhere and to nothing, little mortal Absolutes, secure from question."[9] And the question whether other minds exist, and if so how one could gain knowledge of another consciousness – of its pain, for example – exercised John Wisdom in particular as the chief item on the analytical agenda. Our thesis of Promethean atheism involves attention to the Western tradition since Descartes, in a special way. It sees this as the intellectual locale where a postulate of human being as by definition exclusive of others entailed a new isolation from the divine. And it concludes that such solipsism, atomism or monadology of the person is the leading clue to understanding the nature of modern atheism.

David Hume considered Descartes a *sceptique malgré lui*.[10] For him the Cartesian doubt remains "entirely incurable" in view of the empirical theory of perception. He rejects Descartes's argument for immediate consciousness of one's own self and substitutes his view of the stream of perceptions that deny the simplicity, continuity and identity that might postulate such selfhood. The shift to critical and empirical epistemology reflects the new scientific method much better than did Descartes, or even Bacon. This alternative "radical" will be taken over and worried through by those philosophers, notably Kant, who recognized the inescapably scientific nature of modernity and the need to provide theoretical, perhaps even metaphysical, foundations for that enterprise and its language.

Deism and Atheism

English deism especially developed theses that gained attention on the Continent and that Kant could assume in his own treatment of the same issues.[11] Most significant are the substantial identity of natural and revealed religion and religion as essentially the acceptance of moral duty as divine command. Even those theological innovators in Germany called neologists agreed in reducing revelation to reason and in determining religious truth by experiential test, if not explicitly moral. One can see here the validity of the shorthand definition, which takes "deism" as belief in an impersonal, and "theism" belief in a personal, deity. One also grasps the necessary distinction between deistic natural religion, with its corollary of absent original Designer whose continuing "rule" is one of absence rather than presence, and that "natural theology" of classical theism, which cooperated with grace in positive and quite other ways. Aquinas's *Gratia naturam non tollit sed perficit* was a sentence that deism could hardly utter. As Alexandre Koyré has put it, the God of the Sabbath succeeded the workaday God of classical theism.

Lord Herbert of Cherbury, called the father of English deism by Thomas Halyburton in *Natural Religion Insufficient* (1714), enunciated those religious "common notions" that form the basis for rational religion. Herbert's *De Veritate* (1624) had stated five chief notions: there is one supreme God; who should be worshipped; divine worship consists chiefly in virtue and piety; we should be sorry for and repent of our sins; divine goodness dispenses rewards and punishments both here and hereafter. These theses summarize a movement evident in two of the most representative and influential books: John Toland's *Christianity not Mysterious: Or a Treatise Showing that there is Nothing in the Gospel Contrary to Reason, Nor above it: And that no Christian Doctrine can be properly call'd a Mystery* (1696) and Matthew Tindal's *Christianity as Old as the Creation: Or, The Gospel A Republication of the Religion of Nature* (1730).

Deism had flourished so far by 1677 that Bishop Stillingfleet felt constrained to deliver a sharp attack, *Letter to a Deist*. He writes because the adherence to theories of divine existence and providence go hand in hand with holding Scripture and Christianity in but "mean esteem." It is curious that the first Boyle lecturer, Richard Bentley, could produce *The Folly of Atheism and what is now called Deism* in 1692. No doubt this agreed with Robert Boyle himself: that "sceptical chemist" (after the title of his 1661 book) thought that "by being addicted to experimental philosophy a man is rather assisted than indisposed to be a good Christian" (*The Christian Virtuoso*, 1690). By "experimental philosophy" he means Bacon's method, which he compares favourably to the older chemical concepts of hypostatical "principles" (Paracelsus), although he is less critical of the four elements of Aristotle. At times his scepticism of science pushed revelatory knowledge to a form of fideism, as in *The Excellency of Theology, or the Pre-eminence of the Study of Divinity above that of Natural Philosophy* (1674). Yet his mechanical interpretation (second causes are sufficient for scientific explanation) proved stronger than his theological ideas for later generations.

The Boyle Lectures, "for the defense of Christianity," became a haven for rational apologetics, and for deism. The second lecturer, Samuel Clarke, provides the model. His two series, 1704 and 1705, are entitled "A Demonstration of the Being and Attributes of God" and "A Discourse Concerning the Unchangeable Obligations of Natural Religion, and the Truth and Certainty of the Christian Revelation." Clarke's natural theology is typical in that his "chain of propositions" argues from "something has existed from all eternity," as "one, unchangeable and independent being," to the third and crucial statement: "That unchangeable and independent being, which has existed from eternity without any external cause of its existence, must be self-existent, that is necessarily existent." In an early defence of freethinking, Anthony Collins remarked that until Clarke undertook to demonstrate the existence of God nobody had ·ever entertained any doubts on the subject.

In his *Letters on the English* (*Lettres Philosophiques*) Voltaire called Clarke "une vraie machine à raisonnement." He includes Clarke in his letter (VII) "On the Socinians, or Arians, or Antitrinitarians" whom he sees beginning to revive in England, Holland and Poland. Voltaire's admiration for such "Socinianism" is ambiguous (along with the label itself),[12] but his shrewd judgment correctly identifies the chief point in deism: its natural religion is based on belief in a remote and unitary *Deus* little suited to any form of trinitarian theology. A similar charge was made against the Boyle lecturers by Henry Dodwell, whose *Christianity Not Founded on Argument* (1742) accused the rationalist lecturers of succeeding only in spreading infidelity. He reasoned that since external proofs lack evidential weight, they argue toward probability only. Therefore one is free to believe what one wishes, a two-edged sword indeed.

English deism, and in a sense the Age of Reason, fell under the intellectual critique of David Hume and the "emotional" critique of John Wesley. Continental deism, with which one can identify, with certain qualifications, both Voltaire and Rousseau, did not satisfy the *philosophes*. Their militant atheism disturbed those two worthies, as well as Hume on his visit to Paris. The *Encyclopédie* of d'Alembert and Diderot trades on its atheistic line, and measures the distance now dividing the French intellect from that of both England and Germany. In Germany deism is usually attributed to Reimarus (*The Principal Truths of Natural Religion Defended and Illustrated*, 1755) and Lessing, whose *The Education of the Human Race* (1780) espoused natural revelation despite his later thoughts on pantheism.

Reimarus was influenced by the "physico-theological" circle gathered about his father-in-law, J.A. Fabricius (1688-1736). Immanuel Kant remains the most significant figure, and we will see later how he builds the two basic theses of deism into his system.

In America the influence of English and French deists is marked in thinkers such as Franklin, Jefferson and Washington. Franklin's personal "Articles of Belief and Acts of Religion" resembles "The Jefferson Bible" in that both stress moralism to the exclusion of dogma. Washington once acquiesed in a statement of the American consul in Algiers, that "the Government of the United States of America is not in any sense founded on the Christian religion." Thomas Paine became famous by his *The Age of Reason: Being an Investigation of True and Fabulous Theology,* published 1794-96, which intends to rescue deism from association with atheism, but does so by a stringent attack on revealed religion.[13]

Prometheus Pursued

What has been happening to Prometheus along the way? The age continues to regard the myth as a story about creation, with Pandora prominent. Milton compares her to Eve:

> What day the genial angel to our sire
> Brought her in naked beauty more adorn'd
> More lovely than Pandora, whom the gods
> Endow'd with all their gifts, and oh, too like
> In sad event.
>
> (*Paradise Lost* IV.5.712ff).

On the other hand, Milton's Satan is sometimes compared with Prometheus, since the energy of this poetic creation assumes heroic and titanic proportions. This theme continued to interest literati: Shelley, as we will see, notes the comparison closely: "Milton's Devil, as a moral being," is "far superior to his God." And in his own *Prometheus Unbound* he states that "the only imaginary being resembling in any degree Prometheus, is Satan." Elizabeth Barrett Browning, however, takes an opposite view: "the Satan of Milton and the Prometheus of Aeschylus stand upon ground as unequal as do the sublime of sin and the sublime of virtue."[14] By her time we will be in the heyday of romanticism, when the truly evil one, for many if not for the gentle "Portuguese," is God, whether Zeus or Jehovah.

The seventeenth century was an age of discovery and

expansion, herald of Enlightenment. Galileo saw Jupiter's satellites through his telescope in 1609, reinforcing the Copernican heliocentric theory of the previous century. The Renaissance came late to England, and it was fitting that, being spared the Thirty Years' War, the country should crown the spirit of humanism by its intellectual vigour and practical inquiry. To be sure, chemists would still be sometime alchemists and the breed of astronomer maintained his love of astrology – the foundation stone of the Royal Observatory at Greenwich was laid on August 10, 1675, at the precise minute determined as most favourable by astrological charts.

The first two decades of the century gave posterity the greater plays of Shakespeare, and the King James Version of the Bible. Shakespeare may represent the age that led to Enlightenment in a special way. Kenneth Clark has given a disturbing pen portrait, in which he mentions the influence of Montaigne: "But Shakespeare's scepticism was more complete and more uncomfortable . . . Shakespeare must be the first and may be the last supremely great poet to have been without a religious belief, even without the humanist's belief in man." After quoting typical soliloquies ("What a piece of work is man! . . . man delights not me;" "a tale / Told by an idiot; full of sound and fury, / Signifying nothing"), Clark concludes: "How unthinkable before the break-up of Christendom, the tragic split that followed the Reformation; and yet I feel that the human spirit has gained a new greatness by outstaring this emptiness."[15]

The new mood that prepared for Enlightenment was a displacement of the humanist acceptance of Fortune and ambiguity about freedom to pursue ideals, by a clear statement of human freedom as power. The practical science of the Renaissance takes a Baconian form as the means to make us "masters and possessors of nature." This aim suited England as well as the Continent: Lord Shaftesbury (a disciple of John Locke) looked for the "wise and able man" to make himself "the architect of his own life and fortune."

The advance of empirical thought can be measured also by what was happening to medicine. It was shedding its old-fashioned quackery and links with alchemy and barber-ism. Peter Gay states: "medicine was philosophy at work: philosophy was medicine for the individual and for society."[16] The first clause means that medicine was being empiricized and rationalized; the second that rational thought was considered the cure for that disease called Christianity. The *philosophes*, medical doctors among them, applied medical and pathological analogies to the subject of religion. It is an illness, a "sacred contagion," a "sick man's dream," a germ and source for epidemic fanaticism and persecution.

Signs of the Times

A different type of spirituality is on view in the Cambridge Platonists, better termed "latitude men" since not all were Cantabrian or
even Platonist. Their moderacy helped them survive the turbulent
century of civil war, commonwealth and Restoration. The leadership
of Benjamin Whichcote established their intellectual centre at
Emmanuel College, Cambridge. Here also Ralph Cudworth
(1617-88) was fellow and then tutor. Cudworth's immense though
fragmentary *True Intellectual System of the Universe* (1678) is a sustained polemic against atheism. The first part boldly claims for itself:
"Wherein All the Reason and Philosophy of Atheism is Confuted,
and Its Impossibility Demonstrated." The chief example of atheism,
for Cudworth and his allies, was Hobbes, with Spinoza nearby.

Thomas Hobbes (1588-1679) has come to fame in modern
times for teaching crass materialism and enlightened self-interest. As
is usual with caricatures, both truth and error attend the portrayal.
At times he extends the use of reason to religion and appears quite
the deist: "In religion, we are not to renounce our senses and experience; nor (that which is the undoubted word of God) our natural reason. For they are the talents which he hath put into our hands to
negotiate until the coming again of our blessed Saviour; and therefore not to be folded up on the napkin of an implicit faith, but
employed in the purchase of justice, peace and true religion" (*Leviathan* III, 43). Such "calculated hypocrisy," as this and similar statements have been called,[17] is balanced by his analysis of the Reformation and his conclusion that religion is rooted in irrational fear: "In
these four things, opinion of ghosts, ignorance of second causes,
devotion towards what men fear, and taking of things casual for
prognostics, consisteth the natural seed of *religion*" (I, 12). Again:
"*Fear* of power invisible, feigned by the mind, or imagined from tales
publicly told allowed, [is called] RELIGION; not allowed
SUPERSTITION" (I, 6).

Our myth is socialized by Hobbes, who sees Prometheus as a
symbol of political rebellion and founder of democracy, less preferable than order or "natural" rule (*De Cive* 10.3). His commitment to
empiricist method and his unswerving loyalty to the materialist conclusions which his reductive logic seemed inexorably to involve, mark

him out as a chief figure of controversy in an age that was itself controversial in political as well as intellectual life. To find a place for value in the world of facts remains the crucial problem for today's positivist, especially when "judgments of value" are taken as products of "possessive individualism," as C.B. Macpherson terms the root of English capitalism.

Cudworth's attack on atheism was a work of erudition, recalling historical sources and types of fatalism, materialism and atheism. His earlier sections make much of the "atomical physiology" of Leucippus and Democritus, which those two philosophers subserved to atheism, whereas Plato and Aristotle rejected the physiology while accepting the "Theology and Pneumatology of the Ancients" (I, 43-46). Later chapters examine the grounds for atheism, in particular the hylozoists and corporealists, a combination of the two making atheism certain (III, 1-3). The Cambridge Platonists insisted on the rightful use of reason in religion – a "religious reason" opposed to the naturalism of Bacon as well as the fideism of most Calvinists of the day. In the debate on determinism precipitated by Hobbes they argued for liberty, and it is to be noted that the quest for freedom had led, in Hobbesian speculation at least, to its denial. They argued also for a recognition of mystery beyond that rational world inhabited by the deists. Cudworth's attempt to relate the new science and its philosophy to the best of Christian teaching found more help in Descartes than in Bacon. But in developing his idea of a "plastic nature under God," he is breaking new ground. He avoids the concept of *anima mundi*, but thinks that organic terms are necessary to offer the integrative description required by a reasoned faith. His intellectual system was of substantive influence on the great naturalist John Ray, whose *Wisdom of God in the Works of Creation* (1691) endorses the doctrine of plastic nature.

It was fitting that the argument from design should come into prominence at this time. The new philosophy of nature replaced former analogies of creation as artistic works of beauty or organisms with life and teleology of their own. It substituted a new and powerful analogy of an Inventor or Designer who causes mechanisms to operate and to continue according to their intrinsic operational model. In its atomistic or corpuscular form, this theory ran the danger of materialism, a danger acknowledged by experimenters and explicitly refuted by Cudworth and others, notably Robert Boyle. Boyle rejects the Epicurean notion of atoms producing the world by accident. He credits God with the design of such mechanisms as the human eye, and with the origin of motion. He also introduces what will become – like the example of the eye – a notorious case study and problem for later generations, the analogy with a watch or clock to explain the role of the Creator. He chooses the most famous instance of the day, the Strasbourg cathedral clock: "The several pieces making up that curious Engine are so fram'd and adapted, and are put into such motion, as though the numerous wheels and other parts of it knew and were concerned to do its Duty."

Isaac Newton (1642-1727) shows the "reasonable way" with the cosmo-logic beloved of the Age of Reason. "This most beautiful system of the sun, planets, and comets, could only proceed from the counsel and dominion of an intelligent and powerful Being."[18] For Newton, Absolute Space constituted a divine *Sensorium*, derived from the analogy of body-mind interaction in the sensorium of the brain. "Does it not appear from Phaenomena that there is a Being incorporeal, living, intelligent, omnipresent, who, in infinite Space, as it were in his Sensory, sees the things themselves ultimately . . . and comprehends them wholly by their immediate presence to himself?" But neither God nor world affects the other in this sort of scheme. The divine functions as a point of absolute rest, providing a "form of inactivity" or inertial force (*vis inertiae*), a passive reference system. This is the fateful "combination of deism and dualism" (T.F. Torrance) that reinforced the growing subjectivism, the scepticism about "an objective rational order independent of man."[19]

Newton was not only the dominant sage of his time; his approach is typical of the careful method of the new science. "I make no hypotheses," he remarked (*Hypotheses non fingo*), and his diffidence in producing solid argument for his theories suggests the painstaking integrity of the emerging discipline. He judged it "better to do a little with certainty" than to attempt too much. He typifies that stress on induction that Einstein applauds as appropriate to the "youth" of science. Whether Newton would have followed Einstein from special to general theory and thence to the quest for unified field theory, is a nice question. As a private citizen, the earlier scholar enjoyed alchemy perhaps as complement to the minimal stance he assumed in public. But it is the latter that forms his legacy. It was Newtonian mechanics that constituted the new paradigm, one which Kant thought it necessary to rationalize metaphysically. The Newtonian world-machine with only occasional need of tinkering by its architect (the notorious "God of the gaps") has replaced the medieval world-drama in which God and humanity were starring actors.

Thus did the age of deism both magnify and reduce the

concept of God the Creator. It may have matched the new and expanding knowledge of experimental science, especially optics and astrophysics, but it captured the divine being within the rational net of inferential argument. The further step to full-blown Enlightenment mentality, with God reduced even further and finally dispensable, was but a short one. Meanwhile, the Promethean spirit of mastery over all skills and science was growing, and its peculiar next step – to defiance of all gods – proved equally short.

The Study of Mankind

"Know then thyself, presume not God to scan; / The proper study of Mankind is Man." Alexander Pope's famous lines from *An Essay on Man* reflect more than the staid and orderly cadences of the neoclassical period in English letters. This age of "natural religion," of deism, well agreed with freedom of the will, as Pope's *The Universal Prayer* displays. "Through nature to nature's God" seemed a self-evident way by the eighteenth century, now that the dust had settled over that road after the stormy innovations of the seventeenth, and the Age of Rationalism was truly come. Joseph Addison's hymn "The Spacious Firmament on High" is typical – and was published first in the *Spectator*, quite at home with Sir Roger de Coverley. There were enough exceptions among the literati to remind us that no period can be summarized simply – Christopher Smart and William Blake, for instance. It is worth quoting Samuel Johnson's observation about Smart (author of *A Song to David* and the wondrous product of his insanity, *Rejoice in the Lamb*). Boswell records as follows:

> Madness frequently discovers itself merely by unnecessary deviation from the usual modes of the world. My poor friend Smart showed the disturbance of his mind, by falling upon his knees, and saying his prayers in the street, or in any other unusual place. Now, although, rationally speaking, it is greater madness not to pray at all, than to pray as Smart did, I am afraid there are so many who do not pray, that their understanding is not called in Question.[20]

The Age of Reason was more complex than that title suggests. Perhaps Voltaire (1694-1778) reflects its spirit yet maintains this complexity in his own pilgrimage, acquainted as he was with *philosophes* of many kinds, and erudite beyond most. His preface to *The Lisbon Earthquake* (1755) – translated into English with notes by Tobias Smollett – acknowledges Pope's *Essay on Man* as having "expounded in immortal verse the systems of Leibniz, Lord Shaftesbury, and Lord Bolingbroke." It is not Pope's own optimism he challenges so much as "the abuse of the new maxim, 'whatever is, is right'." His *Candide*, of course, is now a classic text on "the problem of evil," a *reductio ad absurdum* of the Leibnizian idealism, whether or not it is cogent.

Voltaire attracts us because of his incisive portrayal of religion, particularly in *La Dictionnaire Philosophique* (1764). Despite the hyperbole of Goethe in extolling him ("Depth, genius, imagination, taste, reason, sensibility, philosophy . . . brilliancy, rapidity, gaiety, pathos, sublimity, universality, perfection, indeed – behold Voltaire") or popular antipathy to his demand, "Ecrasez l'infâme!," he remains inescapable in understanding the Enlightenment. But his very ambiguities remind us of his time and place, with little choice between superstition and unbelief; his call to d'Alembert to crush the infamy continues: "You know well that I speak only of superstition. As for religion, I love and respect it as you do."[21]

Voltaire's dictionary entries are significant. The French critique of religion calls in question the famous judgment of Marx at a later date, that the critique has reached its highest form in Germany. For Voltaire the age of reason means the end of religion, leaving at most a deistic hypothesis linked to teleological evidence of the science of his time. On religion he opens with a testimony to his recognition of "the immensity, the movements, the harmony of those infinite globes which the vulgar do not know how to admire," and his faith in "the intelligence which directs those vast forces." With such faith he contrasts the intolerance and fanaticism of popular religion which believes things "because they are impossible." Using his familiar science-fiction motif (see *Micromegas*) he records a journey on which he meets the shades of immortals, at last encountering Socrates and then Jesus. In both cases it was wicked and hypocritical "priests and judges" who killed them. The gentle and moralistic message of Jesus is explicit: true religion consists in loving God and your fellow creature as yourself. Voltaire confesses, "I take you for my only master." Jesus makes a sign of consolation; the vision disappears, "and a clear conscience stayed with me."

On superstition Voltaire laments the fanatic hatred of other sects, which is characteristic of every religious institution; he concludes: "less superstition, less fanaticism; and less fanaticism, less misery." This echoes the burden of the article on sect in which the rivalry of sects can be overcome only by subscription to that "universal religion" espoused by philosophers: "There is a God, and one must be just." And although this point of agreement is true, "the systems through which they differ" are false. The positive expression of his faith is found clearly in the article on theist.

> The theist is a man firmly persuaded of the existence of a Supreme Being, as good as He is powerful, who has created all beings that are extensive, vegetative, sentient, and reflective; who perpetuates their species, who punishes crimes without cruelty, and rewards virtuous actions with kindness.

Once again a distinction obtains between the faith of the "primitive" and added systems: "His religion is the most ancient and the most widespread, for the simple worship of a God has preceded all the systems of the world." Moreover, a belief in Providence is entailed by this simple faith, "although he perceives only a few effects and a few signs of this Providence."

The apparent deism of Voltaire may be explained as Karl Marx did in his shrewd observation that Voltaire taught atheism in his text and faith in his footnotes, and that the people believed the texts rather that the notes.[22] Voltaire was the Enlightenment figure who revived the Prometheus myth, in his *Pandore* of 1740. Billed as "une allégorie sur la chute de l'homme," the work features Jupiter as "tyran jaloux et tout-puissant." He is denounced as the cause of evil, "Eternel persécuteur / De l'infortune créateur." The theme is the divorce between heaven and earth when Prometheus accepts the titanic challenge, "Ose former une âme." The creator thus rebels against Jupiter by his act of creation, whereas humanity is the result of this cosmic dispute, this titanic revolt against heaven.

By this time our myth has assumed the form of a creation story. Like Plato's demiurge, Prometheus is responsible for a weak and ambiguous creature, the subject dearly beloved of poets, dramatists and philosophers who bid us strive for survival, for mastery, for perfection. In the mid-sixteenth century J.C. Scaliger had taken a fateful step by calling the poet himself an *alter deus*. After all, poesy is literally a making, readily comparable to the *creatio ex nihilo*. A name of significance in this development is that of Anthony, third Earl of Shaftesbury (1671-1713), whose aesthetics pictures Prometheus as creative artist, a sure step toward the definitive *Schöpferischen Künstler* of Goethe. Shaftesbury's "Soliloquy or advice to an author" and dialogue "The Moralists, A Philosophical Rhapsody"

handle the myth as the tale of a "dangerous man-moulder" who inter-
fered with Jove's plans. A philosopher would respond that "whether
Prometheus were a name for chance, destiny, a plastic nature, or an
evil demon, whatever was designed by it, 'twas still the same breach
of omnipotence."[23] In the dialogue, the sceptic Philocles berates
Palemon for being "so transported" with the myth, chiefly because he
wished "such an operation as this for mankind." Shaftesbury's philosophy agrees that the product of "thy stolen celestial fire, mixed with
vile clay" is "a wretched mortal, ill to himself, and cause of ill to
all." But like his friend Pierre Bayle, he uses doubt as entrance to
truth, to an optimistic belief in human potential. He accuses theologians of using Prometheus as scapegoat, along with doctrines of original sin and Satan, to solve the problem of evil. But what he contributes to the cumulative tradition of Prometheus is his estimation of
the literary genius: "Such a poet is a second maker; a just Prometheus, under Jove."[24]

The Promethean spirit is much less noble in those *philosophes* who adopted materialism as part of a world-view that resem-
bled the *jeux de salon* of which they were so fond.[25] They were not
serious philosophers so much as practical unbelievers, given to scan-
dalizing the establishment by showing the absurdities of "superstitions" when judged by "nature." The influence of Baron d'Holbach's
Système de la nature (1770), the "dogmatics" of materialism, for
instance (on Diderot and later Shelley), is little deserved, as he
repeats the simplistic reductionism found earlier in La Mettrie's
L'Homme machine (1747). The saving doctrine was "matter in
motion," an axiom not to be explored in depth until perhaps Lenin.
A key passage illustrates the ascription of divine attributes to nature:
"The idea of nature necessarily includes that of motion. Whence did
nature receive her motion? Our reply is: from herself since she is
the great whole, beyond which nothing exists" (I.2).

In d'Holbach's *Système* Nature or Reason is all-sufficient and
self-explanatory. The typical theme of protest against tyrants –
divine as well as earthly – is heard, along with a significant point:
religion is a drug and an illusion. Materialism trades on the subtle
exchange of Nature for God: divine attributes are not so much
denied as transferred, as in Rousseau's *Volonté Générale*. Everything turns on the definition of nature, the natural. For Enlightenment thinkers it seemed clear that creation is either senseless or the
result of an evil deity (Zeus-Jehovah) so that humans are called to
build a new creation (Prometheus-Christ). Thus develops that "vocation of the subjective will" that we take as the essence of Promethean

atheism. Its progress in France maintained the primacy of technique, from the speculations of the *philosophes* to the vision of social physicists such as Saint-Simon and Comte: the engineers have triumphed, enrolling us all in a cosmic Ecole polytechnique.[26] The property of *aseitas* has now been shifted from God to matter and its conscious knower, the human subject. Human aseity will function as autonomy in the post-Kantian age, the free will of an absolute subject who constitutes his selfhood and his world. Whether the defiance of Prometheus or the demonic pact of Faust, the self-appointed role appears entirely fitting: it seems so "natural."

David Hume (1711-76) shows how the crucial question of the limits of knowledge makes the primary quest "a science of man." Locke and Berkeley before him had traced the lines of British empiricism, but Hume is more complex in one sense: he wishes to understand the relationship among reason, will and passion, since all conduct is moved by passion. His theory of the self and its moral judgment is an alternative to the rationalist account. On the freedom of the will he may be classified as soft determinist, since his treatment parallels that of causality: the appearance of freedom masks the fact that volition is determined by the passions, rather than "reason become practical," as Kant will urge.[27]

On religion, Hume was cautious, perhaps dissembling, certainly provocative. Calling himself a "speculative sceptic," he directed his critical approach to the "superstition" of popular and dogmatic religion, and to its chief "proofs," the arguments from miracle and from prophecy. It was above all an age of teleology. Both John Toland and Matthew Tindal, as well as Butler's *Analogy of Religion*, built on the argument from design to establish inferential proof of Christianity's truth. The cult of reasonableness, especially in Britain, encouraged gentlemanly discussion and a distinct antipathy to enthusiasm – the Church of Scotland virtually invented the idea of moderacy. Hume is hard to pin down personally, lacking dogmatic fervour, yet makes it clear that the argument from design does not permit one to conclude that there is moral governance in the universe. In the *Dialogues concerning Natural Religion*, published posthumously in 1779, his sort of scepticism finds dramatic expression. Doubt is a strategy; it is not equated with denial; therefore the three dialogists are no cardboard figures. Butler is perhaps Cleanthes, and Hume speaks chiefly through Philo (with Samuel Clarke cast as Demea). A teasing ambiguity haunts the pages of these wonderful dialogues, with a poignancy at the end where the power of the Design is recognized and a softening of Philo's position noticeable.

Certainly Hume is against the latitudinous moralism of the age, against the deism that relies so much on a specious causality in its teleological argument, and against enthusiasm. He is an empiricist, "the 18th-century Ockham" (A.C. Crombie), attacking rationalism yet without quite solving the problem he inherits. It is one thing to hold that the mind cannot think *a priori* any concepts involving necessity; it is more serious yet to hold that empirical reason cannot secure the will because of the role of the emotions. On this point Leszek Kolakowski observes that Hume's philosophy "reflects the impotence, so to speak, of the Enlightenment, its helplessness in the face of the questions it raised."[28]

The Energy of Reason

"The whole eighteenth century understands reason in this sense; not as a sound body of knowledge, principles, and truths, but as a kind of energy, a force which is fully comprehensible only in its agency and effects."[29] Ernst Cassirer's study of the philosophy of the Enlightenment sees a shift in its understanding of reason away from such a one as Giordano Bruno, who pits the human mind against infinity. The identity and unity of the ego is now guaranteed by the "spectacle" of the world, whose phenomena constitute the objects of the human subject.[30] This egocentric view is reinforced by the Cartesian revolution. By the Enlightenment, philosophers could assume that reason is energy. The familiar scholastic definition – *veritas est adaequatio rei et intellectus* – has made way for the new concept of constitutive rationality, as Kant would explain it definitively.

The Enlightenment view of energetic reason is a clear signal of the arrival of Promethean man, for whom the Age of Reason is really a "*cult* of reason" (Molnar). Overcoming the passions with his reason, he regards his ego as the clue to reality, so that the "science of man" takes precedence, and the "despotism of theology," as D'Alembert called it, must be overthrown.

Thus a Baconian reasoning assumes a dynamic posture, capable of a renovation of all things, which reverses the consequences of the Fall. The new humanity is virtually called by divine vocation to unite all things in a cosmic harmony. Reason and will work together in a synergism that mirrors the ultimate maturation of the race. Where once the energetics of theological sanctification and reconciliation were thought to ameliorate the worst effects of human creatureliness and fallenness, now a new age of enlightened and mature leaders holds the promise of liberation and control. There are familiar analyses of this phenomenon by both Leibniz and Kant. In Leibniz's treatise *On Wisdom* this summary of the German *Aufklärung* appears:

> Now unity in multiplicity is nothing but harmony, and because one thing agrees more nearly with this than with that, order arises, and from order beauty, and beauty awakes love. . . . Now when the soul feels within itself a great harmony, order, freedom, force, or perfection, and is accordingly delighted, this causes joy. . . . Such joy is constant and cannot deceive or cause future sorrow if it is the result of knowledge and accompanied by light; from this joy there arises in the will an inclination toward the good, that is, virtue. . . . Thence follows that nothing serves happiness more than the light of reason and the exercise of the will to act at all times according to reason.[31]

Here is an ideal of unity in multiplicity, with the mind mirroring reality not in the passive sense of French and English psychology (the theory of impressions) but as "a living mirror of the universe" (Cassirer). The ideal was to provide German thought with that thoroughness and unifying epistemology on which Kant would build. In Christian Wolff, "preceptor of Germany," this Germanic form of Enlightenment egocentric and autonomous reason was perfected; despite his reference to "dogmatic slumbers," Kant owed Wolff the formulation of the problems and the systematic method with which he approached the impasse between rationalism and empiricism.

Immanuel Kant

In Kant's own essay *Was ist Aufklärung?* the kernel and the motto of the age are given concise expression.

> Enlightenment is man's emergence from his self-inflicted minority. Minority [*Unmündigkeit*] is the inability to make use of one's understanding without the guidance of another. This minority is self-inflicted [*Selbstverschuldet*] when its cause lies not in lack of understanding, but of the determination and courage to make use of it without the guidance of another. *Sapere aude!* Have the courage [*Mut*] to make use of your own understanding! is therefore the motto of the Enlightenment.

Here are the crucial words, the motto Dare to Think! (borrowed from Horace) backed up by analysis of that autonomy linked to adulthood that shows a world come of age (*die mündige Welt*), as the "secular theology" will later phrase it.

The challenge recalls that of Diderot (1771): "Have the courage to free yourself from the yoke of religion." Kant (1724-1804) embodies the spirit and the goal of Enlightenment in his *Transzendentalphilosophie* because he dared to assign reason the power to determine its own limits as well as the power to determine knowledge, according to its own categories, within those limits. His ideal of "Philosophie als strenge Wissenschaft" expresses the flowering of the Enlightenment, "the joyful affirmation of the actual capacity of human reason," even to achieve "an enlightenment of the Enlightenment about itself."[32] This suggests the proper interpretation of that compelling sentence in the preface to the second edition of the first critique: "I must, therefore, abolish *knowledge*, to make room for *belief*." By this Kant means that critical philosophy – the established epistemology of the modern era – rejects both theism and atheism as constituting genuine knowledge.

Thus two ideas converge in the history of philosophy: reason and freedom. Kant seeks to account for human freedom, and his epistemology leads him to posit the noumenal self as causal. Freedom is not irrational therefore, since despite the difficulty in providing a scientific account of noumena, this form of selfhood remains rational: it is "(pure) practical reason." Only rational beings can be free: only free beings can be rational.

In the *Critique of Practical Reason*, Kant deals with autonomy in a significant way. Autonomy means personal interest; self-interest is ruled out as heteronomous, for it is hedonism, happiness defined as "mere states." True happiness consists in seeking the good, for interest is connected with duty. The test of universalizability is crucial for Kant's ethics, therefore. "Act so that the maxim of your will can always at the same time hold good as a principle of universal legislation" (31/7). This "fundamental law of the pure practical reason" is the fountain of the moral law. In this context – as in the following theorem – Kant relates the concepts that will have considerable influence from now on, particularly in shaping the self-consciousness of Promethean man: autonomy and heteronomy.

> The *autonomy* of the will is the sole principle of all moral laws, and of all duties which conform to them; on the other hand, *heteronomy* of the elective will not only cannot be the basis of any obligation, but is, on the contrary, opposed to the

principle thereof, and to the morality of the will.
(33/8, Theorem IV)

Freedom in willing consists in the negative sense of independence and in the positive sense of self-determination. Here are the two categories of the earlier passage on Enlightenment: the self-inflicted minority or tutelage is replaced by self-determined independence. "Thus the moral law expresses nothing else than the *autonomy* of the pure practical reason; that is, freedom."

Heteronomy results as much from dependence on some "physical law" (the necessity to "follow some impulse or inclination") as on the externally imposed will of another. If the latter case is the key to the Promethean form of atheism, the former is the key to Kant's concept of freedom in morality. In Jean-Paul Sartre, as we shall see, the two forms of heteronomy are posited as one. Since the criterion of universalizability reflects the motivation for the moral law, Kant insists that the proper motive or "spring [*elater animi*]" of autonomous willing lies in the agreement of the moral law with the subjective will itself. He recognizes the circular argument involved: "an insoluble problem for the human reason . . . identical with the question how a free will is possible." Lewis Beck notes: "The problem is to determine a law that the will can obey without losing its freedom through that very act of obeisance to law." Or as Michael Polanyi puts the case: "The freedom of the subjective person to do as he pleases is overruled by the freedom of the responsible person to act as he must."[33]

In this context happiness derives from satisfying those inclinations termed self-regard (*solipsismus*), which pure practical reason monitors and cleanses from mere selfishness. Thus does the moral law function as "the form of intellectual causality," the same as freedom. Thus also does duty appear as "moral constraint" determining the will in respect for moral law and "reverence for its duty." This occasions one of Kant's few rhetorical passages, in which Duty is apostrophized. (One recalls J.G. Hamann's *Metacritique of the Purism of Reason* in response to the first *Critique*, about which Kant's friendly enemy addressed him: "I write in epic style because you cannot yet understand lyric language.")

> *Duty*! Thou sublime and mighty name that dost embrace nothing charming or insinuating, but requirest submission, and yet seeks not to move the will by threatening aught that would arouse natural aversion or terror, but merely holdest forth a law which of itself finds entrance into the mind . . . what origin is there worthy of thee, and where is to

be found the root of thy noble descent?[34]

Kant's noble duty, guided by the teleological judgment of the Kingdom of Ends, leads him back to an emphasis on the doctrine of creation. Thus in *Religion Within the Limits of Reason Alone* (1793), the contemplation of "the profound wisdom of the divine creation" transports the mind into "the sinking mood, called *adoration*, annihilating man, as it were, in his own eyes." Its power so elevates that words "pass away as empty sound"; the "emotion arising from such a vision of the hand of God is inexpressible."[35] Once again the Ciceronic phrase *elater animi* can describe the quasi-mystical experience. Paul Tillich's term *ecstatic reason* comes to mind, knowledge beyond the subject-object dichotomy. But for Kant a sinister dimension is lurking near. His crucial "limit" is in jeopardy, because "radical evil" so threatens even critical reason that only "the hand of God" has liberating power – a new kind of "transcendental unity," to be sure!

In his book Kant is passing from rational theology to historical theology: God is less the originator of moral law and more the founder of the true community where we are at home with one another. For this reason Michel Despland concludes: "Thus Kant truly began the transition between the rationalism of the Enlightenment and the birth of modern theology located in Schleiermacher."[36]

Kant's final words thus turn to the flaw in Enlightenment rationale. "Radical evil" is established, even by such rational religion, as a "natural propensity to evil." This is in fact the opening gambit of the work: "Concerning the indwelling of the evil principle within the good, or, on the radical evil in human nature." The *propensio* is qualified in the second edition by the scholastic term *concupiscentia*. Moral evil is properly only a determination of the free will so that the propensity consists in "the subjective ground of the possibility of the deviation of the maxims (of the will) from the moral law." Kant is wrestling with the familiar theological problem of the paradox between universality and responsibility. He wishes to insist that the propensity is universal, hence "Natural," yet to be moral it must be freely chosen, responsible. He concludes that it is "a *radical* innate *evil* in human nature (yet none the less brought upon us by ourselves)."

One can appreciate the horrified reaction of Goethe to this teaching: Kant has "slobbered" on his philosopher's gown, leaving on it "the shameful stain of radical evil" and inviting Christians "to kiss its hem." It is not so much that Kant insists on quoting St. Paul and indicating his complete agreement with the apostolic doctrine; rather the radical evil so conflicts with our good maxims that help can come not from further good maxims but only from a redemption (a "reform of the disposition") outside what is rational. Having agreed with Paul's doctrine of sin, the philosopher now finds himself forced to agree in large measure with the Apostle's doctrine of salvation.

The second part of the book concerns "the conflict of the Good with the Evil Principle for Sovereignty over Man." Here Kant struggles with traditional problems of the weight of sin and the inescapable debt, echoing Anselm's categories in *Cur Deus Homo*. For Anselm the principle was *aut poena aut satisfactio*; for Kant it becomes the fact that "satisfaction must be rendered to Supreme Justice, in whose sight no one who is blameless can ever be guiltless." The key to satisfaction lies in that "change of heart" for which Kant finds no better description than Pauline phraseology as to dying unto sin, being crucified in the flesh and putting on the new man. The "moral disposition" follows the example of the Son of God; but Kant can go further and "personify this idea" by which the Christ acts as "vicarious substitute" or "saviour" and "advocate."

Kant's further sortie into the Kingdom of God on earth as realized in the Church (or at least in a Church dedicated to "pure religious faith") leads Karl Barth, in his incisive study of the philosopher whom he calls "the flowering of the Enlightenment," to ask:

> Does Kant after all perhaps know what justification is, in the sense of the Reformation? This question at least one cannot possibly escape, after carefully analysing the multifariously involved utterances of this, the work of his old age – and it is inescapable at this point in particular. It is, of course, impossible, in face of the Kantian re-interpretation of the Christological dogma, to answer this question in the affirmative. But how can it be denied, when it is so plain that it was none the less precisely the Christological dogma by means of which he has here interpreted the text, that text, he alleges, which was the only one which interested him of practical reason?[37]

The text in question echoes Paul – "a righteousness not our own." Kant agrees that this is the only conceivable (that is, by reason) answer to the dilemma of the moral disposition, which is enabled and strengthened to sacrifice self to God and receive from him a new self clothed in the righteousness of another.

Kant escapes his dilemma even here by reckoning such "mysteries" of grace and redemption as *parerga* of religion within the limits of reason alone." They remain adjacent or cognate to this religion: "Reason does not dispute the possibility or reality of the objects of these ideas; it is just that it cannot include them in its maxims for thought and action." His definition of such a "holy mystery" is significant of his solution: "something *holy* which may indeed be *known* by each single individual but cannot be *made known* publicly, that is, shared universally." As holy it is moral, "and so an object of reason," known from within for practical use; yet as mysterious it cannot be shared and therefore remains "not for theoretical use."[38]

The significance of Kant for our thesis is twofold. First, his critical philosophy heralded the end of metaphysical theism and its God of necessary reasons – as Marx, a kind of post-Kantian Hegelian, saw clearly. For instance, the notorious passage in the first *Critique* on "unconditioned necessity" as "an abyss on the verge of which human reason trembles in dismay" reveals Kant's recognition of the *aporia* entailed in the concept of freedom. For when reason reduces this to its limit, both freedom and reason suffer the pain of absolute limit.[39] Traditional arguments for the existence of God – ontological, cosmological and teleological – are contradicted by the non-necessity of their Subject according to critical philosophy. Thus classical theism reaches its dénouement at the hands of its own child.

Second, as the *Atheismusstreit* associated with the names of Fichte and Forberg implies, practical belief may coexist with theoretical unbelief: the autonomy of morals is at least possible on Kantian grounds. Probing the epistemological wound opened by Kant, Fichte posited a noumenal will to overcome the subject-object split. The Kantian ethics of duty filled him with awe. Here was human vocation, destiny (*Bestimmung*). "Not merely TO KNOW, but according to thy knowledge TO DO, is thy vocation." Kant's own postulatory moralism moved from the distinction between phenomena and noumena, required to circumvent the third antinomy of pure reason ("A causality of freedom is also necessary" / "There is no such thing as freedom"), to the dilemma of noumenal freedom. Now "a free will is the same thing as a will that conforms to moral law."[40] Therefore the opposition of heteronomy and autonomy occurs within the human will, as noted earlier. The moral argument for the existence of God cannot appeal from the human to posit an outside Being. And indeed, Kant's moral proof describes a "God" who functions as "the practical moral reason giving laws to itself – I will that there be a God."[41] Transcendental philosophy in this theological mode is both critique and revision of classical theism.

Fear of Death and Fear of Life

The new Enlightenment autonomy has produced creatures of Prometheus with upward mobility, drawn by the moral ideals intrinsic to their human being. The ambivalence of such anthropology is seen in Goethe, more the critic than Kant himself, more committed to the creative act of the individual. Faust's famous revision of the biblical text is his motto: *Am Anfang war die Tat* – In the Beginning Was the Deed.

Goethe's Faust suffers from the fear of life, *Lebensangst*. His upward striving reflects his creator's idea of the cosmic forces that attract and repel, impelling all things through gradations of ascent (*Steigerung*). Parallel to this view was a theme of the *Aufklärung* that religion, on the other hand, springs from the fear of death. Diderot, for one, held that an enlightened person substituted future generations for the eschatology that sustained classical theism: "What posterity is for the philosopher, the other world is for the religious man." The classical authors on whom the *Aufklärer* drew, in their opinion sought to set men free from the fear of death so that they would be beyond superstition – nor would tyrants have any hold on them.[42] The death of Socrates was a favourite example, while discussion of the justification of suicide found a hearing once again. We should remember when viewing this scene that the *philosophes* were a new breed of professionals seeking a very personal freedom – freedom from patronage. From this sense of personal independence sprang a sense of the good of freedom as a general virtue, and the basis for maturity.

Allied to the quest for freedom was a strain of nostalgia, as Nature and "natural man" were idealized and exalted. Rousseau is famous for this tendency, indulged in by many others including Diderot, and expressed classically by Dryden:

> I am as free as nature first made man
> Ere the base laws of servitude began,
> When wild in woods the noble savage ran.[43]

The romantic theme of wilderness is perennial, of course – Cicero's *O tempora! o mores!* crops up in Enlightenment writings.

But nostalgia does not lose the enmity for religion, since "religion" was being identified with "superstition." The example of Condorcet is apt: despite his own experience of the fate of enlightenment thought in revolutionary action, himself proscribed and in hiding (it is now 1793), he developed a philosophy of history in which his anticlericalism increases. Socrates is now persecuted by "the preachers." Peter Gay comments: "here clerical villainy is manifest and prophetic: Condorcet presents the death of Socrates as the opening skirmish in the great war between philosophy and superstition that still rages."[44]

The Enlightenment ranged reason against superstition: freedom from superstition is the route to independence, maturity, the cultivation of wisdom. Hence the clue to religion or superstition as fear of death provided an excellent hold on the weapon considered adequate to every task, human reason. The essential otherworldliness of religion was thought to be the point of vulnerability for the attack of reason. This thought obtained at least until the Marxist critique and remains a touchstone for certain philosophers today, particularly in the tradition of linguistic analysis. Yet the *philosophes* themselves did not necessarily succeed in replacing fear of death by love of life. For one thing, their attack on the religious view of nature, including human nature, made it imperative for them to develop a "science of man." The Genesis account of the creation of the race gave human nature a definite root (*natus*) and essence. Because of the strength of the doctrine of original sin in classical theism, the story of Creation and Fall was of one piece, so that a return to nature would banish the theological stress on the corruption of nature and dependence on supranatural help. But – as existentialists still maintain – it banishes also any concept of a human nature.

As the battlelines were formed in the Enlightenment, so they have continued among philosophers to this day. On one side are supposed those who accept myth and superstition, entailing suspicion of the world and the flesh and reliance on supernatural powers for daily life in the world; on the other are those who affirm the sufficiency of reason for human existence, who see humanity as alone in the universe so far as resources for living are concerned, and who challenge us to acknowledge that fact as the beginning of wisdom. Heinrich Heine would later call these parties Hebrews and Hellenes, positing an irreconcilable conflict between them. The trick in developing a science of the human, however, as Hume saw clearly enough, is that it runs counter not only to superstition but also to rationalism.

– 6 –

Romance and the Firekindler

L'Explosion du "Moi"

The Sturm und Drang movement was a protest against philosophy of order on behalf of passion. J.W. von Goethe (1749-1832) said that the Lisbon earthquake had released the demon of Fear; its occurrence in the middle of the eighteenth century was a reminder that the ideals of classicism might not suffice for all occasions. It was Goethe also who replied shortly to a question about the difference between the two great polarities in culture: "Classicism is health, romanticism disease."[1] Yet Goethe himself symbolizes the power of individual genius, of the creative spirit – *esprit créateur, Geistschöpfer* – which considers itself equal with God (*ebenbürtig*) and hence independent of divine command. Prometheus finds companions in the figures of Niobe and especially Faust.

Our distinction between reason and romance, between light-bearer and firekindler, is not a separation in reality. With this caveat, we note that the early Goethe is a typical romantic, with Faust inhabiting a Gothic world and Prometheus a classical stage. This period begins Goethe's love affair with the myth. His "Frankfurter Prometheusdichtungen" owe much to Rousseau's monodrama *Pygmalion*, which the young admirer described as "zwischen Natur und Kunst," a noble challenge to higher existence. Goethe may begin with Aeschylus, but he has a different theme in mind: the Titan's hatred and contempt of Zeus. He considers Shakespeare a Promethean genius and creator (*Rede zum Schakespears Tag*, 1771). In his fragment *Prometheus* (1773) and the *Ode* of the following year, Goethe shapes the classical myth in his own image. His pantheistic bent, akin to that of Spinoza, considers Destiny a superior but impersonal power, like all divinity including that of orthodox

---

Notes to Chapter 6 appear on page 318.

Christianity. He rejects the tyrant God by substituting for the Creator of the Bible his new Prometheus. "Le Promethée de Goethe n'est plus Promethée, image poétique extérieure a l'esprit qui la pense, mais Goethe même, artiste de genie qui trouve en soi son flambeau."[2]

Goethe's metaphysical revolt rejects heteronomous deity in behalf of human independence, freedom. In the monologue Prometheus taunts the gods for their irrelevance to his earth and for their wretched cult. It closes with the moving and expressive verse quoted earlier:

> Hier sitz' ich, forme Menschen
> Nach meinem Bilde,
> Ein Geschlecht, das mir gleich sei:
> Zu leiden, zu weinen,
> Zu geniessen und zu freuen sich –
> Und dein nicht zu achten,
> Wie ich!

> [Here I sit, shaping man
> After my image,
> A race that is like me,
> To suffer, to weep, ·
> To rejoice and be glad,
> And like myself
> To have no regard for you!]

One ponders these words, weighted with consciousness of the potential of humanity, retelling an old story with a new point, skilfully bringing forth the profound hope of Enlightenment man; one sees the grandeur and the pathos of Goethe and his times. The "mythological point" where Prometheus appears became for Goethe a "present and lively Fixidee." For him it is "hermetischen, mystischen, kabbalistischen," the best symbol of defiance and displacement of Jupiter, who negates freedom and is "der salto mortale der menschlichen Vernunft."[3]

Part of the greatness of Goethe is his variety of talents and roles. The public that greeted the young romantic author of *The Sorrows of Young Werther* (how many youthful suicides followed Werther's example!) were nonplussed by classical works such as *Tasso* and *Iphigenie*, to be followed soon by the sensual themes of the *Roman Elegies*. How to apply Goethe's dictum of "classicism healthy, romanticism sick" to his own work? Especially *Faust*, the first fragment of which (1790) created an enthusiastic following, only to be repelled by the increasing sobriety of the finished Part I (1806) and the posthumous Part II.

Goethe's preoccupation with the Faust legend spanned sixty years. As he worked and reworked this drama, and his principal novel on Wilhelm Meister, the individualistic philosophy was taking shape in the movement from naive romanticism to mature appreciation of the complexity of life and the power of hope. Between the Walpurgis Night and Faust's ascent to heaven lie years of mature thought and action, including *Pandora*'s critique of the current physicotheology (1789). His ambiguous attitude to religion is summed up in a famous remark: "We are pantheists when we study nature, polytheists when we poetize, monotheists in our morality."[4]

Sturm und Drang, led by the twenty-four-year-old Goethe in 1772, featured a truly Promethean poetry. J.G. Herder (1744-1803), Goethe's friend and colleague in those years of proleptic romanticism, exploited the theme of Prometheus and the New Humanity. This critic (who also wrote a *Metakritik*) of Kant, indeed of Enlightenment foundations, promotes his view of the hero as *skaldriche Prometheus*, the inspired poet-shaman, until his mature work on Prometheus unbound (*Der entfesselte Prometheus*), the genius both poetic and patriotic. Like Goethe, Herder's interest in Prometheus was lifelong, from his paraphrases of Greek literature to *Der entfesselte* of the year before his death. A "portrait" of our favourite Titan is developed, a "most instructive emblem," one which provides "a poetic résumé of the author's ideas on human destiny," in Herder's own words. The climactic appeal of the Firebringer rings out in address to us who receive his gift – "die Flamme der innerfortgehenden Menschen-Bildung:" "Make use of the fire which Prometheus brought for you! Let it shine forth with increasing light and splendour! for it is the flame of enduring human culture."[5]

Poet as Titan

> Many are poets but without the name,
> For what is poesy but to create
> From overfeeling good or ill; and aim
> At an eternal life beyond our fate,
> And be the new Prometheus of new men,
> Bestowing fire from heaven, and then, too late,
> Finding the pleasure given repaid with pain,
> And vultures to the heart of the bestower,
> Who, having lavish'd his high gift in vain,
> Lies chain'd to his lone rock by the sea-shore?
> 　　　　　　(Byron, *The Prophecy of Dante*, IV.v.10-19)

In his perceptive essay "Metaphysical Rebellion," Albert Camus has a devastating section on what he calls "The Dandies' Rebellion."[6] Following the lead of de Sade – "the perfect man of letters. He created a fable in order to give himself the illusion of existing" – men of letters compose out of hatred and negation, lacking positive content. "Romanticism, Lucifer-like in its rebellion, is really only useful for adventures of the imagination." Its defiance of God derives from the same Enlightenment reasoning that divinity robs humanity of goodness and freedom. Yet it sinks into fatalism, the romantic hero blending good and evil in headlong career toward his own destruction.

Camus's perception of romanticism provides corrective for much of the sentimental approach familiar to students of literature. Falling into love and falling into melancholy are two chief moods associated with the term *romantic*. In the English poets of nineteenth-century romanticism, however, we meet a striking form of Prometheanism. From Byron to Bridges, the Titan has inspired a robust poesy that attests the perennial attraction of the myth. We are now in the company of Prometheus *Pyrkaeus*, the Firekindler. This was the name of Aeschylus's satyr-play after the Promethean trilogy. The very idea of satyric crudity and buffoonery may seem inappropriate for the mostly serious and high-minded poets before us. But the mythological creature itself was ambiguous in both form and role: its duplicity reflects its origin in the primitive contest, the *agōn* between Summer and Winter. Yet here lay the beginnings of both Tragedy and Comedy, as Aristotle maintained (*Poetics* 1453a). Moreover, the final speech in Plato's great dialogue *Symposium* (215-22) is that of Alcibiades, praising Socrates in a figure that compares him to the masks of Silenus: "Your face is like that of a satyr." Likening the Socratic irony to the latter's unwelcome attention, he concludes: "And this is what I and many others have suffered from the flute-playing of this satyr." For the questioning of Socrates in his role as *eiron* was a means of dis-illusioning, emptying. Its satyrlike behaviour is therefore close to the poetic and romantic humour that attacks through the deliberate indirection of its language.

The spirit of the age is not simply "romantic," however. Kenneth Clark's study of romanticism in painting takes two writings in mid-eighteenth century to indicate the constant interplay of classicism and romanticism. Winckelmann's *Reflections on the Imitation of Greek Art* (1755) and Burke's *Philosophical Inquiry into the Origin of Our Ideas of the Sublime and the Beautiful* (1756) categorize the two approaches and suggest that they are complementary. Clark himself treats both classic and romantic artists in his work, and the chapter on William Blake reminds us of that "fearful symmetry" that the strange artist-poet strives for, a symmetry which includes Prometheus. For the energy of the defiant Titan is preserved in the manifestations of "Orc," of which Jesus was the chief. It is the Promethean fire that will burn up the "opaque" world at the End; it is the tyranny of Zeus-Jehovah against which both Prometheus and Jesus rebel.[7]

Blake's mythology reflects a variety of sources, but despite its individual religious meaning, it links with the poets now under review. For him, Jesus can exhaust the attributes of divinity, and in turn so can ordinary folk. The famous lines "Thou art a Man God is no more / Thy own humanity learn to adore" reflect his identification of divinity with human imagination, so that God as Creator is truly "Man." He rejects the "Jewish" servile worship of Nobodaddy, capricious and malevolent, and welcomes the vision of God as the God-Man, Jesus. Blake's esoteric symbolism may be unpacked sufficiently to appreciate the familiar tension between the God whose attributes demand human servitude and the polar opposite of such a deity, a humanity either fearfully alone or so divinized that the self-reliance of a Titan becomes possible.[8]

The heritage of eighteenth century rationalism provides a stage for romantic poetry: the Christian God is called Jehovah, a proper name for an all-powerful tyrant, equivalent to Zeus. Jehovah-Zeus is the origin of evil, and an emotional theodicy develops centred on Promethean assertion of freedom and human potential. Romantic titanism was compounded of love of the classical era and hatred of Christianity.[9] God as creator of evil, or bumbling demiurge, is one answer to the problem of evil. Voltaire speaks of "l'infortune créateur" (*Pandore*), while other writers proceed to exalt Satan as friend of humankind. Milton's Satan, of course, is familiar as a heroic figure of Promethean dimensions:

> . . . and thou, profoundest hell,
> Receive thy new possessor; one who brings
> A mind not to be changed by place or time.
> The mind is its own place, and in itself
> Can make a heaven of hell, a hell of heaven.
> (*Paradise Lost*, I. 251-55)

Milton's drama is a conflict of power, an opposition of wills for the possession of dominions. Therefore the question of good and evil hangs on the resolution of such conflict through conquest or betterment. It was easy for the post-rationalist age to align itself with antitheism and with the persona of the Antichrist. This was explicit with Leconte de Lisle and the French Parnassus group (*Le Parnasse contemporain*, 1866-76) and quite compatible with the revolutionary poets in general.

Gilbert Highet has given a profile of the anti-Christian polemic of the age.[10] The Graeco-Roman ideal was thought to provide a model of energy and life-affirmation lacking in Christianity. The latter was associated with gloom and weakness – one thinks of Swinburne's "pale Galilean" appropriately addressed in "Hymn to Proserpine:"

> Thou hast conquered, O pale Galilean;
> the world has grown gray from Thy breath:
> We have drunken of things Lethean, and
> fed on the fullness of death.

The impotent Jesus symbolizes the religion of vengeance and victimization, a clear contrast to the manifold deities of classical nature-worship and the exaltation of human strength and virtue (the masculine *vir*).

Highet gives three arguments in use. One is that Christianity is Oriental, foreign and correspondingly barbarous. Gibbon's closing gibe at "the triumph of Barbarism and Religion" matches Renan's description of the "foreign cult," with Paul "an ugly little Jew, speaking the greek of the Syrians" (even *koinē* Greek is repudiated). A second argument equates Christianity with repression, paganism with liberty. Whatever the historical errors of such a view, the sketch provided earlier suggests its power. A third compares the strength and intensity of paganism with Christian timidity and weakness, a theme to be used with vigour by Nietzsche, another whose love of Greece led him inexorably away from Christianity.

Byron

George Gordon, Lord Byron (1788-1824), represents the romantic spirit in an exemplary way. His reputation as model for his own *Don Juan*, his loves and travels and adventures, underline the posturing and dramatizing of genuine romanticism. Several of his poetic creations reflect facets of Prometheus. *Childe Harold's Pilgrimage* is rich in the themes to be developed. There is mystic harmony with Nature, and an apathy symbolized by the waters of Lethe. There is praise of Rousseau, Gibbon and Voltaire in Canto Third, rising to the hymn to freedom and to reason ("the faculty divine") in Canto Fourth. Indeed, Gibbon and Voltaire are "Titan-like" in their work of sceptical inquiry:

> Thoughts which should call down thunder
> and the flame
> Of Heaven, again assailed, if Heaven the
> while
> On man and man's research could deign
> do more than smile.
> (Canto Third, CV)

And there is also the price to be paid for reflection, those "ceaseless vultures" of concern and remorse which afflict whomever dares to think (II.59).

Manfred suggests further self-projection: the brooding figure on the mountain and in the tower calls on the spirits of earth, ocean, air, night, mountain, wind and his own star in his quest for "forgetfulness" and "oblivion." His lost love appears like the ghost of Samuel to Saul, and at the end he dies defiant of the shades of destiny and death itself. Manfred stands possessed of his own will; to the spirits he can cry in pride:

> Slaves, scoff not at my will!
> The mind, the spirit, the Promethean
> spark,
> The lightning of my being, is as bright,
> Pervading, and far darting as your own,
> And shall not yield to yours, though
> cooped in clay!
> (153ff)

Moreover, even in *Don Juan*, Byron's lighthearted play – its ottava rima at times descending to bathos – affords him vehicle for the familiar themes of liberty, apathy and poetic licence. Of special note is the familiar burden of courtly love, honoured in the Renaissance, encouraged by Ronsard – fire as symbol of love.

> And life yields nothing further to recall
> Worthy of this ambrosial sin, so shown,
> No doubt in fable, as the unforgiven
> Fire which Prometheus filch'd for us from heaven.
> (CXXVII)

It is in the *Prometheus* fragment (1816) addressed to the Titan that we hear serious echoes of Aeschylus. The description of the suffering hero leads into Byronic rationalism:

> Thy Godlike crime was to be kind,
> To render with thy precepts less
> The sum of human wretchedness,
> And strengthen Man with his own mind.
>   (35ff)

His Prometheus is "a symbol and a sign" in calling humanity to resistance against its "funereal destiny." His hope and vision is that with "a firm will" the human spirit may be "Triumphant where it dare defy, / And making Death a Victory."

Byron's theme of titanic resistance raises a question about the romantic sublime as philosophy of life. The rhetorical or literary sublime in the classical tradition of Longinus was revised by the romantics in behalf of a "natural sublime" responding to great and awesome objects. Burke's *Sublime* moved the ideas toward the negative pole. John Keats's aesthetics sought to sublate (*sublim*ate?) the "disagreeables" through poetic representation of essential qualities. His identification of essence with Beauty/Truth reflects his redefinition, following Hazlitt, of sublime as creative activity. The imagination serves Poesy by its telling narrative of the rise and fall of Titans. Keats's own voracious reading served his "speculation," which sought to explore and exorcise the "World of Pains and trouble." How is "the burthen of the mystery" to be endured? In a famous letter (December 21, 1817) he declares that one must prove himself "capable of being in uncertainties, mysteries, doubts, without any irritable reaching after fact and reason." Such "negative capability" characterizes tragic sublimity – the resignation of *To Autumn*, for instance, or the divine twilight of the *Hyperions*.

For Byron, of course, the tragic is less a conscious mood and more a studied manner. His is the romantic egoism, the arrogance of absolute free will. Pechorin, Mikhail Lermontov's "hero of our time" (1840) exemplifies the type of larger-than-life figure beloved of romantic inspiration. Iris Murdoch has related the romantic hero to the modernist myth in which the psyche is like a machine, limited in perspective and in choice. But this restriction is combined with a sense of unlimited freedom, "the illusion of jumping out" of its conditions. The tension is almost palpable in the life and work of Shelley.[11]

Shelley

Percy Bysshe Shelley (1792-1822) develops the Promethean theme in a more profound and significant manner. Like Byron, he was impressed with the polemic against Christianity and the praise of classicism mentioned before. Like Byron also, he is famous for amours and exile. Both poets shared a passion for freedom, notably the cause of Greek liberty then at issue of arms. Shelley's *Hellas* (1821) begins with one of his inimitable prefaces, in which he states: "We are all Greeks. Our laws, our literature, our religion, our arts, have their root in Greece. . . . The human form and the human mind attained to a perfection in Greece . . . those glorious beings." He also adopted the equation of Jehovah with Zeus (Jupiter, Jove) and the concomitant equation of freedom with atheism.

Shelley's brief life is marked by his espousal of atheism from the youthful *The Necessity of Atheism*, which led to his expulsion from Oxford in 1811, to the *Essay on Christianity*, its companion piece published posthumously in 1859. It may be that we ought to take the undergraduate essay less seriously than his own sensitive generation did, since there is evidence that it was a case of youthful exuberance and rebellion rather than serious theology. A decade later, in the more significant *Defence of Poetry*, he dissociated himself from the atheism of "some of the French writers," a sentiment echoed in his repudiation of the "materialism" of his youth. He is also reported to have commented on *Necessity* that it was "villainous trash."[12] Shelley was not a materialist, since a growing idealism of Bishop Berkeley's variety led him to posit a "Spirit of the Universe" that allowed to Christ only attributes of human virtue.

The Necessity of Atheism is noteworthy more as a prelude to his notes on *Queen Mab* than as a contribution to theology. Shelley defends the thesis "There is no God" as rejecting "a creative Deity" but not "a pervading Spirit coeternal with the universe." He laments "the annoying idea that theology gives of a capricious God," clearly the clue to his early anti-Christian stance. Later, in *A Refutation of Deism* (1814), he will attack the God of vengeance and of battle, a God who could be enclosed in a little box "brought home in a new cart." In the *Essay on Christianity* he concentrates more on the negative attributes of classical theism: "The universal being can only be described by negatives. . . . Where indefiniteness ends, idolatry and anthropomorphism begin." This sounds like a good beginning for negative theology, or even the concept of analogy as mean between agnosticism and anthropomorphism, but for Shelley it supports his kind of idealism or near-pantheism. Positively put, he states his creed thus: "There is a power by which we are surrounded, like the atmosphere in which some motionless lyre is suspended, which visits with its breath our silent chords at will. . . . This power is God."[13]

Queen Mab was printed privately in 1813, Shelley's first major poem. His *Notes* reflect the earlier essay and develop his idealism or monism as against all ideas of a personal God who works by "a peculiar Providence." In place of providential oversight he sees "Necessity! thou mother of the world!" (V.198) – a chain of cause and effect "immense and uninterrupted." The defence of "There is no God" is repeated (VII.l3), followed by an excursus on belief (the God-hypothesis fails every criterion of evidence) and quotations from d'Holbach, Pliny, Newton and Spinoza as in the *Necessity*. He uses his text "I will beget a Son, and He shall bear the sins of all the world" (VII.l356) as occasion for a lengthy exposé of Christianity as supernatural fable doomed to extinction. "If God has spoken, why is the universe not convinced?"

The poem itself opens with Voltaire's motto, *Ecrasez l'infâme*! The Spirit of Nature emerges as focal point of his protest against slavery and poverty, induced by "priest, conqueror or prince." His utopian hope awaits the time "When man, with change-less Nature coalescing / Will undertake regeneration's work" (VI.42f). Book VII is crucial: the Spirit tells of seeing "an atheist burned," occasioning a passage which teaches an immanentist and reductionist view of religion. There are various names: "Seeva, Buddh, Foh, Jehovah, God, or Lord," but for Shelley "God" still stands for "tyrant." Ahasuerus cries: "Is there a God! – ay, an almighty God, / And vengeful as almighty!" (84f). God is an "almighty Fiend," characterized by "tyrannous omnipotence." This lengthy section is a caricature of classical theism in which the blind revenge of God is met by the sacrificial death of Christ. It rivals Lucky's speech in *Waiting for Godot* as parody.

Such early writings suggest the background and preparation for Shelley's understanding of Prometheus. It was in company with Mary Godwin and while visiting Byron – three exiles in Switzerland – that a curious circumstance occurred, famous for the production of Mary Godwin Shelley's book *Frankenstein* (1817). The three companions staged a story-writing competition among themselves, with Mary's sketch leading to her novel. Its full title is *Frankenstein, Or, The Modern Prometheus*. In her later introduction the author describes the circumstances of its origin, and the conversations between Shelley and Byron on "the nature of the principle of life," the possibility of its being discovered and communicated, and "the experiments of Dr. Darwin." Such was the climate of thought some two years before Shelley began work on his *Prometheus Unbound*, to be published in completed form in 1820.

Dr. Frankenstein's monstrous creation is analogous to the creative power of Prometheus. It is interesting that in Mary Godwin's mind was the threat and the ambiguity of such power, the dystopia that might well result from manipulation of elemental forces through technology. The rebinding of Prometheus is evident in the scientist's desire to benefit humanity, yet able only to mirror his own solipsism and egoism in his creature's vices, "children of a forced solitude." For Shelley, however, the Promethean model illustrates rather the potential for good, the utopian vision to which he is committed. His hero is deliberately fashioned after Aeschylus; there is little ambiguity about his confidence in the modern Prometheus to use his power for good, to effect what he wills.

Shelley's preface to *Prometheus Unbound* makes clear that he is not attempting to recreate the lost play of Aeschylus of the same title. The supposed plot was the reconciliation of Zeus and Prometheus, the latter disclosing his secret (the danger threatening Zeus's dominion by the consummation of his marriage with Thetis) as the price of his release. Shelley comments: "I was averse from a catastrophe as feeble as that of reconciling the Champion with the Oppressor of mankind." The "moral interest" of the fable, he suggests, "would be annihilated if we could conceive of him as unsaying his high language and quailing before his successful and perfidious adversary." He then compares Prometheus to Satan, judging him "a more poetical character" than "the Hero of Paradise Lost." For "Prometheus is, as it were, the type of the highest perfection of moral and intellectual nature, impelled by the purest and the truest motives to the best and noblest ends."

Here, then, is the romantic manifesto: both Satan and Prometheus revolt against the wicked God, with Prometheus singled out as archetypal rebel, truly romantic in his vocation and suffering, his noble qualities and pure motivation. His role as Firekindler, of course, includes that of Lightbearer, *Lucifer*. The lyric poem is a praise of freedom and of a form of titanism as the solution to the problem of evil, a titanism "rationaliste . . . melioriste, scientiste et toujours anthropocentrique."[14] Such an interpretation of the myth has been challenged and even ridiculed by critics who charge the nineteenth century writers with transforming the original into a revolt against evil for the social good, the typical romantic quest.[15] Mary

Shelley's notes to her late husband's poems stated that he regarded evil as an accident, "not inherent in the system of the creation." Therefore,

> Shelley believed that mankind had only to will that there should be no evil, and there would be none. . . . . That man could be so perfectionized as to be able to expel evil from his own nature, and from the greater part of the creation, was the cardinal point of this system.

In the poem such a destiny is personified by Demogorgon, who topples Jupiter from his throne and conducts him into the abyss. Prometheus is set free by Hercules, having persevered in defiance. The final speech is reserved for Demogorgon, who extols the new day after "Heaven's despotism," when "Gentleness, Virtue, Wisdom, and Endurance" flourish.

> To suffer woes which Hope thinks infinite;
> To forgive wrongs darker than death or night;
>   To defy Power, which seems omnipotent;
> To love, and bear; to hope till Hope creates
> From its own wreck the thing it contemplates;
>   Neither to change, nor falter, nor repent;
> This, like thy glory, Titan! is to be
> Good, great and joyous, beautiful and free;
> This is alone Life, Joy, Empire, and Victory!
>   (IV: 572-80)

Zeus-Jupiter-Jove is a two-dimensional figure in the poem – "Monarch," "almighty Tyrant," "Heaven's fell King," "Crime, where it sits throned / In brief Omnipotence," who gloats in his total power at the very moment Demogorgon ascends to be his doom. Prometheus, on the other hand, is credited in Asia's moving speech (II.4, 31ff) with the strength of defiance, the wisdom to grant freedom, and the grace to give gifts. Even as outcast, "from adamantine chains" he cursed God. And hearing, God "trembled like a slave." Therefore Asia demands of Demogorgon: "Who is his master? / Declare is he too a slave?" (108f).

In Shelley's vision, the world is transformed by the defiance of tyranny, which in itself is an act of freedom, reversing the master-slave relationship. The poem thus parallels his *A Philosophical View of Reform* (1819) and has the same history in view: from revolution to Restoration. The ironical issue of the French Revolution in a further form of despotism was a source of deep disillusionment to the literati of the time. Like Byron, Shelley exhorts his generation to struggle for freedom not only in the exotic lands of Italy and Greece but in the homelands too, once bright with hope and now again in shadow. If Demogorgon represents Necessity (Shelley's only Absolute, as it were), then Asia, the bride of Prometheus, represents love, without which blind necessity will miss the mark.

Shelley is much more programmatic and political than many of the romantic poets. His atheism is a practical ingredient in his recipe for liberty, since only as the tyrant deity is denied and overthrown will those human tyrants who derive their power from his – specious as he considers the derivation to be – be likewise dislodged from mastery. It is a noble vision and a just cause. Moreover, the age of "the divine right of Kings" was not long gone, and its heritage remained. If the German critical philosophers could point to Lutheran doctrine and Prussian usage to support their identity of divine and human tyranny, in England too church and state reinforced one another in a class structure and an oppressive society. The French Revolution stood for radical cure in the minds of Wordsworth and Coleridge, of Byron and Shelley, of Robert Burns.

The pathos of revolution's outcome reflects the personal dilemma of nineteenth century intellectuals. After all, "Le Romanticisme, c'est la Révolution." In this respect our poets embody romanticism not as love of nature or as melancholy, but as enthusiasm, gift of the Firekindler: not poems to a skylark, nor an ode on melancholy, but hymns to revolution. The self longs for deliverance, individual and social, but must rely on agents of change which traffic in worldly power. Shelley's passionate hope vacillated with moments of despair. His "Lift Not the Painted Veil" of 1818 acknowledges our "twin Destinies":

> Lift not the painted veil which those who live
> Call Life . . .
>   behind, lurk Fear
> And Hope.

For others too the dogma of progress was too good to be true. James Thomson's "The City of Dreadful Night" (1870-74) symbolizes the doom of the romantic era, a bleak vision of the new metropolis without purpose. Even that Promethean battler W.E. Henley, anticipating the school of "dark realism," is more Stoic than optimist in his familiar lines: "I am the master of my fate: / I am the captain of my soul" (*Out of the Night*, 1875).

The Romantic Spirit at Large

Romanticism as historical phenomenon may be contrasted to classicism, but also seen as response to Enlightenment. In this sense one might state that romanticism stands in tension with classicism and on the side of rationalism. George Steiner suggests that the historical case should be made as follows:

> It is not between Euripides and Shakespeare that the western mind turns away from the ancient tragic sense of life. It is after the late seventeenth century. . . . It is the triumph of rationalism and secular metaphysics which marks the point of no return.

Such interpretation of the development must qualify the popular image of romantic emotionalism. For surely the paradigm should not be Prometheus but Dionysus? One might well understand Schelling in this way (indeed he subsumed the two under one symbol) or Schiller and certainly Novalis.[16] Yet Prometheus was a source of fascination and inspiration to them, a reminder that our academic labels distort while enlightening. A standard of criticism is present in the romantic spirit, as the behaviour of Beethoven indicates.

Shelley's situation regarding the French Revolution has a distinct parallel in that of Beethoven's attitude toward Napoleon. The composer had dedicated his Third Symphony to "Bonaparte." But before its first performance in 1804 – so the story goes – he received the news that Napoleon had proclaimed himself Emperor. In anger he tore up the dedication and wrote a new title: "Heroic Symphony to Celebrate the Memory of a Great Man and dedicated to His Serene Highness Prince Lobkowitz." The *Eroica*, like his earlier ballet music *Creatures of Prometheus* (1800), from which he took the theme for the final movement, reminds us of the general romantic spirit of human greatness and the recognition of genius. And like *Fidelio* it recalls the constant theme of freedom. The finales of Beethoven's Fifth and Ninth symphonies have been compared with the Third in heralding "the emergence of a strong and free human society," while the *Eroica* is singled out as "a veritable musical arch of triumph through which the image of a liberated humanity joyfully passes in review."[17]

It is this praise of Prometheus that later music echoes in its thematic use of his story. Franz Liszt, A.N. Skriabin and Carl Orff have explicit works in this mode. Skriabin, simulating the play of fire in his "clavier à lumières," depicts the final triumph of good as humanity melds with the cosmos. Orff produced a musikdrama based on the text of Aeschylus, developing themes of divine and human passion. Part of Orff's triptych along with Antigone and Oedipus, Prometheus here recovers something of his original classical symbolism.[18] We are reminded of Nietzche's thesis about "the spirit of music."

We might note that we are in the age of Karl Marx, who was learning Manchester School economics at first hand in London. And while Marx can quote Shakespeare on occasion, there is no evidence to show that he had read Shelley, and we do not suggest direct influence. Still, when he called Prometheus "the noblest of saints and martyrs in the calendar of philosophy," it was some twenty years after Shelley's poem was published, and when Napoleon had been hailed as the new Prometheus. It was also about the very time when a strange book was published in England: *Prometheus Britannicus, or John Bull and the rural police.* This work by J.L. Brereton was in fact a reaction against the Reform movement, but is significant in depicting the typical Englishman as one who suffers under tyranny.

The meliorist aspect of Prometheanism is clearly before us, and the reason why Napoleon – particularly before he became afflicted by imperialism – was associated with the mythical figure. In Edgar Quinet's *Napoléon* he is "nouveau Prométhée," and in Monti's *Prometeo* he is superman, rebel against tyranny, liberator.[19] We saw how the romantic poets politicized their theories about the Titan's role. For Victor Hugo also Prometheus is "le libérateur enchaîné." We may recall further the trilogy of Quinet, his christianization of Prometheus already noted in the chapter "Prometheus and Christ."

Thus a marked contrast obtained for the romantics between the "pale Galilean" and the muscled martyr of the Caucasus. The one might be symbolized by Holman Hunt's *Light of the World*, the other by Peter Paul Rubens's *Prometheus Bound* – the meek and patient Christ and the unyielding captive (there pre-Raphaelite, here baroque). It seemed a choice between two objects of faith, the one otherworldly and escapist, the other life-affirming, joyfully accepting the battle against evil. In a sense, two theodicies are set in juxtaposition, two answers to the problem of evil. When religion is defined according to the first alternative, as escapist, a mere bowing to the revealed will of Providence, it is little wonder that modern advocates of the betterment of society found it almost self-evident that one must choose the part of rebellion against God, with his command to submit and obey. And since modern science appeared quite antiprovidential, further reason was given to the war against God. Louis

Menard's *Prométhée délivre* (1843) carries the case against religion to its logical conclusion: "Les temps sont maintenant accomplis: Zeus est mort. / L'Idéal est en toi: Voila le Dieu suprême."[20] The hatred of the Christian God is voiced in work after work, often in Promethean guise. Raymond Trousson's exhaustive research provides striking confirmation of the power of the myth in the late nineteenth century, especially in France and England. Typical is the assessment of A.R. Eagan (*Prometheus*, 1877): "But Zeus is Lord of Death and King of Pain, / And curbed his foe with vulture and with chain." The Titan symbolizes the human hope (e.g., Delarue's *Le Prométhée de l'Avenir*, 1895) and inspires a passionate rejection of God, an affair of the will quite in line with Nietzsche's program.

Carl Spitteler's *Prometheus und Epimetheus* deserves special mention, not least because of C.G. Jung's commentary on this work of 1881. Spitteler seizes on the ancient myth of Prometheus, Epimetheus and Pandora in order to explore the two philosophies of existence stemming from Goethe's *Pandora*.[21] Spitteler's allegory involves a dialogue of the two brothers with "soul." The angelic offer of a present kingdom in exchange for their souls results in Epimetheus's acceptance of the soulless world, while Prometheus refuses, choosing a future possibility over the present. This neglect of the world brings him suffering leading to atonement. Thus Prometheus is for Spitteler the pre-eminent martyr (*Dulder*).

Jung's analysis relates the brothers to his familiar psychic categories of introversion and extroversion. While he insists that both are present in every individual, the Forethinker chooses soul over world, and the Afterthinker the opposite. But for Jung the two represent a deeper dimension, explored best by Goethe both in the Prometheus-Epimetheus-Pandora myth and in the Faust legend. "The divine wager between good and evil is accepted. Faust, the medieval Prometheus, enters the lists with Mephistopheles, the medieval Epimetheus, and makes a pact with him."[22] Satan is Epimethean in reverting to chaos, "thinking in terms of 'nothing but' which reduces All to Nothing." For Spitteler the ultimate reconciliation between the two brothers is through a divine child Messias, not unlike Jung's transformation of types in enantiodromia. In the latter concept, the twinning of Foresight and Hindsight leads to proper rule of one's "kingdom;" the Messianic reign is the goal of integration.

Somewhat similar to Spitteler is André Gide, whose *Prométhée mal enchaîné* (1899) is a youthful oeuvre bouffon. Its epigraph is a quotation from Victor Hugo: "An eagle, or a vulture, or a dove." The eagle functions as conscience – Prometheus grows to love its beauty, but finally eats it. The other character is Miglionare or Zeus, an ostensible banker. But his wealth brings power, which he uses in a gratuitous manner, as a form of gambling: "I alone, he alone whose fortune is infinite, can act with absolute disinteredness; man cannot. Hence my love of gambling; not of gain, you understand me, but of gambling; what could I gain that I do not possess already?" This is a brilliant reduction of the Christian understanding of divinity – only the omnipotent can grant his grace as truly gratuitous, and therefore, for Gide, irrational and unjust. The final dénouement has Zeus laughingly tell Prometheus that he has no eagle (conscience) himself – "why it's I who give them to others." For he is "God Almighty."

Gide's Prometheus is scandalized by this capricious use of power. Since Gide's concern is that moral sense that constitutes human freedom, his Prometheus rejects Almighty God, grace which is a form of gambling, and even some universal conscience (collectivity) that may be imagined to function in quasi-divine manner. Trousson compares Gide with Spitteler, concluding that "Avec eux Prométhée devient égocentrique, il réduit l'âme universelle au Moi unique. . . . Prométhée devint le Dieu de Prométhée."[23]

Modern poets continue the fascination with the myth, and the pride in the role of this heroic rebel. Robert Bridges's *Prometheus the Firegiver: A Mask in the Greek Manner* (1883) is significant in that at the end the altar inscribed to Zeus has "words newly writ," the name of Prometheus. Here too we meet "the mighty Zeus our angry king," against whom the wise and patient protagonist brings fire to earth and exhorts us to strive against the divine power. Such works suggest the truth in Vincent Muselli's poetic address to "montée sublime, heure prométhée." Yet it is far from the last word.

It is true that the modern form of Promethean heroism turns on the rejection of the Christian God, at least in his image of the Almighty. We will see this also in Nietzsche, Camus and Sartre. Others, however, wish to turn back from the Titan to the Christ whom he anticipated – Alex Craig and Edwin Muir, for example. Now some observers would agree with those who see our age as quite godless, with a consequent poverty of myths and heroes. But others would argue quite otherwise – that myths express the perennial wisdom at the root of consciousness, of thinking. Elsewhere we have suggested some implications of mythological reflection.[24] In particular the recurring symbol of Leviathan-Behemoth, for both biblical and poetic imagination, offers an alternative to Western theodicy. If, as Eliade suggests, myth may be distinguished as creation and quest, then the notion of contest, *agōn* provides thematic unity to *rites de passage*, the journey of Everyman, the labyrinthine route toward the centre of Being.

The modern poetic spirit, however, seems spurred by a new nihilism, which informs so much of our "entertainment" industry.[25] In such vogue the stage on which Aeschylus saw Prometheus bound yet defiant has shrunk; the modern Prometheus is bound once again, this time by the chains of his own chosen role as divine Man. The romantic vision cast Jehovah as Zeus and demanded freedom. Their successors suffer from an absolute freedom. They lack an Other who might dispute the passage with us. If there is no Godot to expect, human history seems a darkening stage, and the firekindler a diminishing presence. He survives to light revolutionary tinder, as in the Man of Fire of José Orozco, the Mexican painter and muralist. Fitting as that may be in its situation, the modern torchbearer suggests what a long day's journey we have come from the Titan *agonistes* of Aeschylus.

In its issue in Enlightenment and the consequent return of idols, the Promethean bearer of light and fire comes close to that haunting vision of Dante's *Inferno* (Canto 34). There Lucifer, "Emperor of the dolorous realm," is a giant frozen to the chest in ice, his six huge wings stirring the frigid air of his prison in token defiance. Both fire and light extinguished, the parody of antitheism ends in chilling darkness.

PART III

THE END OF
ENLIGHTENMENT

– 7 –

The Speculative Death of God: Hegel, Feuerbach

On Behalf of Absolute Spirit

After Kant the way of romanticism offered one option for European intellectuals. Hegel opened up another, although in a sense it is the logical end of romanticism, the rationalization of its philosophy of identity. Child of the Enlightenment, G.W.F. Hegel (1770-1831) gave new shape and impetus to a dialectic that continues to influence most of our world. The Age of Reason tended toward a minimal definition of deity, God as bare *être suprême*. It also adopted the Renaissance view of knowledge as utilitarian. On both counts Hegel claimed to take the inheritance and raise it to a higher power. This act of dialectical transposition, the famous sublation (*Aufhebung*), in which the phenomenon of a lower order is both annulled and preserved in a new and higher form, represents his philosophical theology of reconciliation, *Versöhnung*. It is the archetypal category of Hegel's system, inasmuch as it shows the central Christian doctrine "raised" to the power of abstract and theoretical thought as Idea or concept (*Begriff*).

Hegel's systematic comprehension of reality under the sign of Idea is, in his own eyes, the logical outworking of Absolute Spirit. In the process, Nature comes to self-consciousness in Humanity, as the Absolute moves through its dialectic to produce a society, a Kingdom. Hegel's complex tracing of the process through stages in history, and the rough approximation of that process itself in the familiar triplex of thesis-antithesis-synthesis (analogous to Kant's use of the *Triplizität*) is not our direct concern here.[1] Yet to understand his contribution to the development of Promethean atheism, we need to look at some of his primary concerns, keeping in mind how they

---

Notes to Chapter 7 appear on page 320.

were interpreted by his disciples on both right and left in the ensuing debates.

Hegel's early and crucial work is *Phänomenologie des Geistes*. It was published in 1807, but completed the previous year when Napoleon overran the city of Jena where Hegel was teaching. Immediately we face a thorny question, whether to translate *Geist* as "Mind" or "Spirit."[2] Among anglophone philosophers the former has been preferred, thus avoiding the appearance of theology or spirituality. Yet for Hegel himself, theology is what he claims to be doing, and throughout the work he presents a sort of taxonomy of theological processes. At the same time, his grasp of theology is completely within the terms of idealistic philosophy, so that his sublation of the matter of theology to philosophical conceptuality must seem a compromise in the eyes of the theologian. Such judgment underlines the fact that in Hegel we have not only Enlightenment but also the means for going beyond the limits – or rather, of extending the limits of reason to include the supposed "transcendent." Hegel's self-confidence is reason's confidence in itself.

Only *Geist* is real. Spirit is characterized by freedom, a freedom guaranteed by the infinite (limit-less) nature of the subject, in its absolute form as Spirit *or* Mind. Further, such Mind is self-conscious because only so is freedom raised to its highest power. It follows that perfect freedom is attained only by the philosopher, who is self-conscious in all his acts of thinking, bringing these acts to their highest form as *Begriffen*. Thus his grand scheme: "we state the true form of truth to be its scientific character – or, what is the same thing, when it is maintained that truth finds the medium of its existence in notions or conceptions alone" (preface to *Phenomenology of Spirit*). Hegel's theory of the concept or notion thus weds the two decisive themes of Prometheanism: subjectivity and freedom.

Dialectic : Cow with Three Stomachs?

To achieve this end, the process of sublation involves a dialectical movement involving the classical moments of positive and negative. Since reality and Idea are synonymous, this "dialectical idealism" sees reality as a sort of cosmic argument moving itself through the process. Absolute Spirit posits itself, moves outside this posit, so to speak, in an alternate form, then returns to itself but in a higher form. The familiar thesis-antithesis-synthesis pattern, although never a complete (or even proper) picture, aptly shows Hegel's dialectic, earning Kierkegaard's charge of "cow with three stomachs." Hegel regularly discerns a triadic pattern in phenomena. The *Encyclopedia*'s Logic, Nature and Mind reflect his developed theory of contradiction and reconciliation. The second moment, the Idea in its otherness (*Anderssein*), is the critical moment for both philosophy and theology – literally "crucial" for the Christian approach.

In those early works posthumously published as *Hegels Theologische Jugendschriften*,[3] we see how the youthful theologian was already interpreting Christianity in abstract or nonhistorical terms. He attacks the "positivity" of biblical religion, its heteronomous nature.[4] He prefers a Kantian moralism, ethical truth encapsulated in historical narrative. And here is the key to Hegel's stimulation of the Promethean stance, even if in his case it is not atheism but antitheism.[5] He seeks to sublate the God who exists independently of human subjectivity, in behalf of the latter as the constitutive principle of deity. Hegel identifies the precise respect in which Prometheanism means not the death of "God" but the divinization of "Man."

> Thus the despotism of the Roman emperors had chased the human spirit from the earth and spread a misery which compelled men to seek and expect happiness in heaven; robbed of freedom, their spirit, their eternal and absolute element, was forced to take flight to the deity. [The doctrine of] God's objectivity is a counterpart to the corruption and slavery of man, and it is strictly only a revelation, only a manifestation of the spirit of the age.[6]

This famous passage could stand as a motto of the new faith in humanity emerging after the Enlightenment, much as Kant's *Sapere aude!* passage served as rubric for that precursor stage. For if Kant is the flowering of *Aufklärung*, its logical end, Hegel is its dénouement, its logical *Aufhebung*. He accepts its new subjectivity, the ego that makes its own world (that makes the world its own). He casts it in the leading role in the world-historical drama he is directing, Absolute Spirit coming to self-consciousness. In this drama, the Kantian ethics, which Hegel had mastered in his youth (the "Life of Jesus" casts the Nazarene as a Kantian philosopher), is in turn displaced, like the Judaism it resembles, by the new law of love.[7] The move from *Positivity* to "The Spirit of Christianity and its Fate" is well known, from negative to positive attitudes toward the gospel. According to the latter, Abraham lives for law rather than love, so that world is mediated to him "as simply his opposite . . . sustained by the God who was alien to it."[8] Even Kant's "Duty" fails to rise above law, lacking the dialectic of the Sermon on the Mount, which "exhibits that which fulfils the law but annuls it as law and so is something higher than obedience to law and makes law superfluous."[9]

The ingredients for the Hegelian recipe are now assembled. There is an initial positivity, a transcending negation and a new position in a higher key. From law to love is the logic of the Hegelian life-process, a conflict between positive and negative in behalf of *Geist* transcending itself. There is also the master-slave relationship so fateful for subsequent Marxist interpretation. And an objection to a Kantian concept of autonomy in which the latter dictates submission to the moral law. This imperative, for Hegel, would mean that we are not really free but divided against ourselves. Kant's categorical imperative is reduced to hypothetical level when compared with Jesus' different kind of "shalt" based on a living father-son relationship.[10]

There is a unity of essence between divine and human that is peculiarly visible in Jesus, but present in all. Love is sign and sacrament of such common union. "The culmination of faith, the return to the Godhead whence man is born, closes the circle of man's development." The dialectic of faith has its rise in fearful acknowledgment of "gods outside itself," the alienation of traditional superstition. After isolation and separation, "it returns through associations to the original unity."[11]

Emil Fackenheim relates this dialectic to Hegel's concept of the Trinity, indeed two trinities linked by love.

> Christian faith (reinforced and completed by theological thought) makes the ultimate affirmation of a *total* and *gratuitous* divine Love *for the human*: a total identification with the human, by a Divinity *which does not need it.*

This "pre-worldly trinitarian play" moves into history and conquers death "by suffering it."[12] The traditional distinction between economic and ontological-immanent levels within triunity is thus honoured by Hegel's rethinking. The irony we are tracing in this work appears in high relief as we ponder this Christian theologian, articulating the doctrines of Fall, alienation and reconciliation, and then espoused for his social and political theory, his "worldly" concept of mediation.

Religion as Freedom and Alienation

Hegel's is a social philosophy, attending to history despite the method of abstraction, and committed to the goal of setting us free. As a seminarian at the Tübingen Stift, in company with Schelling and Hölderlin, Hegel celebrated the French Revolution by setting up a "liberty tree" outside the city. His pursuit of liberty informs his entire system. "The general concept of human nature is no longer adequate;" freedom of the will must become the sole criterion. For "human nature is too dignified to be placed at the level of nonage where it would always need a guardian and could never enter the status of manhood."[13] In part this implies the Kantian tradition according to which the pure practical reason moves ahead into liberty through choices deriving from mental structures themselves. It was this aspect of Kant that Fichte elaborated and celebrated as the autonomous will. We have noted that the theme of freedom drives thinkers since Renaissance and especially since Enlightenment.

The young Hegel's analysis of Judaism and Christianity is fixed in this context of the pursuit of liberty. Both religions are cast as otherworldly, a "flight from the finite [*Flucht aus dem Endlichen*]," the result of unhappy consciousness, which encourages submission. Hellenism provides a thesis of serene gods of immanence and order, with the tragic Crucified as antithesis. Synthesis comes as those "heroes of action" thrown up by history and its "cunning of reason" provide handholds for Spirit as it becomes self-conscious.[14]

Hegel's "bright ikon of Greek religion" (James Collins) illustrates his idea of good religion, a positive force for culture rather than a degenerate "positivity" that directs attention away from social reality. Hegel, to be sure, disagrees with the *philosophes* and with Hume who dismissed positive religion as the essential matter. He distinguishes between religion and its defacement in "positive" forms. Thus he hoped to set Christianity free from that positivity resulting from the Augustinian tradition of original sin, which steered the desire for happiness into an afterlife beyond punishment and purification. More importantly, Hegel's early research and writing allowed him to ponder "the conditions required for making a passage from a relatively humane form of Religion to a positivity marked by gloom, suspicion toward natural life, and restriction of freedom."[15]

At this point we are touching on his close analysis of alienation, and the spring from which the powerful theory of Marxism drew its original inspiration. He takes the dynamism of these religious moments and forms, the conditions under which freedom and its loss occur, and sees a type, an exemplary model for social theory. If human alienation is to be fought and overcome, it must first be understood at that point where it cuts most deeply into human being, and here religion alone offers the most lengthy and profound tradition. The Enlightenment had acknowledged Christianity as the sole form of religion worth denying. Whether idealizing Greek religion or no, Hegel set against it the possibility of a purified religion in which the link between humanity and nature, the affirmation of world, overcomes alienation.

Where reason is honoured, there freedom is assured; positivity arises only through nonrational grounds for moral choice. Hegel thinks this dynamic to be quite clear in the case of Jesus, whose teaching "of a purely moral religion" was perverted through the miracle stories which offered new and different basis for doctrine: a supernatural and nonworldly authority.[16] Such is the road to heteronomous authority, by which deity is cast as Lord and Master, a tyrannical Zeus.

Hegel justified his view by taking Judaism (e.g., Abraham) to be a calculated contract by which power is assigned to a quasi-personal deity in order to convince the People of God of their special place and consequent debt of obedience. By alienating themselves from their moral reason, they lose their proper selves. They also lose God, since they remove him from the immediacy of worldly enjoyment. "This is not a truly religious integration of the divine and the human, but a transformation of the divine into an alien overlord and of the human into a well-ordered kingdom of puppets."[17]

Master and Slave

In *Phenomenology of Spirit* Hegel had laid the groundwork for his discussion of master and slave (*Herr, Knecht*). We strive for recognition, for mutual approbation of works and successes. Now to accept otherness as a universal phenomenon is to reinforce one's ego; but to experience the clash of individualities is to feel the threat of the other. In the ensuing struggle division appears between weaker and stronger, those who risk less or more, those who assert themselves to lesser or greater degree. Here lies the origin of every form of human servitude, summarized as "master and slave." A paradox arises: the master uses the slave, benefits by having leisure and so escapes nature in its negating mood. But the slave, meanwhile, must struggle with nature through his work and so learns (gives mind to) and creates where the master merely negates and destroys. The slave transforms things through his work and so can grasp himself as free agent, as universal consciousness: conceptuality has arrived.

Thus mastery over nature, even on the part of slaves, leads to mastery over self: freedom. The capacity to maintain one's independence even in a situation of slavery contributes to the development of Stoicism, a higher stage although something of a retreat from reality (thus similar to the illusion or opium of religion, according to later critics). Almost inevitably, the tension and contradiction of the situation leads to Scepticism. Here the intellectual enquiry continues so far that it mistrusts mind itself and despairs of a reliable reality. Hegel's idea of the "unhappy consciousness" is extended to all halfway religiosity, a positivist stage of subjection to an alien deity as Lord and Master.

When humans substantialize and externalize the concept (*Begriff*) of spirit by re-presenting (*Vorstellen*) it to themselves in the form of a Being (*Sein*) outside themselves, we have Hegel's classic view of positive religion awaiting the transforming touch of philosophy. Only in philosophy is Spirit "truly free and *bei sich.*"[18]

Hegel's system is an attempt to discern and bring to consciousness the unity of all things. "The whole of philosophy is nothing else than a study of the nature of different kinds of unity."[19] This determination of unity (*Bestimmungen der Einheit*) requires a unitive logic, operative in the dialectical process through "negation of negation," to produce a synthesis of opposites. The latter relates to the Christian doctrine of love as that mutuality that unites different wills and lives not by annulling them but by distilling in a higher unity the nonalienated otherness. It will be a question for us later whether modernity understands the possibility of nonalienated otherness. Hegel does. He distinguishes particular from individual: "The universal must pass into actuality through the particular."[20] It is not the realist-nominalist debate here but the healing of individualism by a personalism of loving relationship.

The theological implications of this "pantheism of love," as it has been called, reach even to the doctrine of the Trinity. The triadic process is visible in God himself. A creative Father posits over against himself a creation with its fate of alienating otherness. Within the creation, Absolute Spirit achieves means of grace through union of contradictories in mediation, entailing death and rebirth. Finally, a spiritual community embodies reconciliation of divine and human. Thus Incarnation is the kind of estrangement necessary for ultimate reunion. The dialectical *Aufhebung* of religion into philosophy entails the transformation of dogma into concept, so that reason itself experiences a "speculative Good Friday" as its ritual of passage.

The Death of God

The notorious phrase "God is dead" was for Hegel primarily a line from a Passion hymn, "Gott selbst ist tot." "The highest abnegation [*Entäusserung*] of the divine Idea – 'God has perished, God Himself is dead' – is a monstrous, horrible representation, which brings before the mind the deepest abyss of estrangement."[21] The Incarnation of the Word plunges the Wholly Other into the depths of humanity, identifying with the lowest point of our experience. But it reappears as risen Man, so that the *genus majestaticum* sublates the former attributes in its unity. This classical Lutheran dogmatics reflects the christological teaching, which, as we shall see in Karl Barth's estimate of Feuerbach, may be charged as chief cause of the apotheosis of humanity in German idealism. Since Spirit and Mind are one, we can say also: Universal Consciousness is achieved; reason understanding itself critically attains perfect freedom, "now as a matter of principle the master of all things."[22] Unlike mere epiphanies, the Incarnate One is the self-consciousness of Absolute Spirit. His death therefore cancels his particularity, allowing Spirit to inform the entire human community. Nature and especially history are interiorized, freed from external contingency. Thus the goal of absolute knowledge is achieved, "Spirit knowing itself as Spirit." This finale to the Christian dogmatic drama – described poetically in the closing pages of the *Phenomenology* – means that history is grasped conceptually, *die begriffene Geschichte*. Hegel calls this "at once the recollection and the Golgotha of Absolute Spirit."[23]

This Good Friday of the conceptual process represents the agony of reconciliation. Hegel's philosophy of religion mediates between "positive" Christianity and speculative idealism. It achieves unity through turning the events of Holy Week into concepts, beyond the Cross. At this point, in a sort of philosophical resurrection, religion attains the same content as philosophy, with the latter determining the *Vorstellungen*. Incarnation, seen retrospectively from the height of Notion, was historically necessary but not unique. Its role was to bestow form, through *pneuma*, on every human. It is the divine pedagogy to effect the true object of religion, humanity. The end of religion, its fulfilment through the work of reason, raises it to the abstract level of Idea. It has become Philosophy. Its absolute subject is *human* being.[24]

As Hegel draws our thinking through the historical events of the Christ, he is at once sublating the finite into the infinite or abstract-speculative and transcending the otherness of God, the Divine Being of classical theism. The first accomplishment he calls "this conversion of the finite," as the "pain . . . that God himself is dead" makes way for holiness and "elevation to God."[25] One can appreciate the philosopher's anxiety to overcome the merely historical in the career of his Idea. But the second, the transcending of the Christian "God," has proven much more momentous. It has reinforced the Enlightenment correlation of a heteronomous God with human alienation.

Such complementariness was recognized by Hegel himself in the *Science of Logic*, where *Dasein* emerges from the dialectic of Being and Nothing.[26] It was picked up in earnest by Feuerbach and Marx in their inverted dialectic of alienation and reconciliation. It was noted as accomplished fact by Jean-Paul Sartre in his assumption that the God-question is *passé*. And it has been more recently worried over by the so-called Death of God theologians of the 1960s in the U.S.A. and Germany. It is to Hegel they turn in orienting their modernity, in echoing Bonhoeffer's ambiguous words that we must live "as if God did not exist [*etsi Deus non daretur*]." Eberhard Jüngel has remarked that "the dark statement about the death of God" is based on the axiom of *remoto deo*, or the unthinkability of God. Now this in turn rests on the assumption of divine absoluteness, reflected in Hegel's Absolute Necessity. Such a starting-point leads inexorably to metaphysical *aporia*, so that both faith and unbelief "are overshadowed by the dark clouds of the unthinkability of God" and both "regard these shadows as their destiny." We shall return to this thesis at the end, when we examine the key category of autonomy and its assumption of heteronomy or absolute necessity; here we applaud Jüngel's repudiation of such a starting-point (which appeals even to Pannenberg) by insisting on the "worldly nonnecessity" of God. For then one can begin to argue that "God is not necessary; he is more than necessary."[27] Whatever we think of Altizer's eclectic religiosity, of Hamilton's apparently dilettante handling of his subject, of Van Buren's pilgrimage through and beyond the strictures of linguistic analysis, we see the impressive Idea of Hegel take shape.

Gabriel Vahanian, whose sociological writings gave credence to the notion that "God has died in our time," has articulated a serious theological position that reflects the profundity of Hegel's own approach.[28] And Dorothee Sölle acknowledges the debt to Hegel for a modern who seeks to "atheistically believe in God."[29] Yet it is doubtful whether these disciples have represented Hegel properly. He did not understand his philosophical Golgotha as determining "modernity." Rather it was a moment in the progression of *Geist*, to be reflected upon from the further moment of its sublation. Of course he took seriously the Godforsakenness of Jesus the Christ; but the absolute alienation of the cosmos is what is intended and revealed. It were too light a thing, spoke Hegel, for my Servant to redeem the historical by renewing history; he is a gateway to that which is beyond history. He once remarked that enlightenment, *Aufklärung*, meant clearing out, *Ausklärung*.

The Hegelian tradition proved fateful for the development of the Promethean spirit. Yet ironically the theoretical meditation on the speculative death of God was itself transmuted, even sublated, into the practical. Hegel's thesis that world-spirit moves through history on behalf of the Absolute informed a different mind-set in the new generation. As Aristotle had brought the previous history of philosophy to a climax, so had Hegel for his time; perhaps for all time. As there followed after Aristotle the practical philosophers, so would Hegel be followed by the activists on the Left. Thus it was another of his writings that proved decisive for Karl Marx, the *Philosophy of Right*. Here are the familiar categories of rights, including the right to appropriate property; of contract between two free wills, from which "duty" derives; of the roots of alienation in relationality through property; of the final purpose of the good as achieved through social morality. It was in the preface to the *Rechtsphilosophie* that Hegel described reason as a "*rose* within the *cross* of the present."[30] There is a long tradition of rose and cross, not least in Martin Luther's seal, which bore a cross surrounded by white roses. Hegel's symbolism is significant: reason must turn the events of Holy Week into a "speculative Good Friday," raising Christian dogmatics to philosophy of religion: so he concludes his essay "Faith and Knowledge." If Christ reconciled the divine and the human *de facto*, as it were, now philosophy must achieve the higher reconciliation in thought, *de intellectu*.

Hegel's Absolute Subject heralds the logical consummation of Enlightenment subjectivity. Through the sublation of Christian theology into idealist philosophy he perfected the Promethean thrust of modern thought. The work of Hans Urs von Balthasar on our myth is subtitled *Studien zur Geschichte des Deutschen Idealismus.* For him the titanic symbol encompasses the movement of German idealistic philosophy, and indeed orients it about an eschatological End. Von Balthasar sees modernity as an "apocalypse of the soul" in which philosophy, theology and art converge to effect a revelation of subjectivity well named Prometheus. Hegel, in this scheme, is instrument of kindling the fire and so preparing the way for the Dionysian holocaust of the twentieth century. "The fire which Hegel kindled is thus sacrifice as well as judgment, and both as Eschaton."[31] The power of Promethean skill and science, the subjective self now set free in defiance of transcendence, is but a way of reaching ahead to an alien fire and a strange dance, the sublation of a rival deity named Dionysus. Whether Nietzsche or Marx, Hegel's descendants used the freedom he bestowed to follow other gods, a wild Dionysus on the one hand, a practical Prometheus on the other.

Hegel's Offspring

What is really going on in this vast systematic process of conceptualization? Kierkegaard will complain that the very vastness, the comprehensiveness, of the system is at fault: nothing escapes this "cud-chewing process," the unifying dialectic of both/and. Yet Hegel's contribution is great and manifold – perhaps even the origin of all that is great in the philosophy of the past century, as Merleau-Ponty maintained. Part of this contribution, if not the key to it, is Hegel's direction of both philosophy and theology to worldly affairs, to history. The historical process is the locus of infinity, so that to analyze history and culture is to understand Spirit. The dialectical process evident today in Marxism, in liberation theology, in process thinking, owes a chief debt to Hegel.

The Left Hegelians show an increasingly antitheological stance. One expects it from a convert from Right to Left such as Bruno Bauer, whose hatred for the theologian is reflected in the new tradition, particularly Nietzsche. But Heinrich Heine (1797-1856) had also proclaimed the death of God with literary power in his poems, notably *Götterdämmerung.* He called Kant the executioner who beheaded (belief in) God with the blade of his criticism; for the God about whom we can know practically nothing is therefore "nothing but a fiction."[32] The identification of theism with subservience to an alien will ties in with the revolutionary spirit of the age. In 1800 Fichte had chosen Prometheus over the "old arbitrary God," in light of Goethe's independent Titan. The French Revolution proved symbolic of human autonomy so that religion is cast as antirevolutionary, a sort of intellectual opium to pacify the masses. As we shall see, the narcotic analogy had been current since d'Holbach in 1767. Ludwig Feuerbach used the idea of opiate in his Bayle Book of 1838; Heine seized on it with rhetorical zest in 1839: "Heaven was invented for people who no longer expect anything from earth. . . . Hail this invention! Hail to the religion that poured into mankind's bitter chalice a few sweet, narcotic drops, spiritual opium, drops of love, hope, and faith."[33]

Heine later turned his back on this exuberant atheism and "returned to the common fold after a long period of tending the swine with the Hegelians" (the serpent in Paradise is termed a Hegelian *Privatdozent*). But Max Stirner pushed the new philosophy further, in direct descent from the Kantian dichotomy. In *The Individual and His Property* (1845) man has become "the ego of history," his own and only power, the "unique" person in world history.

The differences among Hegelians came to issue on the moot question of whether Hegel's philosophy of right (which in turn involved his critique of religion) was a support of the civil authorities, indeed of Throne and Altar as expressed in the Prussian state of his day. Whether Hegel's system thus functioned ideologically, as *Realpolitik*, was answered affirmatively by the conservative party. On the other side were those who stressed his dialectical-critical stance, the negative element in the method of *aufheben*. This left-wing group included Bruno Bauer, Heinrich Heine, D.F. Strauss, Max Stirner and Ludwig Feuerbach. Although they subsequently took differing ways, their emphasis on Hegel's critique of church and state prepared for the Marxist thesis that "the criticism of religion is the presupposition of all criticism." For Marx himself it was the erstwhile theologian Bauer whose shift to radical criticism of orthodoxy provided the clue: the gospel masks the decisive reality, the self-consciousness of the early Christians. The group's satire, *The Last Trump over Hegel, the Antichrist and Atheist*, reflects Bauer's influence, from which Marx soon disengaged himself. The split among Hegel's offspring was designated right, centre and left by D.F. Strauss, whose first *Life of Jesus* (1835) helped occasion the division. It claimed to be proper Hegelian demythologization of biblical story and Christian doctrine. But more stringent and more significant was the voice of Ludwig Feuerbach.

Ludwig Feuerbach

> To enrich God, man must become poor; that
> God may be all, man must be nothing.
>
> Man is the God of Christianity, Anthropology
> the mystery of Christian Theology.[34]

Feuerbach's provocative *Thoughts on Death and Immortality* (1830) used Hegelian categories to deny a personal God and immortality, concluding with satirical epigrams. This work ended his hope of a professorship, while later works established his alternative to classical theism and provided inspiration and direction for Marx. The "humanizing of Christianity" in these writings was programmatic: "The task of the modern era was the realization and humanization of God – the transformation and dissolution of theology into anthropology."[35] In fact it was Hegel's essentialism that prepared the ground for Feuerbach (1804-72). W. Pannenberg summarizes: "God is the 'essence' of man as his *transcendent destination*."[36] Feuerbach goes beyond Hegel in locating human essence in immanent spirit, the infinite species-being. What proves decisive is his explanatory hypothesis, the theory of the genealogy of religion. The heart of what appears to be the genetic fallacy in his logic is the concept of projection. What lends it power is the identification of the human in all religious language. After him, those "masters of suspicion," as Ricoeur calls them – particularly Marx, Nietzsche and Freud – will regard religion as the projected illusion deriving from false consciousness. To simplify, Feuerbach's thesis was that if one substituted "man" for "God" in Christian theology, one would be putting things properly. For Man is the *ens realissimum*, the social ideal or the human self-conscious of itself.

Feuerbach himself was called a new Prometheus on the publication of his *The Essence of Christianity* (1841), the left-wing Hegelians acknowledging his authority – "upon seeing God falling from heaven under the assault of this new Titan."[37] His colleague Ruge hailed this "world-moving step" which "with unrouged truth demasks Christian and philosophical hypocrisy." Ruge's own atheistic-republican sympathies were promoted through numerous writings, especially the *Jahrbücher*, which taught a robust atheism, the abolition of religion in behalf of a "humanized world of liberated men." Atheism was now explicit: Feuerbach, Marx and Bauer planned an *Archive for Atheists*, while the indefatigable Ruge celebrated the end of the "religious mask": Bauer, Marx and Feuerbach "have already reached the summit and planted the flag of atheism and morality;

God, religion and immortality are hereby deposed, and the philosophers' Republic, Man, and the new gods of Man Proclaimed."[38]
Feuerbach's original intention to become a theologian had been set aside at Berlin when he devoted himself to philosophy and attended Hegel's course on philosophy of religion. His 1828 thesis (*De ratione una, universali, infinita*) shows his dissatisfaction with abstraction, and attempts to ground ideas in the "sensuous." In correspondence with Hegel he justifies his "materialization" and "secularization" by the plea that it is "time for it," adding that it is grounded in the Hegelian system.[39] He continued to acknowledge his debt to Hegel, as having enunciated the final speculative philosophy. But his criticism grew as he appropriated more of the Hegelian Left program and stressed Hegel's theological side: "The contradiction inherent in modern philosophy . . . that it is a negation of theology based upon theology, or a negation of theology which is itself a theology: this contradiction is particularly characteristic of Hegelian philosophy."[40] In the *Grundsätze* (*Principles of the Philosophy of the Future*) Feuerbach tackles Hegel at the same point that proved vulnerable for Kierkegaard's critique: the abstract self of rationalism, enjoying only a speculative relationship with body, with that concrete humanity that exists before and beyond abstract thinking. He also sees that Hegel's dialectic swallows up all opposition, even including atheism within Christianity, "by making of atheism, the negation, an objective component of God – God as a process, and atheism as one component of this process." His new philosophy, therefore, must negate such speculative reconciliation, which maintains an obsolete theology under the form of dialectical nominalism. He chooses the concrete, a sensuousness that guarantees human selfhood in palpable terms. Human being is understood only in its authentic sexuality, as engendered, relational being. Here is where his powerful statement on I and Thou appears, and the essence of that relationship in love.

> The truth speaks to us, not from within our own preoccupied self, but from another. Only through communication, only through the conversation of man with man, do ideas arise. Two human beings are necessary for the begetting of another human being, spiritually as well as physically. The unity of man with man is the first and last principle of philosophy, truth, and universality. For the essence of man is contained only in the unity of one man with another, a unity which is based upon the real difference between I and Thou. Even in thought and as a philosopher I am a man among others.[41]

The two works that continue to fascinate theologians developed similar themes: *The Essence of Christianity* and *The Essence of Religion* (*Das Wesen des Christentums*, 1841; *Das Wesen der Religion*, 1851). The theological program of this philosopher was suggested by his predecessors, not only Hegel but also Schleiermacher. In both systems, what was stressed was "the non-objective quality of God." Here is the root of his preoccupation with the objective as projection of the subjective, quite different from the objective *I* recognized as fellow ego, a proper *Thou*.

A Lutheran Heritage?

Karl Barth's estimate of Feuerbach is incisive.[42] He notes the role of Hegel and Schleiermacher in that development of doctrine that is virtually identical with German idealism. What Feuerbach "exploded" was "the mystery of the modern doctrine of God – that the being of God is the predicate of the human subject." Feuerbach, on this view, is guilty only of recklessness in exposing what had been going on, the hypostatization of the world of ideas, which "perhaps better be named reason than God." Thus: "The predication of God as personality was necessarily for them the absurdity of which no philosopher or theologian must under any circumstances be guilty."

A particular rendering of Lutheran theology is singled out by Barth as contributing substantially to the idealistic development.[43] Since it operates strongly in the Marxist interpretation of alienation it provides a singular datum in understanding the shift from theology to anthropology. Hegel had appreciated the "kenosis" or self-emptying of the Word of God in Incarnation, following the crucial text of Philippians 2:6-11. It is written there that Christ's "equality with God" was set aside: "he emptied himself, taking the form of a servant." This verse had been translated by Luther as *Sondern entäusserte sich selbst*. Hegel's exegesis of the "death of God" in Scripture and dogma expounds the concept of *Entäusserung*, synonym for the more familiar term for alienation, *Entfremdung*. Indeed the biblical passage contains three "Hegelian" terms: *geeussert* (denied), *gestalt* (form) and *erhohet* (exalted). Moreover, since German puts *Menschwerdigung* for *Incarnatio*, Hegel's rendering takes the Word-become-flesh as God-Man and finally, simply Man. Thus "God" moves over into the opposite form, just as philosophy "empties" history through conceptuality, the speculative Good Friday of the process. At the last, deified humanity emerges: *Homo homini Deus est.*

The distinction between *Entäusserung* and *Entfremdung* is significant. Georges Cottier renders the former by *kénose*, this transliteration of the Greek (Phil. 2:7) intending the objectification of the divine in the human incarnation, while *Entfremdung* is rendered by *aliénation.* He recognizes that Hegel remains ambiguous on the relation between the two, while Marx simply identifies them. Jean Hyppolite prefers *aliénation* for *Entäusserung*, however, and *extranéation* for *Entfremdung.*[44] The Latin *alienus* meant "belonging to another" in contrast to one's own, *suus*. Secondary meanings include the foreign or strange, adverse or inconsistent, and finally distracted or insane (*mens alienus*). After a period when alien and alienist had psychological meaning, generally today the idea of the strange is central.

To be estranged from self, world and God became the classic delineation of the state of fallenness. Now the Augustinian stress on the Fall had tended to relate alienation simply to the causality of sin, producing the false consciousness of the perverted ego. The Lutheran tradition yields somewhat to this temptation, whereas Hegel maintains a more complex causality. It is the finite movement of Spirit that involves human being in that otherness that creates alien forms of consciousness; as other, they may make for positive and creative tensions and results. This ambivalence of the concept of alienation will concern us again in relation to Marx, whose early humanism was more open to the Hegelian dialectic than his later economism.[45]

A clear picture of why "God" threatens human freedom is afforded by Hegel's depiction of the *fremd* God as the Object-God, quite separated from the human. Religion is thus the reign of the Object: the divine will is expressed in Law, before which the human is condemned unless he obey completely. In this guise God is *die Kraft fremd,* an alien and alienating Power. In the *Encyclopedia* Hegel is quite clear on the relationship:

> An evil God, a natural God, has as correlate evil men, natural and without liberty. The pure concept of God, the spiritual God, has as correlate the free spirit. The representation which man has of God corresponds to that which he has of himself and his liberty.[46]

Hence the Zeus-Prometheus correlation.

Marx, and even more powerfully Nietzsche, accepted this "moral" judgment about the kind of God correlative to human freedom. Under the Feuerbachian critique, Hegel's abstract Spirit was bound to yield to a humanized free spirit; and with Marx the fateful step to a new correlation takes place: human freedom and socioeconomic conditioning.

We return to Barth's critique, which recalls the Calvinist quarrel with Lutheran theology. Christology involves the often precious question of the relationship between the divine and the human natures. Not all theology has been as careful as the formula of the Council of Chalcedon, which affirmed the connection without attempting to spell out the way in which they are connected. It states four negations to mark out the limits of speculation, two on the side of identity and two on the side of separation (the likeness to Aristotle's concept of analogy is noteworthy). Calvinists charged Lutherans, in their hot debates of the Reformation and post-Reformation days, with transgressing the limit of identity, while Lutherans aimed the counter-charge at their opponents. Barth finds himself espousing a "Calvinist correction" to Lutheranism, despite his admiration for Luther himself. He thinks that the Lutheran doctrine of Incarnation comes down too heavily on the identity of the natures, as expressed in the *communicatio idiomatum*, the transference of properties between the two. He thinks that the movement in such a christology "leads smoothly and directly to anthropology . . . to the doctrine of a humanity which is not only capable of deification, but already deified, or at any rate on the point of apotheosis or deification."[47] Luther's own early "mystico-anthropological" tendency may have created the historical condition for the development, as Ebeling also states in his work on Luther.[48] In any event, the case of German idealism, moving from theology to anthropology and from dogma to critique, is the subject of which Feuerbach sees himself as logical end. Hegel consummated the history of philosophy in a real sense; Feuerbach was the inevitable progeny. It was no accident that when Marx scored the philosophical "interpretation" of the world, it was a thesis on Feuerbach. But had not Feuerbach already interpreted the Hegelian interpretation as a call to arms, a program of historical action?

Materialism and Method

Feuerbach's philosophy is usually approached through its influence on primitive Marxism. In one sense that is a loss, since it obscures his own alternative to Hegelianism and his bold program for the reform of philosophy. Yet history has decreed that his place is lodged within the derivation of Marxism from Hegelianism through the purgatory of his radical critique of Hegel. Thus Engels would write:

> The spell was broken; the "system" was exploded and cast aside. . . . One must himself have experienced the liberating effect of this book [*Essence of Christianity*] to get an idea of it. Enthusiasm was general, we all became at once Feuerbachians.[49]

And consider the equally famous words, following a quotation from Luther that Marx uses to show that Feuerbach (who called himself Luther II) was interpreting Christianity properly:

> And I advise you, speculative theologians and philosophers: free yourselves from the concepts and prepossessions of existing speculative philosophy if you want to get at things differently, as they are, that is to say, if you want to arrive at the *truth*. And there is no other road for you to *truth* and *freedom* except that leading through the stream of fire [*Feuer-bach*]. Feuerbach is the *purgatory* of the present times.[50]

In the *Critique of the Hegelian Dialectic*, Marx summarizes Feuerbach's "great achievement" thus:

> 1. to have shown that philosophy is nothing more than religion brought into thought and developed by thought, and that it is equally to be condemned as another form and mode of existence of human alienation;
> 2. to have founded *genuine materialism* and *positive science* by making the social relationship of "man to man" the basic principle of his theory;
> 3. to have opposed to the negation of the negation which claims to be the absolute positive, a self-subsistent principle positively founded on itself.[51]

Marx considers Feuerbach as the only Young Hegelian who has considered the problem of method, and therefore the one who has succeeded in moving through the Hegelian dialectic in behalf of a practical issue. The "final" stage of negating the negation remains abstract and so is merely a return to the original theoretical stance. Hegel is caught within the mind, whereas Feuerbach breaks forth into action and so provides "a philosophical basis to socialism."[52]

By acting on Feuerbach's theory of religion as projection of ideal humanity, as the truth of social humanity, Marx re-formed his teacher in a communist image so that today his heritage is not so much the complex "metaphysische Egoismus," involving motivation from dread and hope,[53] as the theory of projection, now more familiar through Freud's application: the gods are the wishful thinking of alienated humans.

To arrive at this extreme conclusion, Feuerbach required the conceptual formulation of dogma at the hands of Hegel. In his *Towards a Critique of Hegel's Philosophy* (1839) he tackled the hard question raised by Hegel's system: how is the material of Logic related to Nature? At the beginning of this early work he puts the issue in significant terms, showing the failure of German criticism to grasp the essence of gospel:

> *Incarnation* and *history* are absolutely incompatible; when deity itself enters into history, history ceases to exist. But if history nevertheless continues in the same way as before, then the theory of incarnation is in reality nullified by history itself.

The context is his thesis that self-conscious spirit is "species existing as species," and that a law of "limitation" (the categories of space and time) limits every appearance within history to species-being. This rules out the singularity claimed for the Incarnation of the Word by Christian theology.

Feuerbach is committed to the universally human, to human being as species-being, derived from Hegel by a left turn from speculative-idealistic thought. In his *Preliminary Theses on the Reform of Philosophy* (1842) he traces the lineage of "modern speculative philosophy" as Spinoza-Schelling-Hegel. Parallel is the movement theism-pantheism-atheism, a progression that Feuerbach sees necessitating his "new philosophy" in which humanity is the "ground and base of the Absolute."

The following year (1843) Feuerbach published *Principles of the Philosophy of the Future* to continue and substantiate what had become a censored document. In the preface he repeats his goal of deriving a philosophy of the human (anthropology) from the philosophy of the Absolute (theology): "to establish a critique of human philosophy through a critique of divine philosophy." In the *Principles* we see the logic of German criticism at work, a logic that Marx will take over uncritically. It assumes that theology is otherworldly, that God has no relation to space and time, to history. This reinforces the earlier statement that Incarnation and history are incompatible, a statement that sweeps away the hard thinking of Christian Fathers (not to mention later theologians) who were not hampered by such dualistic assumption and therefore who were able to think Incarnation and history together. Indeed, the three cardinal doctrines of the early Church were Creation, Incarnation and Resurrection – all three affirming the divine responsibility for and presence within history. One must take account, of course, for the mechanistic model of nineteenth-century science, which informed German criticism from Kant to Marx. This debt hampers such critique from achieving proper perspective beyond the dualism of the inherited tradition.[54]

Feuerbach's theory of projection (e.g., christology is religious anthropology) is a tool for the theory of reduction: talk of transcendence is in reality talk of immanence, talk about the divine is talk about the human, and so on. Because of Feuerbach's commitment to his definition of religion as otherworldliness, a commitment with the force of *idée fixe*, he interprets the doctrine of God, in particular the attribution of qualities, as self-evidently fantasy, an imaginary predication about a fantastic projection. Thus to posit God is to deny him, theology becomes pantheism, and the human component in the pantheistic equation may be separated out by the new philosophy so that human nature is revealed in its species and its truth:

> Speculative philosophy as the realization of God is the *positing* of God, and *at the same time* his *cancellation or negation*; *theism and at the same time atheism*: for God – in the sense of theology – is God only as long as he is taken to be a being distinguished from and independent of the being of man as well as of Nature.[55]

The crux of Feuerbach's critique consists in positing a pure theology that as *theos-logos* enunciates a doctrine of God as he is in himself. This rules out trinitarian doctrine, with its living God who is by this definition relational, with Incarnation as the logic of Trinity. The quarrel, to restate our thesis, is seen as that between a titanic assertion of the glory of humanity against a kind of theism discerned as otherworldly. Feuerbach, to follow the words of Barth, has his own Magnificat to sing, and it is in behalf of "man's apotheosis."[56] If Marx found this new philosophy to be a "static materialism" unable to do justice to objective human activity (Jan Lochman), nonetheless it proved a necessary step on his way to dialectical materialism. In retrospect it seems also an inevitable step, given the condition of Christian theology and its support of the narrow Prussian state, and given the turn to philosophy of religion that Hegel had engineered for theology itself.

Speculative idealism, even with the romantic element securely in its grasp, seemed launched on a voyage of self-discovery, which led unwittingly from theology through humanism to atheism. That voyage, as Hegel saw it, was a sort of "Odyssey of the Absolute;" for Feuerbach the "apotheosist" it was humanity returning to its own birthright. And then there came Karl Marx, who rode this tide of critical philosophy toward shores hidden from his predecessors and who harnessed the critique to a vibrant materialism that still captivates half our world. His view (in the critique of Hegel's *Rechtsphilosophie*) of the process at issue is noteworthy:

> History is thorough and goes through many phases when carrying an old form to the grave. The last phase of a world-historical form is its *comedy*. The gods of Greece, already tragically wounded in Aeschylus's *Prometheus Bound*, had to re-die a comic death in Lucian's *Dialogues*.

The reference is personal: he intends to play Lucian to Hegel's Aeschylus.

The Practical Death Of God:
Marx, Engels, Lenin

Marx before Marxism

> Philosophy makes no secret of it. Prometheus's admission: "In sooth all gods I hate" is its own admission, its own motto against all gods, heavenly and earthly, who do not acknowledge the consciousness of man as the supreme divinity. There must be no god on a level with it.[1]

Karl Marx (1818-83) obtained his doctorate at age twenty-three for a dissertation titled *The Difference Between the Natural Philosophy of Democritus and Epicurus.*[2] From it and the preparatory material included in the first volume of his collected works, we see the significance of Prometheus for the young philosopher. The Titan is the patron saint of philosophy, whose defiance of deity symbolizes the sort of liberation to which German critical thought tends. Not that Marx himself is yet the man of action, who sees clearly the necessary way from theory to practice; he is still a philosopher for whom the Doktorklub at Berlin seems sufficient. But as we saw, the Left Hegelians have become a moving force in militant atheism, and soon Marx is at the cutting edge, Prometheus reincarnate.

The young doctorand had written with passion of the "world-conquering, absolutely free heart" of philosophy. With Epicurus it cries to its opponents: "Not he who rejects the gods of the crowd is impious, but he who embraces the crowd's opinion of the gods." He draws on Aeschylus's *Prometheus Bound* to illustrate his feelings about his hero.

Notes to Chapter 8 appear on page 325.

> And to the wretched March hares who exult over
> the apparent deterioration of philosophy's social
> position it again answers, as Prometheus did to
> Hermes, the messenger of the gods: "I shall never
> exchange my fetters for slavish servility. 'Tis better
> to be chained to the rock than bound to the service
> of Zeus."
> Prometheus is the noblest of saints and martyrs
> in the calendar of philosophy.[3]

Like Fichte and Goethe before him, the young Marx was fascinated by this mythological figure, as reflected in some of his
poems. The *Prayer of Despair* (*Prometheus*) is plaintive if defiant,
railing against God who has "wrecked everything I had": "Proudly
on myself I will avenge me / Against that being lording it on high."[4]
The essential mood of Marx's atheism, resentment against divine
lordship, is visible also in another poem, *Thoughts on God*:

> Like the very gods I dare to roam
> Victorious through their ruined realms,
> My every word is act and flame,
> My breast and the Creator's are the same![5]

Here rivalry of God becomes displacement, apotheosis. The very
euhemerism that seemed to account for the evolution of gods now
encouraged Marx himself to play the divine. How ironic, if fitting,
that the *Collected Works* should open on a depiction of Marx as Prometheus Bound.[6]
The atheism of Marx preceded his materialism, his commitment to economic-social questions. His original revolution was rebellion against all gods, in particular that familiar God of Christian theism, remote and all-powerful over human affairs. Hence the
hypothesis behind the thesis: God is a Zeus-figure, Hegel's symbol
of Absolute Spirit, a "transcendable God."[7] His thesis revived the
Epicurean atheism of antiquity, which he saw as analogous to his
own time: just as after Aristotle philosophy became practical through
schools of materialism and atheism, even so after Hegel philosophy
had reached such speculative and systematic levels that it must similarly become practical.

> Just as Prometheus, having stolen fire from heaven,
> begins to build houses and settle on the earth, so
> philosophy, having extended itself to the world,
> turns against the apparent world. So now with the
> Hegelian philosophy.[8]

The seeds of his critique of Feuerbach and his own move into social
activism are present in his academic work, both the dissertation and

the notebooks he kept, seven of which are extant for our perusal.

A key issue in the dissertation noted earlier turned on the "doctrine of a swerve in the fall of atoms" characteristic of Epicurus but not of Democritus. The early atomists struggled to explain the "persistent rain of atoms" (Lucretius) either by positing a mechanical necessity of events, as Democritus did, or by arguing for a deviation allowing novel complexes and vortex formations, with Epicurus. Such an "energizing principle" opposes individuality, uniqueness, to the mere universality of determinism, and constitutes the "difference between Epicurus and Democritus" in the thesis. Marx rejects, however, the privative nature of the Epicurean individuality, expressed in its ethical negation, *ataraxia*. In this he agrees with Hegel's evaluation of classical philosophy. At stake in this exercise, then, was whether classic enlightenment made room for genuine self-consciousness, for freedom. Indeed, Ernst Bloch holds that in the dissertation Marx was grasping the need for philosophy to become not only critical but practical: "the First and Eleventh Theses on Feuerbach are already present *in statu nascendi* in the references to Epicurus."[9] In the retrospective words of the preface to *Capital*, Hegel's dialectic was found "standing on its head," so that one must turn it on its feet to "discover the rational kernel within the mystical shell."

Critical Philosophy and the Critique of Religion

Marx the young philosopher has a high opinion not only of the general role of philosophy but of the particular task of German philosophy. His critique of Hegel is his own contribution to criticism, his acceptance of his role in the drama of German thinking since Kant. Hegel's place is perhaps ambiguous but certainly crucial in that his system entails its own sublation. Just as the objectivism of Democritus is opposed and thus overcome dialectically by Epicurus's introduction of the subjective factor, so Hegel requires completion by an opposition that will issue in practice.

The highest moment of critical philosophy is its criticism of religion. The famous passage in the "Contribution to Hegel's Philosophy of Right" (1844) describing religion as opium (to which we soon turn) is in a context expressive of Marx's conviction about the history of philosophy. The Introduction has been called "the Magna Charta of the critique of religion" (Van Leeuwen).

> For Germany the *criticism of religion* is in the main complete, and criticism of religion is the premise [*Voraussetzung*][10] of all criticism.
>
> The basis of irreligious criticism is: *Man makes religion*, religion does not make man. In other words, religion is the self-consciousness and self-feeling of man who has either not yet found himself or has already lost himself again.
>
> The criticism of religion ends with the teaching that *man is the highest essence of man*, hence with the *categorical imperative to overthrow all relations* in which man is debased, enslaved, abandoned, despicable essence.[11]

His analysis of the German political situation suggests to Marx that before there can be a practical or political break with "modern state conditions" there must be a break with the philosophical or theoretical "dream-history" preventing the emergence of the "modern." He lauds the "*practical* political party," which demands the negation of philosophy, but wishes it to go further, in good Hegelian fashion: "You cannot abolish philosophy without making it a reality." But the realization of *philosophy* would mean the abolition of *religion*, making an end of the heteronomy of heavenly ideals and so of the worldly state that embodies alienating pseudo-powers. His attack on the Beyond is in behalf of worldly reality: the human species-being (*Gattungwesen*) unveiled by Feuerbach, the universal essence of humanity. In order to posit this Humanum, a negation of God is absolutely necessary.

It is the high view of religion, as reflecting the human condition of servitude in a crucial and ambivalent manner, that makes the criticism of religion the final stage before theory breaks forth into *praxis*. And for Marx it seemed equally clear that the modern "scientific" study of religion, both of world religions and of early Christianity, had established the facts about the origin and development of religion.

Engels On Religion

> Hitherto the question has always stood: What is God? – and German philosophy has resolved it as follows: God is man.[12]

Marx and his friends lived in a heady time of new methods in critical thought, which seemed to promise assured results – a confidence that appears today as rather naive. There was the historical-critical approach to biblical studies, and the *Religionswissenschaftlich* method in comparative religion. Both approaches are much in dispute these days, and the enthusiasm with which the Young Hegelians greeted the theoretical reconstructions of primitive religion, the classical pantheon, the emergence of monotheism and the birth of Christianity, reflects the most uncritical aspect of their critical philosophy.[13]

Bruno Bauer played a signal role in this drama of incipient atheism. Like most of the Young Hegelians, Bauer (1809-82) was entranced by history. He had begun well to the Hegelian Right, with historical studies of the Fourth Gospel and the Synoptics, and ended his literary career, now on the extreme left wing, with studies of revolutionary movements in the eighteenth and nineteenth centuries. Although he was not committed to the practical application of theory as was Marx, he agreed that the "end of philosophy" had come: "If Europe has turned away from metaphysics forever, this same metaphysics has been destroyed forever by criticism."[14]

Friedrich Engels (1820-95) shows his debt in "Bruno Bauer and Early Christianity" (1882). He considers Bauer "worth more than" the theologians who criticize him, having done "more than all of them" about the question of the historical origins of Christianity. Because of such research, Engels thinks it no longer tenable to accept the thesis held by "the free-thinkers of the Middle Ages to the Enlighteners of the eighteenth century," namely that religion derives from "deceivers." Further, Bauer also showed the weakness of Strauss's mythological theory of origins.

Two points stand out in Engels's indebtedness: the supposed lack of historicity in the Gospels and the tracing of Christian ideas and doctrine to hellenistic tradition – Philo "was the real father of Christianity, and . . . the Roman *Seneca* was, so to speak, its uncle."[15] This is a point to which Engels will return in his articles titled "On the History of Early Christianity" (1894-95), where Bauer is again singled out as the champion who has dismissed the errors and given scientific status to the theory of origins. Engels sees a dichotomy in the classical age, with "atheistic materialism" issuing from classic Greek philosophy, in particular Epicureanism, while on the other hand "Greek vulgar philosophy led to the doctrine of a one and only God and of the immortality of the human soul." Now while a dichotomy is observable within the classical tradition, it does not correspond to Engels's happy thought, nor to Bauer's laborious thesis, and certainly not to an elevation of Epicurean thought over the Platonic-Aristotelian ("vulgar"?) tradition. This has been noted in an earlier chapter, and elsewhere we have suggested a different interpretation of the dichotomy, namely that between "Mystery and Tragedy" on the one hand and on the other that "optimistic rationalism" characteristic of the developing Platonism.[16]

Engels disagrees with Marx on the etiology of religion and provides a distinct advance by broadening the explanatory hypotheses. In *Feuerbach* he had adopted the thesis of animistic origins, following Edward Tylor's *Primitive Culture* (1871). The concept of *Naturreligion*, so appealing to the nineteeth century world-view, obtains from *The German Ideology* of 1846 to the *Anti-Dühring* of 1878. In the latter he states: "All religion, however, is nothing but the fantastic reflection in men's minds of those external forces which control their daily life, a reflection in which the terrestrial forces assume the form of supernatural forces." He continues by citing "comparative mythology" on this evolution, which reconstructs phases when these "fantastic figures" are given "social attributes," come to represent history and finally meld into a monotheistic deity. Thus are the lines of typical Marxist-Leninist critique of religion prepared by Engels. Religion is a distorted reflection of the world; and it stems from fear or anxiety. Here medium is clearly taken for message. Here also, the negative motive is isolated from the accompanying elements of the experience of the numinous – Otto's phenomenology of *Das Heilige* – and even more so from the biblical understanding of "the fear of the Lord" as "the beginning of wisdom." The naturalistic account of religion succeeds only in accounting for a poor relation of religion, properly so-called. Its reductionism misses that essential reality that not only believers but its observers consider irreducible.[17]

Like Marx, Engels had begun with a certain attraction to philosophical atheism. The notional complex which this avid researcher and scholar assimilated served to reinforce what his Young Hegelian stance dictated. Later he would add observations concerning the "practical death of God," as we are calling this phenomenon, especially among the working classes. Atheism for them, he notes, is almost "self-evident;" indeed it "has already outlived itself":

> this purely negative word no longer has any application as far as they are concerned inasmuch as their opposition to faith in God is no longer one of theory but one of practice; they have *purely and simply finished with God*, they live and think in the world of reality and are therefore materialists.[18]

Whereas Marx relies narrowly on sociomorphic categories such as class structure and ideology, Engels draws on animistic and evolutionary theories, which he considers quite compatible with, indeed necessarily complementary to, the former. And while Marx does not show awareness of the narrow base on which he operates in his etiology, Engels remains naive about the critique of Tylor and friends already being mounted in his day. As noted before, contemporary scholars of both the history of religions and sociology of religion must find the Marx-Engels reconstruction essentially defective. It is unfortunate that this outdated approach to the data of religion remains foundational for many Marxist philosophers. No doubt this reflects the similarity of their situation to that of Engels himself, whose interest in the topic was meant to serve the historical materialism of Marx.

This real aim of Engels – not to explain religion but to explain every nonmaterialist explanation of reality – becomes clear in his properly philosophical enterprise. The intellectual Engels was quite Hegelian in his articulation of the laws of dialectic – the interpenetration of opposites, the leap from quantity to quality, the negation of the negation. But in his *Dialectics of Nature*, completed in 1886 but not published until 1925, he extends the laws to the natural sciences beyond reason. Nevertheless, one can agree with this estimate of his contribution to Marxist theory: "he was the creator of orthodox Marxism as a system based on historical materialism and on dialectics."[19]

The Reformation: A Case Study

Along with the curious reliance on Bauer and certain theses of the Tübingen school on the subject of early Christianity, one may put the thesis concerning the Reformation developed by the Hegelian Left. Luther, Calvin and Münzer feature in the drama. "*Luther*, we grant, overcame bondage out of *devotion* by replacing it by bondage out of *conviction*." So said Marx in the critique of Hegel's *Rechtsphilosophie*.[20] Marx thinks that Protestantism, while no solution to alienation, provides "at least the true setting of it." This is because it interiorizes the struggle, replacing the external priest by an internal "priestly nature." Secularization of church property will no longer suffice: only a revolution of inward attitude and motivation will overcome alienation. Thus he pays tribute to the advance that the Reformation has brought, even if he considers the solution still to be tried.

John Calvin is given short shrift in Marxist thought, since Engels typified him as "providing the ideological costume for the second act of the bourgeois revolution . . . the true religious disguise of the interest of the bourgeoisie of that time."[21] In his *Socialism: Utopian and Scientific* (1886 introduction), Engels concentrates on the connection between the doctrine of predestination and the new commercialism of Calvinist lands – a point to become notorious after Max Weber and still the subject of scholarly controversy.[22] But he does fault Luther for subservience to rulers while Calvin's "democratic and republican" ecclesiology made for a "republicanized" kingdom of God. In continental lands and then in England, Calvinism inspired revolutionary if bourgeois upheavals.

Thomas Münzer receives treatment especially in Engels's *The Peasant War in Germany* (1850) and has been a favourite of Communist hagiography ever since.[23] Whereas Luther was a "burgher reformist," Münzer is a "plebeian revolutionary." Engels describes his life and theological thought and then his politics. Noting the close connection between the two, Engels states, "Just as Münzer's religious philosophy approached atheism, so his political program approached communism."

Such interpretation of the trilogy of Reformers assumes what it seeks to prove, that class struggle is the clue to history. The two northern Reformers who took opposite sides on the issue of the Peasant War, however, were not victims of class determinism so much as antagonists in a perennial debate. This turned on the question of interpreting the Kingdom of God, what today is called realized and futurist eschatology. Engels insists on treating conditions as causes, a category-mistake· that reinforces the concept of projection. The latter concept, indeed, as if to prove the coincidence of opposites, slips into reductionism. The fantasy of religion is pressed down into the causality of "class." Granted that class structure was indeed marked at the Reformation as well as in the era of Marx and Engels – a structure that hinged on the holding of property – to subsume the movement of Reform (and Counter-Reform?) under this class rubric remains tendentious, to say the least. It abstracts from the rich tapestry of Reformation one thread to the loss of all others. The relation of Reformation to Renaissance, the intellectual history of late medieval Europe, the significance of the emerging city-states as rival authorities to the episcopate (both Zürich and Geneva are signal examples) – these are some of the neglected data. To compare "burgher" with "plebeian" movements of Reform as Engels does loses the complexity of the actual situation. All is reduced to "the reactionary Catholic camp, the Lutheran bourgeois reformist camp, and the revolutionary camp."[24]

The possibility of rebellion exercised medieval and Reformation consciences in a schema which Engels misses because of his assumption that only "substructure" is admissible evidence. The triangle of people, prince and magistrate formed a dynamic of order and authority that limited the liberty of revolt to the lower magistrates. This thesis of Theodore Beza (*Du droit des Magistrats*) is echoed by Peter Martyr Vermigli; they drew not only on the *Corpus Iuris Canonici* and the *Corpus Iuris Civilis* but also the Roman law of treason, *lex Iulia maiestatis*.[25] The legal tradition embodied in such sources is too complex to suffer the simplistic reduction of Engels's *Peasant War* treatise. Just as the moral law led Immanuel Kant to transcendental postulates, so the tradition of civil and canon law had led the Reformers to recognize that the problem of rebellion demands a context of order and also eschatology. But Engels's etiology of religion posits "fantastic reflection" of "external forces" of nature and history, which he regards as sufficient explanation of such historical issues, as well as solving the "confusion" of "comparative mythology."[26]

The three protagonists of Engels's theory are more than his cardboard figures. Martin Luther's notorious reaction to the peasant uprising – that "calamitous jacquerie of 1524" – reflects a theology of the "two kingdoms" and especially of the power of the Word of God, which needs little help from humans, particularly through force of arms. His opposition to Münzer stemmed from a clear awareness of the option of choosing a present Kingdom, the central platform of *Schwärmerei*. When Spirit governs Word, then the *spirituali*, as the Elect of God, govern the world. Münzer's Sermon before the Princes at Allstedt is an example of the practice of revolution in destructive mode that results from apocalyptic theory. Romantic and fanatic, it makes a strange tale for Communist devotions.[27]

Luther knew as well as Münzer the long tradition of realized eschatology, of Chiliasm and particularly of Joachim di Fiore. Of course, there is in Lutheran theology a distinct danger of quietism, of mere submission to authority and the counsel to accept one's lot as from God. This is as true of Calvinism in its tendency toward submissive piety under a strong doctrine of predestination. But against this danger or tendency is the noble and often paramount doctrine of vocation. Luther's insight into the calling of the Christian under God – a calling (*Beruf*) entailing liberty for oneself and for one's neighbours – was followed by John Calvin. The "political and secular" realm was underlined by Luther as one of three callings (along with family and Church) through which we serve God and his creatures. "God gives you office that you may serve." Rather than typify Luther as burgher, one could as well argue that he defends the values of the old order against the social upheavals then beginning. On this thesis, Calvin is the modern, correcting the traditional Aristotelian doctrine that money is barren, limiting interest rates in Geneva, and reminding his followers that hand in hand with this freedom to use the divine gifts for social betterment goes the hard lesson of "discipline" – bearing the cross. The twin doctrines of vocation and stewardship sum up Calvin's "meditation on the Christian life" and cut across the class structure despite the temptations of the emerging bourgeoisie.[28]

Similar opinions to those of Engels are voiced by Marx, for instance in *Capital*, where he identifies "Protestantism, Deism, etc." as those bourgeois developments appropriate to the alienated world of capitalistic society, where human relations are a matter of commodities.[29] Thus develops a typology of religion according to which the roots of religion lie in the alienation of those reduced to impersonal relationships. The primitive fetishism gradually develops into monotheism, always reflecting the "socioeconomic substructure," until at last the refinement of bourgeois society expresses itself in an impersonal deism or a culture-Protestantism. It is at this point that philosophy has fortunately provided such critical analysis that demand for practical transformation becomes overwhelming. To seize the demand in the name of action is the task of the new "social scientists."

So the historical understanding of German critical philosophy becomes programmatic for Karl Marx. Rather than becoming atheist through his materialism, it might be said with greater justice that Marx became a materialist because of his philosophical atheism.

Worldly Philosophy

The Young Hegelians considered themselves "the last philosophers," much as Hegel thought of himself as the last theologian. They also styled themselves "the action party." For if the world has become philosophical, philosophy must become worldly. The last (eleventh)

"Thesis on Feuerbach" put it classically: "The philosophers have only *interpreted* the world variously, the point is to *change* it." Feuerbach himself comes under this critical rubric, since his materialism remained theoretical, abstract. The eleven theses attack such *theoria*, in which even sensuous reality remains "objective," lacking the dialectic of its nature as productive activity, the clue to revolutionary action. On the other hand, Hegel's idealism at least interpreted correctly the dynamism of material production, although leaving this similarly abstract or spiritual.

The practical program of Karl Marx, therefore, derives from critical philosophy as from the stimulus of a partial analysis that leaves the final step outstanding. Whereas Hegel's "Christian" faith allowed him to rest content with a spiritual reconciliation, the atheism of the young Marx dictated an alternative dénouement. Karl Löwith comments on this point: "Marx's criticism of the existing order is not motivated by mere 'desire to change.' It has its roots in a Promethean rebellion against the Christian order of creation. Only the atheism of man with faith in himself must also see to the creation of the world."[30] The Absolute Spirit was regarded as Zeus, an alien and alienating Other that robbed humanity of its rightful autonomy. No statement puts the case for the new Public-Private better than this: "A being does not regard himself as independent unless he is his own master, and he is only his own master when he owes his existence to himself. A man who lives by the favour of another considers himself a dependent being."[31]

It may be thought strange that such total freedom was allied with the new determinisms of the time – social, scientific, evolutionary.[32] Certainly for the younger Marx an authentic humanism is clear, particularly from the Paris Manuscripts, the economic and philosophical papers of 1844, and related works. Ever since their publication in 1932, such writings have stirred controversy concerning Marxist humanism. On one side (beyond the iron curtain) appears a scepticism about the humanistic thesis; on the other, a liberation theologian such as José Miranda can speak of "the Christian Humanism of Karl Marx." Our concern in this book is to stress the philosophical and religious significance of early Marxism as a form of Hegelianism and a revolt against classical theism. In this sense it was not a "scientific spirit" that dictated Marx's own anti-idealistic stance; rather, his philosophical research enabled him to grasp the thrust of critical thought and the historical analogues to his situation. Marx and Engels appear fascinated by historical-critical studies of the Bible, comparative mythology and world religions. They seized on new theories – evolution, fetishism, hellenistic Judaism as the perversion of a socialist Jesus – in their search for explanatory reasons for the fantasy called religion.

The rediscovered humanism was easily related to the programmatic philosophy of actualization. Their data suggested a dehumanizing process requiring replacement by a genuine humanism. In 1856 Marx summarized such a view:

> In our own time everything seems pregnant with its opposite. Machines are endowed with the wonderful power of reducing human labour and making it more productive: we see how they lead to hunger and overwork. The newly released powers of wealth, by a strange quirk of fate, become sources of poverty. The triumphs of art seem to be bought at the price of character. Mankind becomes lord of nature, but man becomes the slave of man or slave of his own base nature. . . . The outcome of all our inventions and all our progress seems to be that material forces acquire spiritual life, and human existence becomes a dumb, material force. . . . We know that the new powers of society, if they are to accomplish good work, demand *new men*.[33]

Such analysis is *Realhumanismus*, human being as it is but with a clear call for the renewal of that being. The Communist revolution, accordingly, concentrates on the proletariat as that class which alone can function as spearhead of what has already been achieved philosophically: "*Philosophy* is the *head* of the emancipation and the *proletariat* is its *heart*."[34]

A caveat has been raised against the idea that the young Marx of social humanism is the clue to Marxism. Louis Althusser's works have attempted to justify developed (and determinist) Marxism rather than to accept as guide the enigmatic texts of his youth. "Voilà donc le *lieu* du débat: le jeune Marx. Le véritable *enjeu* du débat: le marxisme. Les *termes du débat*: si le jeune Marx est déjà et tout Marx."[35] Althusser presses the point that the Marx of the Paris Manuscripts has two themes. One is the cluster of familiar topics: humanism, alienation, social essence of humanity. The other is simply philosophy. In that period, the Hegel under study was a neo-Hegelian figure, resulting in "une philosophie devenant volonté." Thus the formulation of alienation by the young Marx remains within the ideology of socialist humanism, choosing a "humanism of class" as the strategic move.[36]

Althusser's *Contradiction et Surdetermination* and *Lire Capital* submitted the thesis that the youthful formulation gave place to a distinctly different one in *Capital*. The mature Marx attempts a startling reformulation, which Althusser even terms a "rupture," in contrast to the earlier stance. Now the concept of money moves into prominence, the power of those who control the means of production. No longer is the human essence, "socialized humanity," the burden of analysis, but rather those varied human activities "contradicted" by the determinations of the historical process. No longer is the Hegelian *Aufhebung* internalized, as proved possible in the Russian revolution. The latter was explained by Lenin as a case of the weakest link theory: Russia was the most fragile in the "système d'Etats," intensely alienated and ripe for the revolution. So the practical and strategic approach of Lenin is quite consistent with the Marxist theory of a complex of contradictory occasions determining the dynamics of alienation and reconciliation.

In respect to Althusser's "theoretical anti-humanism," we note his caveat, but note further that it touches but little the chief point at issue, namely the theoretical origin of Marxist atheism. Indeed, the new antihumanist atheism of a school of Marxists (and structuralists) can be interpreted in line with our thesis as the final step in the irony of atheism that first replaces theism with apotheosized humanity and then in turn with dehumanized natural effects.

Religion and Alienation

The thesis at work among the Young Hegelians was that philosophy issued in atheism, thus sounding the death knell of a system of mystified philosophy (i.e., theology), which fed on alienated humanity. Whatever idealistic reconciliation had been achieved by Hegel was but the last gasp of those generations that nurtured their hopes on illusion. Both Feuerbach and Kierkegaard recognized the inevitability of a break between philosophy and Christianity, if from opposite sides. For the former, philosophy's task is to expose essential human being, and *ipso facto* to deny Christianity; for the latter there is no ultimate substance to philosophical reasoning in view of the event of the Incarnation of the Word of God. We noted earlier Feuerbach's attack on the contradiction of modern philosophy, "that it is a negation of theology based upon theology, or a negation of theology which is itself theology"; even more significant is the stringent position of Kierkegaard. Together they indicate the crisis for philosophers of the nineteenth century who see themselves as standing on the razor's edge between philosophy in thrall to theology and the new philosophy, which wills its own death in the emergence of revolutionary politics. Yet there is evidence that German idealists, particularly Fichte, Schelling and Hegel himself, are not to be too simply regarded under the rubric of titanic critique of religion. Eugene Kamenka, for one, insists that they "moved with age toward less Promethean positions."[37]

The key to such a radical shift in philosophical consciousness lies in the idea of alienation. For Hegel, this phenomenon was best understood as part of the universal drama of *Geist*. It is social reality, "interpersonal relations" in modern jargon, that imposes alienation, chiefly because persons are reduced to things. The master-slave relationship is symbolic. An initial mutuality of acceptance – both parties need to be recognized, even desired (*Begierde*) - gives place to a stage in which individuality subserves the other, which now appears as a threat to selfhood. Such contradiction of otherness reflects the universal dialectic of Being or Spirit. In various places where such "unhappy consciousness" is described, Hegel unfolds the inner workings of that movement toward otherness which in turn culminates in sublation.[38] But more to the point, Hegel sees clearly that the dynamics of alienation have to do with property relations. If Absolute Spirit represents that freedom which is human destiny, it remains a fact that we have lost this treasure through the acquisition of property. Personal values are exchanged for "dead things," so that we lose ourselves. This "loss of freedom" is what alienation or estrangement signifies: *Entfremdung*.

When Marx turns to the "self-alienation process [*Selbstentfremdungsprozess*]," he has the Hegelian model before him. It is significant that he applies his notion of fetishism to this phenomenon. His analysis of commodities and their exchange value in *Capital* develops its "labour theory of value" and its elaborate dissection of capitalism's errors and shortcomings not without deliberate use of the idea of the "fetishism of commodities." Thus a human-interest story such as that of the seamstress Mary Anne Walkley not only enlivens his text but reminds us of Marx's essentially humanistic orientation, his moral judgment and prophetic irony:

> This girl worked, on an average, 10 1/2 hours, during the season often 30 hours, without a break, whilst her failing labour power was revived by occasional supplies of sherry, port, or coffee. . . .
> Mary Anne Walkley fell ill on the Friday, died on

Sunday, without, to the astonishment of Madame
Elise, having previously completed the work in
hand.
                                    (*Capital* II.15.7)

Similar is his earlier but equally sarcastic treatment of the
legislation on wood-stealing – interpreted to include the gathering of
wood by the poor.[39] "It need hardly be pointed out that the gods of
wood carry the day, and down go the human sacrifices!" Before the
courts both owner and thief are dehumanized because defined only in
terms of the property to which they are "related." The value on display before the court – hence the philosophy of law on view – is the
value of commodities. This is a peculiar form of mystification, which
Marx called "reification [*Verdinglichung*]," elevating the thing to
value above persons, and correspondingly reducing human being to
thinglike or unhuman disvalue. Chief victim of this process is the
proletariat, forced into *dinglich* status and so *Unmenschen*. Describing the conditions resulting from bourgeois capitalism, the *Communist Manifesto* deplores the result, which "has left no other nexus
between man and man than naked self-interest, than callous 'cash
payment'," resolving personal worth into exchange value. The result
is "a class of labourers who live only so long as they find work, and
who find work only so long as their labour increases value."

The third Paris Manuscript of Karl Marx, entitled "Private
Property and Labour," attacks private property as a notion of "fetis-
hists and Catholics." Here occur the famous words:

> *Communism* is the *positive* abolition of *private prop-
> erty*, of *human self-alienation*, and thus the real
> *appropriation* of *human* nature through and for
> man. It is therefore the return of man himself as a
> *social*, i.e. really human, being, a complete and
> conscious return which assimilates all the wealth of
> previous development. Communism as a fully
> developed naturalism is humanism and as a fully
> developed humanism is naturalism.

Human self-alienation has both holy and unholy forms. Philosophy attacks the former first, and then the latter: "Thus the criticism of heaven turns into the criticism of the earth, the *criticism of
religion* into the *criticism of right* and the *criticism of theology* into
the *criticism of politics*" (*MER* 42). Alienation is overcome by correcting idealistic-religious ways of apprehending reality with material-
istic-socialist ways. The displacement of values through the fetishism
of commodities exposes money as chief fetish, "the quintessence of
the alienated world." It is analogous to that "diabolical power of

money" exposed by biblical prophets and apostles. The dynamics of alienation sketched by Hegel's analysis of property relations is becoming fixed within Marxist theories of economic exploitation and class struggle. The early humanism is being suffocated by the economic determinism or socioeconomic ideology. Such concentration on social alienation as sufficient reason for the origin of religion misses those "limit situations" (the Kantian *Grenzfallen*) that moralists and existentialists take as data untouched by the Marxist critique. In his study of Soviet "scientific atheism" James Thrower notes the hard fact for Communist theorists that where social alienation has all but disappeared, "religion not only persists, but appears to be gaining ground." He concludes: "This reluctance to move beyond the now firmly established Marxist-Leninist analysis of 'alienation' is a striking illustration of the closed nature of Soviet study of religion."[40]

The abolition of private property becomes the solution to alienation because the dynamic of depersonalization is identified with the structure of property relations. This links up with the labour theory of value, at once the personalization and the quantification of worth. It is a cluster of concepts that has roots in medieval scholasticism, notably Aquinas and Antonino of Florence, but evident also in Benedictine and Franciscan teaching on property. Thus R.H. Tawney concludes, "the last of the Schoolmen was Karl Marx."[41] In between, of course, lie the shadows of Hegel and of Feuerbach. The one exposed the essential form of alienation as "the alienation of self-consciousness," while the other raised consciousness to the level of social being, *Gattungswesen*. These points are made by Marx himself in the Paris Manuscripts, and he knows that his calling to criticize popular religion may be termed Epicurean or Feuerbachian as well as Promethean.[42]

The concept of alienation has experienced a rough passage since Hegel and Marx. It has carried some of the freight from the Augustinian and Lutheran tradition noted in the previous chapter. It also brings Hobbes's sharp insight into the way the "great Leviathan" of the corporate state attracts to itself absolute properties of independence and power, assuming a reified personality, a species of heteronomous beast. From modern sociology it adds a more generalized sense of unmediated *anomie*, almost identifying humanness with alienation, a kind of secular Manicheeism. There is also a positive use of the term, referring to the gift of creativity or genius. Such variety of meaning leads Joachim Israel to conclude that it is too ambiguous to be helpful, so loaded with "metaphysical presuppositions" as to be useless. (The famous response of the Marlon Brando character in the movie *The Wild One* is apt: to the question "What are you rebelling against?" he replied, "What have you got?") Still, the concept of alienation may identify a constant in any description of the human condition, a universal experience of brokenness, estrangement and lack that demands analysis and prescription in the most profound sense. Whether religion is taken as part of cause or cure, it cannot be denied that alienation immediately raises the question of transcendence.[43]

Søren Kierkegaard

The theme of alienation belonged equally to another Hegelian, too often contrasted with Marx as if he were merely individualistic rather than social, or of the Right rather than the Left. But for Kierkegaard (1813-55) the established Lutheran church of Denmark embodied "Christendom," as much the object of radical critique as classical theism for Feuerbach and Marx. And something of the kind of distance between Marx and Kierkegaard may be measured when one compares the "Eleventh Thesis on Feuerbach" with an aphorism of Kierkegaard:

> The philosophers have only *interpreted* the world, in various ways; the point is to *change* it.
> (Thesis XI)

> What the philosophers say about Reality is often as disappointing as a sign you see in a shop window, which reads: Pressing Done Here. If you brought your clothes to be pressed, you would be fooled; for only the sign is for sale.
> (Diapsalmata, *Either/Or*)

For the lonely Dane too, the enemy was Hegelian idealism, although he lacked companions in his struggle. The dimension of "the individual [*die Einzelne*]" was corrective to that of "the crowd," a generalized humanity lacking subjectivity. Tempting as it is to balance this against the generic man of Feuerbach and Marx, there remains a necessary truth in this passion for the "single one" who may stand out from the mass. As Buber saw.[44]

For Kierkegaard alienation is taken seriously only when one moves beyond the aesthetic or immediate stage, where property relations are merely external. The ethical sphere or lifestyle mediates every relationship through reflection, but only in "religiousness" are categories available to recover the self through relationships, including those of property, in which having and being assist one another. That is, human being is here subject to ontological analysis that cuts behind the categories of Marx. Nor does Kierkegaard neglect the social and political spheres, despite his attention to the individual. The revolutionary events of 1848, for instance, were welcomed because they "cast light on my thesis."[45] Here, then, is an alternative analysis of alienation and reconciliation, still in response to Hegel and by developing his dialectic. Since the prophet of the northern market-town of Copenhagen was lost to history for a century, during which time Marx and his fellows found themselves at the centre of momentous events, his alternative was unable even to assist Christendom in reforming its human relations. Nevertheless, it is salutary to ponder the implications of Kierkegaardian analysis and its distinction between the God of idealist philosophy and establishment theology, and the God of biblical revelation. Thomas Molnar concludes:

> Kierkegaard also unmasked the concept of alienation. Man cannot be alienated from the true God, only from the Hegelian Absolute of which he is supposed to form a part. Had the scholarly world followed, among Hegel's critics, Kierkegaard rather than Marx, we would have been spared the pseudo-problem of "alienation."[46]

Opium of the People

> *Religious* suffering is at the same time an *expression* of real suffering and a *protest* against real suffering. Religion is the sigh of the oppressed creature, the sentiment of a heartless world, and the soul of soulless conditions. It is the *opium* of the people.

Much has been written on these words, in pain or in joy or in perplexity.[47] The punch line, of course, is still to be heard: "The abolition of religion as the *illusory* happiness of men, is a demand for their *real* happiness."

A familiar point in exegesis of the passage is that Marx is stating two things about religion, one negative but the other positive.[48] As both "expression" of suffering and "protest" against suffering, religion functions in a twofold way. Subsequent use of the term restricts meaning to the former, to the neglect of the latter. It is this simplistic reduction of Marx's understanding of religion to merely narcotic or soporific role – especially when interpreted as a deliberate feeding of the masses with the drug of piety – that is misleading. Jan Lochman reports that the Czech Marxist historian and philosopher Robert Kalivoda "rejected as a deplorable misunderstanding the assumption that the sentence by Marx on religion as opium of the people . . . was an adequate statement of Marxist theory of Christianity."[49]

Religion as opium of the people is a notion that Marx knew from a general idea of Feuerbach's, used also by Moses Hess. In *The Essence of Christianity*, chapter 12, "The Omnipotence of Feeling, or the Mystery of Prayer," Feuerbach's program of humanization identifies the God of political community with Law, and the God of "unpolitical, unworldly feeling" as Love. Hence "God is the Love that satisfies our wishes, our emotional wants. . . . God is love: that is, feeling is the God of man, nay, God absolutely, the Absolute Being." And since Nature is deaf to his prayer of anguish (how quickly the human condition is typified by pain among the Young Hegelians) he turns inward, praying to his deepest self.

> This open-air of the heart, this outspoken secret, this uttered sorrow of the soul, is God. God is a tear of love, shed in the deepest concealment over human misery. "God is an unutterable sigh, lying in the depths of the heart"; this saying is the most remarkable, the profoundest, truest expression of Christian mysticism.

The "saying" comes from Sebastian Franck, the sixteenth-century German mystic. Feuerbach contrasts belief in creation and miracle with mystical faith, both in the text and in the appended notes, replete with quotations from the theologians. His shift of the object of faith from God to self entails a shift in the key doctrine of prayer from dialogue with transcendent Love to the sigh of a distressed, indeed alienated, heart.

That religion should have a consolatory function is hardly surprising, nor in itself a criticism. Indeed, the opposite would seem to hold: that a religion that offered *no* consolation to believers must be false. But the point at issue is hardly touched by the debate: such a function is "not of itself a signal of unreality unless one accepts a view of reality which rules this out, arbitrarily, from the start."[50] The proper case against religion, apparently, is put much better by those Christians who have denounced the misappropriation of the consolatory function, especially when ruling classes have sought to placate their underlings through pious deeds and ritual provisions. Such a self-interested use of religion has been the subject of prophetic condemnation since at least the Hebrew protesters of the eight century BCE such as Amos. That protest often remained peripheral or underground, to be sure. And with the advent of the Constantinian era, when Christianity became official and privileged, the unity of church and state made it the easier to "use" religion in this way. Privilege and cant go together, and the tragic history of persecution of the Jews remains the chief symbol of the abuse.

Religion functions not only as consolation and therefore patient of severe abuse by privileged groups but also as protest, a form of practical social criticism in its own right, and therefore patient of effective use by prophets who protest injustice and inhumanity.

The chief weakness in the Marxist interpretation of religion, therefore, is not the identification of its consolatory function with consequent abuse, nor even its relative neglect of Marx's own recognition of the complementary function of protest. Rather, as noted earlier, it is the failure to examine critically its own acceptance of those ideas belonging to the spirit of its age that provided reductionist explanations of religious phenomena. There is the projection theory of Feuerbach, linked certainly to the development of German theology and perhaps explicitly, as Karl Barth held, to Lutheran christology; there is the historical-critical method espoused by Bruno Bauer, which thought to reduce biblical story to "myth"; there is the incipient *Religionswissenschaft*, which suggested a historical line from natural or "primitive" religion through polytheism to monotheism, all related to the fear of alien Nature; and there is the new evolutionary theory, which promised such great things that it informed all the above. So Karl Marx found grist for his polemical mill, especially when one remembers his constant notion that everything is product, that man as producer is the key to reality. Thus Ernst Bloch explains the reaction of Marx to the classical theory of knowledge for which thought is passive, receptive (*visio, theoria*) and so is "alien to work and does not reflect the labor process."[51] The Marxist approach, on the contrary, advances a sort of "labour theory of knowledge." The "Theses on Feuerbach" criticized that philosopher for clinging to the classical epistemology:

> The chief defect of all materialism up to now (including Feuerbach's) is, that the object, reality, what we apprehend through our senses, is understood only in the form of the *object* or of *contemplation;* but not as *sensuous human activity*, as *practice;* not subjectively.
>
> (*Thesis 1*)

He had also criticized Democritus for this fault, in his dissertation. Thus the distinctively modern, Promethean concept of knowledge deriving from Kant and Hegel is present under the form of production, human labour.

If the "practical death of God" seems replete with theoretical constructs and ideological superstructure, this opening act in the drama of communism soon ended. A genuine man of action appeared at centre stage, forcing the critique of religion into stronger lines, assuming strategic priority. Religion is no longer an ambivalent phenomenon, patient of dialectical treatment. It is now a simpler case, of fideism, an irrational illusion grounded in fear and helplessness. It is to be refuted on behalf of "sacred matter." We will approach Lenin through his earlier countryman, Fyodor Dostoevsky.

Dostoevsky's Russia

Fyodor Dostoevsky (1821-81) is the type of literary genius who can speak through contradictory characters. But all the wild and wondrous creations attest their author's paramount concern for the fundamental issue of human existence, the precarious balance between belief and unbelief. "God has tormented me all my life," cries Kirillov, one of "the possessed." We know that the author's dream was to compose a master work entitled *Atheism*, of five volumes, tracing "the life of a great sinner" (the hagiographical nuance is not to be missed). This would propound "the chief problem . . . that has consciously and unconsciously tortured me all my life: the problem of the existence of God."[52] If his plots and characters seem larger than life, they trace in bold strokes the varied pattern of belief and unbelief. In the brothers Karamazov, including the half-brother Smerdyakov, there shows forth the partnership of good and evil, faith and its rejection. One needs to assimilate all this brotherhood to grasp Dostoevsky's understanding of the reality of divine and human being. This greatest and last of his novels (1879-80) seems to give the best lines to Ivan the rebel. He articulates the dilemma of antitheism, with its axiom of "All or Nothing" and its conclusion: God does not exist, therefore everything is permitted. His brothers "paraphrased" this, Dmitri in one way, Smerdyakov in quite another, and fatal, manner. Must positivism lead to nihilism, and liberty to licence? What is goodness without God, and to Whom can one offer thanks for the good earth and the simple joys? Is suffering punishment or purification or something more profound than either? These are the questions posed by this brotherhood of dark destiny. Dostoevsky's last words provide a strange testament to a faith in which "sorrow and then pancakes" symbolize a terrible joy beyond the confines of nihilism or idealism, a hope beyond rebellion.

Henri de Lubac has described our topic as "the drama of atheist humanism." It may be appreciated in terms of three statements proposed as theses or assumed as axioms at various stages of play. The typical expression of heteronomy is, "God can do anything he wants to." Kirillov puts the chief options well: "If there is a God, then it is always His will, and I can do nothing against His will. If there isn't, then it is my will, and I am bound to express my self-will" (*The Possessed* III.6.ii). The Grand Inquisitor of Ivan's imagination claims that the first means "Nothing is required" – the second entails Ivan's own "Everything is lawful." This Promethean creed struggles with a third view, that of secular humanism, the novelist's foil – "Something is demanded." The latter suggests the Kantian problematics of antinomy explored by Louis Shein, who notes the fact that before leaving for Siberia Dostoevsky asked his brother to procure a copy of the *Critique of Pure Reason*. Finally, the novels themselves develop a fourth thesis, that "Everything is given and therefore all is accountable," a form of the All-*and*-Nothing argument we shall meet later. Ivan may collect stories of innocent suffering as the dossier to prosecute God; he begets not only a murderer but the Devil himself, who delights in rational discourse and draws the logical conclusions to Ivan's theories: "Man will be lifted up with a spirit of divine Titanic pride and the man-god will appear."[53]

Dostoevsky saw Ivan as typical of the bourgeois-atheistic Westernism imitated by the Russian upper classes. Thus, in Slavophilic fashion, he looked to the peasants to save his country. Father Zossima states: "One who does not believe in God will not believe in God's people. . . . Only the people and their future spiritual power will convert our atheists, who have torn themselves away from their native soil."[54] The turmoil and the passion of Holy Russia are caught in his novels. To kiss the earth is an act of faith, but for Orthodoxy it is much more. It is an acknowledgment of the strength of the people, who embody the Truth manifest in flesh. Ivan Karamazov is armed with a rationale that accuses theism of "Euclidean nonsense" in its attempts at theodicy. But Alyosha does not plead a theodicy; he has no "answer" to the problem of evil. He accepts Father Zossima's perspective with its tension of belief and unbelief, of knowing and ignoring. Or again, Stavrogin tests every possibility, "since God does not exist," but at the last even he cannot live with personal disintegration.

The clues that the author provides – in spiritual elders and holy fools, *startsi* and *yurodivye*, in holy earth and in the possibility of resurrection – suggest the richness of his heritage. In large part this reflects the unbroken tradition of Orthodoxy, with its liturgy centred in Light and its Gates of Heaven opening on Life. No doubt the emphasis became channeled into otherworldly hope like that of the classical theism of the West. This was indeed a dreadful aberration, but it gave substance to Lenin's charge that "during all the years of [Christ's] so-called worship he has been the tool of the oppressors."

Dostoevsky was not unaware of the temptation of religion – the Grand Inquisitor is his testimony to bad faith. But he recognizes the complexity of atheism, its varying texture and terrible logic in a Raskolnikov or a Stavrogin or a Kirillov. He knows better than Lenin how wrong religion can be; but he knows also that he cannot escape its claim nor turn its power into its opposite. The Inquisitor had substituted happiness for freedom, had rejected the "terrible gifts" of the Christ, which only the few had strength enough to accept: "those children of freedom, of free love, of free and splendid sacrifice for Thy name." And so he serves the anti-Christ, the substitute idol who grants peace to those who submit and obey.[55]

Mother Russia offers dense paradox: light and darkness, freedom and slavery, belief and unbelief. When Stavrogin confesses, Bishop Tykhone observes, "Perfect atheism is worth more than worldly indifference." If Kirillov struggles against a God defined by his "arbitrariness," Mitya Karamazov rejoices in One who inspires the "privilege of giving joy." But Dostoevsky himself respects both positions, speaks through both. Shortly before his death he responded to criticism of his *Karamazov*: "You might search Europe in vain for so powerful an expression of atheism. Thus it is not like a child that I believe in Christ and confess Him. My hosanna has come forth from the crucible of doubt."[56]

Surely Lenin inhabits the same religious space as these characters. For him too Mother Russia provides a context of paradox and pathos. It is as if he steps out of these pages, a brother Karamazov, a member of the circle of the Possessed, raw and underground, obsessed with the morality of crime and punishment, justice and freedom and earthy matter. He too is repulsed by a specious theodicy, compelled by a passionate rebellion. Just as Dostoevsky's characters continue to haunt our imagination, so Lenin is a spectre that "haunts the world" in Robert Payne's words.

Vladimir Ilyich Ulyanov: Lenin

> Tyrannical toward himself, he must be tyrannical
> toward others. All the gentle and enervating senti-
> ments of kinship, love, friendship, gratitude and
> even honour must be suppressed in him and give
> place to the cold and single-minded passion for rev-
> olution.

These words are from *The Revolutionary Catechism*, subtitled *The Duties of the Revolutionary toward Himself* and written by Sergey G. Nechayev. It surfaced after his trial in 1873, when the *Nechayevtsi* were rounded up – 152 were arrested – and their plans and secret papers discovered. A senseless murder of a fellow student and revolutionary brought Nechayev to trial in person and imprisonment for the rest of his days in the Peter and Paul Fortress (where Peter the Great had murdered his own son Alexis). His *Catechism* (1868?) taught "only one science, the science of destruction." This "apostle of absolute immoralism" (Vincent Miceli) defined as moral "everything that contributes to the triumph of the revolution." His story is documented in the notebooks of Dostoevsky and the novel *The Possessed*. Most important of all, Nechayev was of profound influence, well before Marx, on Lenin.[57]

The earlier Marx-Engels views on religion suffered from category-mistakes and genetic fallacies perhaps, but they preserved a certain ambiguity in which religion was not merely sop but protest, symbol of the need for revolution. But with Lenin (1870-1924) a dramatic shift takes place, prepared by the revolutionary spirit of Russian anarchism and nihilism and by the unhappy soil of Russia itself with its history of hereditary serfdom, which oppressed Lenin's own father in his early years. The circumstances in which the Gospel of Marx found a home as the liberating Word for a nation of serfs hardly European has been noted by many as a peculiar irony of history. Lenin both adopted and adapted the teaching of the German philosophers, whose subtle reasoning on the origin and role of religion held little relevance to his own land. The chief teaching on religion he could use was the connection of faith with class. The rulers drew legitimation from religion, while in it the serfs found other-worldly solace.

Lenin showed extreme harshness toward religion, an intolerance of what he considered a corrupt church built on an irrational faith. Religion in his eyes is merely fideism, lacking reasonable foundation and traceable to feelings of helplessness and fear. He also considered philosophical idealism to be only a subtler form of fideism, hence his assurance in attacking it, as he tended to do with all opponents, with passion rather than argument. His commitment to materialism owes as much to the influence of nihilism as to an achieved philosophical stance. His chief attempt at discursive reasoning, *Materialism and Empirio-Criticism* (1909) consists of attacks on fellow Marxists with scorn and spleen.[58] In particular, Alexander Bogdanov's union of idealism and socialism in *Empiriomonism* is subject to ridicule and vituperation: "idiocy," "madness" – "What a pity that this superb philosophy has not yet found acceptance in our theological seminaries, where its merits would have been fully appreciated."

Lenin felt himself called to a redemptive task – the religious imagery is appropriate to one who spoke of bearing a cross too heavy for his shoulders, and of the expected peace and plenty of the future. This vocation combined with his native energy and mistrust so that he laboured under a terrible burden all his days. Breaking in health, he yet preached his rejection of the religion and morality that he identified with class privilege and superstition. Lenin's legacy is a hardening of the position on religion worked out by Marx and Engels, a kind of revision indeed, becoming even clearer in his philosophical disciple Stalin. Lenin's article "On the Importance of Militant Materialism" proved most influential on future development, with its call for study of the history of materialism and of atheism. There followed the expansive research and writing on the history of religion, particularly with S.A. Tokarev, including the strange spectacle of a thorough syllabus on religion required of all students in higher education.[59]

Yet Lenin deserves a second hearing. For one thing, his materialism is not that of a Hobbes, nor simply a form of positivism. He developed a philosophy of matter-in-motion, with attributes suggesting that we are still within the parameters of a religious interpretation of Marx-Leninism. Lenin and Stalin endorsed as "A very good statement of the principles of dialectical materialism" the saying of Heraclitus (*c.* 530-470 BCE): "The world was not made by gods or men, but it was and will be ever-living fire, self-igniting and self-extinguishing, according to measure or law."[60]

Of importance is the commentary by Arthur Gibson, who treats Lenin under the heading "Faith in Matter."[61] Gibson locates Lenin's materialism within the response provoked by Berkeleyan-Hegelian idealism, which so subordinated matter to mind that the external reality of the material world was radically questioned. Combining Berkeley's *Esse est percipi* with Hegel's "the real is the rational and the rational is the real," Gibson considers the Marxist anti-Hegelian reaction something "salutary and illuminating to matter-shy theists."[62] Already in Engels's *Dialectics of Nature* there occurs a "well-nigh mystical attitude to matter as ultimate and matrix of all that is." For Engels, matter is eternal and cyclical – quite Heraclitean this – and responsible for the emergence of conscious mind and all such transformations:

> we have the certainty that matter remains eternally the same in all its transformations, that none of its attributes can ever be lost, and therefore, also, that with the same iron necessity that it will exterminate on the earth its highest creation, the thinking mind, it must somewhere else and at another time again produce it.[63]

Lenin develops this theory of the inner dynamic of matter, partly in reaction to what he perceived as the "crisis in modern physics" expressed by Henri Poincaré and other physicists because of the new electron theory of matter. The redefinition of matter as energy seemed to imply that "mass disappears." In that first decade of our century this did indeed seem to be the case to many, those on the religious Right welcoming the return to a spiritual universe. Lenin's words are interesting: he quotes with approval a saying of Valentinov that this would be an "offence against sacred matter." Thus matter is characterized by that ontological ultimacy hitherto reserved for the Transcendent, whether expressed in religious or in moral terms. This is a metaphysics of matter, and as such prone to the critique of nonmaterialist philosophers.[64] Yet what Lenin is attempting is a refutation of idealism in order to "save the appearances" of material objects as objects. His *Materialism and Empirio-Criticism* pinpoints the problem admirably: "The new trend in physics regards theories only as symbols, signs, and marks for practice, i.e. it denies the existence of an objective reality independent of our mind and reflected by it." And this point is a constant refrain: mind reflects objects, which exist independently of their being thought. Therefore he laments the replacement of materialism by "idealism and agnosticism." Lenin refuses to say *what* matter is: it exists as the limiting *that* of human knowledge. Gibson calls this move Lenin's "epistemologizing of essences" with distinct analogies to the Christian concept of God.[65] His concept of matter may be seen, therefore, as "less a rigorously antispiritualist bias and far more an existentialist bias over against idealism of all ilks."

Lenin's materialism, then, may be interpreted more kindly than, say, that of Bakunin. The anarchist's theory of revolution hinges on his reinterpretation of the Fall: Satan appeared in time in order to raise man, in defiance of the God who wished to keep him servile. "But then comes Satan, the eternally revolted, the first *libre penseur* and emancipator of the world."[66] Bakunin's is a materialism in the service of revolution; his break with Marxism (he was expelled in 1872 from the International Workingmen's Association) concerned the use of politics in revolution. He distrusted all state power, including that of the proletariat. Thus he was regarded as an anarchist rather than a collectivist. Yet his pan-Slavism and his grasp of the dynamics of social revolution symbolize the situation in Lenin's Russia.

Opium for the People

> Religion is opium for the people. Religion is a kind of spiritual intoxicant, in which the slaves of capital drown their humanity, and blunt their desire for a decent human existence.[67]

In *Socialism and Religion* (1905) Lenin moves one step beyond Marx and Engels. Religion is reduced to "a private matter," yet one that is impossible for the socialist. The latter is aware of the lack of "conscience," indeed the "obscurantism" of religious belief. Against the "religious stupidity" of workers, therefore, an "ideological struggle" is called for. In this key essay and in other writings and speeches, the "fight against religion" is promoted as a strategic necessity in the socialist cause. It is no longer a case of the inner dialectic of a religion that expresses protest as well as consolation, and that is bound to disappear. It is now perceived as a matter of the false alternative to class-consciousness and proletarian liberation, an illusory faith that hinders the achievement of the social good.

In Nikolai Berdyaev's judgment, Lenin was "an imperialist and not an anarchist," "an anti-humanist as he was an anti-democrat."[68] Thus his programmatic dictatorship of the proletariat led with iron logic into the coercion of Stalinism. This agrees with the assessment of Eric Voegelin, that the "organizational centralism" of the original movement is the clue to the political success from Marx to Stalin. "Beyond the conflict of personal ambition lies the profound antagonism between the authoritarianism of Marx and Bakunin's truly revolutionary existence."[69]

Such authoritarianism helps explain Lenin's attitude toward the so-called god-builders (Gorky, Lunacharsky, etc.) as much as his strategic attack upon religion. Maxim Gorky had talked of creating God anew, of making a religion out of socialism. Lenin replies: "For some the statement 'socialism is a religion' is a form of transition from religion to socialism; for others, it is a form of transition *from* socialism to religion."[70] Gorky's maxim, "Gods are not sought – *they are created*," set him apart, so he claimed, from god-seekers such as Berdyaev and Sergei Bulgakov. But Lenin's correspondence with Gorky reveals his antipathy to this entire way of seeing things. The distinction between god-seeking and god-building is a dispute over blue devils compared with yellow, and such talk betrays a hostility to scientific socialism.[71] The material origin of ideas is clouded by this philosophy, akin to Bogdanov's idealism. The latter posited God as a "complex of ideas" orienting society toward its future shape. Along with Bazarov and Lunacharsky, he was named by Lenin as the sort of "Empirio-critic" who relapses into a form of Berkeleyan idealism rather than follow Engels's materialism. For Lenin, however, matter is ontologically primary, existing independently of consciousness. Reflecting on two of his favourite targets, he declares: "The idealists will always join the halfhearted Avenarius and Mach in attacking materialism!"[72]

Lenin opposed Gorky and friends for another reason, more significant because it reveals the inner necessity of his idea of matter. Whereas the Machian tradition courted solipsism and issued in reconciliation, Lenin believed that matter moves through permanent dialectic. Dialectics was a theme of his *Philosophical Notebooks* (published posthumously) commenting on Hegel's *Science of Logic*. Dialectics, he writes, is "the study of contradiction in the very essence of objects." The "self-movement of matter" is the basis of all change and hence the core of dialectics.[73]

The "practical death of God" reached a certain impasse with Lenin. His strategy for helping religion achieve its self-destruction proved abortive, even under the heavy hand of Stalin. Therefore the phenomenon of revisionism marks a distinct evolutionary phase in Marx-Leninism, with a view of religion both critical of and advancing beyond Marx, Engels and Lenin. Its vision includes a positive assessment of Christianity and its Scriptures; and a fresh look at Prometheus.

– 9 –

Re-Visioning Marxism

Marxism as Religion

> Now the old guard was used up; the logic of history
> ordained that the more stable the regime became,
> the more rigid it had to become, in order to pre-
> vent the enormous dynamic forces which the Revo-
> lution had released from turning inwards and blow-
> ing the Revolution itself into the air. . . .
> Revolutionary theory had frozen to a dogmatic cult,
> with a simplified, easily graspable catechism, and
> with No. 1 as the high priest celebrating the mass.
> (Arthur Koestler, *Darkness at Noon*)

To interpret developed communism as surrogate religion is nothing
new. Koestler once joined Silone, Gide, Spender and others in a
lament for "the God that failed."[1] We suggested above that the mys-
tique of Holy Russia provided a matrix for the substitution of one
absolutism for another. Thus we see numerous rituals implicitly or
explicitly borrowing from Orthodox liturgy. Most famous is the pilgrimage to a divinized Lenin, eternal in his formaldehyde immortality. At school opening, flowers are placed on Lenin's tomb, accompanied by genuflection. Babies are officially blessed, and couples
"go to ZAG" (acronym for the Registry of Marriages) where ritual
and music derived from the Liturgy make an occasion of the wedding
ceremony.[2]

    Such development through ideology to religion may be con-
sidered consistent with Marx's own stance, a logical conclusion as
proclaimed strongly by Robert Tucker, for example.

Notes to Chapter 9 appear on page 332.

> The religious essence of Marxism is superficially
> obscured by Marx's rejection of the traditional
> religions. . . . [but] denial of the transmundane
> God was merely a negative way of asserting that
> "man" should be regarded as the supreme being or
> object of ultimate concern. Thus his atheism was a
> positive religious proposition.[3]

Tucker analyzes Marxist structural elements, which demand religious interpretation. He considers Marx to have followed Hegel's lead in his metamorphosis of the theological notion of the soul's salvation. In technical terms of classical theism, this is the Divine Economy, the threefold drama of salvation from creation through redemption to reconciliation. The shift from divine initiative to human is noted in the "self-deification" of Faust, imitated in the Marxian struggle for unalienated humanity, "that corresponds to the master-theme of salvation of the soul in the Christian theology of history."[4]

Tucker's thesis is that analysis of Marxism now places less emphasis (or credibility) in the "social scientific" nature of the enterprise, and shifts to a different approach: "The search for understanding of the deeper springs of his world-view increasingly becomes a search for its moral or religious meaning." Such a thesis may draw largely on the cruciality of the Paris Manuscripts, but it fits in with the stream of Russian commentary that sees Marxism as a counter-religion. Sergei Bulgakov in 1907 proposed to see "Karl Marx as a religious type," developing the "anthropotheism" of Feuerbach.[5] And Berdyaev, as we have seen, is diligent in tracing the outlines of religiosity in Marx and his movement.

A most significant step occurred with the death of Lenin and the events following, manipulated by Josef Stalin. Robert Payne sums them up as "the apotheosis of a God" and cites the liturgical versicles and responses that Stalin prepared in eulogy. The refrain "we vow to thee, comrade Lenin" is a devotional expression of total commitment. "With these words, Stalin announced himself as the high priest of the cult of Lenin, and the commander of the faithful." It is this cultic stage that Koestler has documented with literary skill and passion, and that led in part to the disaffection of E.P. Thompson and Leszek Kolakowski, among others.[6]

Such a religious aura, such a particular spirituality, as that which came to characterize Russian communism and its satellite parties, called up the spirit of Prometheus in an obvious manner. An early work by John Lehmann, *Prometheus and the Bolsheviks*,[7] is an account of Soviet Georgia in which the Titan appears to the author in a dream. Reclining on a deck chair of the ship that traverses the

Black Sea, Prometheus tells of his release, a hundred years after Shelley's poem ("I was very much flattered by Bysshe's attitude"). One of his revolutionary "liberators" says, "What you have dared, we have now achieved: the forces of production are now in the hands of the people, who alone can use them justly and fully." At the end, Prometheus announces a momentous, if obvious, decision: "I have decided to join the Party!"

More serious is the continuing mythologization of communism in Promethean terms. Hans-Gerhard Koch has documented the process, beginning with the "archetypal" use of the myth by Karl Marx.[8] Books published in Russia and East Germany, notably those intended for children and youth, make explicit use of Prometheus's scorn of the gods and his example of human autonomy. The 1957 Festival of Youth book *Unser Deutschland* called Goethe's *Prometheus* "the poetical manifesto of German enlightenment," and asked for renunciation of childish belief in a personal all-powerful God. In *O World in Light* (*Du Welt im Licht*, Berlin, 1954) Stalin is likened to Prometheus, a hero bringing fire, light and warmth to earth and whom no earthly power can shackle. And in 1957 the oration at the Friedrich Schiller University at Jena marking the communist anniversary included these words: "The great socialist October revolution in 1917 marked the hour when Prometheus man was freed for ever from the fetters with which philistinism had bound him. It was the hour of liberation for the Prometheus spirit, the hour of the emancipation of science. It represents the greatest triumph so far of scientific thinking in control of the historic process."

Such was the situation, the hyperbole, the religious overtones of communism, until the end of the Stalinist era and the call for revision. A new chapter in the history of Marxist atheism is presently being written, and an age of Marxist-Christian dialogue begun. Its fate still hangs in the balance, as we reserve judgment on the ultimate significance of the new Soviet policy of openness, *glasnost*. But it is now our task to acknowledge the dialogue and study the revision.

Ernst Bloch

Recent writers within the Communist faith, particularly those bearing the heretical (or schismatic?) label "revisionist," have emphasized the early or humanist Marx and have reinforced the "religious" dimension of Marxism. That is, either they acknowledge the common schemata of theology and communism, or they interpret Marx's theory of religion and therefore the role of atheism in a variety of ways. In the recent phenomenon of Marxist-Christian dialogue, particularly in Czechoslovakia, strange results are to be seen in a more positive assessment of religion on the part of Communist philosophers, and the general agreement by both sides that reformation is in order. One might say: the Communists have only interpreted religion in various ways; the point is, to change it.

First we should look at Ernst Bloch (1885-1977), who antedated such dialogue with his thesis that an "esoteric Marxism," forced underground by Communist orthodoxy, mounts a critique on the crass materialism of modern communism and calls for a shift in the appreciation of religion. He thinks that the Paris Manuscripts have vindicated this position.

Among Bloch's earliest writings are two that anticipate the burden of his mature years. In 1921 he published *Thomas Münzer als Theologe der Revolution* and two years later *Geist der Utopie*. Best-known for the three volumes of *Das Prinzip Hoffnung*, published from 1953 to 1959, Bloch left Eastern Europe in 1961, regarded as a revisionist, and rightly so if one considers his influence among the participants in Marxist-Christian dialogue in Europe.

To recall Bloch's own pilgrimage is apt, for he is a man of stories and images – and the human journey is the moving image of Absolute Future. In *A Philosophy of the Future* there is a beautiful passage on "The Journey that is Knowing: the 'Faust' Itinerary. The Walk."[9] Taking off from Schiller's poem *The Walk*, Bloch ponders the magical cloak that enabled Faust to make his wondrous itinerary. This reminds Bloch of the stages of mystical ascent, leading him from Nicholas of Cusa's dialectical reconciliation of contraries to Hegel's *Phenomenology* with its steps on the way of Spirit.

> And the subject of the *Phenomenology* is from the start a Faust-like "self," for it extends itself to the cosmos (when writing the *Phenomenology*, Hegel produced an appropriately cosmological image in his description of Napoleon as "the world-soul . . . on horse-back").[10]

Both Goethe and Hegel lead his imagination a further step to the mystical theology of Richard of St. Victor, whose *Mentis itinerarium ad Deum* moves from carnal *cogitatio* through inner *meditatio* to spiritual *contemplatio*. Cusa's *sensus, ratio, intellectus* and *visio* also resemble Hegel's way.

Bloch wishes to trace the human journey under the rubric of the future's gravitational pull. One of his mottoes is "S is not yet P," which Bloch once suggested as the summary of his philosophy.[11] By this he means a sort of existentialist working out of future essence, defined in terms of hope: *spero ergo sum.* "Without atheism, there is no place for messianism." It is the *Novum*, the pull of the *Futurum*, that establishes human being, who engages in action on behalf of the utopian vision and promise.[12]

For Bloch the key to religion and its true origin lies not with Creation but with the next word of Genesis: *Eritis sicut Deus.* The "You shall be as gods" signals the hope for deification, the future to which humanity moves. He sees this word as opening on "a religious critique of religion," denying the ontological God beyond humanity, and calling for a program of increasing unity: "until a son of man himself replaces the image of Yahweh." He agrees with Hegel that the *Cur deus homo* of Anselm needs this reply: the Greeks made their gods not too human, but not human enough. Therefore: "This *Eritis* is clearly the most subversive word in all myths open to an anthropocentric interpretation – from the serpent up to Prometheus."[13] Here again – as in Feuerbach's case – we see a form of christological interpretation, drawing on the *homoousios* of the Fathers but leading it into a form of christomonism, according to which the Incarnation is such turning of God into human form as to constitute a literal deification, the *theōsis* to perfection. (In fact the Hebrew *Elohim* in the passage can mean not only gods but great humans.) Bloch cannot tolerate "the fiction of God the Creator and the hypothesis of God in heaven;" his substitute is a vague That-ness (*Dass-Antrieb*), an *Ens perfectissimus*, an ultimum resembling romantic metaphors much more than either Christian theology or Communist ideology.[14]

What sort of philosophy is this, what doctrine of humanity and of God? For one thing, Bloch maintains that Marxist atheism must remain a tentative and tactical critique of the divine hypostases, in particular those that threaten human freedom. Hence "atheism is always a relative concept." Bloch therefore states: "Only an atheist can be a good Christian," which Jürgen Moltmann has reversed to read, "Only a Christian can be a good atheist."[15] On one level, and astonishingly enough, Bloch is in dialogue with the Christian Fathers, those ancients who hammered out trinitarian theology by developing a subtle christology involving union of opposites and negative theology at the heart of definition, in the Chalcedonian formula most explicitly. Just here the theologian must fault Bloch – and Moltmann and Cox and those others who follow his lead too quickly – for a shallow reading of patristic doctrine. Here is no hint of the *perichorēsis* obtaining among the *personae* of the Trinity (that cosmic dance embracing earth, matter, human history in its loving grip, a partnership of joyful glory); nor of those twin concepts of *anhypostasia* and *enhypostasia*, which saved christology from a reduction to absurdity. Therefore Bloch misses what is crucial in trinitarian doctrine: the role of that Word intending to become incarnate, the *Logos incarnandus*, and the implication of this role for the reserve necessary in discussing the formula "God became man." Once again the Hegelian use of Philippians 2:2 is on view, the dilemma of otherness and of how God is able to move over into a second modality of being while maintaining the original. Bloch, like Marx, follows the Lutheran christology at this point, itself a variant of the Augustinian-Western tradition. An alternative is that of Orthodoxy, following the Cappadocians and Gregory Palamas (and ultimately Origen rather than Augustine) with a different distinction, namely that between essence and energies, to depict the divine play of being. This option was lost to the view of German philosophy, where the Lutheran decision to exhaust the role of Christ in virtual enfleshment bred strange results.[16]

Yet such critique passes too quickly over the solid contribution Bloch makes to our appreciation of biblical Christianity. Recognizing the "mystery" symbolized by the cryptic reply to Moses on the Mount of revelation (*Eh'ye asher eh'ye*, I shall be who I shall be: Ex. 3:14), Bloch breaks with that Western tradition of classical theism that turns this into a nominative rather than a verbal self-definition: He Who Is.[17] Here, rather, is the "Exodus God," a deity in motion, a "spirit of the Exodus." But this insight suffers an unhappy alienation in the Church. God's People completed their exodus, found a land of promise in which to settle, and so "nationalized" their God. In passage after passage Bloch inveighs against the Church of the upper classes, which "bristles at see-through blouses, but not at slums in which half-naked children starve, and not, above all, at the conditions which keep three quarters of mankind in misery." It postpones deliverance to "St. Never-Ever's Day" or beyond.[18]

This critique is expressed well in *Atheism in Christianity*, which takes the Bible as "the priests' bad conscience." But just as there are "two Bibles," one for the rich and privileged and another *biblia pauperum*, so are there two churches, and two Gods. The critique of religion, therefore, is not the absolute rejection by "vulgar

Marxism," which lacks the subtlety of Marx himself and takes the opium passage out of context. That context included "protest" as well as "sigh" and so was "clearly not just a question of putting to sleep."[19] Religion can adopt Prometheus as saint too.

Bloch, man of many images, is fond of the image of Prometheus. He rejects gnostic myths of heavenly-angelic archetypes in behalf of a heroic perspective that puts "man on his own," outside heteronomous rulers or gods.[20] Prometheus assures this perspective, and so does Jesus, according to Bloch. He distinguishes myths that hypostasize from those that posit a future, the utopia possible to humanity. Prometheus secures this *novum et ultimum* as the type of rebel who features in "crypto-Messianic myths."

> We can see this in the Bible versus Zeus, who brought a murderous deluge down on man, and dashed the light-bearer Prometheus against the cliffs, like a cross – the Lord-of-the-world, against whom the Promethean in man always rebelled, being better than its God. The Prometheus myth appears again, still far from standing properly on its feet, but for the first time fully understandable now that it has broken away from static Greek thought. And able now to break through into the *Futurum*, thanks to the power of the *Novum* which first came into its view (into the Utopian dimension of its view) through the Bible.[21]

Bloch relates Prometheus also to the figure of Job, whom he wishes to rescue from its reduction to "a model of resignation" at the hands of Jews, Christians and Muslims.

> That is the Titan who challenges God, and who needs no demi-god to be his champion (after the model of the Greek tragedy against Zeus), but who places himself fair and square in the fight and takes his stand as a man against an enemy he believes to be almighty.[22]

A certain weakness is apparent in Bloch's taking the figure of Satan as decisive in the biblical account, relapsing into traditional theodicy. Yet his seriousness about an exegesis that will enlighten Moses, Job and Jesus by using Prometheus as foil allows him to probe the Marxist critique of religion in a stimulating fashion. Atheism is now seen as "meta-religion," an evaluation of the religious "inheritance" that isolates its function as "protest" and relates it positively to the Bible. Bloch's understanding of the prophets enables him to approach the genre of apocalypse as the logic of a religion that takes history seriously and locates its faith in a future revelation of divine justice. In this regard he can even identify "the specifically Hebrew element – Prometheus."[23]

Ernst Bloch, regarded as religious by atheists and as atheist by the religious, has given us a startling profile of a "heroic" view of Bible, Christ and Church. For him, the Prometheus myth is quite capable of Hebraicization and quite in the line of Moses, Job and the Hebrew prophets. Religion as protest, the Bible as biased toward the poor, the Church as open and free, God as truly human – an impressive doctrinal system that has proved to be a positive catalyst in Marxist-Christian dialogue. If we have accused his thinking of certain errors, this is not to diminish the stature of one who found himself in no-man's-land between antagonists, homeless between ideological worlds, sharing Christian hope and values but insistent on a metareligious interpretation that remains atheistic. How has such a stance fared in the dialogue?

Marxist-Christian Dialogue

Revisionist Marxists, condemned by Communist orthodoxy, find sympathetic partners in dialogue among Christian theologians who appreciate the ambiguity of Marxist attitudes toward the Church, typified in the rich thought of Ernst Bloch. We shall mention only a few of such dialogists, notably Jan Lochman, Milan Machoveč and Vitězslav Gardavsky. But first the work of Leszek Kolakowski forms a good introduction to the general approach of the new generation of revisionists.

Kolakowski, philosopher and playwright, was expelled from the Communist party of Poland in 1966 and from his teaching position at the University of Warsaw in 1968 for his views and support of student rebels. Material evidence at that time included the article "What Socialism Is Not."[24] This brief and staccato piece resembles Luther's Ninety-five Theses in its catalogue of errors and its bold attack on corruption. Its negations are countered by refreshing positions in his other works, of which the theme of "The Priest and the Jester" is probably most familiar in the West.[25] Here he contrasts the sacerdotal role of the preserver of the past and servant of the cult with the relative "outsider" who criticizes and jeers at the established order because his imagination allows him to consider alternatives. The former is, to use one of Kolakowski's titles, a "man without alternatives," so bound by tradition that he serves an ideology. The jester is free, liberated by his concern for the human and therefore at odds with "a state that produces superb jet planes and bad shoes," as he says in "What Socialism Is Not." This reflects what Kolakowski terms a "concept of the left," according to which there is always a Left to challenge the established order; it is a functional term rather than a substantive one. The functional approach allows him to recognize the religious dimension in communism, in particular its priestly caste with the consequent establishment of cult and proprietary laws. He writes: "A rain of gods descends from heaven on the funeral rites of the one unique God who outlived himself. Now atheists have their saints and blasphemers are building chapels." His commitment is not to ideology or party but to "Marxist Humanism" and the free spirits that title intends.[26]

It is significant that Kolakowski criticizes those who oppose revision (the Leninist and Stalinist hard-liners who made *revisionist* a term of abuse)[27] for believing their doctrine or method is exempt from revision, and therefore devotees of "theology" rather than "science." The latter term (*nauka*), like the German *Wissenschaft*, is broader than our English *science* and therefore capable of carrying his humanistic meaning. One of his enemies, indeed, is that "positivism" that descends from Hume's negation of the power of reason: Kolakowski considers this philosophy to reflect the "impotence" of the Enlightenment, its "helplessness in the face of the questions it raised."[28]

In Kolakowski, then, we see something of the revisionist school of Marxist thinking today. Both Bloch (more explicitly) and the revisionists have prepared the soil for dialogue, which was matched by the emergence of theologies of liberation in Catholic and Protestant circles. The dialogue in Czechoslovakia, related to the "spring thaw" of 1968 is a case in point, its hope and its tragedy apparent.

Spring Comes to Prague

Czechoslovakia, where once Jan Hus raised a mighty protest against corruption in the Church (and paid with his life), experienced a thaw in between two ice ages of rigid communism. During that brief period of "socialism with a human face," the courageous voices raised on both sides to protest corruption and rigidity were able to join in partnership on behalf of truth. Now the curtain has fallen again, but their words endure. Their legacy is a bold and creative way through the traditional cold war psychology of enemy against enemy. They challenge both sides to re-examine assumptions and conclusions, both their own and the other's, to see where a common search for truth might lead.

An earlier spokesman, mentor to such theologians in the dialogue as Jan Lochman and Milan Opočenský, had paved this way by his teaching and writing. In a little book composed at the end of the war, Josef Hromádka (1889-1969) considered the parting of ways at which his country stood, between fascism and communism.[29] He took Stefan Zweig as "a parable of modern civilization." The humanist author's suicide letter (1942) explained that he would like to have begun again: "But after one's sixtieth year unusual powers are needed in order to make another wholly new beginning." Other figures whom Hromádka treats in this work include T.G. Masaryk, Dostoevsky, Kierkegaard and Karl Barth.

Masaryk, philosopher and statesman, is noteworthy for his insight into the European cultural tradition. From his early work *Suicide* (1881) to his mature writings on politics and religion, Masaryk was convinced that German idealism led to "the cosmic illness of modern humanity" as Hromádka calls it.

> The modern man suffers under the suicidal agony because of the lack of energy, because of weariness and fear coming from spiritual and moral isolation, from Titanism and the cult of superman. Militarism is an attempt of this superman to escape from his own illness; but by the attempt the disease grows.[30]

Masaryk traced the development of such spurious titanism in Kant's rationalistic ethics, leading to both the romantic heroism of "the heartless, callous, sophisticated Faust" and to "the militaristic egoism of the Prussian architects of Germany." Nor is the cold-blooded scepticism of Hume to be absolved, in his judgment. Perhaps only Dostoevsky grasped the tragic condition of modernity – for instance in his portrayal of Raskolnikov, "a helpless, miserable Titan, an impotent rebel." This protagonist of *Crime and Punishment* embodies the "humanistic Titanism" that first exalted reason and then – in reason's name – denied its own powers, declaring humanity to be "a powerless by-product of the processes of nature or of the social environment."[31]

In Hromádka's *Gospel for Atheists* he moves clearly into the new arena.[32] More than a decade has passed since his little nation found itself in the Communist camp in opposition to the West. He calls for "a new beginning," since an age of "uprootedness, bewilderment and skepticism" is upon us on both sides of the iron curtain. But the beginning lies with the Church, to confess its guilt for the corruption of society, for its contribution to the European catastrophe. The solidarity in guilt must be faced and confessed if the Church is to regain confidence as healer: "We Christians have actually become untrustworthy, we carry the responsibility and guilt for those lacking hope; the skeptics and the nihilists, the atheistic communists as well." Hromádka traces the European pilgrimage from Christendom to secularism, its thinkers treading the borderline between belief and unbelief: "Even the 'God' of Hegel and the 'Christ' of Tolstoi reflected the titanic attempt of the modern world to possess God and to become His lord." His programmatic appeal warns against assuming that both sides constitute opposing worldviews, *Weltanschauungen*. Even communism, he insists, "is not primarily a Weltanschauung," inasmuch as its revolutionary view of man, political tactics, and even its "atheism," "were only means, means used by the communists in order to help man and human society." He admits that some Communists, like some Christians, put their world-view out in front of the confrontation; this is to play the wrong game and to promise "tragic failure." States in themselves are neither atheist nor Christian. For sometimes atheism is a "radical humanism" promising melioration of social conditions, while sometimes Christians have opposed such melioration. Therefore the Christian cannot in principle say no to "a state led by atheists."

Hromádka's appeal is for a nobler gospel than that of mere no-saying based on a dogmatic world-view that brooks no reformation (the Christian word for *revision*). He calls for a return to the authentic gospel, which spells freedom, including the promise of liberation to the communist and atheist. This mission must lay aside the traditional role of Churches as authorities, "power blocs" that confirm the Marxist view of religion and Church. It must recapture the vision of loving service that comes directly from Jesus himself.

Christus oder Prometheus? – Lochman

Jan Lochman continues the major themes of Hromádka. A leading participant and spokesman for the dialogue, since 1968 he has been professor of theology at Basle. He underlines the need for the Church to signal "the end of the Constantinian era," as it is called, that name standing for the establishment of Christianity as the official religion of society, the *corpus Christianum* or the "Christendom" of Kierkegaard. As defender of the faith, such institutionalized religion is guilty of approaching others as "patronizing *patres et magistri*, fathers and teachers, presenting their infallible answers in the spirit of self-centred dogma and monologue."[33] Such a Church hides the gospel under a basket; to renew the credibility of Christian witness, it has to go. Reflecting on Hromádka's *Gospel for Atheists*, Lochman hails the new dialogue as a way to restore credibility. The former age was "replete with fixed battle lines and battle cries and marked by a mutual 'demonizing' of the other side."[34] He makes three points about the "relativity" of atheism. One concerns historical relativity, since those called atheists were often merely the opponents of established religion, like Socrates or the Christian Polycarp. When the latter was asked to cry "Down with atheists!" he did so, but giving the words an opposite meaning. A second is psychological relativity, inasmuch as atheism is at times a "dialectical phase of life" on the way to belief. A third is theological relativity, as affirmed in Scripture: the covenant depends on God's faithfulness, regardless of the unfaithfulness of Israel.

In his book *Encountering Marx*, Lochman notes the "biblical heritage" common to both sides in the Prague circle, and the significance of the numerous books on religion by Marxists in recent years: Bloch's *Atheism in Christianity*, Machovec's *Jesus for Atheists*, Fetscher and Machovec's *Marxism and the Jesus Affair*, Konrad Farner's *Theology of Communism* and *Marxist Salt for Christian Earth – Christian Salt for Marxist Earth*.[35] Such titles show an amazing rapport between the two sides as to what constitutes the heart of the mutual challenge of Christianity and Marxism.

For our purpose, Lochman's importance carries through in his analysis of Prometheus. He sees the alternative as "Christ or Prometheus."[36] Such stark phrasing reduces the issue to its essentials, not the false alternative of theism-atheism (which must be demythologized) but that of two christologies, as it were. Instead of "Theismus/Atheismus?" we should ask "Christus/Prometheus?" Lochman is amazed at the breaking of Marxist "silence about Jesus" now that the "warm stream" of revisionist and utopian thinking has arrived. He thinks of Gardavsky and especially of Ernst Bloch, with his *prometheische Christologie*.[37] Bloch contrasted this theology of the cross based on eschatological revolution with the traditional pessimism and patience that characterized classical theism. We must compare Christ as Lamb, an antirevolutionary symbol (and therefore contributing to the charge of opiate) with Christ as serpent, a threat to every complacency and oppression.[38]

Is there, for Christians, a distinctive and creative challenge of the Prometheus myth as developed by Marxism? Lochman thinks so, and takes it up in detail.[39] "Prometheus *has* a place in the Christian calendar," he states emphatically. Since, in his view and following that of Paul Ricoeur, the biblical God is not Zeus, nor biblical humans Greek, there may be room for a complementary myth consistent with the human figure of Jacob (Gardavsky) and even with Jesus as Prometheus (Bloch). Basic to Lochman's thesis is the conviction that the authoritarian class structure behind the Zeus-Prometheus model is not biblical. Thus human emancipation is not an affront to God, a threat to his glory, but on the contrary is the very meaning of his revelation, what his glory is *for*. Moreover (moving from *Gotteslehre* to *Sündenlehre*), sin is not simply *hybris* - the God of exodus and of Resurrection displays free involvement in history, working with humans as his co-workers in behalf of liberation from bondage. Finally (the moment covered by *Rechtfertigungslehre*) grace and human work issue in creation and history, in the travail of new creation that prevents a relapse into what Bonhoeffer called "cheap grace."

Lochman's conclusion about Prometheus is that the myth requires demythologization: Marxist and Christian disagree about the role ("Saviour or Pioneer?") and therefore about the symbol itself. Yet positively there remains a profound and common appreciation of the mythical figure, to which Lochman returns in a later article. He writes:

> The fundamental issue between Marxists and Christians concerns the question: *Is there a place for Prometheus in the Christian calendar?* Are the biblical-Christian and the Promethean-Marxist perspectives of man mutually exclusive? Is Christ an antipode of Prometheus? This is a crucial question for any Christian-Marxist dialogue. If Christ and Prometheus were two exclusive alternatives, then the only responsible encounter between Christians and Marxists would be a confrontation and not a real dialogue.[40]

He notes that in the classical age Prometheus challenged the ontocratic-hierarchical order; that age concurred in his punishment – Zeus was right. Marxism can reinterpret the myth because of a radical shift in world-view, "a new conception of the role of human creativity within the order of creation." This un-Greek, Hebraic conception makes Prometheus stand for the revolutionary, for humanity as "the creative subject of history." And therefore "for such a man there is a place exactly in the Christian calendar."

Yet this is not Lochman's last word. He faces squarely the problem of Marxist atheism and concludes that it remains true that "this philosophy is consciously and organically an atheist creed."[41] Insofar as Prometheus dis-places Christ, he has no "place" in the Christian calendar. "If the final hope of man is in a Promethean salvation, then there is no real place for the biblical God." Thus while refusing to be identified with certain traditional "theistic-ontological structures," Christians should beware of identification with Marxist humanism as if this is an unambiguous philosophy. Christian witness to God's transcendence involves *metanoia* - repentance or self-critical rethinking. It prevents the subtle call of *eritis sicut deus*, which binds us within a new myth, the ideology of dogmatic politics engaged in an apocalyptic struggle. And it encourages a humbler vocation, *eritis sicut homines*: you will be human. If such a humane mission is consistent with the Promethean myth, Lochman holds, it can be shared by Marxist and Christian alike.

How Dead Is God? – Gardavsky

> In January 1967, when *Time* magazine was reporting on the death of God, the Czechoslovakian magazine *Literarni Noviny* was publishing a series of articles under the title "God is Not Yet Dead." How curious that in the West God's death should be heralded and that in the East it should be announced that it was not quite so.[42]

Vitĕzslav Gardavsky has been philosopher and professor and, after Dubček's fall, stoker. His book *Hoffnung aus der Skepsis* contrasts Greek and Hebrew myth, cosmos in the former and time in the latter.[43] To have time is to be involved in work: yet this is not the hard and alienating labour of a dualistic cosmos, but the joyful work of creation. Indeed, he can say that it is play rather than work because it creates: *Ein Spiel, keine Arbeit: Schöpfertum!* Only with such creative playing does the possibility of civilization arise.[44]

Gardavsky's understanding of the biblical cluster of creation, word and work as play and hope constitutes a significant contribution to the dialogue and to Christian theology itself. He sees the "I" established in the creative act as the only guarantee of freedom. This forms a sort of surplus (*Uberschuss*) of the Word, the Word of both creation and future promise. Such a view rescues Marxist thought from denying human freedom in behalf of generic liberation, and from the limiting effects of its doctrine of surplus value. In this theory of the hope that derives from scepticism, moreover, we find an unusual kinship to the recent "theology of play," as it might be called, among Christian writers who insist that only a doctrine of "free grace" can establish a comedic view of human existence.[45] Such is his *atheistische theologie*.

Gardavsky is better known, however, for his book *God is Not Yet Dead*.[46] Similar views appear here, of course, in particular the contrast between hellenic and Hebraic mythology. Only the latter properly establishes the sort of genuine transcendence that gives rise to subjectivity. This is his burden: "God is not quite dead. Man is not quite alive." First comes a section analyzing five "Monuments": Jacob, Jesus, Augustine, Aquinas and Pascal. The chapter on Jacob is most significant, for Gardavsky's aim is to find what in the Bible makes it "seem close to us and intelligible," and in Jacob he finds the clue to the doctrine of human being. That is, he refuses to select the harsher aspects of Yahweh as tyrant and instead concentrates on the Hebrew experience of "a past which is yet to come." The future orientation provided by crucial events of the past thus affords a transcendent horizon. In Jacob-Israel he finds perfect embodiment of this orientation, confronting the Lord of Time in battle and in covenant and in promise. Jacob's condition, beset by time with its uncertainty and limits, is the context for his freedom in choosing his way ahead. His courage is virtually the substance of his faith, reminiscent of Tillich's definition of "the courage to be." For Gardavsky, Jacob is a Promethean figure in his stubborn wrestling with the will of God, and in his suffering.

Jesus is also an attractive figure in Gardavsky's book, preaching the Kingdom of God through acts of love, which often turn into miraculous occurrences. His thoroughly apocalyptic role leads quickly into the book of Revelation, so beloved of Marxists since Engels's time. Gardavsky sees the tragedy of Christianity in that "false mystical interpretation" of Augustine and others that forfeited the apocalyptic vision of Jesus. Thus: "According to Pascal, the answer did not lie in talking about action, but in talking about Jesus. That is his tragedy, and the tragedy of those who come up with the same answer as his."[47]

The "mystical" interpretation – a favourite critique of Marxist and humanist alike – renders Christianity heteronomous, in that divinity so lords it over humanity as to represent in itself alienating power and command. Since the Enlightenment was essentially a bourgeois movement, its critique is but another form of false consciousness – Gardavsky is at his best when analyzing types of atheism of recent centuries. He sees two forms of outmoded atheism, the antitheism of Enlightenment, which turns to irrationality and cynicism,[48] and that "optimistic atheism – totally committed, inflexible, pedagogic" of early Marxism, particularly in Czechoslovakia.

Gardavsky's typology lists five categories of atheism: practical, conformist, anticlerical-antitheist, abstract humanist and Marxist. It is significant that his initial assumption about all five is presented uncritically: "An atheistic conviction is the product of reasoning alone, even if it is a form of consciousness, and indeed, in the best cases, of self-consciousness."[49] He qualifies the statement by adding that both theism and atheism depend on one's "circumstances" and on how one has "internalized" them. Yet it remains true that the Marxist theory of human dependence on circumstances throws into questionable relief its claim to rationality and science. In Gardavsky's explanation of his types we see a better logic at work. The first two (practical and conformist) are dismissed because of their unreflective nature. Anticlericalism and antitheism are flawed because they uncritically accept a blanket description of the evils of religion so that their caricature plays into the hands of their "enemy." While the next type, abstract humanism, overcomes this fault, it still fails to measure up to genuine Marxist atheism because its recognition of human weakness leads to "emotion" rather than to political action.

What, then, is Marxist atheism? Gardavsky has already attacked certain errors in earlier Marxism, particularly the antireligious crusade of Lenin.[50] Certainly the situation inside Russia posed a dilemma for Lenin, faced with the need to reject religion. He opted for a harsh and "unscientific" militant atheism, appropriate as tactic perhaps but prolonged and intensified both by Communists and by the reaction of the Church. But instead of that harsh type, Gardavsky promotes one that is "not automatically anti-clerical or antitheist." The profile here presented is almost romantic in its idealized cult figure who is critical of religion but only where justified (e.g., only where the Church fails in loyalty to the socialist state), who agrees with Marx that religion is both expression of suffering and a protest against it, but who is "also aware that this coupling of the religious with the social is conditioned by history." Thus the social relationships apart from which human nature is unintelligible (as against the approach of "abstract humanism") force the Marxist into an atheism that functions as metaphysics, "first philosophy" in Aristotle's sense.

Gardavsky's final chapter is entitled "Marxist Atheism as Metaphysics." He must first distinguish such an enterprise from religion, which it resembles, and from dialectics, which it does not. On one hand he thinks that Marxist metaphyics is free from even the "religious illusion;" on the other, it is not the "bad metaphysics" that Engels attacked but a dialectical way of meeting the deepest questions, the "eternal" questions posed in every age by reflective humans. "In this sense, metaphysics represents in objective terms a social requirement." Marxist metaphysics hinges on the relation between present and future, espousing an "open future" consonant with human creative action. And it is based on two certainties:

> Marxism, precisely because it is also atheism, knows that man possesses no more than two basic pieces of insight into himself of which he is absolutely certain: I am a social being who is capable of transcending himself; I know with absolute certainty that I must die.[51]

Hence the dilemma of Marxist atheism: "subjective identity and transcendence" remain "materialist and dialectic" because of the fact of death. Facing death squarely in these final pages, Gardavsky is unrelenting: the individual has no hope of immortality and therefore must rest content with the community as that to which he transfers his value and his hope. His vaunted "practical activity" is held to sublate both Greek and Hebrew theories – here Gardavsky seems sadly inconsistent with his book on hope, where he acknowledges the play of creative work deriving from the biblical tradition. He closes with a poignant portrayal of "love," a secularized and hope-less echo of Paul's hymn to *Agapē* in I Corinthians 13. And he ends with his motto, the atheist answer to the ancient saying *Credo quia absurdum*: "We do not believe in God, *although* it is absurd."

In Gardavsky we have one who remains atheist after considerable reflection on Scripture and by adopting many Hebrew and Christian insights. He feels free to approach even Marx, Engels and Lenin critically; in this he is truly revisionist. But he remains atheist, despite the evident attraction of Christianity. He represents a new breed of Marxist philosopher, breaking the traditional "silence about Jesus," as Lochman put it. And in Milan Machoveč, a fellow Czech philosopher, we have an even more explicit voice after silence.

Jesus for Atheists – Machoveč

The book *Jesus Für Atheisten* (1972) has been called "a minor but indispensable classic which will replace Kautsky's as a study of Jesus."[52] Now Karl Kautsky's *Foundations of Christianity* (1908), while using the obligatory theory of socioeconomic conditioning, was sympathetic not only to the revolutionary elements in Jesus' preaching of the coming Kingdom but also to the clearly communist dimension of the primitive Church (Acts 2:44f, 4:33ff). Interestingly enough, Kautsky detected Essene community influence at this point, but went on to posit advanced communism in diocesan sees with bishops as treasurers – an interpretation of the "consumer communism" of the Jerusalem congregation more appropriate than most Christian exegesis.

Milan Machoveč goes beyond Kautsky in his effort to grasp the *theological* import of Jesus. He admits that traditional Marxists have been guilty of hostility toward religion merely on principle – "since their position is not something which is open to questioning, but is rather a self-evident truth upheld by the ideologically closed institution."[53] In this context he explains the materialism of Marx as "by no means a 'cult of matter' or 'physicalism'," since it referred strictly to the supremacy of the *human*. Likewise, his atheism is "not something affirmative but something *critical*." Atheism has meaning only as a critique, "limited in place and in time." And since the classic Marxist readings of religion were critiques of nineteenth-century representations of God, now modified radically by certain theologians, "Marxists no longer know whether we are still atheists or not in this regard." At the least he warns not to "create a new 'dogma of the non-existence of God'" for all eternity.

Machoveč maintains sympathy with Jesus despite the rigid "historical-materialist methodology" that dictates Marxist approach: "This is how in the end all Marxists think, and they cannot think otherwise." Strange as this sounds, it recalls Gardavsky's flexibility as he bids Marxists use the method in an open and intelligent manner. Taking both men's statements at face value, and remembering that they are now *personae non gratae* to Communist orthodoxy, we note the positive value assigned to the person and work of Jesus. Here is the theology of the Cross again, especially since Machoveč knows that "power was used so thoughtlessly in the Marxist movement, and indeed abused." So the Cross, "the deepest mystery of the New Testament," is not mythology but "a profound and highly relevant truth." Once the socioeconomic roots are exposed, the task of *metanoia* and

of preparing the way of the Kingdom remains. Machoveč sees himself able to support both sides along this way: he has "opted positively for the 'Christian cause'" yet remains "a disciple of Marx."

Jesus' call for repentance, *metanoia,* is seen as "a deep
experience of every honest 'philosophy of man'." The Christ, for
Machoveč, is the Hebrew Son of Man – not its mystified and ele-
vated "fate" in subsequent hellenized dogma – who addresses his
people in behalf of the Kingdom of God. Like Job he is a suffering
Messiah. This emphasis on the humanity and passion of Jesus does
not entail a reduction in significance of the resurrection, however.
On this belief, acknowledged to play a central role in early Christian
thinking, the author provides a sympathetic treatment of Mystery that
tries to avoid the easy explanation of both extremes – either a simple
materialism (of Christian fundamentalism), or an existentialist appeal
to "Easter faith."[54]

Once again we stand before a formidable and gracious
attempt at understanding on the part of an "outsider." Once again we
note obvious problems, especially with the limiting method thrust on
Marxists because of ideological assumptions about the nature of "scientific" explanation. Yet again we acknowledge the profound insight
into biblical religion resulting from close study, and the critical atheism that allows so great a degree of openness to the heart of religion
and to Christ as Founder. The dialogue made possible by such openness enjoyed a sudden moment of light, brilliant if brief, which sheds
its rays on all continuing efforts at dialogue.[55]

PART IV
THE RETURN OF IDOLS

– 10 –

The Complex of Oedipus – Freud

> Three masters, seemingly mutually exclusive, domi-
> nate the school of suspicion: Marx, Nietzsche, and
> Freud. . . . These three masters of suspicion are
> not to be misunderstood, however, as three mas-
> ters of skepticism. They are, assuredly, three great
> "destroyers." But. . . . It is beyond destruction that
> the question is posed as to what thought, reason,
> and even faith still signify.[1]

In his major work on hermeneutics, *De l'Interpretation*: *Essai sur Freud*, Paul Ricoeur continues to expound his "philosophy of the will" by examining Freud as interpreter. He identifies two kinds of interpretation. One is the familiar "recollection of meaning," by which faith seeks understanding in a fresh way; this may be termed "postcritical" and "a second naiveté." It tears away the masks which hide meaning; it "reduces disguises." Beside this stands another sort of interpretation, which Ricoeur calls "exercise of suspicion." It is the latter that bears on our thesis because of its role in the apparent "atheism" espoused by Freud, and the Promethean form of his Oedipus complex.

Sigmund Freud (1856-1939) understood himself to be a kind of scientist, at least in its exploratory function; Ricoeur considers him an exegete. Similarly with Marx and Nietzsche: they are diligent interpreters of what they see as hidden meanings, masked through falsehood either deliberate or unconscious. If the truth is to make us free, they feel called to make the truth free. Since we chose to examine Marx earlier, in relation to the Hegelian movement, we now turn briefly to Freud and Nietzsche, keeping in mind this orienting category: masters of suspicion.

One commentator has warned against "the hazards of reading Freud," while another thinks it necessary to include the section "How to Read Freud" in his analytic.[2] Such caution is salutary lest we seize on Freud's familiar negative categories and miss the value of

---

Notes to Chapter 10 appear on page 337.

his cathartic contribution to the study of religion. Nor should we forget the sage advice of Joseph Jastrow: Freud cannot divest himself of the professor's gown, while Jung always wears a surplice. Thus the love affair that some theologians carry on with Jung may be a temptation to error, while dialogue with Freud may provide needed therapy.[3]

Atheist and Jew

Freud's attitude toward religion is a complex, symbolized by the twin figures of Oedipus and Moses. Like Marx, he remains ambivalent on the subject; indeed, we argue that the shift from ambiguity to ambivalence toward his Jewish inheritance provides the best clue to interpreting Freud's dream. In this we follow recent research, which enlightens the religious dimension of Freud's own "unfinished journey" in a new way, as Justin Miller suggests.[4] The definitive biography by Ernest Jones described him as "an unrepentant atheist," and remarked that "he felt himself to be Jewish to the core." This latter point was accorded new attention in the controversial work of David Bakan, who located Freud solidly within the Jewish mystical tradition ("Freud spent his whole life in a virtual ghetto"). His Jewishness may have remained largely cultural inheritance, but it provided a "source of energy," an intellectual milieu, as well as - here is the striking thesis - an interpretation of dreams. Thus Bakan casts Freud as modern Joseph, consulting the Kabbala for clues in exegesis of the human text. Despite strong opposition to this thesis, support has been given by Klein's *Jewish Origin of the Psychoanalytic Movement* and other analyses of Freud's correspondence and writings that suggest the continuing weight of his religious heritage.

Freud first presented his embryonic thesis on dream interpretation at the weekly game of taroc, a card game based on the Kabbala. It was appropriate, perhaps even symbolic. For Jewish mysticism had layered the school exegesis of Torah with a complex method involving association of ideas and self-knowledge, mixed with certain emphases from the Kabbalistic document, the Zohar, such as numerology and the significance of sexuality and family relationships. Lest we seize on this connection alone, we recall earlier research on the unconscious that influenced Freud, notably that of his teacher Franz Brentano (the only nonmedical lectures he attended at Vienna) and of Schopenhauer on the will.[5] Still, the dynamics of Judaism past and present in his life, the "virtual ghetto" of the early psychoanalytic movement (underlined by Jung's defection) and the rise of virulent anti-Semitism, suggest the human and ideological environment in which he pursued his vocation as therapist, that is, master of suspicion.

The familiar notion that the child is father to the man is extended by Freud to the phenomenon of religion: "god at bottom is nothing but an exalted father." A further development is the parallel between individual childhood and the evolution of the race. The maturing individual regresses to childish ways of coping with problems and fears by turning to religion; civilization is hampered in its development by the illusion of religion. In both cases the same problem of authority obtains: dread of superordinate power. For Ernest Becker this explains Freud's Oedipus complex - "man is the greatest tyrant over man," and selfhood derived from "transaction with *others*" is a dilemma solvable by flight to Oedipal behaviour. Becker draws on Wilhelm Reich's idea of "character armour," "the arming of the personality so that it can manoeuvre in a threatening world."[6]

A different assessment of Freud's theory is given by psychologist H.C. Rümke, who takes seriously *homo religiosus* as the normal maturer who meets with obstacles to his religious development. Such "interruptions" prevent the "basic trust" familiar in psychology from reaching its proper level of maturity. Indeed, one of the weaknesses of the Freudian theory of the origin of religion lies in the acceptance of a phylogenetic model; overpowered by the hostile forces of nature, the individual "gives them the character of a father" and "turns them into gods."[7]

The concept of projection, so important for reductionist theories of the genesis of religion, and familiar in Feuerbach and Marxism, appears strongly in *The Future of an Illusion* (1927), where "the effect of religious consolation may be likened to that of a narcotic." Following the "infantile prototype," "a store of ideas is created, born from man's need to make his helplessness tolerable and built up from the material of memories of the helplessness of his own childhood and the childhood of the human race."[8] In this same book Freud defends this theory as being no different in substance from his earlier view of totemism's rise (*Totem and Taboo*, 1912-13). If anything, his outlook on nature including human nature has become even more pessimistic.

> When the growing individual finds that he is destined to remain a child for ever, that he can never do without protection against strange superior powers, he lends those powers the features belonging to

> the figure of his father; he creates for himself the
> gods whom he dreads, whom he seeks to propiti-
> ate; and whom he nevertheless entrusts with his
> own protection.

Freud distinguishes illusion from both error and delusion. For both are false, whereas illusion may be true: "Thus we call a belief an illusion when a wish-fulfilment is a prominent factor in its motivation, and in doing so we disregard its relations to reality, just as the illusion itself sets no store by verification." By "wish-fulfil-ment" Freud means the emergence in consciousness of the deep desires of the unconscious, so that our apparently reasonable attitudes and expectations are in reality dominated from below. Freud is careful to note that because an idea satisfies a wish we should not conclude that it is false. Yet his reliance on the concept of project-ion (from unconscious into consciousness rather than from earth to heaven, as was Feuerbach's notion) and his relating it firmly to the concept of fulfilment of desire take him well along the way of etiolo-gical explanation of the phenomenon of religion.

The role of the father in Freud's theory is decisive, for it applies both within the family unit and in the history of the race, the primal father. But a difficulty attends the paternalist model. For it cuts both ways, and thus suggests an ideology rather than a testable theory. For one thing, as Gordon Allport remarks:

> It seems curious that while Freud insists that belief
> in God is a projection of dependence and love
> associated with the earthly father, he overlooks the
> fact that by the same token atheism may be con-
> strued as the projection of ambivalence or hatred
> associated with the male parent.[9]

For another, as we shall see, the projection of father into primal father remains mere speculation with no evidence from "primitive" study.

Another aspect of religion is actually more significant for Freud's growing sense of the importance of social issues (*Kultur*): religion is a hindrance to the development of civilization because it is not only an illusion but a neurosis. Just as childhood involves a neu-rotic phase in the maturation process, so (phylogenetically) does the history of the race. On these grounds:

> Religion would thus be the universal neurosis of
> humanity; like the obsessional neurosis of children,
> it arose out of the Oedipus complex, out of the
> relation to the father. If this view is right, it is to
> be supposed that a turning-away from religion is

bound to occur with the fatal inevitability of a process of growth, and that we find ourselves at this
very juncture in the middle of that phase of development.[10]

The idea of religion as a universal "obsessional neurosis" goes back to his first essay on religion, "Obsessive Actions and Religious Practices" (1907). Another decade of research convinced him that attitudes to totem animals and to human fathers were analogous, as were relations among totems, primal fathers and God-figures.

The Oedipus complex was noted as early as *The Interpretation of Dreams* (1900) as the crucial example of the "two typical dreams" of incest and murder - love of mother and death of father. In the 1910 lectures on "The Origin and Development of Psychoanalysis" it was called the "nuclear complex [*Kernkomplex*] of every neurosis."[11] The repressive origin of religious ritual is now well advanced, and religious phenomena are understood on the model of neurotic symptoms of the individual. It might seem easy to criticize Freud's dependence on evolutionary theories of the emergence of religion (between animism and science), in particular his stubborn loyalty to Robertson Smith. The latter's speculation on totemic behaviour patterns, especially taboos on incest and murder, contributes to what V.P. Gay considers the "weak model" of obsessional neurosis in the book. Hans Küng concludes: "It was precisely this ethnological explanation of religion and this evolutionary scheme of the early classical writers on the history of religion which Freud adopted."[12]

The work in question, however, is quite open in admitting the speculation involved, noting that it attempts only a reconstruction of *psychical* history on psychoanalytic grounds and is not to be misconstrued as offering a "single source" theory of religion. Moreover, in defining taboo at the beginning of the second chapter, Freud notes its duality. On one hand is the sense of "sacred, consecrated." Today this is termed *mana*, the Melanesian companion term for the positive pole of which taboo is foil. Their combination recalls Otto's *mysterium tremendum et fascinosum*, or sense of the "numinous." The negative is Freud's chief interest - "uncanny, dangerous, forbidden, and unclean." In 1919 he had delineated the dimension of the Uncanny (*unheimlich*) traditionally regarded as culturally peripheral or underground, yet containing a dynamism best seen in the phenomenon of Surrealism. (André Breton is a chief influence in relating Freud to the surrealist movement.) Oscar Dominguez once produced a deck of surreal playing-cards. The suit of spades is renamed "dreams," its master card entitled "Freud, Magus of Dream."[13]

Archaic Heritage

> I have repeatedly been led to suspect that the psychology of the neuroses has stored up in it more of the antiquities of human development than any other source.[14]

Freud would add to neuroses the world of dreams as preservers of mental antiquities. He coined the term *archaic heritage* to describe this innate but unconscious lore, of "phylogenetic origin," roughly analogous to Jung's "racial unconscious," although with less positive function. Human consciousness is a kind of text, and Freud's theory of false consciousness, like Hegel's unhappy consciousness, means that we are mutilated texts, the truth hidden under masking layers that require an appropriate method of removal. Freud considered himself to have uncovered the third of the human traumas, the "narcissistic wounds" self-inflicted by humanity: he sees the end of anthropocentrism with the Copernican revolution, of privileged status with Darwin, and of rational primacy with the Unconscious.

It is in this context that dreams receive special attention from Freud. He takes them as his model, the model "of all the disguised, substitutive, and fictive expressions of human wishing or desire."[15] Hence the importance of his 1900 work, *The Interpretation of Dreams.* Paul Ricoeur concentrates on the *Traumdeutung*, particularly chapter seven with its quasi-physical "topography." He sees in Freud a struggle to articulate the passage from the dynamics of desire to the semantics of meaning.[16]

On Ricoeur's view, Freud is a symbolist: he is understood adequately not when reduced to sexologist but when grasped as exegete. If dreams occupy a "privileged place" in his topography of the unconscious, it is because they revert to our childhood and thus allow us to recover the heritage still so powerful in its repressed form. The call for oneiric interpretation in symbolic mode, sometimes termed "anagogic," suggests Freud's kinship to theological exegetes who struggled with similar problems of hidden meaning and surface masking. And if we substitute the idea of sin for that of desire, we find even closer parallels.

> Since desires hide themselves in dreams interpretation must substitute the light of meaning for the darkness of desire. Interpretation is lucidity's

answer to ruse. We touch here upon the source of
any theory of interpretation understood as the
reduction of illusion.[17]

Another theological commentator on Freud agrees with Ricoeur's interpretation. Hans Küng notes the new reductionist physicalism that was overthrowing the idealist philosophy of nature (*Naturphilosophie*) at the very time Freud was developing his theories and moving from physiology to psychology, from neurology to psychopathology. Hence the task of therapy as exposition of repression, and the decisive place of the interpretation of dreams.[18] Yet this very faith in science complicates the positive appraisal of Ricoeur and Küng, despite their recognition of the complication. Some psychologists seem more critical than the theologians. Heije Faber, for one, underlines Freud's agnostic approach to the study of religion (a fact noted also by Ernest Jones as well as C.G. Jung): "Freud himself never struggled with the question of religious truth. . . . His observations do not rest on empirical investigation."[19]

Oedipus and the Religious Illusion

In approaching "illusion," Paul Ricoeur notes that believers may "sidestep his radical questioning of religion" in view of Freud's scientism and agnosticism, while unbelievers "may confuse psychoanalysis with this unbelief and agnosticism."[20] Ricoeur's escape from the dilemma is by way of the iconoclastic nature of psychoanalysis: "this 'destruction' of religion can be the counterpart of a faith purified of all idolatry." Iconoclasm remains the end of psychoanalysis. What lies beyond - faith or unfaith - is neither its concern nor its decision.
    Freud's own iconoclasm may be related to the problem of alienation already encountered.

What Feuerbach wanted from the philosophical
standpoint and Marx from the political-social,
Freud sought from the standpoint of depth psychology: emancipation, comprehensive liberation, more
humanity on the part of man. It meant in particular opposition to tutelage, domination, oppression
by religion, Church, God himself.[21]

Freud was concerned with the "fall" obvious between the child and the adult: the downward way from curiosity, the vital energy of sexual awakening, to mental inhibition and alienation from oneself. That he sees this so largely in terms of sexual instincts and their repression should not hide the profound truth about the alienation process that he uncovers.[22] Where sexual energy is sublimated into positive expression, it continues the spirit of freedom, of investigation and experimentation. Since the Oedipus complex is the *telos* of childhood sexuality, its proper resolution provides the key to therapy, including that required by the religious illusion.

We are taking Oedipus as Freud's symbol for the Promethean will, which overcomes domination and establishes personal autonomy.

> King Oedipus, who slew his father Laius and married his mother Jocasta, merely shows us the fulfilment of our childhood wishes. . . . Here is one in whom these primeval [*urzeitlich*] wishes of our childhood have been fulfilled, and we shrink back from him with the whole force of the repression by which those wishes have since that time been held down within us.[23]

Here is the familiar story of rebellion against minority status, external power and authority (heteronomy). It explains, according to Freud's theory, that our "two fundamental taboos," incest and murder, derive from "the sense of guilt of the son," the psychic power that is "nothing else than Kant's Categorical Imperative" (*T-T* 191, 6).

Now as Joseph Jastrow notes, "the classic Oedipus myth happens not to fit the Freudian circumstance at all. . . . *Oedipus* the king of old, could have had no 'Oedipus' fixation" since he did not know his real mother until his doom was working itself out. More importantly, Jastrow charges Freud with sexualizing the family relationship, importing sexual categories and interpretations into what can be analyzed more properly and simply without them. He finds "no warrant in biology, physiology or psychology" for the complex as described, "with its infantile sexuality and the ubiquity of 'Oedipus'." Nevertheless, Freud's theory constituted a radical critique of Enlightenment views of human freedom and autonomy. Rationalistic optimism was confronted with a theory that the ego is not master in its own house, a determinism incompatible with therapeutic liberation. Both humanistic and existentialist psychoanalysis reacted to this "crisis of autonomy." They accused Freud of inconsistency, of holding a theoretical assumption about human autonomy contradicted by his clinical discoveries about the determinism of human behaviour.[24]

Thus we may query the sexual emphasis that Freud gives to his theory, while noting that it stands for the arena of maturation and autonomy in his system. And perhaps it itself masks a phenomenon familiar to theology, if recently neglected. For while ego and id struggle for supremacy, we have a situation strikingly analogous to that described by historical theology as concupiscence.

The most familar name in regard to this concept is that of Augustine, although he has suffered a very bad press on its account. Like Freud, he recognized that human motivation and behaviour suffer from a structural fault, a perverse willing; also like Freud he acknowledged a primary role to human sexuality in the energetics of such willing. He saw two kinds of love, with corresponding volitions and even entire kingdoms or Cities working out their fateful dynamics. Authentic love is *dilectio* or *caritas;* its reverse or perverse form is *cupiditas* or *libido.* The distance between them may be measured by the difference between true desire for genuine "ends" and mistaken desire for mere means taken by an illusion for ends in themselves. That which is to be used (*uti*) is thus enjoyed, and that which should be enjoyed (*frui*) is used as means. Such exchange reduces God to a utilitarian role and - most significantly for our thesis - contains an implicit hostility that is the hallmark of pride (*superbia*), the root of sin.[25]

While Augustine's psychological analysis is much like that of Freud's, the role of sexuality is not. No doubt the popular image of the great Christian Father as identifying sin with sexuality is informed in large part by his tendency to illustrate concupiscence with sexual lust. Yet he could protest that his adversary Julian wrongly attributed to him such a restricted concept. Because his analytic maintains the phenomenon of pride at its centre, he can distinguish a concupiscence that is "praiseworthy" and a rightful "desire of wisdom." Moreover, the description of human being with heart curved back on itself (*cor incurvatus in se*) challenges Freud's interpretation of human selfhood as a determinate structure faulted by an illusory freedom. Since Augustine follows the classical understanding of freedom as self-determination, the move from pride to self-love and thence to self-idolization seems not so far. In her work *Freud and Original Sin*, Sharon MacIsaac states: "Concupiscence is self-alienation - self-alienation which has its roots in appetitive autonomy."[26]

The instincts, like the negative pole in energy cells, seek their discharge against the "control" of ego. Yet such an analogy is not so helpful when one considers the dialectical play of id, ego and superego in Freud's mature topography of human nature. For the mastery sought by ego is hampered not simply by the passionate id but by social inhibitions, which function by way of reification, much as in the Marxist interpretation of cultural forms. But the power derives from the energy built up through repression rather than through the distance achieved by projection; herein lies a significant advance of the Freudian over the Feuerbachian-Marxist interpretation of religion as projection. Freud's concern is the shift from ego-libido to object-libido and the "reality principle" at stake in such disputed passage. Further weight is given the contrast when one considers how much Freud speaks of "work" in this connection. The "mechanisms" of both daydream and nightmare constitute work. And it is the work of sublimation that sublates the alienated dimension of such works. Indeed, Freud's economic terminology not only applies to his treatment of artistic genius but extends (seriously) to jokes and humour.[27]

Oedipus at the Crossroads

To commemorate Freud's fiftieth birthday in 1906, the Austrian sculptor Karl Maria Schwerdtner presented him with a bronze medallion bearing his resemblance on the obverse, and on the reverse a Greek design of Oedipus answering the Sphinx, with the inscription from Sophocles: "Who divined the famed riddle and was a man most mighty?" Now the riddle had been posed as to human identity (what goes on four legs, then two, then three?), and Oedipus headed for his destiny in Thebes with the reputation of a Magus. For Sophocles the dramatic irony of the Oedipus cycle consisted in the dialectic of sight and blindness. Tiresias was a blind seer; Oedipus could see but was blind to the truth. And when at last he "saw," he blinded himself in appropriate irony for his dreadful unseeing acts against Laius and Jocasta.

Freud is almost blind to this dimension. For him Oedipus is but a pawn, a two-dimensional figure in his sexology. Similarly, Moses as intermediary between God and Israel, liberator of his people and utterer of Torah, recedes behind the role of apparent victim in the hypothetical drama of primal sacrifice. There is ultimately, however, a blending of the two characters in a broader complex, so that Oedipus/Moses maintains continuity as the clue to the human Torah, the drama of world history itself. Once again the issue has to do with a struggle of wills and the question of who will have the last word.

In Freud's understanding of the dynamism of human development there is a like stress on autonomous willing to that of the Promethean rebellion encountered so far. There are differences, of course, not least the fact that an oedipal personality is a relational one: the self is formed in relation to parents, set free (or not) within the same set of limited choices and reflected on the grand scale of culture. In comparing the Freudian image of man with that of Reinhold Niebuhr, Peter Homans states:

> The Oedipus myth articulates for all men the innermost problematic depths of selfhood and, as such, is the psychoanalytic counterpart of Biblical myth. The energies of a culture, like those of the individual, are circumscribed by Eros (cultural process) and by Thanatos (return of the repressed).[28]

Both phylogeny and ontogeny - the individual and the race - are organized about the oedipal relationships. Here are primal father and archetypal hero, defiance and rebellion, and consequent suffering; here also is the origin of culture, of man on his own. Not that Oedipus is clearly Promethean - he carries too much of the ambivalence of repression and guilt to act the Liberator as Prometheus does. Yet his relational style improves on the lonely Titan and on the dehumanizing effects that his call for total freedom seems to bring.

Erik Erikson has identified this thrust toward wholesome relationships with others as the logic of Oedipus. He is speaking of Freud's relationship to Wilhelm Fliess in Vienna (1887-1902), the transition period from physiological and neurological interest (leaving behind the Helmholtzian, mechanistic viewpoint) to psychoanalysis. Freud called Fliess his "Other one" to whom he could entrust what he was not ready to entrust to "the others." Erikson's account of this phase surveys Freud's working through the universal father image and its distortions; he comments:

> Freud now could break through to the first prehistoric Other of them all: the loving mother. He was free to discover the whole Oedipus complex, and to recognize it as a dominant theme in world literature and in mythologies around the world.[29]

The complex of fantasies making up Freud's Oedipus mirrors the individual's relational development as replication of the racial and ancient drama of desire and patricide. In reference to our thesis concerning the Promethean will as constructor of atheistic autonomy, this oedipal organization of the self symbolizes adaptation to that masculine "inner tyrant" of the patriarch and his social counterparts, further symbolized in the superego. The oedipal crisis thus provides the clue to alienation, and hence to possibility of reconciliation. As the subject experiences the other, the reality principle is allowed its proper play through what has been termed the "coefficient of adversity of things" (Bachelard), the sheer objectivity of world. In turn this is transition from nature to culture, as others are delimited by lawful boundaries. Otherness and Law stand for the normalization of the subject, the passage through Oedipus as complex to culture.[30]

Needless to say, Freud's use of the Oedipus story is so idiosyncratic that it hides the richness of the original myth. Oedipus, as Robert Graves has suggested, may well be a protagonist in a story of advent (*eleusis*), thus participating in the ritual death of the solar king. Far from being evidence for common or universal human experience, it shared rather that theatrical distance from which *hoi polloi* watched - with pity and fear - the strange logic of tragic heroes and divine Furies work itself out to the bitter end.[31] In this sense both Prometheus and Oedipus have suffered as much at the hands of their admiring interpreters as they did in the ancient tales.

Peter Homans appreciates the significance of the Oedipus complex for theology as do few others. He distinguishes mechanism and transcendence as the moments in self-development experienced in the oedipal dimension.

> If such oedipal organization is an important link between mechanism and transcendence, one might expect oedipal sexuality to have a place in theological discussions of the self. But that is not the case. Instead, we find at this point a gap or blank. To move, as these theological discussions do, from a critique of mechanism to the assertion of transcendence without indicating intermediate process and considerations is reminiscent of the characteristic theological aversion to continuity.[32]

Although the context is Homans's comparison of Freud with Niebuhr, he has in mind a general theological stress on discontinuity, on the contrast between nature and grace or Kierkegaard's "infinite qualitative distinction between time and eternity" perhaps. Psychoanalysis, on the other hand, seeks meaning - "imaginative, associational interplay amidst apparently diverse functions and constructions of the self." Homans thus can state baldly: "Freud's psychology is one of continuity, or mediating between the gaps created by theology." For athough theology rightly criticizes the psychological "mechanisms" that function deterministically, it fails to follow through as psychology does in its second stress on continuity. Instead it introduces a new kind of determinism, and with it new gaps: the theological determinism of divine will as (heteronomous) moral force. Thus the superego is "heir to the Oedipus complex" and transcendence means "the transcendence of the superego."[33]

Life Against Death

In Freud's warfare of the instincts, Eros resists Thanatos: the sexual instincts are "the true life instincts" that "operate against the purpose of the other instincts," namely death.[34] Freud's understanding of libido faces the infantile narcissism of its beginnings, but looks for a development from self-interest to a truly relational orientation in which the other is encompassed within life-affirmation. And such development depends on an environment of love. Although Freud's analysis of human love tends to settle for a typology of functional forms, as in the essay *On Narcissism*, there remains the insight that love is the final power and arbiter in human relationships.

Writing to his theologian friend Oskar Pfister in 1910, Freud stated, "As you admit, I have done a great deal for love." And to Einstein in 1933, facing the Nazi menace, he called for a love "without sexual aim" as an indirect way of opposing war: "There is no need for psycho-analysis to be ashamed to speak of love in this connection, for religion itself uses the same words: 'Thou shalt love thy neighbour as thyself'."[35]

If love reconciles the warfare both inner and outer, then Freud's answer to the problem of alienation consists in its unifying power. The filial revolt and its legacy of guilt, taboo and repression may yet lead to a happier issue. The totem meal, which so impressed Freud, may derive from his notion of the Oedipus complex, but it holds the key to the healing of relationships. In *Totem and Taboo* this aspect becomes clarified only at the end; meanwhile there is the mass of speculative material based on Frazer, Marrett, Robertson Smith, Durkheim and others. But in his final chapter ("The Infantile Recurrence of Totemism") he turns to the nature of the sacrificial meal as "an act of social fellowship between the deity and his worshippers." He is quoting the words of Robertson Smith, which are reinforced by subsequent biblical scholarship regarding the covenantal nature of Israel's relation to Yahweh, and the primary role of sacrifice as thanksgiving rather than propitiation. When grace (*charis*) begets gratitude, the result is a communion meal of thanksgiving (*eucharistia*). It recalls the festive finale of classical Comedy, in which marriage inaugurates a new and wider family group - a new society, in fact. The wedding banquet symbolizes this logical end of romantic action. Northrop Frye has described the Bible as "romantic comedy" in genre. He has in mind the structure of romance and its comic resolution. Since "comedy ends in a festive society," he observes: "A comic resolution, in fact, could almost be defined as an action that breaks out of the Oedipus ring, the destruction of a family or other close-knit social group by the tensions and jealousies of its members."[36]

Ricoeur's book on Freud ends with suggestions on "how a path that Freud has closed may be reopened" regarding guilt and consolation; here I suggest that beyond the theme of totemism may lie not the eccentric and precious theme of *Moses and Monotheism* but a recovery of Freud's own better insight into the significance of the holy feast. For he grasped the essential connection: "Sacrifice and festival go together among all races: each sacrifice entails a holiday and no holiday can be celebrated without a sacrifice." The god and his worshippers are "communicants" one with another, as closely bound as to constitute "one bond and one flesh." Thus the emphasis on sacrifice falls on the power of the life offered rather than on the killing. The festal atmosphere (holiday is "a prescribed excess") is thus central to biblical religion, and the motif of renewal through death sounds the same note of life against death as Freud's theory of instincts.

Unfortunately Freud did not pursue this positive insight into the nature of religion. Instead he reverted to his familiar theory of the primal horde of Darwinist speculation and the consequent powerful and jealous father who "keeps the females for himself and drives away" the growing sons. Even though such a "primal state of society has nowhere been observed," he insists that "By basing our argument upon the celebration of the totem we are in a position to give an answer: One day the expelled brothers joined forces, slew and ate the father, and thus put an end to the father horde."

The dynamics of this speculative reconstruction supply the elements of Freud's new myth of Oedipus: the sons repented of their deed, banned "the killing of the father substitute, the totem;" and denied themselves the "liberated women." "Thus they created the two fundamental taboos of totemism out of the *sense of guilt of the son*, and for this very reason these had to correspond with the two repressed wishes of the Oedipus complex." This bold thesis is of the greatest importance for Freud, since he concludes that "the beginnings of religion, ethics, society, and art meet in the Oedipus complex." Therefore his insistence in these pages that "god is in every case modelled after the father . . . god at bottom is nothing but an exalted father" quite overcomes whatever insights emerge concerning other functions for the sacred banquet. His confession that "I am at a loss to indicate the place of the great maternal deities who perhaps everywhere preceded the paternal deities" further weakens the thesis, as does his superficial sketch of Greek religion. Yet he does acknowledge the power of Greek tragedy, the suffering of Dionysus; "one can easily understand how the almost extinct drama was reviewed in the Middle Ages in the Passion of Christ."[37]

The flaw in Freud's approach to religion is perhaps appreciated best by examining the definition of love, of human relatedness, at its core. Erich Fromm has compared it to the competitiveness of modern capitalistic humanity, similar to H.S. Sullivan's description of the alienated, marketing personality for whom sexuality denotes an "egotism *à deux*." Fromm himself pursues the kind of alienation at its heart even further, to compare it with that of the autistic personality. Since Freud's view of love tends to be pathological, it resembles the masochism/sadism polarity later developed by Sartre. But insofar as autism participates in the self-destructive wish for omniscience and omnipotence, the typical withdrawal and disorientation suggests the similarity to the Freudian understanding of personal alienation. Thus Fromm concludes that the modern concept of God befits "the alienated culture of success . . . a psychological device to make one better fitted for the competitive struggle." Freud attempts to correct or dispel this concept, but since he operates with categories of alienated selfhood it proves difficult indeed to recover much of substance.[38]

Freud's contribution to the Promethean will in its rejection of religion may remain ambiguous, but his popular influence has convinced many that a sufficient explanation of religion lies in the immature wish for an authoritarian father-figure. Other psychologists disagree. Gordon Allport recognizes the partiality of any "single formula" explanation of religion, and notes that the "developed person will not fabricate his religion out of some emotional fragment but will seek a theory of Being in which all fragments are meaningfully ordered." Psychoanalyst Otto Rank had questioned the rationalizing attempt of psychology whereas "man is born beyond psychology and he dies beyond it, but he can *live* beyond it only through vital experience of his own - in religious terms, through revelation, conversion or rebirth." Another psychoanalyst, J.C. Flügel, has made a significant point, that "Christianity is predominantly a son and brother religion and not a father religion."[39]

Here is the clue to a revaluation of the death of Jesus. Freud selects a specific theory of atonement, the "substitutionary," according to which the death of God's Son is the necessary expiation for the weight of sin (*pondus peccati*) sundering human from divine. In Anselm of Canterbury's famous formulation, the question *Cur deus Homo*? is answered by the need for a God-Man to bear the burden from each side to the other. It is a transactional model, the heart of classical theism, and therefore offered to Freud an apparent instance of the totemism he found in both "savages and neurotics." Thus Freud's theological option was a fateful decision for his view of religion. He missed the alternative and complementary theories of atonement, assigning privileged status to the one compatible with his preconception of the function of sacrifice as expiatory. The "weight of sin" is translated into the weight of guilt, with tragic consequences since genuine satisfaction is almost impossible when covenant basis and sacrificial cult are so dissevered.

Freud's case for atheism, then, is as ambivalent as his Oedipus complex. His pursuit of speculative theory to explain the origin and development of religion is less helpful as both psychology and theology explore the complexity of human being. This distinction has been formulated by theologian Karl Barth, between exact science and dogmatism. Writing of "man as an object of theological knowledge," he notes the kind of "scientific anthropology" that assists this task, and the speculation that hampers:

> the exact science of man cannot be the enemy of the Christian confession. It becomes this only when it dogmatises on the basis of its formulae and hypotheses, becoming the exponent of a philosophy and world-view, and thus ceasing to be exact science.[40]

From Oedipus to Moses

Freud's Moses, like his Oedipus, develops along a trajectory related to our motif of prometheanism. We noted before how the question of Freud's relationship to his Jewish heritage has been enlightened by recent studies that draw on the resources of his correspondence with

Jung and others, published since 1960. An important contribution of these studies concerns the hermeneutic that the young Freud brought to the work and world of our dreams. Orthodox study and interpretation of Torah was a fruitful source of his oneiric exegesis. Writing to Martha Bernays in 1882, he states: "My old Jew provided several more ingenious attempts of the kind to explain and support the Scriptures. I knew the method."[41]

Thus without drawing lines of strict causality between the early scriptural studies and the *Traumdeutung*, we may look for similarities in content as well as method. If Freud remains something of an "infidel Jew," it is the less surprising that he soon moves the motifs of Oedipus and Hamlet back to the figure of Moses as to the archetype behind such ektypes. Here is his truly heroic Titan, about whom such fundamental and essential crises gather that he stands forth as the virtual centre of world history. Marthe Robert's work *D'Oedipe à Moïse* regards the essays on Moses and monotheism as "Freud's dream." They were motivated by the wish to cleanse himself of his father Jakob and of the paternal (patriarchal) Jewishness. The anxiety over anti-Semitism forms a substantive part of this motivation, on her thesis, related to the fundamental tension between the universal and the particular, the conflict between "Rome and Judaism." In a letter to Arnold Zweig he noted that his original intention was to entitle the first essay "The Man Moses: A Historical Novel." This literary genre would leave him free to reconstruct a persona beyond the issues of incest and murder, beyond Oedipus, Jocasta and Laius to Gentile and Jew, to Moses the Egyptian adopting the Jews as his chosen people and being murdered by them - that is, by Freud the author. As Oedipus was for him "that mythological lawbreaker," so Freud himself is able to "break" the Lawgiver in this dreamwork. (He had long possessed a little collection of "graven images" on display in his study.) The Jewish heritage of guilt advanced in *Totem and Taboo* is reaffirmed and sharply personalized. "Moses is the symbol of orthodoxy, the author of the Law, the figure responsible for imposing its heavy yoke."[42]

Freud recounts ("Der Moses des Michelangelo," 1914) his fascination with the statue by Michelangelo, returning to San Pietro in Vincoli daily during three weeks in Rome in 1913, as to the place of revelation. Details of interest to other observers - the phenomenon of the horns (in Rabbinic lore, cones of light signifying the prophetic authority), the symbolism of the central place in the tomb of Julius II between Rachel and Leah (*vitae contemplativa et activa*) - are less important than the striking focus of the eyes, and the hand grasping the tables of Law, the index finger on the beard suggesting a hasty action corrected. For these belong to the cryptic message Freud seeks to decode. As he stands in contemplation before the work of genius, he reflects on the "almost oppressively solemn calm" emanating from it, its "sublime repose." He concludes (providing sketches by way of illustration) that Michelangelo has caught his subject in the moment of calm after his violent outburst against the Jewish abomination with the golden calf, and quotes the explanatory passage Exodus 32:7-35. Freud comes to regard Moses as having withheld punishment, as the superego restrains its wrath. To his view, "Michelangelo has placed a different Moses on the tomb of the Pope, one superior to the historical or traditional Moses." The artist displays the "frozen wrath" of one who has won an inward victory "for the sake of a cause to which he has devoted himself."

So Freud's journey from the archeology to the teleology of the human psyche comes to rest at length on his "overinterpretation" of the central character in the Jewish drama. Like Michelangelo, Freud has "had the presumption to emend the sacred text." In a letter to the B'nai Brith lodge of which he was a member for thirty years, he called this Jewish heritage one of "dark emotional powers." Moses became for him a truly "Freudian" father-figure. In Paul Ricoeur's words, "this Moses had to be glorified as an esthetic fantasy and liquidated as a religious fantasy." But the price was high:

> One can guess how much it cost Freud to run counter to Jewish pride at the very moment when the storm of Nazi persecution was breaking out, when his books were being burned and his publishing house ruined, and when he himself had to flee Vienna and take refuge in London: all this must have been a terrible "work of mourning" for Freud the man.[43]

The puzzle of human being to the unravelling of which he had dedicated his life turns finally on the mosaic symbolized in the Jewish figure of titanic proportions. The complex named Oedipus has now encountered another godlike being, both victim and victor, both id and superego. Heteronomy has been displaced, but autonomy carries with it the tragic sense of a loss maintained by a living memory and a continuing tradition. If the child is father to the man, so also are one's fathers to the child. And their collective name, for Freud, is Moses.

- 11 -

The Dance of Dionysus - Nietzsche

> And do you know what "the world" is to me?
> Shall I show it to you in my mirror? This world: a
> monster of energy, without beginning, without end;
> a firm, iron magnitude of force . . . my *Dionysian*
> world of the eternally self-creating, the eternally
> self-destroying, this mystery world. . . . This world
> is the will to power - and nothing besides! And
> you yourselves are also this will to power - and
> nothing besides!
>
> (*WP* 1067)[1]

Someone who takes as the meaning of *world* the category "will to power"; who announces the death of God; who seeks to replace the Christian "slave" morality with that of "the Overman"; whose key symbol is the eternal recurrence of the Same; who preaches Dionysus against the Crucified - surely he is the great modern exemplar of Promethean atheism. Thus Friedrich Nietzsche (1844-1900) appears to disciples and enemies alike. Walter Kaufmann summarizes his significance as "Philosopher, Psychologist, Antichrist."

The Will to Power

Nietzsche sees three "images of man" dominating modernity, those of Rousseau, Goethe and Schopenhauer. The first led to a popular and revolutionary power; Goethe represents the height of theoretical man ("Faust the liberator of the world becomes a mere world traveller"); Schopenhauer's pessimism and his concept of recurrence provide key ideas for Nietzsche's thought.[2]

Notes to Chapter 11 appear on page 342.

Arthur Schopenhauer (1788-1860) deserves more than a note in these pages, yet perhaps he is best appreciated through Nietzsche. He is famous as the modern pessimist, although his major work, *The World as Will and Idea* (*Die Welt als Wille und Vorstellung*, 1819), resembles Kant's attempt to locate the limits of knowledge and to secure an alternative to merely rational understanding. For Kant this was the practical or moral reason; for Schopenhauer it is the will. Enlightenment theories of knowledge had followed the classical tradition that reason rules passion. Schopenhauer advances the voluntarist alternative by showing the connection of epistemology with psychology, as did Hume. I grasp the phenomenon of my bodily existence through my will; by a "great extension" of the same sort of willing representation, all phenomena are constituted a world. A distinct ambiguity remains concerning his philosophy, since his concept of *Vorstellung* entails a pessimism about the reliability involved even in the process of willing.

Nietzsche follows Schopenhauer rather than Kant, attributing the latter's assumption of moral universals to his love of symmetry in reasoning rather than to genuine insight into the nature of morality. He agrees with Schopenhauer's category of *Erbsünde*, the essential fault "at the heart of existence itself." It is this perception that demands renunciation, the free choice of the tragic hero. Yet his "pessimism" is methodological. In the end he rejects the pessimist, along with that "unjustified generalization" of will that he attributes to psychology. But if not psychology, where does willing belong? Within epistemology. Willing is a reaching out, a mastery; not mere physical "force" but the specific affect that invests world with reality. Nietzsche's theory of knowledge traces the way from truth to art, in which the decisive move is art as the "distinctive form" or "configuration" of will to power. We shall return to this theme. Here we wish to note in a preliminary way how the will to power plays a revolutionary role in the philosophy of Nietzsche.[3]

The time of Nietzsche was a time of revolution, rejection of things past, buoyant hope in the potential of the freedman of the new age. For instance, Richard Wagner's summons to revolution in art (*Die Kunst und die Revolution*, 1849) was matched by his fervour in revolutionary events - Leipzig 1830, Dresden 1849. His views echo the Promethean free will:

> I desire to destroy the rule of the one over the other, of the dead over the living, of matter over the spirit; I desire to shatter the power of the mighty, of the law, and of property. Let man's *own* will be his master, his *own* desire his only law, his

own strength his total property, for *the free man alone is sacred*, and *nothing* is higher than He . . . the living revolution, *man become God*.[4]

Nietzsche's early admiration for Wagner was transformed by the *reichsdeutsch* program of Bayreuth. He rejected the Christian-Germanic hero in favour of a different replacement for Christ, namely the Dionysus of *Die Geburt der Tragödie*. At this time Nietzsche was becoming aware of the work of Bruno Bauer and Max Stirner. Such men heralded the birth of a post-Christian age through their radical critique of biblical and historical religion and the development of the man-god from the God-Man. The "surmounting of man" led to the idea of the Overman (*Übermensch*) first bruited in Stirner's circle. The latter's thesis is the familiar opposition: if Christ is Overman, man cannot be truly an "I." Setting free the human ego is the new program Nietzsche shares with the successors of the Young Hegelians.

Beyond Nihilism

The will to power is Nietzsche's answer to what he detects as the crisis of modernity, the onslaught of "European nihilism." By this he means the end of the Christian God, the transcendent Being with power over all beings, "the movement whose essential interpretation he concentrates in the terse sentence: God is dead" (Heidegger). Christianity granted to human being an absolute value, thus reversing the truth about our "smallness and accidental occurrence in the flux of becoming and passing away." Its morality provided "the great antidote against practical and theoretical nihilism" (*WP* 4). Does Nietzsche's utter rejection of Western morality imply a nihilism, whether axiological or metaphysical? This is a difficult question; but we may conclude that he seeks a free and conscious confrontation with nihilism in order to revaluate the human project, reorder it according to rational possibilities. The will to power must serve the new and higher truth: the eternal recurrence of the same.[5]

The year 1888 was most significant for Nietzsche - it was the year before insanity overtook him, the year of *The Case of Wagner*, *Twilight of the Idols*, *The Antichrist* and *Ecce Homo*. He had intended to proceed with the four-part *Revaluation of all Values* (itself a replacement for the projected *The Will to Power*), but only the preface and initial essay, *The Antichrist*, were completed. The working title of the second essay was "The Free Spirit: Critique of Philosophy as a Nihilistic Movement." Instead, he turned to that final outburst of megalomania, which nonetheless contains the deepest truth about modernity. He identifies himself with Dionysus, now himself a crucified figure, the sacrifice required for the fate of Europe ("Why I Am a Destiny").

In *The Birth of Tragedy* Dionysus represented the negative pole in the creative dialectic necessary for Apollo's engendering of tragic genius. From this early aesthetics Nietzsche gradually developed a Dionysus charged with polar energy in a synthesis of both classical gods: "in tragedy this antithesis is sublimated [*Aufgehoben*] into a unity."[6] This positive stance is described with reference to Goethe:

> Such a spirit who has *become free* stands amid the cosmos with a joyous and trusting fatalism, in the faith that only the particular is loathsome, and that all is redeemed and affirmed in the whole - *he does not negate any more*. Such a faith, however, is the highest of all possible faiths: I have baptized it with the name of *Dionysus*.[7]

In the closing sections Nietzsche criticizes Winckelmann (his old Basle colleague) and even Goethe for viewing the Greeks too rationalistically, missing the Dionysian orgy, particularly the affirmation of life and "the eternal joy of creating":

> All this is meant by the word Dionysus: I know no higher symbolism than this *Greek* symbolism of the Dionysian festivals. Here the most profound instinct of life, that directed toward the future of life, the eternity of life, is expressed religiously - and the way to life, procreation, as the *holy* way. It was Christianity, with its *ressentiment* against life at the bottom of its heart, which first made something unclean of sexuality: it threw *filth* on the origin, on the presupposition of our life.

How does this serve to surmount the age, to go beyond nihilism? By foretelling the nihilistic shape of what must come after the collapse of Christian belief and its ethical corollaries, Nietzsche not only warns of doom but also calls to decision. And as one who has "lived through his nihilism to its end" - who has it "behind him, beneath him, beside him" - he is worthy of a hearing. He addresses us through a mask. The prophet Zarathustra was founder of the dualistic Persian religion (Zoroastrianism) with its clear-cut warfare between light and darkness, good and evil. On behalf of the moral deity - Ahura Mazda, "Wise Lord" - he preached against the evil spirits of the reigning polytheism who served *Druj*, "the Lie." Nietzsche's reason for taking this name as mouthpiece is irony, as he explains in *Ecce Homo*:

> I have not been asked, as I should have been asked, what the name *Zarathustra* means in precisely my mouth, in the mouth of the first immoralist: for what constitutes the tremendous uniqueness of that Persian in history is precisely the opposite of this. . . . Zarathustra *created* this most fateful of errors, morality . . . what is more important is that Zarathustra is more truthful than any other thinker. . . . The self-overcoming of morality through truthfulness, the self-overcoming of the moralist into his opposite - *into me* - that is what the name Zarathustra means in my mouth.

Nietzsche's choice of Zarathustra may reflect in part the popularity of the twelfth-century Persian poet Omar Khayyam, although commentators do not seem to note direct influence.[8] The familiar translation of Edward FitzGerald (first edition 1859) introduced the sceptical mysticism of the Sufi through quatrains (*ruba'is*) extolling the goal of liberty beyond "the tyrannous wheel." FitzGerald's generation, playing with classical ideals of epicurean autarchy, welcomed the sad and bold creed whose central symbol of wine could be taken literally or allegorically. Two German translations were available from the 1880s, by G. von Schack (1878) and F.W. von Bodenstedt (1881). In any event, it is the ancient tradition of Iranian aphorism, the Rubaiyat, that comes closest to the utterances of Zarathustra. In Nietzsche's hand the old prophet is transformed into herald of a new gospel: through the will the past can be redeemed from the resentment of not having willed it. To will the past is to will the new future and so to accomplish the mission of Overman. Thus speaks Zarathustra.

This program or destiny is illustrated by Zarathustra's first discourse, "Of the Three Metamorphoses": "I name you three metamorphoses of the spirit: how the spirit shall become a camel, and the camel a lion, and the lion at last a child." The camel enters the desert laden with the heaviest of questions, including the moral heteronomy of the past. In the desert it finds freedom through metamorphosis into a lion. For the lion is able to utter "a sacred No even to duty." Thus the "thou shalt" is transformed into "I will!" "Once it loved this 'Thou shalt' as its holiest thing: now it has to find illusion and caprice even in the holiest, that it may steal freedom from its love: the lion is needed for this theft." With Christian belief and ethic behind it, the liberated spirit now undergoes a third change, into the child.

> The child is innocence and forgetfulness, a new beginning, a sport, a self-propelling wheel, a first motion, a sacred Yes.
> Yes, a sacred Yes is needed, my brothers, for the sport of creation: the spirit now wills *its own* will, the spirit sundered from the world now wins *its own* world.

Thus fate-destiny and creation with its "accidental" sports are melded in the child-like Overmen or "master-men [*Herrenmenschen*]." Such new men provide the bridge over the destruction of the old masses degraded by religion. Taking up the arguments of earlier critics, Nietzsche attacks Christianity at the point of its doctrine of sin, interpreting the universality of guilt (*Das Schuldgefühl*) as a sign of that "equality" that the mob wishes to force on the Higher Men.

> The advent of the Christian God, as the maximum god attained so far, was therefore accompanied by the maximum feeling of guilty indebtedness on earth. Presuming we have gradually entered upon the *reverse* course, there is now small probability that with the irresistible decline of faith in the Christian God there is now also a considerable decline in mankind's feeling of guilt; indeed, the prospect cannot be dismissed that the complete and definite victory of atheism might free mankind of this whole feeling of guilty indebtedness toward its origin, its *causa prima*. Atheism and a kind of *second innocence* belong together.[9]

Genealogy and Morality

Nietzsche's deconstruction of values follows a genealogical method, similar to Freud's archeological. In seeking to expose the origin of religion, he is close to committing the genetic fallacy in logic. He avoids it narrowly, remarking that "the more insight we possess into an origin the less significant does the origin appear" (*GS* 345; cf *WP* 647: "Against Darwinism"). His aim, with special reference to "philosophers" who miss the point about truth and valuation (e.g., *GS* 351), is a "critique of moral values" of a truly radical sort. The root of all valuation is the locus of authority, the origin of judgment - "the value of these values themselves" (*GM* Pref. 6). It is this method that recalls us to Ricoeur's thesis that Nietzsche is a master of suspicion, operating through a hermeneutics of will. Behind the apparent or "willed will" lurks the "willing will" in need of deciphering. A. Nehamas has remarked: "It is essential to Nietzsche's conception of genealogy that it is explicitly modelled on the interpretation of texts." This relates to his perspectivism, the contrary of positivism's dogma "There are only facts": "No, facts is precisely what there is not, only interpretations" (*WP* 481). Arthur Danto concludes that Nietzsche remains a philosopher of nihilism - "there is no order and *a fortiori* no moral order in the world." By asking the question of origins, Nietzsche raises the proper question of definition. The good, for instance, means not only the contrary of evil but also of what is base or contemptible (*GM* 1.16, *BGE* 260). He does not intend the metaphysical question "What is?" but the genealogical question "Which one?" - not the *quid* but the *qui*.[10]

His thesis on the genesis of religion follows the familiar Enlightenment tack of driving a wedge between Jesus and Paul. Jesus is the moral hero whose simple Kingdom philosophy is seized on by "that disastrous wrong-headed fellow" on behalf of Jewish values. The latter are world-denying, the spawn of "revenge and hatred," of *ressentiment* (*GM* I.8). This is slave morality, reacting to a hostile world by beliefs that bring feelings of power. For "slaves and semi-slaves *desire power*." They ransom themselves in imagination, then demand recognition, justice, privilege and at last, "absolute power." Their self-serving religion creates a God of similar revenge and hatred, purveyor of reward and punishment (*BGE* V.195, *WP* 158ff). The resulting "holy lie" involves ideas of God the "Paymaster," an afterlife "in which the great punishment machine is first thought to become effective," conscience, morality as "denial of all natural processes" in behalf of "morally conditioned" events, and truth as revealed, identical with priestly teachings (*WP* 141). Like Feuerbach he sees, particularly in Germany, an unholy alliance between questionable forms of theology and philosophy.

> The Germans immediately understand what I mean
> when I say that philosophy has been contaminated
> by theological blood. The Protestant pastor is the
> grandfather of German philosophy, Protestantism
> its *peccatum originale*. . . . It is only necessary to
> say the words "Tübingen School" to understand
> what German philosophy is at heart: insidious the-
> ology.[11]

A chief strength of Nietzsche's attack lies in his appreciation of the connection between belief and ethics. Since in Christianity's case both turn on the Crucifixion, a clear line runs from the Crucified to life-denying values. If one is to oppose the values, only a thorough revaluation will do, which must rest upon a parallel displacement of the Crucified by Another. It is clear that the Resurrection remains unrelated to the Crucifixion for Nietzsche's understanding. Thus the Dionysus proclaimed by Zarathustra is a proper substitute or anti-Christ, the Greek preposition signifying not only "over against" but also "instead of." "I am the *anti-ass par excellence* and thus a world-historical monster - I am, in Greek, and not only in Greek, the *Anti-Christ*" (*EH* III.2). The death of God poses a peculiar irony in that for Nietzsche the Crucified lingers on in decadent forms of negative morality; to introduce the Overman sponsored by Dionysus, this pale God must be done away with. (Fortunately for this scheme of things, Christians themselves seem bent on deicide.)

Nietzsche's "war against the Christian ideal" required attack on that God who is "no more than a faded word today - not even a concept." In *Beyond Good and Evil* (1886) his critique achieves a consistent statement.[12] Christianity is "self-mutilation," sacrificing freedom, pride, self-confidence, chiefly because of "an over-ripe, manifold and much-indulged conscience." It is important to note that for him morality involves "tyranny" or "protracted constraint," and mere "timidity." Moralizing is indicative of a bad conscience; it necessarily suffers from crypto-Puritanism. British utilitarianism (especially the "pig philosophy" of Mill) is included, for it betrays "that old English vice called *cant*, which is *moral tartuffery.*" The book's scope leads inevitably to the most significant distinction, between "master morality" and "slave morality." Needless to say that Christianity exemplifies the latter to absurdity. Nor does this preserve the dialectical richness of Hegel's categories. Master must displace slave, in Zoroastrian manner.

Thus the attack on faith and its values leaves a gap: "beyond good and evil" means, among other things, the acceptance of the nihilating human will as supreme, and so the coming of a new (if higher) nihilism. This is why Nietzsche's thought is against humanism as well as theism. The "mangodhood" not only attacks the God-manhood of Christian theology but also entails "the self-destruction of humanism." This is Berdyaev's judgment, based on the connection that we maintain as one premise in our thesis, namely that "where there is no God, there is no man either." Karl Barth reinforces this premise by treating Nietzsche within his section on the basic form of humanity. For Barth it is not the atheism that is significant but the anthropology - deicide entails homicide. This is what Iris Murdoch intends when her fictional philosopher John Robert Rozanov remarks that "The point of solipsism, so often missed, is that it abolishes morality."[13] (We might put it that the inevitable correlate of a-theism is an-anthropology.) Barth agrees that Nietzsche saw Christian morality clearly and singled it out as the enemy. His "heart was not in contesting the existence of God"; the "central attack . . . was upon what he called Christian morality." Against this he revolted as aesthete, philologist, hellene, modern: "We undoubtedly have to say of a Feuerbach or a Strauss that - more akin to Nietzsche - they suffered all their lives from Christianity, and made it their main task to combat it" (240). But the chief point is one to which we will turn later, namely the "new thing in Nietzsche . . . the development of humanity without the fellow-man." This was a departure that followed the relentless logic of the Cartesian ego and the subsequent stress on the deconstructive will. It is in this respect that we take Nietzsche to represent Prometheanism, and his Dionysus no longer the collective or communal *élan* but the isolated individual, a willing monad.

Barth's judgment resembles that of Camus, whose "Nietzsche and Nihilism" in *The Rebel* credits him with having conferred new meaning on the word: "A nihilist is not one who believes in nothing, but one who does not believe in what exists."[14] Nietzsche's "mission" is to transform passive into active nihilism; as such he is "the most acute manifestation of nihilism's conscience." Rebellion leads inevitably to asceticism because acceptance of this world ("earth") imposes its own limitation: "A profounder logic replaces the 'if nothing is true, everything is permitted' of Karamazov by 'if nothing is true, nothing is permitted'."

Camus sees Nietzsche's program arising from the initial proposal to "concede the innocence" of the world because it "pursues no end." Lacking intentionality, no value judgments are in order about it, no morality applies. Only "absolute assent" and total "allegiance to this world" can obtain in this new asceticism.

> Thus from absolute despair will spring infinite joy, from blind servitude, unbounded freedom. To be free is, precisely, to abolish ends. The innocence of the ceaseless change of things, as soon as one consents to it, represents the maximum liberty.

For Camus such "liberty" is spurious since it "ends in a deification of fate" and submission to the inevitable. Aspiring not merely to be rid of God but to replace him, the new hero is bidden to submit to earth, to submerge his individuality in the "great cycle of time." It is not that Nietzsche is accused of creating National Socialism and its "submen"; on the contrary, that profound abuse of his ideas suggests their subtlety and difficulty. But on his own ground, according to Camus, he is not the proper rebel:

> The rebel whom Nietzsche set on his knees before the cosmos will, from now on, kneel before history. . . . The great rebel thus creates with his own hands, and for his own imprisonment, the implacable reign of necessity. Once he had escaped from God's prison, his first care was to construct the prison of history and of reason, thus putting the finishing touch to the camouflage and consecration of the nihilism whose conquest he claimed.

"God Is Dead"

> After Buddha was dead, his shadow was still shown for centuries in a cave - a tremendous, gruesome shadow. God is dead: but given the way men are, there may still be caves for thousands of years in which his shadow will be shown. And we - we still have to vanquish his shadow, too.
>
> *(GS* 108)

The phenomenon of the "Death of God Theology" of recent vintage - and short duration - exposed an interesting line of thought stretching from Pascal and others through Hegel and Nietzsche to the contemporary scene. We have mentioned this incident before; here we note Nietzsche's decisive role in the little drama. For whereas idealism had hitherto suggested a dialectical use for the death of God, including Hegel's "speculative Good Friday" as a moment in the sublation of religion in philosophy, Nietzsche proclaimed a post-mortem sadness and astonishment at the deed, recognized first by the Madman but not yet by his generation.

> "Whither is God" he cried. "I shall tell you. *We have killed him* - you and I. All of us are his murderers. But how have we done this? How were we able to drink up the sea? Who gave us the sponge to wipe away the entire horizon? . . . God is dead. God remains dead. And we have killed him. How shall we, the murderers of all murderers, comfort ourselves? What was holiest and most powerful of all that the world has yet owned has bled to death under our knives. Who will wipe this blood off us? What water is there for us to clean ourselves? What festivals of atonement, what sacred games shall we have to invent? Is not the greatness of this deed too great for us?"
>
> *(GS* 125)

The Madman paragraph has been analyzed countless times but still fascinates us with its insight. One thinks of the sacrifice of the Mass, in which God's death is willed as atonement; of speculative idealism, which used the Crucifixion as a timeless truth or symbol for its own "higher" purposes; of secularized Europe, which signals the end of Christendom (according to the theological optimists) but also the end of Christianity (according to Nietzsche). The death of God is no longer part of an essential movement of life through death to renewal; resurrection is hardly mentioned except to be dismissed as legend or as "spiritual" or mental occurrence. The denial of God makes subtle use of the Crucifixion, so that this ambiguity of the term death requires special notice. Nietzsche himself was not much aware of the double irony involved in his treatment. The continuing killing by countless generations of sceptics of one already dead seems a redundant process, so laborious that one wonders at its easy dismissal by historians of philosophy; and by Nietzsche too. (As if even the denial of God has its own Daily Office, its philosopher-priests offering inverse witness to the power and cruciality of the divine Sacrifice).

The Madman is insane because he has experienced the enormity of the deed, both the guilt laid upon him and the challenge to create a substitute infinity. He lights his Diogenes lantern because night has descended, "night and more night coming on all the while." When he grasps the incredulity of his listeners, he throws the lantern down and it breaks. "I come too early, my time has not come yet. This tremendous event is still on its way, still wandering - it has not yet reached the ears of man." Nietzsche is writing in 1883; within a few years he will develop his program for a new religion, but so far he is content only to note the passing of the Christian God. Soon he will issue bulletins from the privacy of his interior hell, sick and seeking, from one locale to another, one admirer to another. This Wanderer will sign his letters "Dionysus" or "The Crucified."

Is this development the logical entailment of his theory of the death of God? The invaluable lectures of Martin Heidegger on Nietzsche warn against taking our aphoristic author literally. In the present case the question is, *which* "god" is dead? Zarathustra is clearly god-less, but he himself observes that "God suffocated from theology; and morals from morality." It is the Prophet's own descent, his symbolic "down-going" at the end of *Gay Science* that poses the God-question. Such act of kenosis suggests an exegesis by which it is the way through tragedy - through God as "a counter-concept of life" (*EH* 790) - to "world." All nay-saying, every negation of the sensuous in favour of a privileged supersensuous, must go. Both Platonic metaphysics and Christian morality assign eternal duration to Being; but Nietzsche wishes to follow his favourite Heraclitus in "the play of life." His program is "To *stamp* Becoming with the character of Being - that is the supreme *will to power*" (*WP* 617).

Heidegger considered the Madman passage to be the necessary consequence of that tendency of modern thought to extreme subjectivity: the human will must extend value to everything, including God. All value-judgments (*Werturteile*) stem from perspectival will to power. Here we may note the gap between Heidegger's destructive interpretation and Derrida's deconstructive: the latter subsumes the Heideggerian "dis-closure" in a concept of the closure of Western thought. Derrida's *différance* involves both the different and the deferred. He takes Nietzsche's eternal return to imply "the sameness of difference and of repetition" and therefore an "incessant deciphering" of the traditional onto-theology of presence. Such valorization (*Wertsetzung*) through willing therefore constitutes "truth."[15] Karl Jaspers reinforces this view ("Only when there is no God, will man become free") with reference to *Zarathustra* II.2: "Willing liberates: that is the true doctrine of will and freedom. . . . This will lured me away from God and gods." The modern European philosophy, which Hegel and his disciples considered to have achieved enlightenment, appears here as the transformation of the *cogito* into a *volo*. Cornelio Fabro places Nietzsche in the line from Feuerbach, Bauer and Marx, if more radical in seeing Christianity as deviation. Thus the Cartesian *cogito*, the Kantian autonomy, the Hegelian awareness "considered as a nihilating activity" all contribute to the concept of will to power.[16]

A Dithyramb for Dionysus

"I am the inventor of the dithyramb" (*EH* 762). Nietzsche encloses the tragic modality of Prometheus within his dithyrambs and satyr play. "I am a disciple of the philosopher Dionysus; I should prefer to be even a satyr to being a saint" (*EH* Pref. 2). The final item from his pen - January 1, 1889, two days before his breakdown - was a dedication for his projected *Dithyrambs of Dionysus*, nine poems composed between 1883 and 1888. He also left notes for a dramatic sketch: "Satyr play at the end. . . . Dionysus, Theseus and Ariadne." If the cast is that of Nietzsche, Wagner and Wagner's wife, Cosima (Liszt), we see the thread alluded to in the poem "Ariadne's Complaint." For Wagner is the Sorcerer, and Nietzsche himself is "thy labyrinth."[17] How strangely this finale to his composition reads, reminding one of Ovid's myth of Marsyas. Challenging Apollo to a musical competition, the satyr loses and is punished by being flayed alive. Is this "metamorphosis" a metaphor of Nietzsche's challenge and martyrdom? Satyr-like, he savoured the bittersweet taste of his irony, he suffered for his musical audacity.

The poetic and aphoristic method is appropriate to Nietzsche's intention. He seeks the antidote to the deadening philosophy of otherworldliness, as is evident in his programmatic "gay science." Reflecting on his authorship in *Ecce Homo*, he regards two works as "Yes-saying" - *Dawn* and *Gay Science*. Of the latter he writes, "in almost every sentence profundity and high spirits go tenderly hand in hand." His idea of *Fröhliche Wissenschaft* is better translated "gay science" than "joyful wisdom," considering his subtitle *La Gaya Scienza*, following Provençal tradition. Here is Nietzsche's answer to the masquerade of art as "scientific" knowledge (and morality). His lifelong use of parody is thus strategic, best seen in the liturgical counter-song of the Ass-festival (*Eselfest*) by Zarathustra. Laughter is the way of release from anguish, the cure for despair. Analyses of humour, especially his favourite modes of satire, parody and irony, note the significance of the "distance" that laughter achieves. The play of life that he seeks to understand and to share is to be imitated in the play of ideas and of language, a *Wortspiel*.[18]

Such serious play is evident in his ambivalent relationship to Wagner's heroic philosophy. The symbol of the Ring was for both men one of perfection, completion. The "eternal recurrence of the same" in Nietzsche is echoed in Wagner's development of the quest motif. As the Grail legend gives place to the Nibelungen saga, the knights Parsifal and Lohengrin are succeeded by wilder and earthbound heroes. The former were in service to a holy vessel, themselves made fit by their freedom from sin. The new warriors, Siegmund and Siegfried, are free from *fear*. And in the great aria of Brünnhilde that closes the penultimate opera, *Siegfried*, she yields to love and to mortality: "I shall close the open gates of perpetual becoming behind me . . . redeemed from reincarnation, I shall proceed to the most hallowed land beyond both desire and illusion, the end of the earthly journey. . . . I saw the world end." And so the twilight of the gods moves inexorably to its fiery extinction (once more, the Firekindler). It is the *Abendland* of Nietzsche's cosmol-

ogy, the foil for his own vision of perpetual return to Life. The Val-
kyrie sees that love illumines, transfigures, and laughs at death
("Leuchtende Liebe! lachenender Tod!"). Nietzsche himself states:
"So love that you must desire to live again. This is your duty. . . .
Eternity is worth it!" (*EH* II.10, 712).[19]

In his early thesis *The Birth of Tragedy from the Spirit of
Music* (1872) Nietzsche had stressed the power of the classical myths
in revealing an affirmative world-view. He prefers Aeschylus to
Euripides ("This is the new opposition: the Dionysian and the Socratic") and examines the *Prometheus Bound* in light of Goethe's
poem.

> Man, rising to Titanic stature, gains culture by his
> own efforts and forces the gods to enter into an
> alliance with him because in his very own wisdom
> he holds their existence and their limitations in his
> hands. . . . In himself the Titanic artist found the
> defiant faith that he had the ability to create men
> and at least destroy Olympian gods, by means of
> his superior wisdom which, to be sure, he had to
> atone for with eternal suffering.

Nietzsche's thesis is that Greek tragedy springs from the twofold
inspiration of the gods of sculpture and of music, who inform both
dream and ecstasy. Apollo represents justice and order, the *princi-
pium individuationis* and self-knowledge ("know thyself;" "nothing
in excess"). Dionysus raises the individual above self to universal
and eternal experience. He is "titanic," both pre-Apollonian and
extra-Apollonian ("barbaric"). While on one level the Dionysiac
musician (Wagner?) sublated orderly culture, the greater point is that
Apollo requires Dionysus; even the Prometheus of Aeschylus is "a
Dionysian mask." When he turns to the relation of music to drama,
Nietzsche sees the tension between the two principles in the tempo-
rary casting of Dionysian heroes as Apollonian "individuals," so that
music (Dionysus) merely reinforces drama (Apollo). But in the long
run Greek tragedy achieves a truly Dionysian end, the transcending
of Apollonian effects:

> Thus the intricate relation of the Apollonian and
> the Dionysian in tragedy may really be symbolized
> by a fraternal union of the two deities: Dionysus
> speaks the language of Apollo; and Apollo, finally,
> the language of Dionysus; and so the highest goal
> of tragedy and of all art is attained.

In the preface to the reissue of *The Birth of Tragedy* in 1886,
Nietzsche includes an ominous sentence to the effect that "the right-

ful name of the Antichrist" is Dionysus. He ends by quoting his own Zarathustra on the "crown of laughter" required to replace Christian pessimism. The new title of the work becomes *The Birth of Tragedy Or: Hellenism and Pessimism*. The die is cast: Nietzsche has joined the line of critics who contrast God and humanity. "Perhaps man will be able to raise himself up from the moment he is no longer engulfed in God." Except that for Nietzsche the new Man of the post-Christian era will serve another deity. For even secular humanity, whom Nietzsche saw as the product of European Enlightenment, must pass away.

> And this is the great noontide: it is when man stands at the middle of his course between animal and Superman and celebrates his journey to the evening as his highest hope: for it is the journey to a new morning. . . . *"All gods are dead: now we want the Superman to live."*[20]

The necessity for transition suggests why Nietzsche can call humanity a "disease," "something that should be overcome," and mock the "mob" (*TSZ* 153, 297).

Whereas the earlier typology of Apollo and Dionysus identified dream and rapture as the two "forces of nature and art" (*WP* 1050), later it is the singular power of rapture (*Rausch*) that drives both types; it is the "enhancement of force and plenitude" (*TI* 8.122ff; pp. 71ff). Nietzsche's theory of art is not merely an aesthetics deriving from his concentration on the sensuous. It is his way of recovering both art and truth from the "discordance" they suffer as perspectival modes.[21] Artistic rapture resembles Hegel's sublation of history in philosophy. The program of inverting Platonism means that art as *mimēsis* of truth, of the ideal world (Republic X), is replaced by art as transfiguration of what is true. A cryptic passage from the explosive year 1888 traces the "history of an error:" "How the 'real World' at last Became a Myth" (*TI* 8.82f, pp 40f). The "real" world is subject to Platonic and Christian transcendentalism, then to positivist agnosticism, and finally to Nietzsche's own revaluation:

> We have abolished the real world: what world is left? the apparent world perhaps? . . . But no! *with the real world we have also abolished the apparent world*!
> (Mid-day; moment of the shortest shadow; end of the longest error; zenith of mankind;
> INCIPIT ZARATHUSTRA.)

If we relate this passage to the new edition of *Birth of Tragedy* (1886), as Heidegger does, we see the weight of Nietzsche's shift of truth to art. Its preface states: "the very task of that audacious book ventured for the first time: *to see science under the optics of the artist, but art under the optics of life.*" That is, Nietzsche's project is to see truth (science) under the perspectival character of Being (art) as Becoming (life). One must escape the freezing gaze of Christian Platonism or classical theism, which eternalizes Truth. One must commit oneself to the life-enhancing power of the artistic will. Therefore: "We have *art* so that we *do not perish from the truth*" (*WP* 822).

Ecce Homo Volens

"God is dead: I come to teach you the Overman." To accomplish the creation of Higher Men, the god Dionysus as proclaimed by Zarathustra must be acknowledged and exalted. His service involves the cultivation of that will that revalues all things, using this-worldly "earth" as touchstone. The will to power is the agency for the passage from lower to higher humanity. Its strategy is the affirmation of life, a will to live; but its tactic is submission to necessity, *amor fati,* the will to nothingness. The "self-overcoming" so important in *Zarathustra* is called by Hollingdale "the hinge upon which the theory of the will to power turns from being a nihilist to a positive and joyful conception."[22] For to overcome the old self is to dis-value its world and its deity, to surpass it toward the higher self. *Volo, ergo sum.*

The formal similarity of this process to Christian doctrine is obvious, leading Ernst Bloch to speak of Nietzsche's *Religions-Ersatz.* While Nietzsche scores the ethic of "submission" in favour of "Zarathustra the godless," he cannot escape the "resort to faith" in a quasi-eschatological doctrine, that of "eternal recurrence."[23]

> For behold, O Zarathustra: New lyres are needed
> for your new songs . . . behold, *you are the teacher
> of the eternal recurrence,* that is now *your* destiny!
> Behold, we know what you teach: that all things
> recur eternally and we ourselves with them, and
> that we have already existed an infinite number of
> times before and all things with us.
>
> (*TSZ* 237)

This apparently self-defeating idea (Overman would yield again to barbarism, barbarism to religion, religion to enlightenment, to Overman . . .), which he arrived at in the summer of 1881 while at Sils Maria, replaces the dialectic of no-saying and yes-saying, of freeing spirits from the bondage of priestcraft. Even at the last, Nietzsche could state that the "fundamental conception" of his *Zarathustra* is "the idea of the eternal recurrence" (*EH* 751).

If Nietzsche began by following such leads as his Basle colleague Jacob Burckhardt's exaltation of Renaissance masters, or his own relation to the "master" Wagner, he ended by speculating on a theory that undermines the very purpose of such mastery. His optimism was overcome not by the pessimism of Christianity but by the fatalism of his own thought. The earlier quest for the human was, in his own words describing the *Vogelfrei* songs of *Die Fröhliche Wissenschaft*, "quite emphatically reminiscent of the Provençal concept of *gaya scienza* - that unity of *singer, knight,* and *free spirit* which distinguishes the wonderful early culture of the Provençals from all equivocal cultures" (*EH* 750). But he moved beyond this refreshing vision of singer and dancer, "the aeronaut of the spirit," to a *reductio ad absurdum*. It is this that disillusioned Berdyaev, for whom "after Nietzsche, humanism is no longer possible. He had laid bare all its contradictions."[24]

A similar appraisal of Nietzsche's leading concept is given by a sympathetic critic, Arthur Gibson, who speaks of Nietzsche's "faith in finitude:" "The fulcrum of Nietzsche's entire articulation of a new vision of reality which is to serve as the basis for his 'transvaluation of all values' is precisely finitude."[25] Finitude is the essential thing: eternal recurrence "encapsulates and undergirds" its defense. Gibson distinguishes the materialist revolt against God in which the "epistemologico-ontological dimension" is paramount, from the spiritualist revolt of Nietzsche, in which rebellion is "basically psychological and pre-eminently personal-moral." God *must not* exist: only Man. Deicide becomes the logical end of an anthropology that clothes itself in divine attributes. The challenge and verve of the resulting journey toward Overman constitute the new faith in the capacities of the finite to provide a proper substitute for infinity. When every moment is eternal, then eternal recurrence has achieved the goal of higher humanity. Gibson warns:

> it is less than accurate to speak, in Nietzsche, of infinite time, and totally mistaken and false to speak of eternity as positive timelessness. What we have is, rather, indefinite time, a creation of the unending interplay of finite energy and finite matter.

We may recall one of Nietzsche's metaphors, that of an hourglass. When finitude becomes ultimate, it guarantees not only autonomy and freedom but also repetition: "The eternal sandglass of existence will ever be turned once more, and thou with it, thou speck of dust!" (*GS* 341). Nietzsche goes beyond nihilism not by discovering a "beyond" that offers transcendent meaning to existence but by investing the human will with the power to impose meaning in its absolute freedom, its autonomy raised to a transcendental power. Ernst Bertram comments: "The platonist in him welds the golden moment to Zarathustra's nuptial ring of rings, the Ring of the Return."[26]

The atheism of Nietzsche is almost a pure type of Promethean wilfulness. Its enemy is God, the God of classical theism, interpreted as a tyrannical and demanding superpower. Christianity is cast as evil, a "sick-house and dungeon atmosphere"; along with alcohol, it is one of "the two great European narcotics," a religion of pity, suffering, loss of power. These are random phrases from *Twilight of the Idols* and *The Antichrist*, two of the short books composed in his final period of writing. They reinforce the judgment of G.A. Morgan that "beyond question the major premise of Nietzsche's philosophy is atheism."[27]

Walter Kaufmann's positive portrayal of Nietzsche suggests that "the conception of the overman is inseparable from that of the recurrence," so that the latter is at once a repudiation of life-denying teachings and a "justification" of the painful world that Nietzsche knew personally.[28] Thus, although it remains "this most dubious doctrine," it constitutes Nietzsche's substitute for theodicy, his answer to "the problem of evil" and his rationale for Zarathustra's invitation to the dance.

> I would not know what the spirit of a philosopher might wish more to be than a good dancer. For the dance is his ideal, also his art, and finally also his piety, his "service of God."
>
> (*GS* 381)

> I would believe only in a god who could dance. And when I saw my devil I found him serious, thorough, profound, and solemn: it was the spirit of gravity - through him all things fall.
> Now I am nimble, now I fly, now I see myself under myself, now a god dances within me.
>
> (*TSZ* 68f)

Nietzsche's atheism, however he interpreted his personal history, depended on the stock of anti-Christian images and counter-images ready to hand among the intelligentsia of his time. His early hellenism and his philological discipline, his affection for Goethe and Wagner, perhaps even his experience at five years of age of hearing the terrible tidings, "Dein Vater ist todt!"[29] - the complex and manifold influences cannot "explain" his strident atheism without recourse to the Promethean stream so well appreciated from his earliest work. For him the human will is the gift of fire, the key to the riches of freedom, power, overcoming all things in earth and heaven. And if in the end he settles for a substitute God, drawn from classical antiquity and proclaimed by a borrowed Parsee, on his lips a dubious doctrine that mocks even his own highest hopes . . . still, here is a man to behold, not least in his weakness, his suffering and illness. He sees perhaps too clearly certain elements of the Christian faith that he must reject to maintain his grace of fire. He is himself a master, even if a master of suspicion, and his atheism may prove as therapeutic for mature faith as that of those other masters, Marx and Freud.

Nietzsche saw through the sham of religion based on a yielding of the will through apathy or fear - or feeling of revenge. Like Marx, he recognized the dehumanizing process encouraged by Christian teaching on resignation, submission to authority. Like Freud, he recognized that "our so-called consciousness is a more or less fantastic commentary on an unknown, perhaps unknowable, but felt text."[30] Together, all three recall us from that "first naîveté," which is self-indulgent and self-serving, to a self-critical examination, which moves through the hermeneutics of suspicion to test more solid ground beyond. It asks whether there be a second naiveté on the other side of suspicion, a child-likeness that enjoys the freedom of autonomous decision because the heteronomy of the old gods, including the perverse image of the Christian God, is broken. Nietzsche's "twilight of the idols" (putting *Götzen-Dämmerung* for Wagner's *Götterdämmerung*) heralds a new Dawn, but one that he himself darkens by the theory of recurrence.

For Nietzsche the vestiges of the old God must go, for "If there is a God, how can one tolerate not being God oneself?" But it is not Dionysus who can substitute for the Crucified - Dionysus himself is an outstanding symbol of that dismemberment or "tearing apart" (*ana-lysis*) in ritual devotion that parallels crucifixion.[31] Only if the latter entails a transfiguration of the human will eternity be opened not as a recurring masque but as a New Age. And that enlightenment will reveal a Lord of the Dance indeed.

- 12 -

The Work of Sisyphus - Camus

> Prometheus, in his turn, becomes a master who
> first teaches and then commands. Men doubt that
> they can safely attack the city of light and are even
> uncertain whether the city exists. They must be
> saved from themselves. The hero then tells them
> that he, and he alone, knows the city. Those who
> doubt his word will be thrown into the desert,
> chained to a rock, offered to the vultures. The
> others will march henceforth into darkness, behind
> the pensive and solitary master. Prometheus alone
> has become god and reigns over the solitude of
> men. But from Zeus he has gained only solitude,
> and cruelty; he is no longer Prometheus, he is Cae-
> sar. The real, the eternal Prometheus has now
> assumed the aspect of one of his victims. The
> same cry, springing from the depths of the past,
> rings forever through the Scythian desert.[1]

In *L'Homme Révolté* of 1951 we have the definitive "history of rebellion." The sign of Prometheus is invoked, for "Notre temps aime à
se dire prométhéen." It was the Greeks who "created a touching and
noble image of the Rebel and gave us the most perfect myth of the
intelligence in revolt." Thus Camus's depiction of metaphysical and
historical rebellion constitutes the "surprising itinerary" of Promethean humanity. The itinerary begins with nihilism, itself product of
and reaction to the indifference of things; it ends, as the above quotation makes clear, with the betrayal of Promethean hope by Caesa-
rean reality.

　　An earlier writing, some four years before *Rebel*, was to
appear in *L'Eté* in 1954. The premise of *Prométhée aux enfers* is
that the human skills deriving from the gift of fire have hardened to
produce a mechanical-technological age, a new slavery. While Prometheus may remain the symbol of revolt, he bears another burden,
he is chief of those who suffer, those who are "deprived of fire and
food, for whom liberty is a light that can wait." This sentiment

---

Notes to Chapter 12 appear on page 346.

reminds us of the insight of Franz Fanon on the subject of bread and freedom. We are bound to the rock "in the very name of that humanism of which he is the primary symbol." Once more Force and Violence are in charge; once more a work of rebellion is required. Our task is to attain justice, to reconcile "le coeur douloureux de l'homme et le printemps du monde." The mighty protest of the Titan has settled into a work of secular piety, and pity. Not the cry of Prometheus but the hands of Sisyphus express the human condition.

Indifference and Absurdity

The early writings of Albert Camus (1913-60) include two plays (*Le Malentendu, Caligula*), a novel (*L'Etranger*) and a collection of essays (*Le Mythe de Sisyphe*). Several themes combined to assure the judgment of the age that he was an existentialist, committed to the sort of hopeless quest for inner meaning attributed to Sartre. The Algerian sun, for instance, struck him forcibly as a sign of "the benign indifference of the universe" to which Meursault yields himself at the end of the novel. And the daughter in *Le Malentendu* describes the attitude of the household as "amiable indifference." Light and darkness - including "the great night of Africa" - are recurring symbols of the elemental struggle of life against death and of goodness against evil that preoccupies him: "In the middle of winter I at last discovered that there was in me an invincible summer."[2] His youthful academic study of the problem of evil convinced him that the traditional theodicy of classical Christian theism was no longer credible. His sensitivity about human suffering contrasts sharply with what he takes to be a general indifference.

> What, then, is that incalculable feeling that deprives the mind of the sleep necessary to life? A world that can be explained even with bad reasons is a familiar world. But, on the other hand, in a universe suddenly divested of illusions and lights, man feels an alien, a stranger. His exile is without remedy since he is deprived of the memory of a lost home or the hope of a promised land.[3]

There are plenty of "bad reasons" around, similar to the "bad faith" of Sartre. Only "blind reason" thinks everything is clear. A mind made lucid by "clearsighted indifference" sees that: "This world in itself is not reasonable, that is all that can be said. But what is absurd is the confrontation of this irrational and wild longing for clarity whose call echoes in the human heart. The absurd depends as much on man as on the world."[4] It is not that the world is simply absurd: the absurd appears only in the "moment" when the "absurd man" confronts it clearly and fearlessly. According to R.W.B. Lewis, Camus follows André Malraux's use of the term in *Le Tentation de l'Occident* (1926): "At the centre of European man, dominating the great moments of his life, there lies an essential absurdity."[5] Camus elaborates the term, now understood from its Latin roots as both *surdus* (deaf) and *absurdus* (harsh, grating). The deaf and harsh-voiced servant in *Le Malentendu* (*Cross-Purposes*) is a type.

What is now taken as a normative depiction of alienation was originally neglected until after *The Plague* had brought fame to Camus. *The Stranger* had portrayed, in appropriately sparse and detached style reminiscent of Robbe-Grillet, the proverbial outsider - outside human relationships including the death of his mother, the love of his mistress, the murder of his accidental enemy. The play and the novel underscore the essential irrationality of things. Chance encounters and haphazard events dictate our choices and their consequences. The tragedy of the play is unrelieved by any noble intention or ultimate good; Meursault is condemned as much for his indifference to his mother's death as for his act of murder. It all comes to the same thing.

Lewis has called *The Stranger* an "absurd mimesis of the tragic."[6] Its "philosophical translation," *The Myth of Sisyphus*, portrays in its title essay the legendary Corinthian king as the absurd hero: "His scorn of the gods, his hatred of death, and his passion for life won him that unspeakable penalty in which the whole being is exerted toward accomplishing nothing. This is the price that must be paid for the passions of this earth." Sisyphus had postponed death by a ruse, but his cunning brought punishment - sentenced to roll the rock up the hill only to have it roll down again so that he might begin anew. Camus bids us regard Sisyphus in the moment when he stands watching the stone "rush down in a few moments toward that lower world" yet again: "It is during that return, that pause, that Sisyphus interests me. . . . At each of those moments when he leaves the heights and gradually sinks toward the lairs of the gods, he is superior to his fate. He is stronger than his rock." The struggle itself "is enough to fill a man's heart" as he discovers his own power over his fate, rendering the idols silent. Therefore, Camus concludes, "One must imagine Sisyphus happy." The absurd man recognizes and accepts the unreasoning face of things. By committing himself to a ceaseless struggle without hope of reward he meets the absurd in the only appropriate manner. After all, "Le style, c'est l'homme."

Lutte, toujours!

The Myth of Sisyphus opens with the question of suicide ("There is but one truly serious philosophical problem, and that is suicide") and ends with a call to contest the absurdity of things. Refusing the leap of faith that Kierkegaard, Chestov and even Kafka had made, Camus makes do with "the moral value of lucidity" and denies all traffic with "subterfuge." His is a bleak hope, in this early stage, when rebellion is not yet a clear vocation for him. Caligula, for example, knows that "My kind of freedom is not good." The emperor has not yet appreciated the limits that alone give weight to an absurd style. "The absurd is lucid reason noting its limits." It is close to hopelessness - not the form of presumption as in Prometheus, but that of desperation, even that moral tedium labelled *acedia*.[7] His concern for *la raison* compromises his exploration of evil. "Caligula is a tormented *pícaro* - a rogue beyond all roguery who yearns to be a saint."[8]

A more positive stage develops with the later series of writings (which he dubbed Promethean), particularly *La Peste* (1947) and its form of philosophical commentary, *L'Homme Révolté* (1951).[9] Two plays, *L'Etat de Siège* and *Les Justes*, support these works by presenting theatrically an epidemic and a rebellion. The question posed by absurdity is now sharpening:

> This essay proposes, in the face of murder and rebellion, to pursue a train of thought which began with suicide and the idea of the absurd. . . . The final conclusion of absurdist reasoning is, in fact, the repudiation of suicide and the acceptance of the desperate encounter between human inquiry and the silence of the universe.[10]

The no of the rebel also implies a yes inasmuch as he is making a "gesture of rebellion." His analysis of the dynamics of rebellion leads Camus to a new discernment: "that only two possible worlds can exist for the human mind: the sacred (or, to speak in Christian terms, the world of grace) and the world of rebellion."[11] Since the rebel wants a situation in which "all the answers are human," he rejects grace.

A curious dialectic obtains, according to Camus: the rebel defies God but inexorably seeks to replace deity with himself. This is why the history of Western rebellion is "inseparable from the history of Christianity." Lucretius's hero Epicurus (as we noted earlier) is involved in this contradiction: "By repudiating the unworthy and criminal gods, he takes their place himself." Even de Sade is treated under the same rubric, a rejection of a God who must be "indifferent, wicked, or cruel" according to the test of answering the question of evil. Camus sees de Sade as posing this test in his writings: the innocent suffer and the evil triumph. This is a form of "freethinker wager" replying to Pascal's.[12]

If de Sade's image of God as "a criminal divinity who oppresses and denies mankind" seems extreme, Camus leads us next to Dostoevsky's Ivan Karamazov. The famous rationalist who collected stories of cruelty to children - that is, of innocent suffering - sees evil as essential to creation. Therefore "creation is unacceptable." Justice is a higher principle than God. But this is no longer the Kantian justice, which postulates an ultimate Judge. Lacking this final knot in the thread of justice, virtue slips through and so "everything is permitted." This famous phrase rivals "All or Nothing" and will concern us again. For Camus, "All or Nothing" symbolizes the compassion that cannot accept salvation if even one other is refused; "everything is permitted" signifies the beginning of nihilism.

In a brief section of *The Rebel* entitled "Nihilism and History" this chief point about rebellion as rivalry with God becomes explicit. Paradoxically, the nosayers to creation and morality have "all tried to construct a purely terrestrial kingdom where their chosen principles will hold sway." This reconstruction of creation answers "the desperate appeal for order that rings through this insane universe," especially at the point where death threatens. "The rebel does not ask for life, but for reasons for living. He rejects the consequences implied by death. If nothing lasts, then nothing is justified; everything that dies is deprived of meaning." Thus at the core of metaphysical revolt is the "protest against evil," especially in its ultimate form as death. The passage recalls vividly the words that Gabriel Marcel uses in similar context: to love someone is to say, "Thou shalt not die," for "If death is the ultimate reality, value is annihilated in sheer scandal."[13]

Camus cannot argue from value-theory to immortality: he is too committed to the assumption that "immortality" means only one thing: reward and punishment. Thus he too is caught within the limited horizon of a God who is vindictive, far worse than Kant's impartial Judge, more akin to the perfect sadist. This hard position is put forcefully in *Cross-Purposes*. Martha is addressing Maria, her sister-in-law who has just discovered the murder of her husband by his mother and sister. Martha is now determined on suicide and confronts Maria with the news of the murder.

> But fix this in your mind; neither for him nor for us, neither in life nor in death, is there any peace or homeland. . . . We're cheated, I tell you. Cheated! What do they serve, those blind impulses that surge up in us, the yearnings that rack our souls? Why cry out for the sea, or for love? . . . Pray your God to harden you to stone. It's the happiness He has assigned Himself, and the one true happiness. Do as He does, be deaf to all appeals, and turn your heart to stone while there is still time.

Here is a passage that compresses the absurdity of life into compact and powerful utterance. Neither peace nor homeland . . . cheated . . . blind impulses . . . a God who is deaf, who is like stone - the themes of the absurd view of things are all here. Crucial is the image of God, himself both surd and absurd: deaf, lithic.

The work of Camus is a lament for the unhappy consciousness forced upon him by this position. He sees the inevitable progression of nihilism - "man without God brutally wields power." He makes his whole universe into "a fortress erected against the fallen and exiled deity." And so his verdict:

> Man, at the culmination of his rebellion, incarcerated himself; from Sade's lurid castle to the concentration camps, man's greatest liberty consisted only in building the prison of his crimes. But the state of siege gradually spreads, the demand for freedom wants to embrace all mankind. . . . To kill God and to build a Church are the constant and contradictory purpose of rebellion.

Freedom, then, ambiguous and self-contradictory, dictates both regicide and deicide, activities that Camus documents with painful faithfulness. Revolutionaries took Hegel's history without transcendence, interpreted it as "the struggle of wills bent on seizing power" and dedicated themselves to the master-slave dialectic. This last he calls "the decisive justification of the spirit of power in the twentieth century."[14]

Camus's interpretation of rebellion sees an interior logic at work: God is rejected because of the struggle against evil to which he appears indifferent or even opposed: man replaces God in playing the ultimate role in history; thus "he arrogates to himself the power of life and death over others." At the last, he justifies terror in the name of justice. Now Camus himself seeks to break out of this chain by positing an alternative significance to history. His analysis of "the kingdom of ends" of Marx and Lenin notes the loss of freedom within the dynamism of history.[15] First quality is sacrificed to quantity, then by dialectical (theoretical) inversion, quantity is named quality in "the decision to call total servitude freedom." Against this movement Camus insists that freedom is guaranteed only by rebellion, but such rebellion as remains the perpetual protest against every enslavement of the human. Such a continuous revolt, to be sure, lacks the vision of an alternative kingdom of ends; but it at least recalls rebellion to its nobility of purpose: brotherhood, peace.

The dilemma of the rebel is that he is caught between sacrificing selfhood to God and sacrificing his neighbour to Justice: "between sacrifice and murder." The notes that close *The Rebel* are much less than programmatic and certainly not systematic. Camus hopes for "a renaissance beyond the limits of nihilism" but can define this only in terms of human solidarity.

> Then we understand that rebellion cannot exist without a strange form of love. Those who find no rest in God or in history are condemned to live for those who, like themselves, cannot live: in fact, for the humiliated. The most pure form of the movement of rebellion is thus crowned with the heart-rending cry of Karamazov: if all are not saved, what good is the salvation of one only?

Secular Sainthood

> "Comment vivre sans grâce, c'est la question qui domine le XXe siècle."

The Rebel appeared some four years after *The Plague*, but it is the novel that continues to convey a more positive message with greater significance for our topic. In brief, Camus concludes that when faced with the universal plague of evil, a specific kind of advocacy of human being is called for, a form of "sainthood without God." Lewis calls the position of Camus in the novel "a tenacious theory of compassion . . . his own truncated precept of charity - leaving the Lord to take care of Himself, and being content with loving one's neighbour." He thinks that both books indicate the shift from the solitude of the earlier nihilism and absurdity to "a sense of participation as the only salvageable value and the one trustworthy meaning."[16] Apart from the question of whether such a reductionist humanism is worthy of such valiant efforts to achieve it, the idea of participation is essential to *The Plague*.

The theme of this familiar novel - a favourite of philosophers of religion - is the outbreak of bubonic plague in Oran and the role of a small group of people in the struggle against it. Of the six chief characters, three are singled out for the burden of the author's views: Dr. Rieux, the story's chronicler and chief rebel against the absurdity of the pestilence; Tarrou, who organizes volunteers to fight the plague and himself dies of it; and Father Paneloux, the priest whose two sermons form key passages in the development of character. William Hamilton has appropriately called these three (in reverse order) "the Christian, the Saint, and the Rebel."[17]

Rieux is introduced as one "sick and tired of the world he lived in - though he had much liking for his fellow-men - and . . . resolved, for his part, to have no truck with injustice and compromises with the truth." He experiences "the passionate indignation we feel when confronted by the anguish all men share" and considers fighting the plague simply "doing my job." Meanwhile, two other characters react differently. For Cottard such struggle is clearly "not my job" because he is profiteering under cover of the plague, while Rambert is unsure what his job is and wants only to escape the city. At length, however, he decides to stay, because "it may be shameful to be happy by oneself." "This business is everybody's business." Thus the solidarity of susceptibility to pestilence is matched by the solidarity of struggle - except for those like Cottard who opt out of responsibility and so declare themselves to belong to that which is to be despised rather than admired in humans.

Here too Camus accuses Christianity of operating with an unacceptable image of God. The deity of classical theism is further simplified, almost reduced to one attribute: omnipotence. In one scene Tarrou asks the doctor about the gap between him and Paneloux concerning human suffering.

> His face still in shadow, Rieux said that he'd already answered: that if he believed in an all-powerful God he would cease curing the sick and leave that to Him. But no one in the world believed in a God of that sort; no, not even Paneloux, who believed that he believed in such a God. And this was proved by the fact that no one ever threw himself on Providence completely. Anyhow, in this respect Rieux believed himself to be on the right road - in fighting against creation as he found it.[18]

Is Paneloux guilty of such theological reductionism? His two sermons suggest that Camus allows only two choices: naïve supernaturalism or agnosticism. The first sermon, preached soon after the plague was well established and before the conversation between Tarrou and Rieux, is a stark view of reality. It begins: "calamity has come upon you, my brethren, and, my brethren, you deserved it." Calling the plague the divine "scourge," the priest draws examples from history proving that "plague is the flail of God and the world His threshing-floor." The just need not fear, "but the evil-doer has good cause to tremble." Like Jonah before the gates of Nineveh, Paneloux sees Oran as deserving calamity because of its sinfulness. God has "turned His face away from us . . . we walk in darkness, in the thick darkness of this plague."

It is a precious vignette of clerical rhetoric seizing a time ripe for repentance and using doctrine for that end. And it exemplifies the popular impression of what Christian dogma - particularly Roman Catholic - has to say about the meaning of evil in the form of calamity, namely divine punishment, and of the faithful way to react, namely submission. The sermon obviously suggested to Rieux that the priest gave lip service to the dogma, even if more experience in tending sufferers might move him beyond it.

The portrait of the priest remains unsatisfactory. When first introduced in the novel, he is described as "a stalwart champion of Christian doctrine at its most precise and purest, equally remote from modern laxity and the obscurantism of the past." And he is an expert on St. Augustine (Camus's 1936 thesis at the university of Algiers, supervised by philosopher Jean Grenier, compared Plotinus and Augustine). Would such a man, aware of the Augustinian wrestling with the problem of evil, and free from obscurantism, compose a sermon so limited in perspective and simplistic in idea? Camus is writing a *roman à thèse*, and one appreciates his motives; yet Paneloux is an unconvincing figure, a theologian untouched by the finer points of theodicy, a parish priest innocent of the experience of visiting sufferers. In short, a cardboard Jansenist.

The one-sided depiction of Christianity in the works of Camus is, no doubt, in part at least the result of his youthful exposure to "a religion professed by the moneyed class and practised in fact by women and old men." His home experience (an agnostic mother, a grandmother of cloying pietism) his teachers at *lycée* and university, his reading in his uncle's library (Gide alongside the *philosophes*) - such upbringing explains his remark to the Dominicans in 1948: "I shall never start from the supposition that Christian truth is illusory, but merely from the fact that I could not accept it."[19]

Can one defend Paneloux? Hardly: his theology is reduced to the very obscurantism of which he was declared free earlier in the book. For he advances the most primitive of theodicies (soundly refuted as early as the Psalms and the Book of Job, to name only the most outstanding examples of ancient theological sophistication): if you suffer it proves you are wicked; if you are good you will escape. This position appears to be so far departed from in the second sermon that commentators generally underline the traumatic shift in the priest's thinking. Hamilton, for instance, considers that now "a quite different solution to the problem of suffering" is being offered, and Lewis can state:

> Paneloux, the clerical caricature in *The Plague*, preaches two sermons, in the second of which he helplessly accepts the horrors besetting his parish precisely because they will not yield to human understanding; he makes that "leap" of faith, and enjoins his congregation to make it, that Camus in *The Myth of Sisyphus* excoriated as a suicidal intellectual betrayal.[20]

But in fact the ten pages of dense writing, which include the famous sermon and end with the priest's death, beg a different interpretation. The chapter begins with the change in Paneloux "from the day on which he saw a child die." He tells Rieux that he is preparing a pamphlet entitled "Is a Priest Justified in Consulting a Doctor?" and invites him to the forthcoming Mass, where the sermon's subject "will interest you." After the sermon this treatise is referred to by his deacon as "bolder still" than the sermon. The theme of both sermon and pamphlet, then, is "all or nothing." When he lies dying (not of plague but of unspecified fever) he refuses Rieux's offer to stay with him: "Thanks. But priests can have no friends. They have given their all to God."

The sermon reinforces this radical dualism between God and creation. Paneloux is now prepared to confess the difficulty of looking at Evil, including human suffering and in particular the sufferings of children, "our bread of affliction." He is content to pose questions: "For who would dare to assert that eternal happiness can compensate for a single moment's human suffering? . . . We must believe everything or deny everything. And who, I ask, amongst you would dare to deny everything?"

Positively, he can say only that one must "keep faith with that great symbol of all suffering, the tortured body on the Cross," to attempt to will what God is willing in this "testing" time, and above all to remain with the sufferers and not to flee from the city. This may be called "active fatalism," but he accepts that name. We "should go forward, groping our way through the darkness," choosing either to love or to hate God. And finally:

> the love of God is a hard love. It demands total
> self-surrender, disdain of our human personality.
> And yet it alone can reconcile us to suffering and
> the deaths of children, it alone can justify them,
> since we cannot understand them, and we can only
> make God's will ours. That is the faith, cruel in
> men's eyes, and crucial in God's, which we must
> ever strive to compass. We must aspire beyond
> ourselves towards that high and fearful vision.
> And on that lofty plane all will fall into place, all
> discords be resolved, and truth flash forth from the
> dark cloud of seeming injustice.

The sermon is a strange mixture of rhetorical device and impassioned pleading, and it ends badly. No self-respecting preacher would move from the early declaration of agnostic perseverance to the idealism of the final sentences. The famous encounter between Ivan and Alyosha Karamazov comes naturally to mind, and the fact that Dostoevsky's antagonists handle the dilemma more convincingly. Even there, of course, Ivan has the better arguments while Alyosha gropes for words. This may be because analysis is easier than prescription, or because for Dostoevsky as for Camus the problem of evil threatens the categories of understanding used to formulate it in the first place. Paneloux ends in a way that Ivan has called the "higher harmony" or idealistic reconciliation, unacceptable to the doubter. But is it not rather the point that Paneloux remains saddled with the original kind of simplistic theology that Camus gives us in the form of the first sermon?

The best commentary on the second sermon is the pamphlet on which the priest was working at the very time he prepared the sermon: "Is a Priest Justified in Consulting a Doctor?" This will sound a strange question to most Christians who do not see the point of such disjunctive categories: earlier theology made a distinction between first and second causes, which combined in a more complex causation: God acts only through worldly means. Today it is perhaps Dietrich Bonhoeffer who phrased best the thorny issue of the relation between God and the world:

> We should find God in what we know, not in what
> we don't; not in outstanding problems, but in those
> we have already solved . . . he must be found at the
> centre of life. . . . The Christian is not a *homo
> religiosus*, but a man, pure and simple . . . it is only

by living completely in this world that one learns to
believe.[21]

"All or Nothing" represents a false choice, an improper formulation of the human condition in relation to attributes of God. By
the logic of antitheism, this choice and these attributes are transferred *simpliciter* to the human being that rebels. Balzac's classic
rebel of *La Comédie Humaine*, M. Vautrin, instructs the young Ras-
tignac in similar terms: he is "a man who has considered the things of
this world and discovered that there are only two courses to take:
either blind obedience or open revolt."[22] So also Paneloux: "Il faut
tout croire ou tout nier." Now we are familiar with historical oppositions such as that between Hegel's both/and and Kierkegaard's
either/or. Before us is a different sort of dialectical opposition, perhaps more telling and certainly as significant. The all/nothing of
Paneloux has echoes wherever the image of God as Absolute Power
is assumed - by Ibsen's Brand, for instance. But its counter-image
suffers a strange neglect, despite its great moment for theological
reflection. Its outstanding example is probably that of John of the
Cross, *doctor universalis* - that is, the universal teacher beyond even
the Angelic Doctor. The Spanish mystic developed a theory of
knowledge appropriate to the God who is open to suffering and so to
unitive love. He also recognized a sort of Kierkegaardian repetition,
which recovers the world through, with and for God. Yet the divine
retains its mystery even in its presence. Therefore one embraces
everything but only as accompanied by the Abyss itself. "All *and*
Nothing" - *todo y nada*.

The all-or-nothing philosophy betrays a totalitarian claim at
the heart of both positions, theism and antitheism. We are using the
word *irony* to describe the fate of the Promethean challenge to Christian faith. For Camus it was a case of secularizing the theism he
knew, of divorcing immanence from transcendence, and concentrat-
ing on the virtues that remain. He was unable to accept the logic of
Incarnation insofar as it means a true penetration of this world and
of our flesh by divinity. The Mystery of a divine-human presence
was dissipated by his insistence on All or Nothing. To the Dominicans he said: "If Christianity is pessimistic as to man, it is optimistic
as to human destiny. Well, I can say that, pessimistic as to human
destiny, I am optimistic as to man."[23] This statement reveals his
image of Christianity as otherworldly and therefore life-denying.
And he follows it with this: "And not in the name of a humanism
that always seemed to me to fall short, but in the name of an ignorance that tries to negate nothing."

To typify or label Camus is most difficult; for instance, how to describe this negation, which opposes humanism as well as faith? And what, might we add, would Camus's opposition make of other traditions - Protestant and Orthodox - which differ radically from his image of Christianity, not to mention the new phenomenon of Vatican II religion, with statements such as *Mater et Magistra* and *Pacem in Terris*?[24]

A Kind of Atheism

> I do not believe in God, that is true, but I am not thereby an atheist.[25]

Camus has been called "the most attractive and popular atheist the twentieth century is likely to produce."[26] Despite his reluctance to accept the label *atheist*, his work is clearly a rejection of classical theism and a challenge for modern people to take upon themselves the vocation of serving others as "saints without God."

The kind of atheism properly attributed to Camus involves antitheism spiced with a pinch of that "postulatory atheism" that characterizes Promethean humanity. Arthur Gibson, who is most sympathetic to all the atheists of whom he writes, entitles his treatment of Camus "Faith in Death," noting the comment of Rachel Bespaloff:

> the sentence of death is the central theme of his work. . . . To be a man condemned, with and among other men likewise condemned: therein lies our task. For Camus, this is the province of ethics - of the *we* engaged in a desperate venture, beneath a narrow sky darkened by the plague.[27]

On this view, Gibson delineates certain positive functions for death - or mortality - in Camus. His is a "praise of death" as well as (more briefly) a "critique." He discovers the radical limits of human existence to be both constituted and symbolized by our dying. Rebellion itself is therefore constituted by death, as a protest and defiance. It matches the rage of Dylan Thomas "against the dying of the light." Generated by the primary indifference and absurdity of things, the rebel comes to focus his opposition on the fatalism or defeatism that being-toward-death encourages.

Now Gibson's positive portrayal requires questioning. Camus himself states, "The rebel defies more than he denies."[28] But *défier* carries the sense not only of challenge or dare but primarily of distrust, indeed disbelief, *de-fier*. The risk of defiance may perhaps increase proportionately to the radicalness of the limit. Before death, all may be wagered because nothing is to be hoped for. This is why Camus turns in another direction, toward the other. His atheism becomes a humanism:

> When he rebels, a man identifies himself with other men and so surpasses himself, and from this point of view human solidarity is metaphysical. . . .
> I rebel - therefore we exist.

This quotation is significant in displaying the flimsy foundation for Camus's concept of transcendence. I transcend myself in the direction of the other through rebellion - why, exactly? Because rebellion, so we are given to understand in the opening pages of *L'Homme Révolté*, springs from a new awareness of all-or-nothing on the part of the slave. Arising in individualism, it espouses a total view, which by definition embraces humanity. "The sudden appearance of the concept of 'All or Nothing' demonstrates that rebellion, contrary to current opinion, and though it springs from everything that is most strictly individualistic in man, questions the very idea of the individual." The rebel acknowledges that the universal rights of humanity (the greater Whole?) transcend his own life; his highest values are "the common good." Incidentally, Camus's rejection of the existentialist premise that "existence precedes essence" is demanded by this recognition of "values as pre-existent to any kind of action," so that "a human nature does exist, as the Greeks believed."

Human solidarity has an inverse side for Camus, one that comes close to the Christian doctrine of sin. He knew of this doctrine from his philosophical studies and continued to wrestle with the problem of evil all his days. *The Plague* is explicit in depicting the related solidarities of human existence, human suffering and human responsibility. How can *solitaire* and *solidaire* be related? His short story "Jonas" relates that, after three days and nights in meditation, the protagonist writes one word on his canvas, but it is impossible to tell whether the word is *solitaire* or *solidaire*. The logical connection of the two is articulated best by Tarrou in his lengthy confession to Rieux.[29] Like Jean-Baptiste Clamence of *The Fall*, Tarrou was exposed to the legal profession (in the form of his father in red gown, calling for the death penalty) as the socially acceptable way of "handling" the problem of evil. It is a short step to concluding that there is none righteous, that "I have realized that we all have the plague, and I have lost my peace." Tarrou's answer is to steel his will, the only power that can maintain "attention": "What's natural is the microbe. All the rest - health, integrity, purity (if you like) - is a product of the human will, of a vigilance that must never falter. The good man, the man who infects hardly anyone, is the man who has the fewest lapses of attention."

This will is no longer Promethean in the aggressive sense that Nietzsche assigned to it. For Camus, Prometheus has become Caesar, a master of slaves; "the real, the eternal Prometheus has now assumed the aspect of one of his victims." It is the latter's cry that continues to ring through the desert, bidding us revolt and rescue him from bondage. Clearly it is not Christianity which inspires this call to arms. Camus stands against Christian faith, particularly its doctrine of sin and redemption, thus deserving the title of Henri Peyre's essay, "Camus the Pagan": "There are words that I have never understood, such as sin. . . . there are a number of us in this persecuted world who feel that, if Christ died for certain men, he did not die for us."[30]

At times the vocation of "sainthood without God" espoused by Tarrou descends almost to bathos. One is simply "doing one's job" in fighting the plague, one acts because of "common decency." Camus once stated that *The Plague* was "more anti-Christian" than earlier writings. It is tragic that the form of Christian teaching he knew best was what one commentator has described as "its popular all-or-nothing apologetics (either despair or Christ; Christ was either madman or divine, etc., etc.,)."[31] Thus Paneloux's all-or-nothing theology reflects a caricature easily called in question by the hard fact of innocent suffering. Tarrou can say: "Paneloux is right. . . . When an innocent youth can have his eyes destroyed, a Christian should either lose his faith or consent to having his eyes destroyed."

The missing term that this specious logic implies is the concept of divine omnipotence: God can do everything, therefore he can prevent innocent suffering. Camus returned to his favourite problem in addressing the Dominicans at Latour-Maubourg:

> We are faced with evil. And, as for me, I feel rather as Augustine did before becoming a Christian when he said: "I tried to find the source of evil and I got nowhere." But it is also true that I, and a few others, know what must be done, if not to reduce evil, at least not to add to it.[32]

We have before us a modest proposal for limiting human suffering. At one point Dr. Rieux remarks that in the face of the appalling suffering of plague victims, he would "rather cure than know." Saints without God are bound to settle for a perpetual dark night of the soul, a daily Gethsemane. Convinced that the existence of God is quite implausible because of the irrefutable existence of evil, they fall back on their own resources, the will to limit suffering and the acceptance of a practical agnosticism about evil. It is something more than pathos yet less than hope. And for such a philosophy Camus deserves the noble title: "A Pascal without Christ."

Total Justice: The Judge in Hell

The "atheism" of Camus has metaphysical dimension insofar as it parallels the revolt of the slave against the master.

> The slave who opposes his master is not concerned, let us note, with repudiating his master as a human being. He repudiates him as a master. He denies that he has the right to deny him, a slave, on grounds of necessity. . . . The metaphysical rebel is not therefore an atheist, as one might think him, but he is inevitably a blasphemer. Quite simply, he blasphemes primarily in the name of order, denouncing God the Father as the father of death and as the supreme outrage.[33]

This may be characterized as antitheism rather than atheism on the ground that beyond the negative of atheism stands the positive "program" of indictment. Jean Onimus has written that "antitheism attacks a hypothesis that it pretends to admit; it supposes for an instant the existence of God the better to affirm its rejection of him."[34] The scandal of injustice that motivates Ivan Karamazov, for instance, is finally untouched by the question of God's existence: "I would rather remain with my unavenged suffering and my unsatisfied indignation, *even if I were wrong.*"

In the original drafts for *La Peste*, the priest loses his faith entirely.[35] Paneloux comes close but clings to the absolute demand of "all or nothing." For Camus the inspiration and the essence of Christianity is otherworldliness. In this he shares with Marx and general antitheism a deliberate stress on the eschatological dimension in denial of the creationist and immanentist. His respect for Jesus, the absurd hero dying for an illusion, concentrates in humanist fashion on the final cry from the cross, where "its truth and its greatness end. . . . Tear out the final page of the Gospel and you have a human religion, a cult of solitude and of greatness is offered to us."[36]

Camus refuses the consolation of religion's futurist dimension in behalf of the quasi-heroic rebel. For him, God always remains the mad tyrant who holds all power, all trump cards.

Camus sees the problem of God as joined to the problem of human freedom in a peculiar way. He rejects the concept of "freedom as such"; instead:

> Knowing whether or not man is free involves knowing whether he can have a master. The absurdity peculiar to this problem comes from the fact that the very notion that makes the problem of freedom possible also takes away all its meaning. For in the presence of God there is less a problem of freedom than a problem of evil. You know the alternative: either we are not free and God the all-powerful is responsible for evil. Or we are free and responsible but God is not all-powerful. All the scholastic subtleties have neither added anything to nor subtracted anything from the acuteness of this paradox.[37]

Thus the problem of God turns on the problem of evil, and this on innocent suffering. The theme of *The Fall* (*La Chute*, 1956), Camus's last novel, concerns the need and burden of atheism, as expressed in the earlier play *Les Justes*: "For us who do not believe in God there must be *total* justice or we're stuck with despair." In this account of how things stand, is Camus fair to theism or to atheism? The one operates with an Almighty God and the other with a total Justice, two forms of the all-or-nothing disjunctive logic. The traditional formulation of the so-called problem of evil was a syllogism: if God is both all-powerful and all-loving, whence evil? The assumptions are that he *can* prevent evil and *wants* to. No more than a fundamentalist Christian does Camus wish to suggest any limitation of divine omnipotence. He transfers the same fundamentalism to his atheism, which demands an unqualified All as its ulitmate concern. (Sartre thought that Camus always carried a "portable altar"). The image of blind Justice holding her scales would do for either one. Thus it is appropriate that this final authorship should turn to the subject of judgment. But his last words are ambiguous, for at the bar is a "judge-penitent" whose very name suggests one who proclaims clemency. Now if justice is linked with mercy, if it is to be sought not through strict law but through equity (*epieikia, aequitas*), then "a correction of legal justice" has shifted the ground of debate and qualified the syllogism. This was the judgment of Aristotle (*Nic. Eth.* 1137f), a judgment that proved to be of considerable moment in Western tradition. Camus's opinion reflects his own reading of the history, particularly its theodicy; he has missed the vital point, that the struggle over "evil" contains at its heart a debate that has already moved beyond the polarity of all-or-nothing.

Jean-Baptiste Clamence finds the cross of his guilt in Paris and moves to the Dantesque landscape of Amsterdam, surrounded by canals like the circles of hell. Our judge-penitent was once a successful Parisian lawyer, defending the wretched of the earth. His fall from this Eden was occasioned by sounds of derisive laughter and in particular by his failure to help a drowning woman. The recognition that he was acting a farce (allusions to Napoleon and Don Juan) proves traumatic: he becomes a voice *clamans* to whomever will listen, announcing the universal fall from grace and need for repentance. Camus rehearses the humanistic exegesis of the Fall as rise - deriving from the Christian insight that the beneficial effects of human sin are much greater than the previous state: *O felix culpa*! He here presents a more complex view of things than in *The Plague*. The doves in the Dutch sky signify his new and "stubborn hope." And the noble calling of the rebel Rieux is countered by a deeper sense of solidarity, guilt and compassion in the figure of Clamence.

The Fall caused consternation among its readers: surely we are not *all* guilty - how dare he drive us toward "moral panic." Others see it as evidence for a new stage in Camus's development: "a movement toward God," or "the prelude to Camus' eventual adhesion to the Christian faith."[38] The latter is surely illegitimate, inasmuch as Clamence is rather less negative about religion than clearly positive. He lacks the bitterness of Rieux, and there is no character to match the deplorable priest of *L'Etranger* or the ambiguous Paneloux. For Clamence "the end of all freedom is a court sentence;" this is the unhappy consciousness of one who has fallen. That is why, in his opinion, religion is "on the wrong track" when it moralizes and commands: "God's sole usefulness would be to guarantee innocence."

Such a "huge laundering venture" for religion relates to another haunting passage in this strange monologue:

> Ah, *mon cher*, for anyone who is alone, without God and without a master, the weight of days is dreadful. Hence one must choose a master, God being out of style. . . . I knew an atheistic novelist who used to pray every night. That didn't stop anything: how he gave it to God in his books![39]

Apart from the intriguing question of the reference to the novelist, this speech echoes much of *The Rebel*. There we read of the difficulty of escaping the master-slave dialectic, for even Prometheus turns into Caesar. There also we read of the afterlife of God, still so relevant to revolution despite his demise. In *The Fall* it is salvation that is at stake. Clamence missed his chance when the cry for help addressed him not in his social role but in his deepest being. Now he can but lament: "O young woman, throw yourself into the water again so that I may a second time have the chance of saving both of us!"

More important perhaps is the pursuit of a theme already clear in *L'Etranger*, where Meursault can speak of "the happiness of stones." Clamence now sees clearly (lucidity is still a virtue for Camus) that "to be no longer free and to obey" remains both option and escape for those convinced that there is no longer "law in heaven." The judge finds himself fallen from his paradise into a sort of hell, or perhaps that *purgatoire sur la terre* familiar in French literature. To be guilty without a supreme Judge is irony; to know that only such a One could be your Saviour is pathos.

Camus demanded "total justice" and discovered universal guilt. His last novel suggests a substantive departure from the noble vocation of Tarrou and especially Rieux. And his image of Sisyphus the modern Promethean seems less than convincing: Sisyphus was attributed by Camus with a "silent joy," sharing the happiness of protagonists such as Kirillov and Oedipus. The latter could affirm, "I conclude that all is well." This cry "drives out of this world a god who had come into it with dissatisfaction and a preference for futile sufferings. It makes of fate a human matter, which must be settled among men."[40] But for Clamence what may be settled "among men" entails by relentless logic the dimension "before God." The weakness of this kind of atheism lies in Camus's exhaustion of Christianity in one form, the Monophysitism that concentrates on the divinity of Christ to the neglect of his humanity. His knowledge of the Western Augustinian tradition and its modern form of Jansenism focused his attention on a conflict between passionate belief and passionate disbelief. The latter antitheism is coloured by the original theism that remains as its foil. Jean Onimus has suggested that "From Pascal to Simone Weil, Camus met only with a paradoxical faith, founded on a destructive lucidity that, like his own, was bent on creating a void."[41]

At the conclusion of *The Rebel* ("Thought at the Meridian") Camus spoke of preparing, among the ruins, "a renaissance beyond the limits of nihilism."

> We shall choose Ithaca, the faithful land, frugal
> and audacious thought, lucid action, and the gener-
> osity of the man who understands. In the light, the
> earth remains our first and our last love. Our
> brothers are breathing under the same sky as we;
> justice is a living thing. Now is born that strange
> joy which helps one live and die, and which we
> shall never again postpone to a later time.

Here is Camus's brief confession of faith: the earth, brotherhood, a strange love and a present justice. It seems little enough to ask for one who identified himself so courageously with the human struggle. Yet in another sense it remains the Promethean dream and a program for Titans. His working titles for his groups of works were "The Myth of Sisyphus" for the earlier block, "The Myth of Prometheus" for those including *The Rebel* and *The Plague*, and "The Myth of Nemesis" for the works beginning with *The Fall* and including *The First Man*, on which he was engaged at the time of death.[42] The Prometheus cycle gives way to Nemesis, "goddess of moderation and the implacable enemy of the immoderate." She symbolizes Hellenism, the alternative to Christianity which Camus identified as early as his university thesis. The difference between Athens and Jerusalem is that between nature and history, history which begets the fateful doctrine of Providence, heteronomy. Therefore one must replace "the reign of grace" with that of justice.[43]

In the early period, *Sisyphus* examined, among other credos, the reasoning of Kirillov of *The Possessed*: "If God does not exist, I am god." This is his conclusion from discovering that "the attribute of my divinity is independence." Camus comments, "To become god is merely to be free on this earth, not to serve an immortal being."[44] That is, the denial of God liberates the quality of aseity so that autonomy can be transferred from the divine to the human. The age-old story is repeated, as Camus understands in his feeling for Epicurus. "Lucretius' hero, on the other hand, embarks on a revolution. By repudiating the unworthy and criminal gods, he takes their place himself."[45] Yet autonomy is a "painful independence" since "everything depends on us": the divine burden of care devolves on us. The all-or-nothing of absolute deity is transferred to antitheists. Prometheus begins well but his end is Caesarism, for the fatal flaw of mastery appears again.

Camus chose Ithaca, symbol of this world, this earth, and of human solidarity. He was unable to allow any hint of this-worldliness to Christianity. Yet it remains a strange fact that he went out from this world engaged on the topic of judgment. Presumably this would not have issued in Sartre's obsession with condemnation. What then?

What form of clemency, of redemption, could obtain for this man in revolt? Does his Ithaca offer a homecoming, a peaceful end to his personal odyssey? Must one imagine Camus happy?

- 13 -

The Fate of Orestes - Sartre

ORESTES: . . . every man must find out his own way.
Nature abhors man, and you too, god of gods,
abhor mankind.
ZEUS: That is true; men like you I hold in abhorrence.
ORESTES: Take care; those words were a confession of
your weakness. As for me, I do not hate you.
What have I to do with you, or you with me? We
shall glide past each other, like ships in a river,
without touching. You are God and I am free;
each of us is alone, and our anguish is akin.

(*The Flies*, Act III)

Lord of the Flies

Jean-Paul Sartre (1905-76) provides a compelling existentialist and
Promethean hero in the figure of Orestes.[1] His first play, *The Flies*
(*Les Mouches*, 1943), retells the ancient story of the son of Agamemnon and Clytemnestra who returns to Argos to avenge his father's
murder. The original Oresteian trilogy of Aeschylus (*Agamemnon*,
The Choephori, *The Eumenides*) pursues the theogony that cast Prometheus in the roles of supporter of the upstart Zeus and then victim
of his anger. When peace was restored between the two (once Prometheus told his secret about Thetis) a new conflict developed. At
the wedding of Thetis and Peleus, Eris, the goddess of strife, was not
invited and in revenge cast the golden apple inscribed "For the fair-
est," which involved Paris of Troy in the fateful choice leading ultimately to the Trojan War. Agamemnon returned from the ten-year
conflict only to be murdered by his wife, Clytemnestra, and Aegis-
theus, who succeeded him as king of Argos. Agamemnon's children,

---

Notes to Chapter 13 appear on page 349.

Orestes and Electra, revenge themselves when Orestes kills his mother and stepfather.

The burden of Aeschylus concerns the nature of justice. The old pre-Olympian religion saw justice as compatible with vengeance, symbolized by the Furies who punished sins. The primitive gnome *pathei mathos* reveals the hard lesson that we learn through suffering. Crime and retribution "mirror one another," in Anne Lebick's words. What concerns the playwright is more than this truth about human being; he turns it upon the gods, even the greatest of all, Zeus himself. Can the Supreme Being learn through suffering? The Furies may become the Kindlies, but can the absolute Tyrant become the ultimate Sufferer? Aeschylus believes so; Zeus begins his divine journey in the *Prometheia* and completes it in the *Oresteia*. He achieves understanding (*synesis*); he becomes Friend, Guide, even Saviour. Thus beyond this ancient lore a different idea of justice and revenge through command and compromise was developing at Delphi, where Apollo ruled. Finally, in Athens, at the Areopagus below the Acropolis, a new ideal of justice in the context of suffering and free will was mooted by philosopher and tragic poet, not least Aeschylus: "As *Agamemnon* is dominated by the relentlessness of Fate, *The Choephori* by the command of Apollo, so *The Eumenides* presents the true justice of Athene, expressed in the authority and wisdom of an established court of law, the Athenian Areopagus."[2]

The turn of Orestes to share the tragic outworking of the house of Atreus comes with Apollo's blessing. But as the second play ends, the murderer is pursued by the Furies. The dénouement in the final play is accomplished by Apollo, the Furies and the new and decisive presence of Athene and "twelve Athenian citizens" whose votes are evenly divided. Athene decides for acquittal and persuades the Furies to settle in Athens with honour. *The Eumenides* concludes:

> Now great, all-seeing Zeus
> Guards the city of Pallas;
> Thus God and Fate are reconciled.
>   Then let every voice
> Crown our song with a shout of joy!

For Sartre this dénouement is unsatisfactory. It demotes the crucial issue of freedom in the determination of justice, chiefly because it allows fate, even in the more sophisticated form of Apollo and Athene, too much power over human affairs. His rewriting casts Orestes and Zeus in a situation of conflict concerning whether Orestes is truly free to choose his future being. Thus the *dramatis personae* embody the variety of types that Sartre examines in his philosophical and literary works, a sort of typology of unfreedom, so to speak, with Orestes struggling to make his free decision concrete in a most ambiguous situation.

The masterwork *Being and Nothingness* (*L'Etre et le néant*, 1943) and its commentary *Existentialism is a Humanism* (1946) afford insight into two chief forms of "bad faith." The phenomenon that Sartre terms *mauvaise foi* arises through ambiguity of selfhood: am I really what I seem to be? This reflects the fragile relationship obtained between facticity and transcendence (or appearance and reality if these are taken in idealistic terms). Bad faith is lack of sincerity: I accept "*non-persuasive* evidence" and so fall into a mode of being distinct from that "reflective, voluntary decision" worthy of human freedom. "This original project of bad faith is a decision in bad faith on the nature of faith."[3]

Two dramatic forms of bad faith are distinguishable in Sartre's works, *les lâches* and especially *les salauds*. The former hide behind a façade of absolute standards, whereas the latter use these very standards to serve themselves, "congealed in the insincerity of their virtues and vices." Thus the two types resemble in a striking manner the traditional Christian approach to a typology of sin under the heading of sloth and pride.[4]

To return to *Les Mouches*, first produced in the publication year of *L'Etre et le néant*, here we find characters who represent the types analyzed in the philosophical work. One commentator has suggested that the Tutor of Orestes is guilty of "false spirituality" in contrast to the "false other-worldliness" of Zeus/Jupiter.[5] The Tutor relates falsely to Zeus because he is "metaphysically blind," while Orestes "has an unerring feeling for the presence of mystery" even though he rejects the role of the god as Master. A key exchange in their dialogue (Act III) illustrates Sartre's antitheism. The murders are accomplished; Orestes is content but Electra disoriented, almost willing to give Zeus the penitence he asks for. Since Orestes is adamant that his deed was done in freedom, for the relief of the city, Zeus addresses him with a lengthy apologue of the Lord of Nature. Orestes agrees and adds: "But you are not the king of man."

> ZEUS: Impudent spawn! So I am not your king? Who, then, made you?
>
> ORESTES: You. But you blundered; you should not have made me free.
>
> ZEUS: I gave you freedom that you might serve me.

> ORESTES: Perhaps. But now it has turned against its
> giver. And neither you nor I can undo what has
> been done.
> ZEUS: Ah, at last! So this is your excuse?
> ORESTES: I am not excusing myself.
> ZEUS: No? Let me tell you it sounds like an excuse, this
> freedom whose slave you claim to be.
> ORESTES: Neither slave nor master. I *am* my freedom.

Before exploring what this identification of the human with freedom could possibly mean, we note the familiar natural theology that characterizes the Zeus of the play, with its emphasis on causality and control. Against this weight Orestes is able to reply simply and tellingly: but not master of *human* being.

Electra is a complex figure who nevertheless embodies essential traits of bad faith. She hides the truth from herself, she is near solipsism, she feels shame (*B-N* 48f, 261, 273). Having lived too superficially for too long, she remains unprepared for the true consequences of the deed for which she has been waiting. She hesitates before the relentless logic of her brother, considers the penitential offer of Zeus, experiences the darkness of the Furies. In all respects she is caught within ties to others that spell alienation. She is slave, her being is "dependent at the centre of a freedom which is not mine and which is the very condition of my being" (*B-N* 267).

Now Zeus is described (in terms reminiscent of William Golding's dystopian novel) as "god of the flies and death," and he himself explains to Orestes that the flies invading Argos are "a symbol." Since they feed on decay, especially what has been described as the "murky secretions of the soul," they illustrate a key concept of Sartre's, *les visqueux*.[6] What the flies symbolize is not only the oppressive presence of Zeus but in particular the quality of dehumanization or thing-ness that attends such masterful presence. It is "things and their gelatinous, solid, or fluid matter" that demand that we look behind our first perception - he has Bachelard's psychoanalysis of things, for instance *Water and Dreams*, in mind (*B-N* 600). The viscous is the "slimy" or "sticky," and it flows through the drama of Orestes like a silent witness of warning and doom. Sartre detects a moral quality to viscosity so that there obtains "a symbolic relation between sliminess and the sticky baseness of certain individuals" (*B-N* 605). It is particularly significant that such baseness is an open possibility for Orestes, "like a *leech sucking me*." As part of the being of the for-itself, it offers to bestow itself as the form of our project of being: "From the start then it appears as a possible 'myself' to be established; from the start it has a psychic quality" (*B-N* 606).

The temptation of Orestes is to yield to the pressure of all others around him who repudiate his free choice in the murder of mother and stepfather, reducing it to social order and divine will. Penitence, guilt, submission are the order of the day. His refusal stands as Sartre's sign that freedom is its own absolute and *raison d'être*. The play ends with a question: what will happen? Orestes has thrown the gauntlet to Zeus, who leaves the scene, and to Electra, who is unable to rise to the challenge of going out into the unknown where "an Orestes and an Electra are waiting for us"; she repents. The citizens of Argos listen in silence to his final speech in which he accepts his crime as his own and declares his kingship. They make way as he pipes the flies out of the city. "Shrieking, the FURIES fling themselves after him."

"I am my freedom"

So decisive and pervasive is the concept of freedom for Sartre that Arthur Gibson chooses to treat him under the title, "Faith in Freedom."[7] Gibson helps us appreciate the significance of *Being and Nothingness* by stressing its ethical nature. That is, despite Sartre's own understanding of what he was attempting as "phenomenological ontology," and despite its obvious debt to the properly phenomenological work of Heidegger, *Being and Time* (*Sein und Zeit* was published in 1927), Sartre's book is really "descriptive ontological ethics." Only with this moral category in constant sight do we recognize the meaning of the discussion of nothingness:

> An intelligent and consistent ontology can grant to nothingness no more substantial status than a formal-logical one in the dimension of the human imagination. But a perfectly intelligent and consistent ethic can certainly grant to nothingness a very substantial status indeed; or more accurately can grant to the act of negation of the practical intellect, the will, a power to alter reality very substantially.[8]

Gibson's primary distinction allows us to give proper weight to Sartre's image of the human, especially his Kantian criterion of universalizability, which stands in apparent conflict with his demand that freedom be absolutely and radically free. It is this ethical demand that colours all his thinking, in contrast to Heidegger's original "phenomenological ontology." The latter's *Fundamentalfrage*, "What is the meaning of being? " led to the distinction between two kinds of existence, roughly that of humans and that of things, *Dasein* and *Vorhandensein*.[9] The kinship with Sartre's categories of the for-itself and the in-itself, *pour-soi* and *en-soi*, is obvious, despite considerable difference in their analyses.

Sartre's freedom derives from an analysis of the structure of existence similar to Heidegger's. But the difference is decisive: he remains a Cartesian who willingly goes beyond Descartes in dismissing the idea of God and in transferring the divine attributes to human beings. William Barrett identifies this Cartesian nature best: "This Cartesian God, says Sartre, is the freest God that man ever invented. He is not subordinate to a realm of essences: rather, He creates essences and causes them to be what they are. . . . When God dies, man takes the place of God."[10] The absolute nature of freedom requires the presupposing of "an original freedom" in order to constitute the human will as that "mode of being" that incorporates human freedom most clearly: "If the will is to be freedom, then it is of necessity negativity and the power of nihilation" (*B-N* 442). The will directs the negations, its nihilating power, outward rather than inward (which would be bad faith, *B-N* 48). Thus it achieves that personal autonomy that Sartre struggles to define in distinguishing an absolute, that is nonrelated, *pour-soi* as against the sort of present guaranteed only with reference to the Other.[11]

Man is not *l'en-soi* but *le pour-soi*: he can assign meaning by an act of freedom, a choice. Yet this provides little consolation for Sartre, who is obsessed with the alienating presence of others and the continuous temptation to yield to self-deception. In the final section of this book we will argue that otherness is alienating precisely when and because the Other is absent. Such a thesis is most clear in Sartre's work. God is impossible because to be *causa sui* (the attribute of aseity in classical theism) is self-contradictory, involving a distancing of necessary selfhood over against contingent or hypothetical viewing.[12] For Sartre only nothingness can guarantee absolute freedom, the experience of negation out of which stands a struggle of will - the choice to die (nausea, self-nihilation, suicide) or the choice to live (release, self-acceptance, good faith).

The project called "human" is an escape from oneself to find oneself: from past to future selfhood, from the nothing behind one toward the not-yet ahead. Nothingness creates dread - so far Sartre follows Kierkegaard; but dread is the womb of liberty, the possibility of selfhood through free choice - from this, Kierkegaard's dread and despair are categorically different. For freedom to be the human absolute, all else must become contingent. Few literary works have drawn the consequences of such a view so relentlessly as Sartre's series of novels *Les Chemins de la Liberté*. Its cast of characters explores the nature of freedom in relation to a variety of human types and situations - the *gamin*, the homosexual, the revolutionary, and especially protagonists such as Mathieu and Brunet. There are some stock literary scenes, particularly from modern French fiction, such as self-mutilation (Gide's Lafcadio, Sartre's Roquentin and now Ivich and Mathieu both).[13] But above all stands the journey of Mathieu in quest of freedom, over against the communist commitment of Brunet. Mathieu is a proper existentialist antihero, courting freedom so absolutely that nothing matters, including any possible reason for the free act. His end is like his beginning: the action of shooting at the enemy becomes a statement of defiance and means of liberation.

> This was revenge on a big scale. Each one of his shots avenged some ancient scruple. One for Lola whom I dared not rob; one for Marcelle whom I ought to have left in the lurch; one for Odette whom I didn't want to kiss. This for the books I never dared to write, this for the journeys I never made, this for everybody in general who I dared to hate and tried to understand. He fired, and the tables of the law crashed about him - Thou Shalt Love Thy Neighbour as Thyself - bang! in that bugger's face - Thou Shalt Not Kill - bang! at that scarecrow opposite. He was firing on his fellow men, on Virtue, on the whole world. Liberty is Terror. . . . He fired. He was cleansed. He was all-powerful. He was free.
>
> (*Iron in the Soul* 225)

Mathieu represents the original quest of Sartre, a quest remaining in theory but contradicted not only by his Kantian concept of the universalizability of the moral conscience - the "tables of the Law" - but also by his subsequent interpretation of existentialism as humanism and as the dynamic of Marxism. The former is dealt with in concise form in *L'Existentialisme est un humanisme* (1946), the latter in *Critique de la Raison Dialectique* (Vol. I, 1960).

Sartre's first move in his quest is to insist on the familiar existentialist definition that existence precedes essence. This involves not only the denial of God ("there is no human nature, because there is no God to have a concept of it")[14] but also the denial of lingering idealism, which constitutes the idea of essence, of a "human nature." Thus man must make himself, he is completely responsible for what he is; he is "a project." His next move follows less clearly from the premise of bare existence:

> he is responsible for all men . . . in choosing for himself he chooses for all men. For in effect, of all the actions a man may take in order to create himself as he wills to be, there is not one which is not creative, at the same time, of an image of man such as he believes he ought to be . . . valid for all and for the entire epoch in which we find ourselves.
>
> (*E-H* 291f)

At this point Sartre's "existentialism" has moved from freedom to constraint, for "Resignation is my will for everyone, and my action is, in consequence, a commitment on behalf of all mankind. . . . I am creating a certain image of man as I would have him to be. In fashioning myself I fashion man" (*E-H* 292). Sartre refers the concept of existential anguish to the sense of total responsibility ("a legislator deciding for the whole of mankind"). This form of Kant's categorical imperative is avoided only by self-deception: "the act of lying implies the universal value which it denies." Since strict proof is lacking to such a universal project, the choice involves risk, the saying of "nevertheless." "There is nothing to show that I am Abraham; nevertheless I am also obliged at every instant to perform actions which are examples" (*E-H* 293).

The dilemma of existentialist choice is clear in Sartre's statement of universal responsibility based on the sheer relativism of choosing one possibility over others. For the choice "has value only because it is chosen"; "it is only I who choose to say that it is good and not bad." Naturally Kierkegaard's reference of anguish and of choice to God must be denied: "abandonment" implies divine absence and its radical consequences - as against those who deny God but wish to continue all the ethical corollaries of theism. "The existentialist, on the contrary, finds it extremely embarrassing that God does not exist, for there disappears with Him all possibility of finding values in an intelligible heaven" (*E-H* 294). Man is "forlorn," "man is free, man *is* freedom."

That essay was written just after the Second World War, and not without reflection on the ambiguity of ethics, on the conflicting moral theories that haunted intellectuals facing hard decisions. By 1960 Sartre still could not produce the ethics promised at the end of *Being and Nothingness* in 1943. But now he worked through the Marxist position on the question whether the reign of freedom must not await the solution to the problem of material production. He seems to agree, in that freedom, at least for the many, remains but a hope. But meanwhile he distinguishes two types of Marxism and throws his weight with one against the other:

> Thus living Marxism is heuristic; its principles and its prior knowledge appear as regulative in relation to its concrete research. In the work of Marx we never find entities. . . . The open concepts of Marxism have closed in. They are no longer *keys*, interpretive schemata; they are posited for themselves as an already totalized knowledge.[15]

The latter he terms "frozen Marxism." But he also derides the "abstract" and the "lazy" Marxist who relies on the closed conceptualizations and who, in procrustean fashion, makes individuals such as Flaubert and Valéry to fit the bed made up so tidily by Marx and Engels. Lacking any "hierarchy of mediations" to interpret such individuals, contemporary Marxism displays its "heuristic inadequacy."[16]

Tension remains in Sartre's work, chiefly his formulation of a moral universal (even in *Being and Nothingness*, if we follow Gibson's suggestion) as against his insistence that action is rooted in radical freedom and continues to be validated with reference to nihilation. This tension is illustrated in the contradiction between the acceptance of "humanity" as the intention of moral choice and the alienation inevitably associated with the Other. Before turning more explicitly to the concept of otherness, we should note the controversy concerning Sartre's overture to Marxism. George Novack concludes that Sartre tried to grasp Marx with one hand and Kierkegaard with the other, and since Marxism and existentialism remain in fundamental opposition, he failed: "Instead of subordinating Existentialism to Marxism, as he promises, he virtually dissolves Marxism into Existentialism."[17] Raymond Aron agrees, arguing that Sartre's fidelity to "the dialectic of the solitary individual" prevented his embracing Marxism. Even his use of the term *praxis* may be identified with the for-itself of *Being and Nothingness*.[18] This insight is reinforced by Maurice Cranston's analysis of Sartre's concept of alienation. Although this is developed sociologically in *La Critique de la Raison Dialectique*, it remains an ontological notion, the familiar "conflict" of *L'Etre et le néant*. It is not the Marxist exploitation motif so much as an "existentialized" Hegelianism, the "mutual antagonism" of Sartre's earlier works.[19]

266   *Prometheus Rebound*

"Hell is Others"

"L'enfer, c'est les autres." This famous definition from *Huis Clos* (*No Exit*) serves as motto for the complex theory of otherness and alienation set out in the plays and novels as well as in detail in *Being and Nothingness*. In the latter's phenomenological analysis of "the look [*le regard*]" especially we have on display an uncompromising statement of the inevitable alienation of human being.[20] "For Sartre, every look is a look of hate, every embrace a 'kiss of death'" (Miceli); "The self of the Sartrean man is intimately haunted by the Other" (Champigny); "By perceiving the other, I congeal him into an object, as a thing among things. . . . He and I are two liberties affronting each other and trying to paralyze each other by our look" (Jolivet).

To begin with the individual isolated by Descartes is to ask for trouble. For when others appear on one's horizon they intensify and complicate the pattern of alienation involved in the motion of the ego toward that which is not-itself. If the environing world occasions nausea in the ego, personal otherness sharpens the pain. In *Nausea* Roquentin's odyssey into absurdity begins with his recognition that things - and selves - rob one of freedom: "each existing, embarrassed, vaguely alarmed, feeling in the way [*de trop*]." The "enormous absurdity of existence" afflicts the ego with a loss of the identity won so laboriously by the Cartesian subject. Even more so is it the case when other *persons* move into view. They heighten one's sense of contingency and threaten one's freedom. The dynamics of alienation are strictly conflictual, cannibalistic. The existential project of recovering the self is the same as "absorbing the Other": "While I attempt to free myself from the hold of the Other, the Other is trying to free himself from mine; while I seek to enslave the Other, the Other seeks to enslave me. . . . Conflict is the original meaning of being-for-others" (*B-N* 364).

Thus what Harry Stack Sullivan calls "the psychology of interpersonal relationships" becomes in Sartre's hands a struggle between mutually exclusive wills, engaged not in reconciliation but in following the inexorable motion of alienating otherness to its ultimate conclusion: mutual annihilation.[21] The radical freedom of the individual ranges all phenomena around its need for space; the distance from others, however, is secured best by enslaving them. The fascinating analysis of sadism and masochism in *Being and Nothingness* suggests the hidden agenda for Sartre's conflictual humanity. "The essence of the relations between consciousnesses is not the *Mitsein*, it is conflict" (*B-N* 429). Now Sartre is not accepting a monadic world in which freedom is constantly "on trial" (he refers to Kafka) before the facticity that presents obstacles to be nihilated. Rather he takes account of those other, alien centres of being and therefore of nihilating freedom. The situation is both more complex and more subtle.[22] The key lies in the concept of appropriation. Both sadist and masochist, to give Sartre's own leading examples, seek to use the other by appropriating his being and his freedom in behalf of their own being-for-others, their own transcendent freedom. This is the context for another of Sartre's analyses of *the look*.

> The sadist discovers his error when his victim *looks at* him; that is, when the sadist experiences the absolute alienation of his being in the Other's freedom . . . he can not act on the Other's freedom even by forcing the Other to humiliate himself and to beg for mercy, for it is precisely in and through the Other's absolute freedom that there exists a world in which there are sadism and instruments of torture and a hundred pretexts for being humiliated and for forswearing oneself.

After a quotation from Faulkner's *Light in August*, describing the castration and dying of Joe Christmas, Sartre adds: "Thus this explosion of the Other's look in the world of the sadist causes the meaning and goal of sadism to collapse. The sadist discovers that it was *that freedom* which he wished to enslave, and at the same time he realizes the futility of his efforts" (*B-N* 405f).

Every ego is engaged in "a desperate effort to *be*" - desperate because we are all nihilators defending our fragile project of being, which necessarily involves mutual destruction: "The Other is in principle inapprehensible; he flees me when I seek him and possesses me when I flee him" (*B-N* 408). That is, in relation to others one is caught in hopeless ambiguity, over against them either by objectifying ("trans-descendence" in Jean Wahl's term) or by experiencing their transcendence transcending one ("trans-ascendence"). To pro-ject one's self in opposition to the Other is to remain *de trop* before every other.

It is as if we are isolated in a closed space with no way out. Perhaps like Pierre in Sartre's short story "The Room" our self-deception leads us to create our essence by manipulating others, while they in turn attempt to manipulate us. Or perhaps it is like that more famous room of the play *No Exit*, in which the consequences of otherness require only a few Others to complete the awful circle. Garcin draws the conclusion at last: "all those eyes intent on me.

Devouring me. [*He swings round abruptly.*] What? Only two of
you? I thought there were more; many more. [*Laughs.*] So this is
hell. I'd never have believed it. . . . There's no need for red-hot
pokers. Hell is - other people!"

Thus the human odyssey of Sartre's characters develops individual consciousness at the expense of acceptance of the Other. A
solipsism of being as well as knowledge is involved. This resembles
the concept of "shut-upness" or unfreedom, which Kierkegaard
advances in the context of demoniacal rejection of communication;
freedom, on the other hand, "is precisely the expansive." Iris Murdoch sums it up well:

> In Sartre's world rational awareness is in inverse
> ratio to social integration. . . . The individual is
> the centre, but a solipsistic centre. He has a *dream*
> of human companionship, but never the experi-
> ence. He touches others at the fingertips. The
> best he can attain to is an intuition of paradise, *un
> drôle d'amitié.*[23]

Murdoch has in mind the characters of *Les Chemins de la Liberté.*
Mathieu gives his life for nothing or for nothingness: "Liberty is Ter-
ror." Those like Brunet and Schneider who once put their faith in the
Communist party are disillusioned and therefore conclude: "If the
Party is right, I am more lonely than a madman. If the Party is
wrong, all men are alone and the world is done for."

"I desire to be God"

If human otherness is paradigm of hell, little wonder that Sartre cannot bear the gaze of a divine Other. He expresses the Promethean
defiance and exchange through many characters and in notable passages. Perhaps his most serious exploration of the theme occurs in
Le Diable et le Bon Dieu (1951), in which "prophetic" Goetz says:

> Each minute I wondered what I could BE in the
> eyes of God. Now I know the answer: nothing.
> God does not see me, God does not hear me, God
> does not know me. You see this emptiness over
> our heads? That is God. You see this gap in the
> door? It is God. You see that hole in the ground?
> That is God again. Silence is God. Absence is
> God. God is the loneliness of man. . . . If God
> exists, man is nothing; if man exists. . . .[24]

And in the next and final scene, Goetz declares that "I killed God because he divided me from mankind, and now I see that his death has isolated me even more surely." Thus his exploration of the difference between good and evil, between service of God and service of Devil, halts before the familiar dilemma of the Sartrean subject: all otherness, whether human or divine, appears as threat to one's freedom of being.

Sartre has been called "perhaps the most uncompromisingly atheistic" of existentialists (Padovano), and Régis Jolivet states: "Atheism is so fundamental for Sartre that we cannot grasp the meaning of his philosophy without referring to it constantly as to the thesis characterizing his system."[25] Jolivet suggests that Sartre's atheism was painless, derived largely from the circumstances of his education "and the spiritual poverty of his milieu" and hence resembling that "anarchism" of which Simone de Beauvoir writes. In short, one can point out the similar pattern of childhood and youth to that of Camus. But unlike Camus, who maintained a certain reverent agnosticism toward theism, Sartre accuses God of *looking* with the fatal glance of divine Otherness. He tells how as a child he felt God looking at him: "Indignation saved me. I flew into a rage against so crude an indiscretion, I blasphemed. He never looked at me again."[26]

When writing *Les Mots* in 1964, Sartre commented that the past decade was an awakening from a sort of madness; "a conscript of the absolute - that was my neurosis." His "slow apprenticeship to the real" thus suggested a different context in which to view his youthful petulance at God's crude indiscretion. Yet his lifelong commitment to the Promethean premise is never set aside, the thesis that divine existence would annihilate human freedom.

The Promethean urge we have been tracing sees the issue as a clear-cut choice: either ourselves or God. To be truly human means to rescue autonomy, to assert absolute individual freedom, and therefore to displace the divine will and freedom by the human will and freedom, to substitute the human for the divine reality. Yet Sartre recognizes the irony of the Promethean endeavour:

> God is dead. . . . Hegel tried to replace him with a system and the system floundered. . . Comte by a religion of humanity, and the positivism floundered. . . . God is dead, but man has not, for all that, become atheistic. The silence of the transcendent, and the permanent need for religion in modern man - that is still the major thing.[27]

Sartre follows and extends both the Hegelian master-slave dynamism and the radical existentialism based on Heidegger. The confluence of these streams, along with his activist stress, the *praxis* of his experiment in communism, emerged in a turmoil of desire, a vast sea of infinite longing.

> Fundamentally man is *the desire to be*, and the existence of this desire is not to be established by an empirical induction; it is the result of an *a priori* description of the being of the for-itself, since desire is a lack and since the for-itself is the being which is to itself its own lack of being.
>
> (*B-N* 565)

Now the for-itself projects the desire for the in-itself, or more properly "to become in-itself-for-itself" - that being possessed of full consciousness of itself as the foundation of its own being-in-itself. And so: "It is this ideal which can be called God. Thus the best way to conceive of the fundamental project of human reality is to say that man is the being whose project is to be God" (*B-N* 566). Sartre can say in this same context that it is "God" who identifies and defines us in our ultimate and fundamental project. Because we reach toward that permanent limit through which we know what we are, therefore (he concludes, with a logic involving a *petitio principii*) we "reach toward being God . . . man fundamentally is the desire to be God."

The ontology at work here, in the concluding sections of *Being and Nothingness* particularly, is a tragic one.[28] The human experiment is caught between the nothingness that threatens us at every turn with a variety of "holes," against which we create such reflexes as will create "folds" in being, able to withstand the threat. Between the *trou* and the *plié*, the human project is haunted by the spectre of "God." Each for-itself reaches toward the ideal of in-itself-for-itself, classically expressed by theologians as *Ens causa sui*, the God whose aseity secures his freedom from all contingency, so that even ontological Nothingness remains at rest before him. Since this idea of God is "contradictory" for Sartre - both a projection of desire and a threat of Otherness - the human passion drives us to sacrifice our for-itself in a project doomed to failure. "Man is a useless passion" (*B-N* 615).

The conclusion of Sartre's ontological speculation is clarified in such passages, as well as throughout his later works. The human project becomes the displacement of God, whose classical attributes are now predicated of human being: absolute freedom, self-grounding, the will that creates out of nothing. In short, "Man makes himself man in order to be God" (*B-N* 626). For this reason we may

regard Sartre's project as a new theogony, a creation of god. Karl
Barth grasps this point clearly:

> I cannot imagine how Sartre's existentialism can
> possibly be understood without the realization that
> from the first to the last it involves the extraordi-
> nary but typically mythological spectacle of a theo-
> gony. To be sure, it is a strange, short-lived and
> stunted God who is conceived and born. . . . To be
> sure, this being is only man. Yet we see something
> of the passion of a monotheistic conception of God
> in the way in which man excludes and rejects the
> existence of God, of any other God. Sartre
> thought that in this way he could give man his
> proper place. But this obviously means that he
> gives him the place and function of God, i.e. of the
> true God as distinct from all others.[29]

Barth recognizes in Sartre's project "the apotheosis of man without
God" and the strange new predication - the human receiving "the
attributes of at least the conventional Western conception of God."
Here are aseity, omnipotence, omniscience, even infinity, which
"may be seen in the unlimited nature of the claim which Sartre's
man-God advances for himself."

We have come full circle as we stand before the new creation, the divinized human of Jean-Paul Sartre's speculative ontology.
Here is the Promethean challenge taken up with revolutionary zeal.
Like a new Robespierre, Sartre bids us pledge our lives to Terror,
the violence that spells liberty. Genet's fictional character, Divine, is
for Sartre a striking symbol of deity: "a hole through which the world
empties into nothing . . . when she appears she causes a hemorrhage
of being." To staunch this wound inflicted by the Other, Sartre advocates a negation of the negation - he notes Flaubert's "negative theology," for instance, as an example of the way in which the collapse of
the image of God denies his negation of being. Like Prometheus,
Orestes finds meaning and selfhood in his own nihilating will; his
apophatic theology destroys the image of humanized deity in order to
gain deified humanity. The totally human thus reigns supreme: theology and autology are one.[30]

- 14 -

Conclusion: Faith beyond Zeus-Prometheus

The Lonely "I"

> In the Sunday afternoon of the yard, the men looked as though they were out for the afternoon. On all their scrubbed and freshly shaven faces was the same expression of *absence*. *They were waiting for something*.
>
> (Sartre, *Iron in the Soul*)

Sartre's vision of the prisoners describes the phenomenon of waiting, implying absence, an interlude in which hope supports life - perhaps hope based on evidence, perhaps merely forlorn. This is another way of putting the case so stridently expressed by Nietzsche's "God is dead." Martin Buber has traced this unhappy *fin-de-siècle* mood in his essays *Eclipse of God*.[1] He notes Heidegger's understanding of the three stages in the eclipse of God: from Pascal's "lost God" through Hegel's "God himself is dead" to Nietzsche's "God is dead and we have slain him." Heidegger himself is important as one who explored the modern sense of loss, of absence. In his interpretive writings on Hölderlin he calls ours an "hour of night": "But alas! our generation walks in night, / dwells, as in Hades, without the divine."[2] Buber adds the comment: "Eclipse of the light of heaven, eclipse of God - such indeed is the character of the historic hour through which the world is passing."

Heidegger's essay "Hölderlin and the Essence of Poetry" describes the modern age as "the time of the gods who have fled *and*

Notes to Chapter 14 appear on page 352.

of the God who is coming."

> We are too late for the gods
> and too early for Being.
> Being's poem, just begun, is man.[3]

Thus a double lack is suffered: "the no longer of the departed gods and the not yet of the Coming One." Appearances suggest that there is no god, or at least that we are living through "the age in which God is absent," a time of *Entgötterung*.[4]

The irony of the Heideggerian alternative to traditional metaphysics is that the old subjectivism is replaced by a new. Christendom grounded reality in a God who functioned as *ens realissimum* and thus made room for - and way for - a subjective response. But the resulting ambiguity about the relationship between thinking and being allowed the split of being from thinking, dis-placing Ground from grounded, and leaving the latter on its own. Now sole source of value and truth, the subjective individual finds himself at the mercy of other beings; the logic of Sartre's tragic view of interpersonal relations is present as the fault of Heidegger's anthropology. Here we note the thesis of Thomas Langan concerning "the absence of the other as other." Heidegger wants to "let the *Seiende* be what it is," a laudable intention. But in the final resort, the source of the other's meaning is in fact my own doing, "the projection of Dasein." Metaphysics may be, for Heidegger, the tragic forgetting of being; but as he re-members being, it appears as a forgetting of the other.[5]

Cartesian subjectivism remains the enemy and the temptation. As Sartre saw with unrelenting clarity, only the alienating gaze of an other allows one to exist for oneself. A moral form of solipsism results, and the private will must operate to achieve autonomy over against and despite the threatening visage of others. Prometheus is no longer a champion on behalf of those oppressed by a tyrannical deity, but the symbol of every one for himself. The "irony of atheism" which we are exploring includes this loss of the other. The price of autonomy is not simply the loss of a divine Other but of human others too. Such alienating relationships objectify, de-humanize. The result is "the man without qualities," as Robert Musil described him in his bleak novels, and the "abolition of man," as C.S. Lewis termed it: artefacts rather than humans through the "scientific" acculturation of our age.[6]

The Decline of Sex

Human sexuality, particularly gender identity, has been the concern of recent scholarly and popular investigation. Such clinical authors as Masters and Johnson introduced the mechanistic or technical approach, and writers such as Nena and George O'Neill illustrate the new wave of technique for its own sake in sexuality.[7] But a comment from John Barth's Scheherezade (expert in both lovemaking and storytelling) is apt: "Making love and telling stories both take more than good technique - but it's only the technique that we can talk about" (*Chimera*). Our thesis that the disappearance of God entails the disappearance of humanity is reflected in the modern understanding of sexual contact between isolated individuals. The traditional ideal of marriage as the creation of something new - "one flesh" - from two people (the mathematics of Mystery), is exchanged by the savage doctrine that you are "on your own" even in moments of closest physical contact. Sexuality has been stripped of the dimension of transcendence, reduced to a bestial model, the sado-masochism of Sartre's grim philosophy.

One can appreciate the problem for a modern, raised on a diet of facticity and technical rationality, when faced with a reality traditionally classified as "mystery" or "sacrament" and hedged about with taboo and moral constraint. The quotation from John Barth's Scheherezade indicates part of the problematics of sexuality: to communicate the essence of mystery is impossible, so one concentrates on technique. It becomes a question of sexual engineering, rather like the pathetic role of Don Juan, a substitution of quantity for quality. Leporello's famous *catologo* in Mozart's *Don Giovanni* suggests the genre: conquest, sophisticated rape. The don himself comments about one of his "affairs," "it is over now, and I hope never to see her again. . . . I do not wish to be reminded of my relation to her." Kierkegaard gives these words to the Seducer in what he termed the "aesthetic" existence-sphere (*Stage*) with its categories of immediacy and luck.[8] One could conclude that Don Juan is a classic case of underachiever, knowledgeable in technique or methodology, but unable to measure up to the criteria for meaningful and lasting relationships. He has little to give, after all, and almost nothing in human terms. He has become as inhuman as the hand of stone that grips him to lead him to his doom in the operatic finale. His Eros is so close to Thanatos that his list of conquests turns Woman into an object, a mere thing calling forth not humanity - manhood - but violence, hatred. Jean Genet has explored this connection between love and death, between phallos and murder.

Our view is that such lack of centred selfhood derives from the loss of others. Individuality does not create persons except through mutuality, the positive presence of others - *ad alium*, in Augustinian terms. That Christian Father had understood well that (meditating on the unity of persons in Trinity) *person* is a relational term rather than, with Boethius, a substantival one. Therefore the key to defining human sinfulness is exclusive love of self: a self enclosed within the circle of its "possessions," the heart curved back on itself. Mere in-dividualism is not the road to autonomy, but only to autarchy, even autism.[9] "Tu n'existe pas que par tes liens."

Promiscuity may indicate freedom, as is claimed in authoritative fashion these days. But it may indicate its opposite also: the new bondage of the autonomous individual caught in the fetters of inhumanity. Thus self-centredness involves an inevitable narcissism (always infertile) in which, according to Christopher Lasch, "the ethic of pleasure" has replaced "the ethic of achievement." The new hedonism underlines the fate of sexuality in our technological age. Lacking the proper mirror, fellow humans, we cannot identify with (that is, identify) the other; we tend toward the fratricide of Cain. For narcissism engenders both homicidal and suicidal impulses, autonomy gone mad. When such an individual looks, he sees the other as enemy, as threat. As parable of such exclusivism and isolation, Michel Foucault has suggested that strange edifice, the Panopticon of Jeremy Bentham's imagining. From this tower of silence and sight, the all-seeing eye of asylum keeper or prison warder watches with hostile intent. Here there can be no common good (*res publica*), no shared humanity, because there is neither freedom nor trust.[10]

Autonomy, Heteronomy - and "Theonomy"?

Our survey of Promethean atheism shows the primacy of the will in this type of anthropology. What has become clear is that to will is to be able to say no - one recalls Descartes, Kant, Sartre above all in this refrain. The "freedom of the will" becomes the battle-cry, since it is assumed that "God" functions as tyrant, the Absolute whose omnipotent will cancels human willing and choosing. The only alternative for free will is thus to deny either the supremacy of God or his very existence. The role of Zeus, classical *tyrannis*, is transferred to Jehovah, the Christian God as understood by antitheists since the Enlightenment. Symptomatic of this development is the identification of ego with will. Iris Murdoch, for one, speaking of Sartre as well as philosophers like Hampshire, Hare and Ayer, laments the passing of moral *vision*, for they equate "the true person with the empty choosing will."[11]

It has been remarked by Alisdair MacIntyre that individualism was invented by the Enlightenment. Whether Cartesian ego or Kantian moral conscience, it is indeed the sole individual that occupies centre stage in the drama of creating values, world, selfhood. The dynamics of this kind of individualism, the classical *solipsismus*, are formed by the assumption that "God" is Tyrant. Camus's Paneloux saw God as the inflexible Master who demands "All or Nothing." Spinoza could refer to humankind as God's "absolute slave." Both Sartre and Erich Fromm used Richard Hughes's novel *A High Wind in Jamaica* to illustrate the awareness of self-consciousness. Emily's crisis of identity includes the following query: "But if she was God, why not turn all the sailors into white mice, or strike Margaret blind, or cure somebody, or do some other Godlike act of the kind?" Such is the image of deity, the godlike acts of absolute power, in popular imagination. Lacking all subtlety of qualification, it appears to be almost the opposite of the biblical idea of the God of Creation and covenant, merciful and gracious, present within the world in incarnate form, suffering the agony of redemptive healing in his own person. Yet it thrusts itself forward as the crucial image in the debate about God, in the line between belief and unbelief. E.J. Pratt, theologian and poet, in what Northrop Frye called "the greatest poem in Canadian literature," *The Truant*, contrasts "the great Panjandrum" (to whom "we concede . . . no pain nor joy nor love nor hate") with the "bucking truant with a stiff backbone":

> He has developed concepts, grins
> Obscenely at your Royal bulletins,
> Possesses what he calls a will
> Which challenges your power to kill.[12]

Tyrant and truant: the stuff of heteronomy and autonomy - with a vengeance, as it were.

When Kant explored the logic of heteronomy and autonomy, he settled for much less than classical theism had attained. As noted earlier, the older debate on freedom of the will engaged more complex issues than were allowed by mere opposition of divine and human willing. Louis Dupré's analysis of modern philosophy of religion stresses the Kantian reduction, summed up under three propositions. First, theoretical reason cannot support religious consciousness, because the former is restricted to "the objective, phenomenal sphere." Second, the transcendent can be approached only through "the subject's awareness of itself" rather than through its world, since it does not belong to the latter's objective, phenomenal sphere. The third shows the modern impasse clearly: "Since the subject must be conceived as essentially autonomous, no transcendent reality can ever interfere with the exercise of human freedom."[13] Such restrictive autonomy melds with technological rationality to yield an "alienation of reason" (Kolakowski) if not an "eclipse of reason" (Horkheimer).

Classical theism may have come to emphasize omnipotence in its theology, but the patristic era had promised something better. No less than a commerce and participation (*methexis*) of divine and human reality was thought to be the logic of Incarnation. Origen of Alexandria, for instance, emphasized that to imagine an absolute omnipotence involves logical contradiction, as does the concept of sheer infinity, for finite minds. The tension with which the Alexandrians wrestled is the essential tension of theism, the gap between divine and human, their mutually exclusive properties. Origen's answer was that the Incarnation of the Word of God was an archetypal modality for coexistence, through *katabasis* or "accommodation." And this category proved decisive in subsequent Christian doctrine. Divine omnipotence does not threaten human freedom; rather, the dynamics of its accommodation provide authentic foundation, reciprocal engagement in covenantal union.[14]

The divine "attributes" - more properly "properties" - must not be abstracted from the divine activity. Thus "omnipotence" must be related firmly to the concrete will revealed in acts of love, especially creation and incarnation. The way of abstraction leads to the manufacture of idols, the sparse God - akin to Luther's horror of *deus nudus* - of deism. This remote and absolute deity was thought a kind of "godhead" beyond and behind the God of trinitarian theology (both "immanent" and "economic"). When trinity is conceived of as deriving from unity (rather than coexisting in polarity with it, as the classical doctrine of the triunity phrased it) then formal logic constitutes speculative theology. Charles Hartshorne's critique of "sceptics who argue from a medieval premise" is apt. They begin from the assumption that the divine purpose is "nonrelative" to human decisions, that its "superiority" involves total independence. He asks the pertinent question, why is the concept of independence or absoluteness considered higher than that of dependence or relativeness? What is *"religiously* significant" about it? His own conclusion is that "To be independent, non-relative, is to be meagre in logical content; the maximum of relativity is the maximum of logical content."[15] Thus the *a se et per se* of the Being of God were abstracted from trinitarian acts both *intra* and *extra*. The nominalism of medieval tradition tended to isolate and then separate the attributes, locating them in our subjective ideas. What remained in God as essential was bare "simplicity," a sort of "idol, which, devouring everything concrete, stands behind" the scholastic formulae.[16]

The clash of wills assumed by Prometheanism befits a deistic plot in which a *deus absolutus* must regard every other will as rival and threat. Deism itself, of course, carried the abstraction far enough to cut the knot: God willed Creation but then opted out, its retired Architect. The Christian doctrine of God, on the other hand, takes care to untie this knot of contradictory wills. When divine and human unite in one person, this *unio hypostatica* embodies a unified will, both divine and human. Such an archetype reveals within godhead the possibility of a will of active loving. The motions of grace within deity break out of the logical box that limits and ignores the dynamism of loving. Patristic theology, for instance, stressed that the Trinitarian will revealed in both incarnation of the Word and procession of the Spirit operates *per modum voluntatis*. Such activity conflicts with evil or corrupt willing - the desire to be God, *eritis sicut deus* - but harmonizes with human willing responsive to its covenant. "Autonomy" should not mean freedom to choose (and so to obtain?) whatever one wills, but responsibility for what one chooses.

For Karl Barth the dilemma of divine and human willing is solved by eliminating the lemma of unique and absolute individuality as posited in the Zeus/Prometheus confrontation. For that is condition and cause of their rivalry.

> For all his heavenly divinity each Zeus must con-
> stantly be very anxious in the face of the existence
> and arrival of very powerful rivals. And even when
> the conflict in Olympus is settled, will the God who
> is claimed to be unique and recognized as such be
> able to master the human "in-dividual," Prome-
> theus?[17]

The monotheism and its rival, monohumanism, is always at risk, its *aporia* evident, if not on Olympus then on the earth, which is home to Titans and to humans. Two conflicting autonomies, each a heteronomy to the other: as the biological analogy suggests, autonomic systems cannot be homologous; their laws are irreducible and exclusive. Such is the agonistic setting for the ancient myth of enduring power. But as Eberhard Jüngel has put the case, examining Barth's theology "between Theism and Atheism," there cannot be humanity without God (*keine Menschenlosigkeit Gottes*). Indeed, Barth's famous essay "The Humanity of God" extols this constant theme of "The-anthropology," echoing the patristic *Theandria*, in which the dynamism of a unified personality guarded against reductionism in the two natures theory. By this he means that Christian faith has nothing to do with "God" in the abstract, nor with its equally abstract partner, "Humanity." Emil Brunner also repudiates a doctrine of *Gott-an-sich* and *Menschen-an-sich* in behalf of a relational or theandric reality.[18]

Such christology is significant because it works out in more dynamic categories the ancient concepts of the church fathers. In particular the twin constructs of *anhypostasia* and *enhypostasia* guard the doctrine of "personal union" against reduction to a single will (monotheletism).[19] The former indicates the (anhypostatic) divine condescension required to begin and to sustain the covenant. The latter points to the (enhypostatic) human response and choice, the free willing that fulfils the covenant in the world. It is this subtle christology that atheism, particularly in its Promethean form, tends to miss. It operates with a Monophysite doctrine of Christ as divine intruder, a kind of Hermes or even Hephaistos in helping to bind Prometheus the rebel. Little hint of his humanity, his own suffering for and with others, is allowed to invite more complex analysis. More importantly, the decisive dimension of christology is lacking, the human *sharing* in the person and work of the "proper Man" (Luther) or "real Man" (Barth). Only this final dynamism, honoured by mystical theology, draws on resources that allow revision of classical theism and antitheism.

The problem of divine and human willing also led Paul Tillich (whom Langdon Gilkey has called "master of mediation") toward a unifying category in his early search for a just social reality. He accepts the opposition between autonomy and heteronomy, since the latter is an alien will imposed on the creativity of autonomous reason. Here is the bite in Tillich's ontology. He delineates certain "polarities" in which the structure of being appears to us. Beyond individualization/participation and dynamics/form, he distinguishes "freedom and destiny." Human freedom is effected only in "polar interdependence" with destiny. Since necessity is a category rather than an element, it contrasts not with freedom but with possibility.

Thus the determinism/indeterminism debate applies to things but not to persons. Even the idea of will tends to become reified and so misleads us into the problem of determinism. But freedom belongs not to a function but to the person: "a personal self participates in his freedom." Freedom is not opposed by destiny, which provides its "conditions and limits," but by its true contradictory, fate. (Tillich's complementary categories of "religious substance of culture" and "cultural form of religion" are apposite here also.) Autonomy cannot conflict with destiny, but insofar as it turns in on itself it projects its opposite as Fate.[20]

Tillich insisted that autonomy as such is not "a revolt against God" but simply against false or arbitrary authority. Therefore, he argued for a third term: "Theonomy does not stand against autonomy as heteronomy does. Theonomy is the answer to the question implied in autonomy, the question concerning a religious substance and an ultimate meaning of life and culture." Autonomy seeks its own rationale, its self-legitimation; but it trades on matters of ultimate concern, it points ineluctably to the transcendental meaning, and so to a theonomous partner in its creative drive. Such is Tillich's contribution to the debate, and programmatic recommendation for its resolution. His proposal for rethinking the logic of willing is salutary in view of the presupposition that divine and human willing constitute contradictory opposition, leading to antinomies of the pure will, as it were.

The Paradox of Omnipotence

Our earlier discussion of the scholastic teaching on necessity and freedom indicated that the term *omnipotence* was already acknowledged as highly ambiguous. The concept of analogical predication saved it from univocal interpretation up to Renaissance and Reformation periods. We suggest that since the Enlightenment, however, philosophers have been less than perceptive on this score. They fell into a grave category-mistake: omnipotence came to be understood more simply as all-mightiness, power to do anything. The qualification put well by the scholastics, noted in our earlier section on classical theism, involved distinctions within the concept of power or potency. Their linguistic analysis recognized the appropriatenes of "impotence" in relation to divine power and provided a context of modal logic for its discussion. Now this was lost, and an image of

total control developed. We noted also that this was given possibility
by certain nominalist trends, and credibility by the harder doctrine of
divine will of Calvinism and Jansenism.

Given such a philosophical tradition, the relationship
between divine and human willing could be explored by using the traditional square of opposition of formal logic. This structures four
terms (categorical propositions) according to their opposition and
implications of truth or falsity (or undetermined status). The square
is drawn as follows:

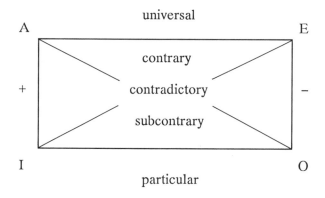

Universals of opposite quality are contraries (A,E); particulars of
opposite quality are subcontraries (I,O). Propositions opposite in
both quality and quantity are contradictories (A,O and E,I). Now
the proposition "God is omnipotent" is a universal affirmative. Its
contrary would be "God is impotent." (This sort of impotence, however, is not the proper privation of Aristotelian and Scholastic teaching.) Although this exhibits the clear opposition of God and freedom
in Promethean logic, it does not take us far. It renders the subcontraries vacuous: God is sometimes. . . . One might substitute the
formula "God is in control" – always (A), never (E), sometimes (I)
and sometimes not (O). Limited freedom is possible (indeterminate)
by the particulars, but the alternative subject (the human) is not
specified. Either *p* or *q;* and *q;* therefore not *p* – this is the horned
syllogism that confronts us. All or Nothing.

To cast the problem in this way is to accept the definition of
a reductive sort of both theism and atheism. (One thinks of Ivan
Karamazov's "Euclidean understanding" of the problem of innocent
suffering, entailing a logical impasse for his theistic belief.) It is to

posit a disjunctive logic reflecting a dualistic ontology. For instance, Mark Taylor uses Derrida's deconstructive categories to illustrate how the "death of God" derives from the "disjunctive syllogism," the logic of simple negation, "which is the logic of repression." Thus genuine otherness, alterity, is a source of fearful withdrawal, as the self turns inward.[21] The assumption is that divine and human willing stand in opposition, according to a model of potency drawn from natural philosophy. And here is the point – it is not omnipotence that presents a paradox to human reason, but power as such.

The root question is, what is the *metaphor of power* underlying these images of divine and human relationships? The philosophical agenda assumes that it is the power of force, of coercion; that God is the Supreme Power exerting total control over human affairs. Certainly, Aeschylus shows Prometheus being fastened with iron chains by Force, servant of Zeus. And still today, our adversarial system in law and politics, our philosophy of force informing sexual and familial dynamics – these signify that the image of power itself is biased and limited. Thus omnipotence is in fact not understood as metaphysically absolute so long as the all-or-nothing paradigm obtains. It is as if there is a limited amount of power (say 100 percent), so that for God to do everything, we can do nothing. It is this "monopolistic" model of omnipotence as "having all the power possible" that process thinking seeks to correct in what Charles Hartshorne calls "social" attribution or "divine relativity." If actual occasions are moved by a divine will that is never determinative but rather persuasive, the idea of power as ownership is overcome in the direction of personalism. Must power always mean "possession"? Is there not an alternative kind of human relationship – as feminists insist so clearly and helpfully – in a consensual rather than coercive form?[22]

Our question is, is there not another logical form which will honour the Augustinian dialectic of coexistence – a "square of mediation," so to say? The concept of theonomy is intended (by Tillich explicitly) to break this deadlock of opposition and introduce just such a mediating term. Older formulae suggested a fruitful tension between omniscience and nescience, demanding a "coincidence of opposites" for release. It was insisted, moreover, that free will is possible only in a cosmos, an ordered universe "determined" by law, by causal connections. Indeterminism would breed not freedom but chaos. Today, quantum probabilities in modern physics offer similar analogue: the behaviour of electrons is a matter not of freedom but of randomness. Friedrich Waismann has noted the implications of quantum theory's "uncertainty principle" for traditional logic: a radical critique is required, shifting to a three-valued quantum logic, for instance, or a "logic of inhomogeneity" (Elsasser). Such moves would honour the sort of "kinetics" that T.F. Torrance identifies as the key to conceptualizing the worldly interaction of divine and human being and willing.[23]

Authentic freedom of human willing is not understood properly in a context of coercive force. The relationships obtaining in a square of opposition will not do. It were better to trade on other categories, starting from modal or deontic logic. One might try a semantic tableau – "If A then (B but not C)" – by which theonomy includes autonomy but not their common contrary, heteronomy. Among many diagrams proposed as isomorphic clues to the propositional calculus, that of C.S. Peirce may prove most helpful. He identifies opposition and reconciliation with a more complex network than the traditional square. Heteronomy (B) and autonomy (C) may be set in relationship to theonomy (A) according to this model, as in the formula A (B(C)). Hence the figure:

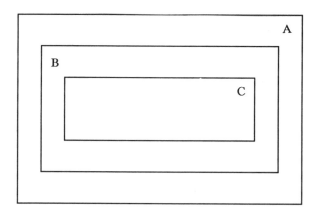

Again, one might follow Venn's lead and ask about the existential import of propositions of which the subject is omnipotence. Then one could utilize the semiotic square. The latter (*hexagone logique*) simplifies the terms by subordinating universal to existential propositions: from "Either A or E" to "Neither I nor O, or both I and O." Thus a new perspective is suggested, from which both divine and human willing may share the same modality of freedom, or better, mutual determination. Such modest mediation is in line with classical analogical thinking and with the negative status of attributes such as omnipotence. The limiting cases remind us of what John Macquarrie calls "a group of divine attributes which together try to express the *overwhelmingness* of God." And here we confront the contemporary debate on the "paradox of omnipotence," as J.L. Mackie has termed it.[24]

Mackie states the paradox as follows: "can an omnipotent being make things which he cannot subsequently control?" If he cannot, he is not omnipotent, and if he can, he ceases to be so. This has taken two forms: impersonal (can God make a stone he cannot lift?) and personal (can God create beings whom he cannot control?), the latter relevant for the Free-will Defence. Both forms imply that the idea of an omnipotent being is self-contradictory or logically impossible. Mackie argues that a logical inconsistency characterizes traditional theism on the point, and his thesis has sparked considerable debate among philosophers. Macquarrie's solution reflects the subtler dimension of the theological tradition that is missed by most philosophers. Alvin Plantinga, on the other hand, stays within logical categories to argue that one can state "It is possible that (God is omnipotent and it is possible that God is not omnipotent)" is either true or false and that neither case counts against divine omnipotence. In short, the grounds of philosophical debate have shifted from a simpler model of formal logic to modalities which allow mediation at least by negation. There is still limitation to assertive propositions, thus missing the point of recent philosophy of language, notably illocutionary logic; but it marks a considerable advance on Enlightenment thinking.

In particular, the debate on the paradox recalls us to the sort of revisionary theism we are discussing. The category of theonomy suggests a way of mediation in which "All" is sublated in "Both" – heteronomy is denied, but not the presence of divine willing, while autonomy (defined in absolute terms) is denied, but not the freedom of human willing. In fact, the divine will (Tillich's "religious substance") provides the possibility of human selfhood and, therefore, choice and consent. Theistic theology, informed especially by biblical studies, insists on divine freedom as that which constitutes and demands human freedom – the opposite of the antitheistic assumption that divine will robs humanity of voluntary choice. "But it is this very monstrous conception of a God who is an existent being equipped with omnipotence and omniscience, which atheist criticism attacks in the name of human freedom."[25] Such a God plays the role of Zeus, inevitably calling forth his partner in crime, Prometheus, to defy his alien will and to establish his own selfhood in contradiction to that of Olympian divinity. What is to be the outcome of this tragic struggle? The choice between heteronomy and autonomy is a hopeless one. Is that all we have, we humans caught between the clash of unyielding wills? Either Zeus or Prometheus – who can deliver us from this either/or?

Neither Zeus nor Prometheus

> For Marx the dilemma is either Prometheus or Zeus. He chooses Prometheus, and he is right. But he is mistaken when he imagines that the problem of God presents itself to every man in the form of this dilemma.
> The Christian chooses both Prometheus and God, but he rejects Zeus.[26]

We have argued that antitheism assumes something about the Christian God that is not so. It takes omnipotence to mean heteronomy, as the contradiction of autonomy – witness the humanist tradition, its scepticism reacting to this very assumption (from *Prometheus* Press).[27] In the typology of atheism advanced in our Introduction, it was recommended that the most fruitful way of understanding modern atheism and its challenge for faith would be to concentrate on the tradition of postulatory atheism symbolized by the figure of Prometheus. Our analysis of key historical figures and movements was an attempt to illustrate this type of atheism and to suggest the sort of critique in order, either from the resources of classical theism itself or from the contemporary revision of theism.

Such revision emphasizes certain concepts concerning selfhood, willing and being. These include the crucial role of "participation" in Orthodoxy as well as Western theology, particularly the renewed concept of covenant.[28] Or again, the doctrine of God in European theology with its reinterpretation of the attribute of unchangeableness and the dynamics of "glory," not so unlike process thinking in regard to divine immutability.[29] Even more significant is recent rethinking of the doctrine of divine impassibility, so that suffering is attributable to deity without the ambiguity and circumlocution of traditional teaching. Noteworthy formulations on the topic, sparked by biblical exegesis as well as by human experience, are Kazoh Kitamori's theology of "the pain of God" and Jürgen Moltmann's of "the crucified God."[30]

An equally significant development in the tradition of Judaism has produced a remarkable emphasis on "hearing the Word." In particular the Patmos Circle provided foundation for what Franz Rosenzweig called "new thinking." In his attempt to displace the older philosophy he resembles Feuerbach, to whom he declared his indebtedness. Rosenzweig's understanding of communication through speech-events, of the life of dialogue and being-with-others, informed the consciousness not only of his own circle but of the now familiar teaching of Martin Buber and Abraham Heschel. The point in this matter is that an alternative paradigm of knowing is being advanced: hearing rather than seeing. Ben Jonson is credited with the saying, "Language most shewes a man: speak that I may see thee." This was taken up by J.G. Hamann in particular.[31]

Martin Buber suggests that the hellenic habit of "thinking with the eyes" is a major contributor to the modern disbelief in transcendence, including the transcending presence of the other person. Western science, for example, has been predominantly observationist and phenomenalist. It has required a traumatic "paradigm shift" (Thomas Kuhn) to adapt to the new invisible data which demand exploration of imageless relations and structures. T.F. Torrance recommends the substitution of "audits" in our epistemology for the kind of "percepts" that necessitated pictures and world-views and led to a "visual epidemic" (A.D. Ritchie). Richard Rorty also scores "the historical phenomena of mirror-imagery, the story of the domination of the mind of the West by ocular metaphors." He notes that this "mirror of nature" doctrine of what philosophy is, with its "vocabulary of contemplation, looking, *theoria,*" fails us at the decisive point of contemplation and theory. For when the contemplative mind "takes large views, its activity is more like deciding what to *do* than deciding that a representation is accurate."[32]

The above relates to the "speech-thinking" of the Patmos group, whose acoustical theme makes word, Logos, the focus of evidence for personal existence. Such a personalist approach denies the impersonal axioms of philosophical analysis when this isolates person from body, *parole* from *langue*, commandment from law. Emile Fackenheim is eloquent on this point, recalling us to recognize the "commanding voice" addressing us through epochal events such as the Holocaust. Divine "commandments" are not reducible to impersonal "laws"; there may be rebellion, but not heteronomy.[33]

The Ambivalence of Atheism: A Double Irony

Karl Barth's theological appraisal of atheism deserves notice. It is typified by the curious and even notorious section "Religion as Unbelief" in the first volume of the *Church Dogmatics* (1938).[34] Here we read that the road of unbelief forks into a "twofold way of mysticism and atheism." Mysticism is "esoteric atheism," existing in dialectical relation with dogmatics and ethics, even though its goal of union with the All is a negative modality of knowledge. Obviously Barth has in mind one kind of mysticism, the "oceanic feeling" of abstract nonduality, as compared with more concrete and personalist forms (cf Meister Eckhart's *deitas* and *deus*). Yet it is significant that he insists, in these prolegomena to his theology of Word, that even an apparent friend such as mysticism must be tested against the negation of the negation, the Incarnation of the Word of God. By contrast, atheism is "an artless and childish form of that critical turn," "blabbing out the secret" of negation, shouting it to the world. "And its whole interest is in the denial as such. That is its artlessness. It fails to see what mysticism does not fail to see: that absolute denial would have no meaning except against the background of a relative affirmation."[35]

Twenty-five years later Barth's debate with Max Bense in the *Zürcher Woche* develops his theory.[36] Bense writes of "the necessity of atheism at the present day," an argument patently elitist, for the "reasons and problems of the intellect" which guide him "exist only for intellectuals." He mentions certain philosophers – "Peirce, Russell, Wittgenstein, Schlick, Carnap, Stegmüller and others" – who deny intelligibility to statements about God. Against the "phantom world" of theology he puts the "objectivity" of scientific-technological reason. He concludes that "the invasion of methodical rationality into every field of provincial irrationality is an urgent necessity."

"The Rationality of Discipleship" is Karl Barth's reply. He wishes only to "make a peaceful little attempt to state my position." He does not think that Bense is in direct opposition, for his blows, "though aimed at me, do not threaten, let alone hit me." This is because Bense is also a believer and Barth also an unbeliever. Bense believes "pretty vigorously" in what he has called "existential determinism." It functions like a deity, its elite constitute a church – "the blessed band of persons who live above a 'definite level of intelligence'" – and they protest against any disbelief that denies the sovereignty of Bense's "thinking individual."

Barth's thesis concerning the rationality of belief turns on his familiar insistence on the *fides quaerens intellectum* of Anselm as "the way of theology." The Christian thinks "rationally in the wake of the act and word of the living God." It is response, gratitude, obedience and love, and as such, in Barth's opinion, might be "the model for all rational thought." But his chief point is to contrast such a humble following of the logic of data with the sovereignty of Bense's "thinking individual." Mere human autonomy remains "incompetent and impossible in relation to the living God because it is blind."

Barth's final point is somewhat different, and prepares for his last meditation on the subject of atheism, pursued explicitly in the closing years of his life. "I know the rather sinister figure of the 'atheist' very well, not only from books, but also because it lurks somewhere inside me too." There is a "rather fiery form of atheism" in the East, related to dialectical materialism, as well as Max Bense's form of "the older, Western, cold type of atheism that is essentially defensive." But both live off a "third form" of atheism – "the fact that we are not better Christians." He concludes:

> The atheism that is the real enemy is the "Christianity" that professes faith in God very much as a matter of course, perhaps with great emphasis, and perhaps with righteous indignation at atheism wild or mild, while in its practical thinking and behaviour it carries on exactly as if there were no God.

This little article has been examined because it provides the theme on which Barth was working at the time of his death in 1968. The "lecture fragments" published since then constitute part of the "ethics of reconciliation" which would have completed the fourth part of the *Dogmatics*.[37] They indicate that the topic of atheism is much on Barth's mind, its crux being the atheism of the People of God. In this he follows the New Testament, whose profile of unbelief has in view "almost exclusively the man of the community, Christian man." Thus the New Testament does not "look or talk through the window" at outsiders, but addresses believers in their unbelief. Their object of faith is "the known and unknown God" – known because of the "objective knowledge of God in the world," whether accepted or rejected, but coexisting with an "ignorance of God," which trades on the positive, which "lives only by what it negates." The result is an "ambivalence with which God is well known in the world and yet still most suspiciously unknown."

The ignorance of God is rooted in the primitive form of "intellectual godlessness" or "theoretical atheism," which denies the existence of God, whether or not it issues in "practical atheism." Such denial affects the "deity of philosophy" or similar human constructs, one of the "data of human experience."

> The true and living God, however, is not a "datum" of ours. He is his own "datum." Only thus, only as he is his own "datum" and reveals himself, is he there for men. He is the one whom the world does not know (I Jn. 3:1). This is why the atheistic negation – which negates only a God who, if he exists, has to be a "datum" of ours – does not touch him. (128)

Most interesting of all for Barth is the belligerent nature of theoretical atheism. Its "confession" and excited struggle against the concept of God suggest its threatened position – "instead of being happy and content with various kinds of anthropomonistic mysticism and morality." Barth's lifelong distrust of human "religion" reappears in these end notes. The worst form of godlessness turns up in religion. Here it is hidden, hypocritical, a human way of dealing with "surrogate" deities as images and substitutes.

Both atheism and religion, for Barth, are forms of "an attempted 'nostrification' of God." Putting God to use, humans display that idolatry that the Old Testament prophets regarded as far worse than mere atheism. And such nostrification has a fateful consequence, revealing the connection with human being noted throughout the present work. He who does not know God "does not know his fellow man either."

> His ignorance of God culminates and manifests itself in his ignorance of his fellow man. He regards him as an object to whom he as subject may or may not be in relation according to his own free choice and disposal. . . . He does not know him as a fellow subject whom God has set unavoidably beside him, to whom he is unavoidably linked in his relation to God, so that apart from him he cannot himself be a subject, a person. (131)

Barth's passage from Wholly Other to others has been likened to "the argument to the other" of Emmanuel Levinas. The latter contrasts the narcissism of the Same with the moral heteronomy of otherness: illeity instead of ipseity. His anti-Heideggerian *Totality and infinity* (1961) carries as motto: L'absolument Autre, c'est Autrui. Both men underscore the inescapable connection between others and the Other. Atheism of the Promethean type means practical inhumanity. To sum up: the logic of presence demands a critique or "delimitation of ontology (of presence)" as Derrida describes

Nietzsche, Freud and Levinas. Classical theism was followed by the onto-theology implied in Cartesian and Kantian problematics. Even Husserl's critique, for instance, assumes the "solitary mental life" we have noted as the context of Promethean willing. If selfhood is impossible without others, if ipseity demands alterity, then neither the distant Enemy nor the absent Emptiness of traditional formulations of transcendence is acceptable – only a surprising and joyful presence of the Other.[38]

Prometheus Ascending

Prometheus did not deny the existence, only the will, of Zeus. But Prometheanism developed a totalitarian world-view, effecting an atheism of the human will in its sovereign role. It is thus not so much a denial of God as the substitution of humanity, a change in Subject rather than predicates: only a divinized humanity can secure the confidence of wilful atheism. In this sense the figure of Prometheus, ineluctably bound with that of Zeus, cannot serve as the model hero. Merleau-Ponty so argued, that *L'Homme* has displaced Prometheus, while Jean Brun sees Prometheus as opening the drama of modern technology only to make way for "le retour de Dionysos."[39] R. Heilbroner agrees that the Promethean spirit is endangered, but rather in his view by the failure of the human prospect: "For it is not only with dismay that Promethean man regards the future. It is also with a kind of anger. If after so much effort, so little has been accomplished; if before such vast challenges, so little is apt to be done – then let mankind suffer the end it deserves."[40]

Prometheus's rebellion against Zeus has succeeded. The end of Zeus opens the possibility of a God beyond the omnipotent Tyrant, and so beyond the dialectic of Aeschylus. Indeed, inasmuch as Zeus himself was subject to Necessity, he remains penultimate. Thus one may choose Prometheus, but only insofar as one rebels against every penultimate tyranny named Zeus. What Paul Tillich termed "ultimate concern" denotes a "God beyond 'God'." In this sense also dialogist Jan Lochman claims that Prometheus may be a leading saint in the theologian's calendar too. Henri de Lubac and William Lynch, among other authors noted earlier, agree that the archetypical rebel demands baptism by Christian theology.[41] Only thus will true humanity be recognized as partner with the God more ultimate than both Zeus and Prometheus. And only thus will Prometheus himself be set free from tyranny, his own as well as others'.

By *Prometheus Rebound*, our title indicates another form of irony. Rebinding the Rebel, our analysis suggests, is what comes of playing him off as ultimate humanity over against idols named Zeus. The foundational category-mistake of antitheism plays into the hands of a self-binding anthropology without transcendent root or relationship to others. Moreover, in a colloquial sense of "rebound," Prometheus is caught in the reactionary movement of negativism, nihilism, as he acts out his no-saying against Zeus. On the rebound he becomes a spent force as the trajectory of his revolt loses momentum. He is bound for death, he has no future of his own. He is not like the giant Antaeus who proved invincible so long as he maintained contact with his mother Earth. For Prometheus descending there is no such resilience; no *Spring*.

If we imagine ourselves once again in that theatre of Dionysus in ancient Athens, we behold the descent of our protagonist into "Hades' rayless gloom." Now that is hardly the last word of Aeschylus. Yet not even the trilogy's conclusion, with Prometheus unbound, proud Firebearer for humanity, provides resolution. For Zeus and Prometheus merely continue their sterile debate between heteronomy and autonomy, the dance of death. Perhaps only the satyr-play traces an authentic hope. Here is the Dance of Life in its fertile power, the way of the negation and affirmation of images that inspired Dante to cast his players in a *commedia*. The gravity of grace has brought forth the levity of gratitude. The god-walk is now empty, the machine at rest. A new and startling *skēnē* reveals itself. We find that we ourselves are on stage, we recognize the others (they include Prometheus and company – Oedipus and Dionysus and Sisyphus and Orestes) as belonging to the troupe; together we enact the play of release and thanksgiving, we share in its comic finale. In such manner we ascend to the everyday, where suffering is endured and sublated in our comic drama of society, family, the *komos* of common rituals of survival. Through this festal procession, through its motions of grace and gratitude, we engage our destiny, our *Hilaria*. So may Prometheus live again as master of rebellion and saint of humanism; but only if Zeus passes away in the shadow of God the living and the true, "whom to serve is perfect freedom."

NOTES

Bibliographical Note

The scope of our work makes a full bibliography difficult, and bibliographies provided in the literature on our topic render it less than necessary. In particular one should cite that provided by Cornelio Fabro, *God in Exile: modern atheism; a study of the internal dynamic of modern atheism, from its roots in the Cartesian cogito to the present day* (ET by Arthur Gibson, Westminster, MD: Newman, 1968), pp 1155-1202. Such an extensive listing supplies sufficient data for both general and specific aspects of the subject of atheism. What remains is for us to remark on certain works of significance because of their coverage or their pertinence.

The definitive study of the Prometheus myth is surely that of Carl Kerényi, Böllingen series LXV.1, *Prometheus, Archetypal Image of Human Existence* (NY: Pantheon Books, 1963), ET by R. Manheim of *Prometheus: Die menschlich Existenz in griechischen Deutung*, 1959. Excellent surveys of the myth's development are provided by Louis Séchan, *Le mythe de Prométhée* (Paris: Presses Universitaires de France, 1951), Raymond Trousson, *Le Thème de Prométhée dans la Littérature Européenne*, 2 vols. (Genève: Librairie Droz, 1964) and Laurent Prémont, *Le Mythe de Prométhée dans la Littérature française contemporaine (1900-1960)* (Qué: Les Presses de l'Université Laval, 1964).

Several multivolume works survey the ground. *L'Ateismo contemporaneo*, ed. by the Facoltá della Pontificia Universitá Salesiana di Roma (Torino: Societá Editrice Internazionale, 1967-69), 4 vols., provides working definitions of theoretical and practical atheism (Intro.) including surveys of literature and cinema (Vol. 1), contemporary philosophy (Vol. 2) and specific philosophical problems (Vol. 3), with a concluding volume of analyses from perspectives of theology and comparative religion. A French trans. under J. Girardi covers the first half of the material: *L'Athéisme dans la Vie et la Culture Contemporaine* (Paris: Desclée et Cie, 1967-69), 3 vols. More thematic is Fritz Mauthner, *Der Atheismus und seine Geschichte im Abendlande* (Hildesheim: Georg Olms Verlag, 1963; original 1922-23), 4 vols. It includes good sections on Rinascimento, deism and Aufklärung. A Marxist approach characterizes Hermann Ley of the DDR, *Geschichte der Aufklärung und des Atheismus* (Berlin: VEB Deutscher Verlag des Wissenschaften, 1966-78), 3 vols. Noteworthy is his handling of Lenin, historical roots of Enlightenment (Vol. 2/1, 1970), and Zwingli and Calvin (Vol. 3/1,

1978). The *Concilium* series (NY: Paulist Press) includes numerous articles or entire volumes on the topic, as noted throughout our work. Both atheism and humanism are served by Prometheus Books (Buffalo, NY) but with little solid research or bibliographical work; see Peter Angeles, ed., *Critiques of God* (1976), Bibliography 369-71.

Thus the Notes that follow do not rely on a formal bibliography. Those for each chapter indicate resources used; publishing data on books referred to in quite separate chapters are usually repeated to assist the reader.

Introduction

1   For Pericles see Thucydides, *The Peloponnesian War* ii.43; for Plato, *The Republic* VI.511Df.

2   R. Kroner, *The Primacy of Faith* (New York: Macmillan, 1943), 25. Schubert Ogden has remarked this phenomenon of a sort of Kierkegaardian "acoustical illusion": classical theism claimed to be the only theism, echoed in the modern claim to total atheism, "The Christian Proclamation of God to Men of the So-called 'Atheistic Age'," in *Is God Dead?* (New York: Paulist, 1966, Concilium 16), 93.

3   Cf. Paul Edwards, *Encyclopedia of Philosophy* (New York: Macmillan, 1967), I:182f.

4   Sir Leslie Stephen, *An Agnostic's Apology* (New York: G.P. Putnam's Sons, 1903). The context is the Victorian debate on "the ethics of belief" – cf. G.D. McCarthy, ed., *The Ethics of Belief Debate* (Atlanta: Scholar's Press, 1986); W.K. Clifford's foundational essay "The Ethics of Belief," 19ff. and Leslie Stephen on "Belief and Ethics," 103ff. J.C. Livingston has explored "the agnostic principle" (Flew) in "British Agnosticism," *Nineteenth Century Religious Thought in the West*, ed. N. Smart, Clayton, Katz and Sherry (Cambridge U.P., 1985), II:231ff, with good Bibliography; cf. his earlier book *Modern Christian thought* (New York: Macmillan, 1971), Ch. 2, "The Religion of Reason." Thomas A. Huxley's own essays on agnosticism appear in vol. 5 of his *Collected Works* (New York: Appleton and Co., 1894): Agnosticism "expresses absolute faith in the validity of a principle, which is as much ethical as intellectual . . . that it is wrong for a man to say that he is certain of the objective truth of any proposition unless he can produce evidence which logically justifies that certainty" (310).

5   E. Gilson, "The Idea of God and the Difficulties of Atheism," *Philosophy Today* 13 (Fall 1969): 174-205; cf. Jean Lacroix, *The Meaning of Modern Atheism* (New York: Macmillan, 1966), ET by G. Barden, 41ff "Ethical Atheism"; S. Paul Schilling, *God in an Age of Atheism* (New York: Abingdon, 1969), 71ff, "atheism as axiological protest."

6   A. Plantinga, *God, Freedom and Evil* (London: Allen and Unwin, 1975), Part I "Natural Atheology." In discussing "other atheological arguments" (65ff) he agrees with our thesis that traditional ideas of God, particularly omniscience, were interpreted as threats to human freedom. Cf. Flew and MacIntyre, *New Essays in Philosophical Theology* (London: SCM, 1955), 96ff for the "university discussion" on theology and falsification. Flew's famous question is: "What would have to occur or to have occurred to constitute for you a disproof of the love of, or of the existence of, God?"

7   *Why I am Not a Christian and Other Essays* (New York: Simon and Schuster 1957) 23: 115f; the latter essay, "A Free Man's Worship," was published in *Mysticism and Logic* (London: Longmans, Green, 1918). Cf. M. Colin Grant, "Bertrand Russell, Dogmatic Atheist" in *Studies in*

Religion 12/1 (1983) 71-83 on Russell's agnosticism, involving an ambiguous assessment of theoretical and practical religion.

8   Quoted by Henri de Lubac, *The Drama of Atheist Humanism* (Cleveland, Ohio: World Pub. Co., 1966), ET by E.M. Riley, 27. For Scheler there is a Prometheus of technology and also "moral Prometheuses" who explore the value-cosmos. The moral Prometheus is a tragic figure, suffering "guiltless guilt [*schuldlöse Schuld*]" – quoted from *Zum Phänomen des Tragischer* by A. Deeken, *Process and Permanence in Ethics: Max Scheler's Moral Philosophy* (New York: Paulist, 1974), 70f.

9   Ignace Lepp, *Atheism in Our Time: a Psychoanalyst's Dissection of the Modern Varieties of Unbelief* (New York: Macmillan, 1963), 35ff. His analysis of "rationalist atheism" concludes that belief in autonomous reason "does not bear up experimentally" (177). Gabriel Marcel, "Philosophical Atheism" in *International Philosophical Quarterly* 2 (1962): 501-14.

10   Stephen C. Pepper, *A Digest of Purposive Values* (University of California, 1947); B. O'Shaughnessy, *The Will: a Dual Aspect Theory* (Cambridge U.P., 1980) 2 vols.; I. Murdoch, "Existentialists and Mystics" in W. Robson, ed., *Essays and Poems Presented to Lord David Cecil* (London, 1970).

11   C. Tresmontant, *Les Problèmes de l'Athéisme* (Paris: Ed. du Seuil, 1972), 243; cf. G. Ebeling, *The Study of Theology* (Philadelphia: Fortress, 1978), 103. This idea of the "no man's land" of scientific investigation is familiar in the debates on objectivity (Popper, Polanyi, etc.). John Courtney Murray credits Thomism with authorizing "a mode of rational enquiry, philosophical or scientific, that was methodologically atheist" – *The Problem of God* (New Haven: Yale U.P. 1964), 89. Also W. Pannenberg, "Types of Atheism and their Theological Significance," in *Basic Questions in Theology* (Philadelphia: Fortress, 1971) I:184ff: "to this extent, the mechanistic world picture of classical physics, perfected in the eighteenth century, which no longer needed the hypothesis of a creator, is the presupposition of modern atheism" (185); M. Polanyi, *Personal Knowledge* (New York: Harper and Row, 1964), 139ff on Laplace.

12   F. Gogarten, *Verhängnis und Hoffnung der Neuzeit* (Stuttgart: F. Vorwerk Verlag, 1953); David Martin, *The Religious and the Secular* (London: Routledge and Kegan Paul, 1969) argues in his work of "demolition" that "secularization is less a scientific concept than a tool of counter-religious ideologies." Bryan Wilson, *Religion in Sociological Perspective* (Oxford: U.P. 1982), agrees about the uncertain status of "the secularization thesis" – "Secularization and Its Discontents," 148ff. L. Shiner, *The Secularization of History: an Introduction to the Theology of F. Gogarten* (Nashville: Abingdon, 1966), provides good background ("Christian Origin," 25ff) as well as conceptual analysis.

13   Andrew M. Greeley, *Unsecular Man: the Persistence of Religion* (New York: Schocken Books, 1972), a "volume of dissent" from the "common wisdom" of contemporary sociology; A.M. Greeley and G. Baum, eds., *The Persistence of Religion* (New York: Herder and Herder, 1973,

Concilium 81); cf. Thomas Luckmann, *The Invisible Religion* (New York: Macmillan, 1967). R. Bellah, *Beyond Belief: Essays on Religion in a Post-Traditional World* (New York: Harper and Row, 1970); *The Broken Covenant: American Civil Religion in a Time of Trial* (New York: Seabury, 1975); also Bellah and Hammond, *Varieties of Civil Religion* (New York: Harper and Row, 1980), esp. IV, "Civil Religion and New Religious Movements"; Bellah and Glock, eds. *The New Religious Consciousness* (Berkeley: University of California, 1976). The papers of the First International Symposium on Belief, Rome, 1969 – Caporale and Grumelli, *The Culture of Unbelief* (Los Angeles: University of California Press, 1971) – include debate between Luckmann and Bellah on the issue. Bellah scores "the objectivist fallacy," which identifies religion with belief, thus missing the entire religious scene where intellectual assent is not necessarily an identifiable dimension (21ff, 42ff). Jacob Needleman, *The New Religions* (New York: Doubleday, 1970); J. Needleman and D. Lewis, eds., *Sacred Tradition and Present Need* (New York: Viking, 1975); Baum and Coleman, eds, *New Religious Movements* (New York: Seabury, 1983, Concilium 161). Charles Campbell, *Toward a Sociology of Irreligion* (London: Macmillan, 1971).

14   Paul Tillich, *The Dynamics of Faith* (New York: Harper and Row, 1957), etc; Karl Rahner, *Foundations of Christian Faith* (New York: Seabury, 1978, ET by W.V. Dych), 177f on "anonymous Christianity."

15   Nicholas Lash, *Theology on Dover Beach* (London: Darton, Longman and Todd, 1979), esp. 3ff "Doing Theology on Dover Beach," his inaugural lecture in the University of Cambridge.

16   W.C. Smith, *Belief and History* (Charlottesville: U.P. of Virginia 1977) Preface and 36ff, "The Modern History of 'Believing': The Drift Away from Faith." For Bellah, see n. 13 earlier.

17   *Beyond God the Father* (Boston: Beacon, 1973), 22ff 39; *Gyn/Ecology* (Boston: Beacon, 1978), Preface xi.

18   A. Flew, *The Presumption of Atheism* (London: Elek/Pemberton, 1976). "Throughout [these essays] I cleave to the Agnostic Principle, that we ought always to proportion our belief to the evidence" (7). Strato (second successor to Aristotle as head of the Lyceum) first formulated the presumption, "received by the young Hume as an emancipating revelation." Cf. the exchange in *Canadian Journal of Philosophy* 2, 1972; Flew, "The Presumption of Atheism" (29-64), Donald Evans, "A Reply to Flew's 'The Presumption of Atheism'" (47-50), and Flew, "A Reply to Evans" (51-53). Cf. Flew, *God and Philosophy* (London: Hutchinson, 1966). For Hume's own typology of scepticism, a good summary and commentary is D.F. Norton, *David Hume, Common-Sense Moralist, Sceptical Metaphysician* (Princeton U.P., 1982), 239ff, "Traditional Scepticisms and Hume's Scepticism." Cf. Flew's *Hume's Philosophy of Belief: A Study of his First Inquiry* (London: Routledge and Kegan Paul, 1961), 214ff, "The Religious Hypothesis." The "recent essay" referred to is "The Burden of Proof" in L.S. Rouner, ed., *Knowing Religiously* (University of Notre Dame, 1985), 105.

19   C. Fabro, *God in Exile*: *Modern Atheism* (Westminster MD: Newman, 1968, ET by Arthur Gibson). The This huge work argues the thesis that a "philosophy of immanence" or Immanentism (92) prevents the very possibility of divine presence, and so is a "structural or constitutive atheism . . . a denial of that transcendence in the epistemological dimension wherein consists the first step of theism rightly and radically understood" (1062). Fabro sees "positive or constructive atheism" as "the quintessential distillation of the principle of immanence" (23). Cf. Martin Marty, op. cit. 64ff, "Two Types of Unbelief." Cf. Chs. 8 and 9 below for the critique of Marxism as false religion, by Berdyaev and others; M. Eliade, *The Sacred and the Profane* (New York: Harcourt Brace, 1959, ET by W.R. Trask) uses his mythological categories to achieve the same end.

20   V. Gardavsky, *God is Not Yet Dead* (Penguin Books, 1973, ET by V. Menkes). 159ff; M. Machoveč, in Caporale and Grumelli, op. cit. 100ff.

21   R.H.L. Slater, *Paradox and Nirvana*: *a Study of Religious Ultimates, with special reference to Burmese Buddhism* (Chicago: University of Chicago Press, 1951); W.C. Smith, "Religious Atheism? Early Buddhist and Recent American," the Charles Strong Memorial Lecture to Australian Universities, 1966; "The Buddhist Instance: Faith as Atheist?" in *Faith and Belief* (Princeton U.P., 1979). Cf. Radhakrishnan and Raju, eds., *The Concept of Man*: *a Study in Comparative Philosophy* (London: Allen and Unwin, 1966), esp. IV and V by Raju; K.S. Murty, *Lectures on the Philosophy of Religion* (Simla: Indian Institute of Advanced Studies, 1973), Annexe I on "A Dialectic of Atheism." J. Thrower, *The Alternative Tradition*: *Religion and the Rejection of Religion in the Ancient World* (The Hague: Mouton, 1980) describes the sceptic-agnostic tradition in India, which Max Müller dubbed "adevism," 38ff.

22   Karl Barth, *Church Dogmatics* 1.2/17.2, "Religion as Unbelief"; see Notes to Ch. 14 later. Walter Stace, *Mysticism and Philosophy* (London: Macmillan, 1961), 124 (107ff., 123ff. on Hinayana Buddhism). Cf. Philip C. Almond, *Mystical Experience and Religious Doctrine* (Amsterdam: Mouton, 1982); Smith, *The Faith of Other Men* (New York: Harper and Row, 1963), 63.

23   Murray, op. cit. 97.

24   MacIntyre and Ricoeur, *The Religious Significance of Atheism* (New York: Columbia U.P. 1969); R. Bultmann, "Protestant Theology and Atheism" in *The Journal of Religion* 52 (1972), 331-35; Paul Holmer, "Theology, Atheism, and Theism" in *The Grammar of Faith* New York: Harper and Row, 1978), 159ff; Johann Figl, *Atheismus als theologisches Problem* (Mainz: Matthias-Grünewald Verlag, 1977): his summary of the state of the question includes secularization/secularism, Vatican II, the Death of God, atheism as antitheism (W. Dantine), the anthropological problematic (Pannenberg, Rahner, Welte) and "A-theismus als Voraussetzung der Theologie" (Braun, Sölle, Moltmann).

25   J.B. Metz, "Unbelief as a Theological Problem" in Metz, ed., *Fundamental Theology*: *the Church in the World* (New York: Paulist

Press, 1965, Concilium 6) 59; K. Rahner, ed., *The Pastoral Approach to Atheism* (New York: Paulist Press, 1967, Concilium 23); A. Charron, *Les Catholiques Face à L'Athéisme Contemporain* (Montreal: Fides, 1973). Peter Hebblethwaite, *The Council Fathers and Atheism* (New York: Paulist Press, 1966) conveys in short space the background, chief speeches and texts of the topic. Also R. Gibellini, "Beyond Atheism: A Dossier of the Secretariat for Non-Believers on Religious Indifference" in Jossua and Geffré, eds. *Indifference to Religion* (New York: Seabury, 1983, Concilium 23). The Secretariat published *L'indifferenza religiosa* in 1978.

26   W. Pannenberg, *What is Man?* *contemporary anthropology in theological perspective* (Philadelphia: Fortress 1970, ET by D.A. Priebe); *Basic Questions in Theology*, 3 vols. (vol. 3 has five essays from *Gottesdanke und menschliche Freiheit*); quotations are from II.184 ("Types of Atheism and Their Theological Significance") and 202 ("The Question of God"). Pannenberg continues his commitment to his starting point in his recent *Anthropology in Theological Perspective* (Philadelphia: Westminster, 1985, ET by M.J. O'Connell). "This concentration on anthropology in dealing with the problems of fundamental theology reflects the modern development of the philosophical idea of God" (11). He follows Arnold Gehlen in taking Herder as point of departure for modern philosophical anthropology, and so to theology: 43ff, "Openness to the World and Image of God."

27   E. Jüngel, *God as the Mystery of the World: on the Foundation of the Theology of the Crucified One in the Dispute between Theism and Atheism* (Grand Rapids: Eerdmans, 1983, ET by D.L. Guder), vii, 17ff.

28   Paul Roche, Introduction to *Prometheus Bound* (New York: Mentor, 1964).

1: Loaded Questions

1   Cf. Kerényi, *Zeus and Hera*: *Archetypal Image of Father, Husband, and Wife* (Princeton U.P. – Böllingen Series LXV.5, 1975; trans. C. Holme); C. Seltman, *The Twelve Olympians* (London: Pan Books, 1952), 32ff.

2   Texts of *Prometheus Bound* used include the Greek text, with fragments of *Prometheus Unbound*, by N. Wecklein (Boston: Ginn and Co., 1891), and ET by Philip Vellacott (Penguin Classics) and by Paul Roche (Mentor Classics). For the myth in general, Carl Kerényi has been prolific: *The Gods of the Greeks* (Penguin: Pelican Books, 1958); *Prometheus, Archetypal Image of Human Existence* (New York: Pantheon Books, Böllingen Series LXV.1, 1963; trans. R. Manheim from *Prometheus: Die menschliche Existenz in griechischer Deutung*, 1959); cf R. Trousson, *Le Thème de Prométhée dans la Littérature Européenne* (Geneva: Librairie Droz, 1964), 2 vols.

3   W. Jaeger, *Paideia: the Ideals of Greek Culture* (New York: Oxford U.P., 1945), I:252. But E. Voegelin notes that Zeus is *tyrannis* in the technical sense of pronouncing appropriate doom "in order to uphold Dike" (*The World of the Polis*, vol. 2 of *Order and History*, Louisiana State U.P., 1957), 256. The character of Zeus is complex, not only because of a clear ambivalence in his nature, but also because of a development at the hands of Aeschylus. Of the former, Jane Harrison notes that he is both gentle and stormy: "Maimaktes-Meilichios is double-faced like the Erinyes-Eumenides"; *Prolegomena to the study of Greek Religion* (New York: Meridian, 1955), 12ff, "The Diasia." At the Diasia he demanded a whole sacrifice rather than the shared communion as in Homer. As to Aeschylus, the Zeus of the *Suppliants* is protector of the weak and the innocent, whereas his dealings with Prometheus show a "harsh" master (as Hephaistos calls him). The theme of the *Oresteia* seems to follow this line, with a Zeus now virtually equated with the Unmoved Mover – he is the "Accomplisher," Cause and Doer of all. See Leon Golden, *In Praise of Prometheus*: *Humanism and Rationalism in Aeschylean Thought* (Chapel Hill, NC: U.N.C., 1962), Ch. 5 "Religious Drama," 100ff. The ultimate resolution can come only when the problem of justice is handed over to the human court, and the Furies have become the Kindlies. From Erinyes to Eumenides is doubtless a key shift in the dramaturgy of Aeschylus, in praise of Athena, symbol of Athenian justice. (See Ch. 13 later).

4   Hegel, *Aesthetik* II.51f; cf. Jaeger, op. cit., 282 ("Sophocles and the Tragic Character").

5   See Gilbert Murray, *Aeschylus*: *The Creator of Tragedy* (Oxford: Clarendon, 1940), esp. 90ff; C.J. Herington, *The Author of the Prometheus Bound* (Austin: University of Texas, 1970), App. A: The Components of the *Prometheia*, 123ff. For Irony see F.M. Cornford, *The Origin of Attic Comedy* (New York: Anchor Books, 1961), 119f, 183f and N. Frye, *Anatomy of Criticism* (New York: Athenaeum, 1967), 39ff, 223ff. For the "wicked god" see Paul Ricoeur, *The Symbolism of Evil* (Boston: Beacon Press, 1967), II.2, esp. 220ff. Cf. Séchan, *Le mythe de*

Prométhée (Paris: Presses Universitaires de France, 1951), 19ff. "Théogonie et Théomachie" on Hesiod, 69ff "La Prométhéide ou trilogie des prométhées."

6   Ugo Bianchi, *Prometeo, Orfeo, Adamo*: *Tematiche religione sul destino, il male, la salvezza* (Rome: Ed. dell'Asteneo Bizzarri, 1976), 188ff. Cf. 199ff "La Speranza: cur male?" and the discussion of Prometheus as demiurgos (203ff) and trickster *titanico* (207ff.). Paul Ricoeur in *The Symbolism of Evil* op. cit. notes that "the Zeus of *Prometheus Bound* and Prometheus himself are the two poles of the tragic theology and anthropology" (218). But Lucien Goldmann, *The Hidden God* (London: Routledge and Kegan Paul, 1964) considers Sophocles properly tragic whereas Aeschylus remains "classical" – he "still wrote trilogies."

7   Kerényi, *Prometheus*, 19f.

8   G. Siegmund, *God on Trial*: *a Brief History of Atheism* (New York: Desclée Co., 1967; ET by E.C. Briefs), 41.

9   C.G. Jung, *Alchemical Studies*, CW 13 (New York: Böllingen, 1967), 12, 109ff.; *Aion: Researches into the Psychology of the Self*, CW 9.2 (1959), 126ff. Cf. G. Durand for the current revival of philosophical interest in the alchemical tradition – e.g., "Similitude Hermétique et Science de l'Homme," Eranos Yearbook 1973, vol. 42 (Leiden: E.J. Brill), 427-515; "Défiguration philosophique et figure traditionelle de l'homme en Occident," Eranos 38 (1969), 45-93; and M-L von Franz, *Alchemy: an Introduction to the Symbolism and the Psychology* (Toronto: Inner City Books, 1980).

10 Kerényi, *Prometheus*, 38f.

11 See Trousson, op. cit. L. Prémont, *Le Mythe de Prométhée dans la Littérature Française contemporaine (1900-1960)* (Québec: Les Presses de l'Université Laval, 1964); L. Séchan, op. cit.

12 Voegelin, op. cit., 254n.

13 Ibid.

14 See Kerényi, *Prometheus*, for whom Goethe's image provides the approach to Aeschylus.

15 Ibid., 14.

16 Ibid., 17. Cf. Canadian playwright Gary Botting's *Prometheus Rebound* (Edmonton: Harden House, 1972; first produced 1971) in which Zeus has given the power of nuclear destruction, precluding a kingdom "desolate and barren." This reversal of roles awards Prometheus a pyrrhic victory: "I am rebound / Against my will, but this time have the aces / And now I play thy trump."

17 Cf. W. Lynch, *Christ and Prometheus* (Notre Dame, Indiana: University of Notre Dame Press, 1970), 63.

18   Cf. Conrad Hyers, "Prometheus and the Problem of Progress" in *Theology Today* XXXVII.3 (Princeton U.P., 1980), 323ff; M.L. Johnson, *Prometheus Reborn: Countertechnology, Holistic Education, and the Ecology-Energy Crisis* (New York: Libra, 1977), 2ff.

19   G. Bachelard, *La Psychanalyse du Feu* (Paris: Librairie Gallimard, 1938) and L. Séchan, op. cit. 3ff, 19ff (Hephaistos). A different interpretation of the polarity is that of C. Lévi-Strauss, for whom the basic opposition is that between sky and earth. Celestial phenomena appearing on earth constitute mysteries, theme of folk-tales – hence the hearth-fire. See the four-volume *Mythologiques*, esp. *The Naked Man*, 1981. Sir James G. Frazer has interesting data in *Myths of the Origin of Fire* (London: Macmillan, 1930), 193ff and *The Golden Bough*, vol. 2 (London: Macmillan, 1936), Ch. 17 "The Origin of Perpetual Fires" – the fennel stalk for conveying fire continues among Greek peasants and mariners (260).

20   Agni (*ignis*) has some 200 hymns dedicated to him, the highest number after Indra, and is the subject of the first ("I laud Agni, the chosen priest, god, minister of sacrifice . . ."). He is fire in all its forms, including hearth fire in household rituals, and the sacrificial fires. He is priest of the gods and god of the priests. Also the sun, lightning, etc. Cf. Séchan, op. cit., 10ff. for the name Prometheus and its relation to Agni-Pramatih.

21   Bachelard, op. cit., 12; cf. Séchan, op. cit., 3ff.

22   Corbin, *Temple et Contemplation: Essais sur l'Islam Iranien* (Paris: Flammarion, 1980), 62. But Prometheus is ignored in a work such as Paul du Breuil, *Histoire de la Réligion et de la Philosophie Zoroastriennes* (Monaco: Ed. du Rocher, 1984) – cf. 255ff. "Une lumière dans les ténèbres."

2: Prometheus and/or Christ

1   *Adv. Marcion* I.1, 247 (Migne, PL 2, 271f).

2   *The Works of Lucian of Samosata*, trans. H.W. Fowler and F.G. Fowler, 4 vols. (Oxford: Clarendon Press, 1905). "Prometheus on Caucasus" (I:53-62). Cf. "Dialogues of the Gods I: Prometheus. Zeus." (I:62f) and "A Literary Prometheus" (I:7ff). See also J. Duchemin, *Prométhée – Histoire du Myth* (Paris: Soc. d'Ed., "Les Belles Lettres," 1974), 102ff.

3   Lactantius, *The Divine Institute*, II.11.

4   Ibid., Bk I, 11ff.

5   *Clementine Homilies* VI, 14.

6   *Stromateis* 1.134, 5.14.

7   *Contra Haer.* II.14, 134.5 (PG VII, 752). Cf. Tertullian: Pandora is analogy for the Valentinian Pleroma – *Adv. Valent.* XII.562, 84 (Pl II, 598f). K. Weitzmann notes the "popular Roman tradition" of Prometheus as creator, which influenced Christian art, including his pointing gesture – *Age of Spirituality* (New York: Metropolitan Museum of Art, 1978) xxiii, 460 and Fig. 62 (451).

8   Trousson, op. cit., 71ff.

9   *Adv. Marcion* I.1, 247 (Migne, Pl 2, 271f.).

10   Quoted in *A Christian-Communist Dialogue*, ed. R. Garaudy and Q. Lauer (New York: Doubleday and Co., 1968), 55.

11   A. Koestler and J.R. Smythies, *Beyond Reductionism* (New York: Macmillan, 1969).

12   Cf. Jean Seznec, *The Survival of the Pagan Gods: the Mythological Tradition and Its Place in Renaissance Humanism and Art* (New York: Pantheon Books, Böllingen Series 38, 1953).

13   In L.W. Barnard: *Athenagoras* (Paris: Beauchesne, 1972), 25.

14   T.F. Torrance, *The Ground and Grammar of Theology* (Belfast: Christian Journals Ltd., 1980), 53f.

15   C.C. Richardson, *Early Christian Fathers*, LCC I (London, SCM, 1953), 293.

16   E. Quinet, *Préface à Prométhée* (Paris, 1857); cf. J. Duchemin, *Prométhée*, op. cit., 112ff.

17   E.R. Dodds, *The Greeks and the Irrational* (Berkeley: University of California Press, 1951), 28ff. Cf. A.O. Lovejoy, "'Pride' in Eighteenth

Century Thought," *Essays in the History of Ideas* (Baltimore: Johns Hopkins Press, 1948) for the ambiguous nature of the idea and the development from medieval thought. Also: J. Kellenberger, "Religious Faith and Prometheus," *Philosophy 55* (Cambridge U.P., No. 214, Oct. 1980), 49ff.

18   E.g., Gordon Rupp, *The Righteousness of God* (London: Hodder and Stoughton, 1953), Part II, "Coram Deo," 81ff; S. Kierkegaard, *The Concluding Unscientific Postscript* (Princeton U.P., 1944), 468ff on guilt as "the decisive expression for existential pathos," 516ff for sin-consciousness as "the expression for the paradoxical transformation of existence. . . . The individual is unable to acquire sin-consciousness by himself, as he can guilt-consciousness."

19   *Hubris, a Study of Pride* (New York: Harper Torchbooks, 1960; revised ed. of *The Wanton Nymph; a Study of Pride* [London: William Heinemann, 1937]).

20   Trousson, op. cit., I.82.

21   There is also a variant tradition in which rebel angels, notably Azazel, taught humankind in defiance of a remote God. Robertson Davies's *The Rebel Angels* (Toronto: Macmillan, 1979) is a fictional work embodying this theme. A further tradition for exploration is the gnostic, in which Heimarmene becomes associated with Zeus in his heteronomy. The revolt of the Titans signifies a higher obedience. Cf. Hans Jonas, *The Gnostic Religion* (Boston: Beacon Press, 1958), 96f, "Prometheus and Zeus."

22   Simone Weil, *Les Intuitions Préchrétiennes* (Paris: Les Editions de la Colombe, 1951), 105f.

23   F. Buri, *Prometheus und Christus* (Bern: Verlag A. Francke, 1945), 174ff.

24   Ugo Bianchi, *Prometeo, Orfeo, Adamo*, op. cit.

25   W.F. Lynch, *Christ and Prometheus: A New Image of the Secular* (Notre Dame, Indiana: University of Notre Dame Press, 1970), 7.

26   Ibid., 53.

27   Paul Ricoeur, *The Symbolism of Evil* op. cit., 218ff.

28   Cf. J.C. McLelland, *The Clown and the Crocodile* (Richmond: John Knox Press, 1970).

29   Murray, *Aeschylus: The Creator of Tragedy*, op. cit., 84ff., 177ff.; Jung, *Answer to Job* (London: Routledge and Kegan Paul, 1954), 4; Friedman, *Problematic Rebel* (University of Chicago Press, 1970), 4, 143, 484f.

30   Thomas Merton, *The Behavior of Titans* (New York: New Dimensions Books, 1961).

31   Ibid., 13.

32   Ibid., 14.

33   Ibid., 21f.

34   *The New Man* (New York: Bantam Books, 1981).

35   Ibid., 20.

36   David L. Miller, *The New Polytheism: Rebirth of the Gods and Goddesses* (New York: Harper and Row, 1974), 33, 71.

3: The Promethean Spirit

1   See Ch. 4, nn. 14, 15.

2   Cf. F. Cornford, *From Religion to Philosophy* (New York: Harper Torchbooks, 1957), Chs. 5 and 6. His thesis is that the Milesian (Ionian) scientific school succeeds the Olympian tradition while the mystical succeeds the Dionysian.

3   Cf. J.C. McLelland, *God the Anonymous*: *A Study in Alexandrian Philosophical Theology* (Philadelphia Patristic Foundation, 1976), 4ff.

4   Bruno Snell, *The Discovery of the Mind*: *the Greek Origins of European Thought* (New York: Harper and Row, 1960), 25, 27.

5   M. Untersteiner, *The Sophists* (Oxford: Basil Blackwell, 1954), ET by K. Freeman.

6   Ibid., 19ff.

7   Cf. ibid., 321ff.

8   C.L. Stough, *Greek Skepticism* (Berkeley: University of California Press, 1969),11f, 67ff (Aenesidemus), 106ff.; cf. T. Penelhum, *God and Skepticism* (Dordrecht: Reidel Pub., 1983) on types of fideism, esp. 52ff "The Pyrrhonist Stance."

9   Ibid., 117.

10   H. Chadwick, *Origen*: *Contra Celsum* (Cambridge U.P., 1965), 429n.

11   Iris Murdoch, *The Fire and the Sun*: *Why Plato Banished the Artists* (Oxford: Clarendon, 1974), 69.

12   E.g. the "likely story" (*eikōs mythos*) of *Timaeus* 29D; cf. *Phaedo* 115: "either this or something like it is true." For the current discussion cf. McLelland, *God the Anon.*, op. cit., 11ff. For Xenophanes see H. Diels, *Die Fragmente der Vorsokratiker*, ed. Kranz (Berlin: Weidemann, 1959, 9th Ed.), fr. 11ff; J. Adams, *Religious Teachers of Greece* (Edinburgh: T. &. T Clark, 1908), 197ff.

13   A.H. Armstrong, *An Introduction to Ancient Philosophy* (London: Methuen, 1965), 130.

14   Gregory Nazianzen, *Theol. Oration* I (Oratio XXVII, IX in NPNF VII, 288A). Cf. Second Oration (XXVIII, VIII, 291A).

15   T. Molnar, *Theists and Atheists*: *a Typology of Non-Belief* (The Hague: Mouton, 1980), 71.

16   G. Siegmund, op. cit., 57.

17   Molnar, op. cit., 30.

18   *Of the Nature of Things*, Everyman Ed. (London: J.M. Dent and Sons, 1947), 57 (307-16); cf. the entire section (62-332) on atomic motion.

19   Molnar, op. cit., 66f.

20   E. Jüngel traces the fateful consequences for modern theism and atheism of the notion of the "unthinkability" of God. Classical philosophy had posited the divine unknowability, which Christian Fathers took over and medieval doctors reinforced – op. cit., vii, 39ff, 100ff. Cf. McLelland, *God the Anonymous*, op. cit., 8ff "Platonism: Optimistic Rationalism?" and 137ff "Heritage and Project." A good survey and analysis of classical theism is provided by H.P. Owen, *Concepts of Deity* (London: Macmillan, 1971). Ch. 1, with discussion of its disputed questions and questioners in Chs. 2 and 3.

21   For this material E. Gilson is helpful, e.g., *The Spirit of Medieval Philosophy* (New York: Sheed and Ward, 1936) and *Reason and Revelation in the Middle Ages* (New York: Scribners, 1938); A. Nygren offers a different perspective in *Agape and Eros*, ET by P.S. Watson (London: SPCK, 1953), IV, "Augustine, the Middle Ages, and the Reformation," 341ff. For the alternatives of school doctrine see W. Principe, *The Theology of the Hypostatic Union in the Early Thirteenth Century*, 4 vols. (Toronto: Pontifical Institute of Mediaeval Studies, 1963-1975).

22   See Paul Vignaux, *Philosophy in the Middle Ages* (New York: Meridian Books, 1959), 27ff for the mystical tradition; *Anselm of Canterbury*: *Truth, Freedom and Evil*; *Three Philosophical Dialogues* ed. and trans. J. Hopkins and H. Richardson (New York: Harper Torchbooks, 1967), including an excellent Introduction by the editors.

23   See Harry McSorley, *Luther: Right or Wrong?* (New York: Newman, 1969), 90ff, excursus on "The Meaning of 'Servum Arbitrium' in Augustine." McSorley follows the distinctions analysed by Mortimer Adler in *The Idea of Freedom: A Dialectical Examination of the Conceptions of Freedom*, 2 vols. (New York: Garden City, 1958-61) for the Institute for Philosophical Research.

24   See also Aristotle – *Eth. Eudem.* Bk 7, 14; Augustine – *De grat. et lib. art.* 17.32, *De Nat. et Grat.* 31, 50. Aquinas – *ST* Ia-IIae, QQ 6 – 17 on *voluntas*, 56ff, and 109-114 (treatise on grace); Anton C. Pegis, "Thomism as a Philosophy" in Gilson and Pegis, *St. Thomas Aquinas and Philosophy* (West Hartford, Connecticut: St Joseph College, 1961); P. Rousselot, *The Intellectualism of Saint Thomas*, ET by J.E. Mahoney (London: Sheed and Ward, 1935); R.L. Patterson, *The Concept of God in the Philosophy of Aquinas* (London, 1933); E. Gilson, *Reason and Revelation*, op. cit., Ch. 3, "The Harmony of Reason and Revelation," 69ff.

25   See *William Ockham*: *Predestination, God's Foreknowledge, and Future Contingents*, trans. Adams and Kretzmann (New York: Appleton-Century-Crofts, 1969). Diogenes Allen has a perceptive remark on our point, that Ockham "turned the problem of universals from the ontological problem of common natures present in various individuals to a question of logic and language. He deals with the terms of propositions

and how they signify" – *Philosophy for Understanding Theology* (Atlanta: John Knox Press, 1985), 156.

26   James F. Ross, *Philosophical Theology* (New York: Bobbs-Merrill, 1969), 5: "The analysis of 'S is omnipotent'," 195ff; Heiko Oberman's monograph is excellent on disputed points of Biel interpretation: *The Harvest of Medieval Theology* (Cambridge, Mass: Harvard U.P. 1963), esp. Prolegomena, 30ff.

27   *Philosophers Speak of God*, Hartshorne and Reese (Chicago: University of Chicago Press, 1953) develops the typology, 15ff, classical theism 76ff. For summary statement of Hartshorne's own position, see *The Divine Relativity* (Yale U.P., 1948).

28   In T. Altizer and W. Hamilton, *Radical Theology and the Death of God* (New York: Bobbs Merrill, 1966), 6. Kaufmann is hardly a fair example of negative "orthodoxy" – e.g., his *Critique of Religion and Philosophy* (New York: Doubleday Anchor, 1961) VI, "God, Ambiguity and Theology." Cf. A. Flew, *God and Philosophy* (London: Hutchinson, 1966) Ch. 2 "Beginning from the Beginning" in search of "a basic concept of God." It is disturbing, however, that philosophers of religion whether theist or antitheist, are able to "presuppose a fairly well-defined and agreed conception of God" – John Hick, ed. *The Existence of God* (New York: Macmillan, 1964), Intro. p. 2. This always includes attributes of omnipotence and omniscience, without explicit qualification (ibid.). Thus J.L. Mackie's sensitive discussion of "arguments for and against the existence of God" can begin by acknowledging Richard Swinburne's (*The Coherence of Theism*) definition "able to do anything (i.e., omnipotent)," etc. (*The Miracle of Theism* [Oxford: Clarendon, 1982], 3.)

4: Rebirth of Will

1   P.O. Kristeller, "The Myth of Renaissance Atheism and the French Tradition of Free Thought," *Journal of the History of Philosophy* 6 (1968), 233-243; Renan's *Averroès et l'Averroïsme*, 1852.

2   J. Thrower, *A Short History of Western Atheism* (London: Pemberton Books 1971), 71. The 1981 Gifford Lecturer, S.H. Nasr, contrasts "pontifical" with "Promethean man," the latter rebelling against heaven and its created human image "from the period of the Renaissance and its aftermath." He agrees with Gilbert Durand's thesis (see Note 19 later) of "the disfiguration of the image of man in the West," defacing the original and traditional image of bridge, *pontifex*, between earth and heaven. He hopes for his return, inasmuch as Prometheanism's "humanism" has produced "the veritably infrahuman which threatens not only the human quality of life but the very existence of man on earth" – Seyyed Hossein Nasr, *Knowledge and the Sacred* (New York: Crossroad, 1981), Ch. 5 "Man, Pontifical and Promethean," 160ff.

3   Cf. J.C. McLelland, ed., *Peter Martyr Vermigli and Italian Reform* (Waterloo: Wilfrid Laurier U.P., 1980).

4   Cf. Trousson, op. cit., I.87ff; Lynch, *Christ and Prometheus*, op. cit., 138ff. for Bruno as Prometheus.

5   *Haec igitur lucra philosophorum, haec est eorum merces*; in Trousson, op. cit., I.104 (*De Fato* III, 7).

6   Ibid., I.105.

7   Marjorie O'Rourke Boyle, *Erasmus on Language and Method in Theology* (Toronto: University of Toronto Press, 1977), 72ff "The Scope of Theology" and 122 for Proteus.

8   *De Sapiente*, 1510 – see J. Seznec, op. cit., 97ff and Trousson, op. cit., I.105.

9   Cf. G.S. Hendry, *God the Creator* (London: Hodder and Stoughton, 1937).

10   *De hominis dignitate*, 1486, ET by E.L. Forbes in Cassirer, Kristeller and Randall, *The Renaissance Philosophy of Man* (University of Chicago Press, 1948) 224f (Sect. 3).

11   R. Coughlan, *The World of Michelangelo* (New York: Time-Life Books, 1966), 91.

12   C. Trinkaus, *In Our Image and Likeness: Humanity and Divinity in Italian Humanist Thought*, 2 vols. (Chicago: University of Chicago Press, 1970), I.xxiff.

13   Luther, *Formula of Mass and Communion for the Church at Wittenberg*, 15; Calvin, *Institutes*, Ch. 1 on "The True Church." For Peter Martyr,

see the sources in App. B of McLelland, *The Visible Words of God* (Edinburgh: Oliver and Boyd, 1956), 267ff.

14　The two key texts, Erasmus' *De Libero Arbitrio* and Luther's *De Servo Arbitrio*, are translated by Gordon Rupp and Philip Watson respectively in vol. XVII of L.C.C.: *Luther and Erasmus: Free Will and Salvation* (London: SCM, 1969). Our quotations are from this edition. Cf. M.O. Boyle, *Rhetoric and Reform: Erasmus' Civil Dispute with Luther* (Harvard U.P., 1983) arguing that what was at stake was the nature of theology itself. Cf. McLelland, "The Reformed Doctrine of Predestination" in *Scottish Journal of Theology*, 8/3 (Sept. 1955). Vermigli saw that the scholastic formulae are less constricting than Luther (or the modern critique of classical theism) suggests. The divine will is *simplex*, manifesting not a *necessitas coactionis et consequentis*, but *necessitas ex hypothesi et consequentiae* (or *infallibilitatis*). All things are ordered according to the *hypothesis decreti divini* so that predestination and free will are not only compatible but correlative.

15　The cluster of ideas (*conformitas voluntatis Dei, unio mystica, imitatio Christi*) was worked out in his first book, *Eyn theologia Deutsch* (1518), the anonymous work which he ascribed to Tauler. I owe this reference to my former student Prof. Dietmar Lage. Cf. McSorley, *Luther: Right or Wrong?* op. cit., esp. 297ff on "Luther's Doctrine of Unfree Will . . . De servo arbitrio."

16　E.g. compare *Institutes* III, Chs. 21-24 with *The Eternal Predestination of God*. With Westphal in mind, Calvin can say: "they plunge themselves into the abyss of the divine omnipotence, in order to extinguish the light of the truth" (*Inst.* 4.17.25).

17　The thesis that Beza, Martyr and Zanchi are responsible for the introduction of Reformed Aristotelianism has been argued by Brian Armstrong, *Calvinism and the Amyraut Heresy* (Madison: University of Wisconsin Press, 1969). Cf. my response in "Peter Martyr Vermigli: Scholastic or Humanist?" in McLelland, ed. *PMV and Italian Reform*, op. cit.

18　Cf. C. Vasoli, "Loci Communes and the Rhetorical and Dialectical Traditions" in McLelland, ed., *PMV and Italian Reform*, op. cit., 17ff.; J.P. Donnelly, *Calvinism and Scholasticism in Vermigli's Doctrine of Man and Grace* (Leiden: E.J. Brill, 1976).

19　After Festugière's pioneering work (*La Révélation d'Hermès Trismégiste*, 4 vols., 1950-54), D.P. Walker has produced *Spiritual and Demonic Magic : From Ficino to Campanella* (London: Warburg Inst. 1958) and *The Ancient Theology* (Cornell U.P., 1972). Apart from individual research on Paracelsus (Walter Pagel), Agrippa (C.G. Nauert) and Francis Bacon (Paolo Rossi), Gilbert Durand has explored the underground tradition with zest – e.g., "Défiguration philosophique et figure traditionelle de l'homme en Occident," *Eranos* 38 (1969), 45-93, "Similitude Hermétique et Science de l'Homme," *Eranos* 42 (1973), 427-515. Cf. also the review article by Stephen McKnight, "The Renaissance Magus and the Modern Messiah," *Religious Studies Review* (5/2, April 1979), 81-88.

20   Frances Yates, *Giordano Bruno and the Hermetic Tradition* (New York: Routledge and Kegan Paul, 1964), 116.

21   R.H. Popkin, *The History of Scepticism from Erasmus to Descartes* (Assen: Van Gorcum, 1960), xii. Cf. T. Penelhum, *God and Skepticism* (Dordrecht: D. Reidel, 1983), 3ff. For Sanchez see H. Butterfield, *The Origins of Modern Science 1300-1800* (Toronto: Clarke, Irwin, 1968), 98.

22   C.G. Nauert, Jr., *Agrippa and the Crisis of Renaissance Thought* (Urbana: University of Illinois, 1965), 208ff. Cf. T. Penelhum, *God and Skepticism*, op. cit., who distinguishes two kinds of Skeptical Fideism, Conformist (Erasmus, Montaigne, Bayle) and Evangelical (Pascal, Kierkegaard).

23   *Academica* 1548, in Popkin, op. cit., 29.

24   T. Molnar, *Theists and Atheists*, op. cit., 43ff., 73ff. esp. For a different assessment of Paduan Aristotelianism see Philip McNair, *Peter Martyr in Italy* (Oxford: Clarendon, 1967), 86ff. Baumer (op. cit., 97) notes that Tommaso Campanella's classification of sceptics in *Atheismus Triumphatus*, 1636, scored the Libertines as the "plague of this age" who denied Christian belief and taught that religions were invented by astute men to keep the masses in obedience. He also thought the heterodox Aristotelianism of Padua to be a main cause of atheism, an Averroism indeed.

25   Molnar, op. cit., 74. For antitrinitarianism see E.M. Wilbur, *A History of Unitarianism: Socinianism and its Antecedents* (Cambridge, Massachusetts: Harvard U.P., 1947).

26   A. D'Andrea, "Geneva 1576-78: The Italian Community and the Myth of Italy" in McLelland, *PVM and Italian Reform*, op. cit., 53ff.

5: Reason and the Lightbearer

1   *The Works of Francis Bacon* (London: 1861), VI:668ff., 745ff. Cf. E. Sewell, *The Orphic Voice* (Harper Torchbooks, 1971), 91ff.

2   *The Essays of Francis Bacon*, XVI of Atheism, XVII Of Superstition (1812).

3   F.H. Anderson, *The Philosophy of Francis Bacon* (University of Chicago, 1948) 53; see Chs. 15 – 17 on the new method of science, and Ch. 25 on "Bacon Contra Aristotle." A.C. Crombie, *Augustine to Galileo: Science in the Later Middle Ages and Early Modern Times* (Penguin: Peregrine Books, 1969), 2:290. Crombie comments, "Knowledge of the form gave mastery over it and its properties, and so the positive task of Bacon's new method was to show how to obtain knowledge of the form." T.F. Torrance, *Theological Science* (London: Oxford U.P., 1969), 68ff.

4   Peter Gay, *The Enlightenment : An Interpretation*, vol. 2: *The Science of Freedom* (New York: Alfred A. Knopf, 1969), 5f.

5   Cf. Popkin, op. cit., 175ff., and Fabro, op. cit., 361ff. on the split symbolized by res cogitans/res extensa. Michel Despland (*La Religion en Occident : evolution des idées et du vécu*, Montreal, Fides, 1979) provides good comparative analysis in Ch. 12, Les bases de la problématique moderne (Contrastes entre Français, Anglais et Allemand, 299ff.) and Ch. 16, Les idées de religion au XVIIIe siècle, 407ff.

6   Cf. Sesonske and Fleming, *Meta-Meditations* (Belmont, California: Wadsworth Pub. Co., 1965). Fabro (26) thinks that this "reflexive Principle" blocks the natural movement to the Absolute. Stuart F. Spicker argues that Descartes himself was not the simple dualist of the tradition: *The Philosophy of the Body*: *Rejections of Cartesian Dualism* (New York: Quadrangle, 1970).

7   J.G. Hamann, in R.G. Smith, *J.G. Hamann* (London: Collins, 1960), 252 (letter to Jacobi of 2 June 1785). Cf. T. Molnar, op. cit., 45, 75.

8   H. Thielicke, *The Evangelical Faith*, trans. G.W. Bromiley (Grand Rapids: W.B. Eerdmans, 1974), I:34. Hans Küng, *Does God Exist*? *An Answer for Today* (New York: Doubleday, 1980), 16.

9   Fergus Kerr, *Theology After Wittgenstein* (Oxford: Basil Blackwell, 1986), 59f. Kerr gives a substantial critique of "the modern philosophy of the self," arguing that Wittgenstein's own view was quite the opposite of the traditional solipsism of the analytical school and that such a view makes for a "theology without the mental ego." Cf. John Wisdom, *Other Minds* (Oxford: Blackwell, 1952) and J.L. Austin, "Other Minds," in the symposium reported in the *Proceedings of the Aristotelian Society*, vol. XX, Supp. 1946, reprinted in *Logic and Language*, ed. A. Flew (New York: Anchor, 1968), 342-80.

10   See Popkin, op. cit., 197ff.; D. Hume, *A Treatise of Human Nature*, I.

11   For this section see, e.g., Ira Wade, *The Intellectual Origins of the French Enlightenment* (Princeton U.P., 1971); C. Fabro, op. cit., 226ff. (Herbert of Cherbury), 273ff. ("Deism Displayed and Flayed [Locke, Toland, Berkeley]"), 250ff. (Shaftesbury) and 315ff. (Samuel Clarke); Lepp, op. cit., 97ff on Rationalist Atheism; F.L. Baumer, *Religion and the Rise of Scepticism* (New York: Harcourt, Brace and World, 1960), 78ff (Strasbourg Clock) 98ff and 112ff; John Cairns, *Unbelief in the Eighteenth Century* (Edinburgh: A. & C. Black, 1981).

12   See R.E. Florida, *Voltaire and the Socinians* (Banbury, O.: Voltaire Foundation, 1974) on the questions why Voltaire maintained such interest in the "anti-Nicene" Protestants of Poland, and whether the movement had direct influence on his thought.

13   Cf. Randall Stewart, *American Literature and Christian Doctrine* (Baton Rouge: Louisiana State U.P., 1958) and Norman Cousins, *In God We Trust : the Religious Beliefs and Ideas of the American Founding Fathers* (New York: Harper and Row, 1958).

14   E.B. Browning, Preface to 1833 translation of *Prometheus Bound* (London: Ward, Lock and Bowden, 1896 reprinting), 8.

15   Kenneth Clark, *Civilization* (New York: Harper and Row, 1969), 164f. For a more tentative judgment see R. Sandler, ed., *Northrop Frye on Shakespeare* (Toronto: Fitzhenry and Whiteside, 1986): "I don't know what Shakespeare believed, but he knew what his audience would buy," 111.

16   Peter Gay, op. cit., 16f.

17   Gerald R. Cragg, *The Church and the Age of Reason 1648-1789* (Penguin Books, 1968), 14. Also Cragg, ed., *The Cambridge Platonists* (New York: Oxford U.P., 1968, Library of Protestant Thought); C.E. Raven, *Natural Religion and Christian Theology* (Cambridge U.P., 1953), I:99ff, "Cudworth and the Age of Genius."

18   Newton, *Principia Mathematica*, Gen. Scholium to Bk. III, Prop. XLII, ET by Motte (544). For the "medieval world-drama" and the "Newtonian world-machine" see I.G. Barbour, *Issues in Science and Religion* (Englewood Cliffs, New Jersey: Prentice-Hall, 1966), 16ff., 34ff.

19   Newton, *Opticks*, Bk. III, Qu. 28; T.F. Torrance, *Christian Theology and Scientific Culture* (New York: Oxford U.P., 1981), 42ff.

20   James Boswell, *The Life of Samuel Johnson*, 1763 (London: J.M. Dent, 1906), I.246.

21   See *Voltaire on Religion: Selected Writings*, ET by K.W. Applegate (New York: Fred. Ungar, 1974); Cf. Will and Ariel Durant, *The Age of Voltaire* (New York: Simon and Schuster, 1965), 116ff.; O. Chadwick, *The Secularization of the European Mind in the Nineteenth Century* (Cambridge U.P., 1975), Ch. 6: "Voltaire in the Nineteenth Century,"

143ff.

22   G. Siegmund, *God on Trial: A Brief History of Atheism* (New York: Desclée, 1968), 149; cf. Stanley Jaki, *The Road of Science and the Ways to God* (Chicago: University of Chicago Press, 1978): "Deism soon became a cover-up for atheism," 7.

23   *Characteristics of Men, Manners, Opinions, Times*, ed. J.M. Robertson (New York: Bobbs Merrill, 1964 – originally published 1711), 16. Oskar Walzel, *Das prometheussymbol von Shaftesbury zu Goethe* (Darmstadt: Wiss. Buchg., 1932), 9ff.

24   Cf. S. Grean, *Shaftesbury's Philosophy of Religion and Ethics* (Ohio U.P., 1967); E. Cassirer, *The Philosophy of the Enlightenment* (Boston: Beacon Press, 1951), 153.

25   Cf. Gaston Bachelard's estimate, in Molnar, op. cit., 47; also C. Becker, *The Heavenly City of the 18th C. Philosophers* (New Haven: Yale University Press, 1932); Paul Zweig, *The Adventurer* (Basic Books, 1974) on "Hero and Anti-hero"; Enlightenment rationalism makes the adventurer a misfit.

26   Cf. F.A. Hayek, *The Counter-Revolution of Science: Studies on the Abuse of Reason* (New York: Macmillan, 1955).

27   *Enquiry Concerning Human Understanding*, VIII. Cf. T. Penelhum, *Hume* (London: Macmillan, 1975), 117.

28   L. Kolakowski, *The Alienation of Reason: A History of Positivist Thought* (New York: Anchor, 1969), 41. One should note also the "counter-Enlightenment" (Isaiah Berlin) symbolized by Giambattista Vico's philosophy of history. For Hume's own stance cf. the differing opinions of Norman Kemp Smith, *The Philosophy of David Hume* (London, 1941) and Intro. to the *Dialogues* (Oxford, 1935) and J.C.A. Gaskin, *Hume's Philosophy of Religion* (New York: Harper and Row, 1978). A careful analysis is that of David Fate Norton, *Hume, Atheism, and the Autonomy of Morals* (Montreal: McGill U.P., 1984).

29   Cassirer, op. cit., 13.

30   Ibid., 38.

31   Ibid., 122 *(Von der Weisheit)*.

32   Karl Barth, *Protestant Theology in the Nineteenth Century* (London: SCM, 1972), 270f.

33   *Critique of Practical Reason*, 73, ET by L.W. Beck (New York: Liberal Arts, 1956), 75; Theorem IV (33ff.) on autonomy and heteronomy; cf. *Groundwork to the Metaphysic of Morality*, ET by John Watson (Glasgow: J. Maclehose, 1908), III.294ff., IV.248. Beck's comment on the *Grundlegung* is from *A Commentary on Kant's Critique of Practical Reason* (University of Chicago Press, 1960), 196. M. Polanyi, *Personal Knowledge* (New York: Harper and Row, 1964), 309. The original is

italicized; its context is "the structure of commitment." Cf. John R. Silber, "The Ethical Significance of Kant's *Religion*" on freedom and the concept of *Willkür* (lxxix – cxxxiv of *Religion Within the Limits of Reason Alone*), ET by Greene and Hudson (New York: Harper and Bros., 1960).

34   *C. Prac. R.* 87 (89).

35   *Religion*, 95f., 170f.; cf. 129ff. on mystery. Cf. *The Conflict of the Faculties*, ET of *Der Streit der Fakultäten* by M.J. Gregor (New York: Abaris, 1979), 95ff. on religion of the heart, 105ff. on the wonder that is felt *(fühlen)*.

36   M. Despland, *Kant on History and Religion* (Montreal: McGill-Queen's, 1973), 226. Cf. *Kant : Lectures on Philosophical Theology*, ET by Wood and Clark (Ithaca, New York: Cornell, 1978), 131ff. on "The Causality of God": when divine causality is "explained through his freedom" we have a *systema liberi arbitrii*.

37   Op. cit., 299.

38   *Religion*, 129.

39   *C. Pure R.*, ET by Meiklejohn (London: Dent, 1950), 357; also in *Philosophical Theol.*, op. cit., 64. Cf. Jüngel, op. cit., 40f.

40   J.G. Fichte, *Der Bestimmung des Menschen*, 1800 (*The Vocation of Man*, ET by W. Smith, Chicago: Open Court, 1910), 93. *Groundwork* 295; cf. *C. Prac. R.* 31ff. For the *Atheismusstreit* see Paul Edwards in *Enc. Phil.* I.189ff; Fabro, op. cit., 29ff., 516ff.

41   *Opus postumum*, quoted by Gollwitzer, op. cit., 208.f and *C. Prac. R.* 144 (149). Cf. *Crit. of Judgment*, 461ff. on the Moral Proof, and J. Collins, *The Emergence of Philosophy of Religion* (Yale U.P., 1967), 89ff.

42   Gay, op. cit., II.84ff.

43   "The Conquest of Granada" 1.1.1, in Gay, ibid., 96.

44   Ibid., 115.

6: Romance and the Fire-Kindler

1   Kenneth Clark, *The Romantic Rebellion*: *Romantic versus Classic Art* (New York: Harper and Row, 1973), 95. Herbert Read once spoke of the debate on romanticism and classicism as "so much weary logomachy."

2   Trousson, op. cit., I.245. On the Frankfurt period, see Oskar Walzel, *Das Prometheussymbol von Shaftesbury zu Goethe*, op. cit., esp. 56ff.

3   Ibid., I.278; Hans Urs von Balthasar, *Prometheus, Studien zur Geschichte des Deutschen Idealismus* (Heidelberg: Kerle Verlag, 1947), 145, 150; cf. 407-514 on Goethe's thought in general.

4   Maximen und Reflexionen, No. 807, quoted in Arnulf Zweig, "Goethe" in *Enc. Phil.* 3.364.

5   Herder, *Werke*, ed. B. Suphan (Berlin, 1882), vols. 26.196 and 32 (*Der entf. Prom.*, 1802, 329-68).

6   Albert Camus, *The Rebel* (New York: A.A. Knopf, 1956), 22ff. G. Durand has noted "l'énorme résurgence du mythe de Prométhée durant toute le période pré-romantique et romantique" – *Univers du Symbole*, op. cit., 21.

7   K. Clark, *The Romantic Rebellion*, op. cit., 19. Northrop Frye, *Fearful Symmetry: a Study of William Blake* (Princeton U.P., 1969), 136ff.

8   Ibid., 207, 225ff. on Orc as Prometheus, and 302f., "the crucifixion of Jesus and Prometheus."

9   For this material see Trousson, op. cit., II.311ff.; Gilbert Highet, *The Classical Tradition: Greek and Roman Influences on Western Literature* (Oxford U.P., 1949), 362ff and 543ff. Cf. Richard Jenkyns, *The Victorians and Ancient Greece* (Cambridge, Massachusets: Harvard U.P., 1980), esp. 87ff, "Tragedy" on the role of Aeschylus for Byron and Shelley.

10   Ibid., 453ff.

11   Cf. W.P. Albrecht, *The Sublime Pleasures of Tragedy: A Study of Critical Theory from Dennis to Keats* (University of Kansas, 1975), 133ff.; Nathan A. Scott, Jr., *Negative Capability: Studies in the New Literature and the Religious Situation* (Yale U.P., 1969), Preface; P.J. Conradi, *Iris Murdoch: the Saint and the Artist* (New York: St Martin's Press, 1986) "Introductory: 'Existentialist and Mystic'."

12   Cf. John Freccero, "Manfred's Wounds and the Poetics of the 'Purgatorio'," 69ff. in E. Glen, ed., *Centre and Labyrinth: Essays in Honour of N. Frye* (University of Toronto Press, 1983).

13   Texts in Shelley, *Selected Essays on Atheism* (New York: Arno Press, 1972). Cf. B. Ellsworth, *Shelley's Religion* (New York: Russell and

Russell, 1964), esp. Chs. 2-3.

14   Trousson, op. cit., II.313.

15   Thus Grillparzer ("Unsinn! eine Absurdidät"); Jacques de Lacretelle ("Prométhée est le premier romantique"); and Roger Caillois – see Trousson, op. cit., II.316. Also W. Lynch, *Christ and Prometheus*, op. cit., 63 on Byron and Shelley.

16   As does H. Urs von Balthasar, *Prometheus*, op. cit.; cf. Tillich, *Perspectives On 19th and 20th Century Protestant Theology* (London: SCM, 1967), Ch. 3, "The Classic-Romantic Reaction against the Enlightenment." For Steiner see *The Death of Tragedy* (London: Faber and Faber, 1961), 192f. Cf. Jean Brun, *Le Retour de Dionysos* (Paris: Les Bergers et Les Mages, 1976): "Les passionés du savoir: Faust et Don Juan," 36ff.

17   W. Fleming, *Art, Music and Ideas* (New York: Holt, Rinehart and Winston, 1970), 290f.

18   Liszt, "Prometheus: Symphonic Poem No. 5, for full orchestra"; Skriabin, "Prometheus: the poem of fire, for grand orchestra and piano with organ, choirs and *clavier à lumières*" (1910); Orff, *Prometheus: Mythos, Drama, Musik*, staged 1968.

19   Trousson, op. cit., II.336ff.

20   Ibid., II.378.

21   Carl Spitteler, *Prometheus und Epimetheus*. Ges. Werke I (Zürich: Artemis-Verlag, 1945), 5-347; *Prometheus Der Dulder*, 353-554. Cf. Highet, op. cit., 528ff.

22   C.G. Jung, *Psychological Types*, V: "The Type Problem in Poetry," Collected Works 6 (Princeton U.P., 1971), 166-272.

23   Trousson, op. cit., II.439.

24   Cf. Joseph Folliet, *L'Avenement de Prométhée. Essai de sociologique de notre temps*, 1950 (Trousson II.46); Alex Craig, *The Prometheans* (London: Fortune Press, 1953); Edwin Muir, *Prometheus* (London: Faber and Faber, 1954). Both poets express yearning for another world suggested by the Incarnation but unclear to their vision. J.C. McLelland, *The Clown and the Crocodile* (Richmond, Va.: John Knox Press, 1970), 61ff.

25   Cf. D.W. Pomeroy, "The New Nihilism," *Theology Today* XXXI.3, 1974 (Princeton), 248ff; also Viktor Frankl, "Reductionism and Nihilism" in Koestler and Smythes, ed., *Beyond Reductionism* (New York: Macmillan, 1969), 396ff.

7: The Speculative Death of God

1   See J.N. Findlay, *Hegel : A Re-examination* (New York: Macmillan, 1958), Ch. 3 "The Dialectical Method"; C. Taylor, *Hegel* (Cambridge U.P., 1975).

2   Cf. A. Kojève, *Introduction to the Reading of Hegel*, trans. J.H. Nichols (New York: Basic Books, 1969); E. Fackenheim, *The Religious Dimension in Hegel's Thought* (Indiana U.P., 1967), 20f; P. Tillich, *Perspectives*, op. cit., 114ff; R.K. Kaeske, "Hegel's Phenomenology: Philosophia Quaerens Theologiam," *Canadian Journal of Theology* XVI, 1 and 2 (1970), 22ff.

3   First published by Herman Nohl (Tubingen: JCB Mohr, 1907) who supplied titles. ET by T.M. Knox and R. Kroner, *On Christianity, Early Theological Writings by Friedrich Hegel* (New York: Harper Torchbooks, 1948) – hereafter *ETW*.

4   "The Positivity of the Christian Religion," *ETW*, 67-181; cf. P. Masterson, *Atheism and Alienation* (Dublin: Gill and Macmillan, 1971), 37: "a religion is positive when it is understood as an arbitrary and authoritarian imposition of a system of dogmas and of commands, by a radically transcendent God."

5   "We shall call this position which denies the existential reality of God 'Antitheism'. . . . Hegel, whom we shall treat as the originator of 'Antitheism,' attacked the 'separate,' or independently existing, God of traditional religion as morally degrading and false and advanced the idea that God is 'subjective' or internally related to human thinking," H.R. Burkle, *The Non-Existence of God: Antitheism from Hegel to Duméry* (New York: Herder and Herder, 1969), 10. Burkle is most helpful in clarifying the terms of the modern development, treating Sartre under the title "the apotheosis of existence" (117ff).

6   "Positivity of Christian Religion," *ETW* 162f. (Nohl 227f.).

7   Cf. Kroner, *ETW* 5ff (The "Life of Jesus" is in Nohl, 73ff). For Hegel on Kant see *Faith and Knowledge*, ET of *Glauben und Wissen* by Cerf and Harris (Albany: SUNY, 1977), 67ff, "Kantian Philosophy."

8   "Spirit of Christianity," *ETW*, 187 (Nohl, 247).

9   Ibid., *ETW*, 212 (Nohl, 266).

10   Ibid., *ETW* 213f (Nohl, 267f). Note that it is in this context that Hegel comments on Matt. 19:23, "How hard it is for a rich man to enter the Kingdom of Heaven" (221 – Nohl 273f). "The fate of property has become too powerful for us to tolerate reflection on it, to find its abolition thinkable." Here "life is bound up with objects," the wholeness of religious reconciliation is impossible. Wealth is caught in the clash of rights, of opposites, and so excludes the unifying power of love.

11   *ETW*, 273 (Nohl, 318).

12   E. Fackenheim, *The Religious Dimension in Hegel's Thought*, op. cit.,
        153.

13   "Positivity," *ETW*, 169, 80.

14   V. Miceli, *The Gods of Atheism* (New York: Arlington House, 1971),
        22ff.

15   James Collins, *The Emergence of Philosophy of Religion* (New Haven:
        Yale U.P., 1967), 229.

16   "Positivity," *ETW*, 71ff.

17   Collins, op. cit., 233.

18   C. Taylor, op. cit., 512. For the above see *Phen.* IV, 217ff; also R.
        Dunayevskaya, *Philosophy and Revolution* (New York: Delacorte,
        1973), 25ff.

19   Quoted by T. Munson, "Hegel as Philosopher of Religion," *The Journal
        of Religion* XLVI.1 (Jan. 1966).

20   *History of Philosophy* I.85. The argument is well developed in the *Lec-
        tures on Philosophy of Religion III* (AAR: Scholars Press, 1979, ET by
        P.C. Hodgson), 3, "Differentiation and Estrangement."

21   *Phil. of Rel.* III.1, 157. Cf. *Faith and Knowledge*, op. cit., Conclu-
        sion; Jüngel, op. cit., 55ff.

22   Barth, *Prot. Theol. in 19th C*, op. cit., 393.

23   Cf. *Phen.* VIII, "Absolute Knowledge"; *Phil. of Rel.* (*Begriff der Rel.*
        156: "to make himself objective for himself").

24   Cf. Taylor, op. cit., 209, 495.

25   *Lectures on Hist. of Phil.*, 3:5; cf. H. Küng, op. cit., 140ff on the theme
        "Hegel understood atheism as postatheistic."

26   *Science of Logic*, 1812-16; cf. Taylor, op. cit., 226ff; Claude Bruaire,
        "Hegel et l'athéisme Contemporain," *Revue International de Philosophie*
        24 (1970), 72-80.

27   E. Jüngel, op. cit., viii, 18ff, etc.

28   E.g., *The Death of God: the Culture of our Post-Christian Era* (New
        York: Braziller, 1961); *Wait Without Idols* (New York: Braziller,
        1964); *No Other God* (New York: Braziller 1966); *God and Utopia* (New
        York: Seabury, 1977). In the second work Prometheus symbolizes the
        apotheosis of artistic humanity; the third speaks of "Promethean, or
        blasphemous, metaphysical rebellion" (46); the contrast with Abraham
        increases, until "Abrahamic iconoclasm" develops as the clue to

eschatology, that which sets Prometheus free "from his own myth." On nonexistence see H.R. Burkle, *The Non-Existence of God*, op. cit.; R. Ross, *The Non-Existence of God: Linguistic Paradox in Tillich's Thought* (New York and Toronto: Edwin Mellen, 1978). A fresh interpretation of the same phenomenon is offered by Mark Taylor, *Deconstructing Theology* (AAR/Studies in Religion 28; New York: Crossroads Pub., 1982) in view of Derrida's deconstruction of the subject-object construct of Western thought: "the death of God is the (a)theology of Deconstruction" (xix). That is, a "metaphysics of absence" replaces that of presence.

29   Dorothee Sölle, *Atheistischen an Gott glauben* (Walter-Verlag Olten u. Freiburg im Breslau, 1968).

30   Karl Löwith, *From Hegel to Nietzsche* (New York: Holt, Rinehart and Winston, 1964), 14ff.

31   Von Balthasar, op. cit., 563. The projected second volume had the title *Dionysos*.

32   Siegmund, op. cit., 243ff.

33   Ibid., 247.

34   *Essence of Christianity*, App. 22

35   *Principles of the Philosophy of the Future*, 1843, 1 (177 of *The Fiery Brook: Selected Writings of L.F.*, Z. Hanfi (New York: Anchor Books, 1972)).

36   *Basic Questions* II.191.

37   Miceli, op. cit., 24; cf. E. Kamenka, *The Philosophy of Ludwig Feuerbach* (London: Routledge and Kegan Paul, 1970), Ch. 1, "The Promethean Background."

38   Siegmund, op. cit., 257; cf. Löwith, op. cit., 83ff; Marcel Neusch, *Aux Sources de l'Athéisme Contemporain* (Paris: Ed. du Centurion, 1977), Ch. 2, Feuerbach, "Père de l'Athéisme Moderne."

39   Löwith, op. cit., 72.

40   *Grundsätze der Philosophie der Zukunft*, quoted in Löwith, op. cit., 77.

41   *Grundsätze*, in Löwith, op. cit., 80. Cf. M. Buber on Feuerbach – "Das Problem des Menschen," *Werke* I.309ff.

42   For this paragraph see Barth, *Church Dogmatics* II.1, 287ff. on "The Being of God as the One who Loves," esp. 290, 293. Barth's essays on Feuerbach are preserved in *Theology and Church: Shorter Writings 1920-1928* (New York: Harper and Row, 1962) 217-237 (from lecture series at Münster, 1920) and in *Prot. Theol.*, op. cit., 534-540.

43   See esp. *C.D.* IV.2, 77ff and *Theol. and Church*, 229ff. An excellent case study of Hegel's exegesis is given by Georges Cottier, *L'Athéisme du Jeune Marx: ses Origines Hégeliennes* (Paris: Librairie Philosophiques Vrin, 1969), 28ff and by Dorothee Sölle, op. cit., 9ff: "Gottes Selbstäusserung . . . Eine Meditation zu Philipper 2, 5-11." See also Werner Schilling, *Feuerbach und die Religion* (München: Evang. Presseverband, 1957), esp. 147ff. "Feuerbach im Lichte Martin Luthers und der Bekenntnisschriften der lutherischen Kirche."

44   Cottier, op. cit., 34ff., "Aliénation et Kénose."

45   See "Religion and Alienation" in the next chapter; also J. Israel, *Alienation from Marx to Modern Sociology* (Boston: Allyn and Bacon, 1971). Both Luther and Calvin at times come close to equating finiteness with sinfulness, although subsequent doctrine, including seventeenth century scholasticism, taught that the possibility of sin (as an act of falling) is located in the "mutability" of the created order as well as in the perverse will. E.g., H. Heppe, *Reformed Dogmatics* (ET 1950) XV, "Sin or Man's State of Corruption," esp. 328ff. on Cocceius's distinction between *libertas* and *mutabilitas*.

46   Quoted in Cottier, op. cit., 39. Cf. J. Thrower, *Marxist-Leninist "Scientific Atheism" and the Study of Religion and Atheism in the USSR* (Berlin: Mouton, 1983): "the two must be kept logically distinct," 29.

47   *Barth, C.D.* IV.2, 81f. For the debates, cf. McLelland, "Lutheran-Calvinist Debates on Christology and Eucharist," *Marburg Revisited*, ed. Empie and McCord (Minneapolis, Minn.: Augsburg Publishing House, 1966), 39-54.

48   Ibid., referring to Ebeling, "Die Anfänge von Luthers Hermeneutik" *Z.Th.K.*, 1951, 172f.

49   F. Engels, "Ludwig Feuerbach and the End of Classical German Philosophy," *Marx and Engels on Religion* (Moscow: Foreign Languages Publishing House, n.d. 224.

50   Reply of January 1842 to articles in the *Deutsche Jahrbücher* (by Max Stirner?) – Easton and Guddat, *Writings of the young Marx on Philosophy and Society* (New York: Doubleday Anchor, 1967), 93ff. But see Küng, op. cit., 216.

51   *Frühe Schriften* – see Bottomore, op. cit., 196ff (*MEGA* I.1 (1) 175).

52   Letter to Feuerbach of August 1844 – D. MacLennan, *Marx Before Marxism* (Penguin Books, 1970), 250.

53   M. Schilling, op. cit., 88ff.

54   Cf. Schilling, ibid. on *Weltbilden*, 46ff; T.F. Torrance, *The Ground and Grammar of Theology* (Belfast: Christian Journals, 1980), 15ff, 75ff.

55   Feuerbach, *Principles*, Thesis 14.

56   Barth, *Prot. Theol.*, op. cit., 537; cf. Masterson, op. cit., 63ff; but F.C. Fiorenza modifies this position – "The responses of Barth and Ritschl to Feuerbach," *Studies in Religion* 7/2 (1978), 149-166.

8: The Practical Death of God

1   *Karl Marx, Friedrich Engels: Historisch-Kritische Gesamtausgabe* (Berlin: Marx-Engels Verlag, 1932) I.1.1,10 (hereafter *MEGA); Marx and Engels on Religion* (Moscow: Foreign Languages Publishing House, n.d.; New York: Schocken Books Inc., 1964), 15 (hereafter *MER*). A major resource in this and the following chapter has been the three volumes of Leszek Kolakowski, *Main Currents of Marxism* (Oxford: Clarendon, 1978): I. The Founders, II. The Golden Age, III. The Breakdown (hereafter *Currents*).

2   *MEGA* I.1.1, 1-52 (Notes 83-144), ET by N. Livergood (The Hague: 1967).

3   Foreword to thesis, op. cit.

4   See G. Siegmund, op. cit., 264ff; L. Althusser, "Sur le Jeune Marx," *La Pensée*, mars-avril 1961; G. Cottier, op. cit., 145ff; B. Delfgaauw, *The Young Marx* (New York: Newman Press, 1967, ET of *De Jonge Marx* 1962), 101ff for the 1837 letter to his father; D. McLellan, *Marx Before Marxism* (London: Penguin, 1972), Ch. 2.

5   Ibid., 265. After wrestling "through many nights," he writes: "A curtain has fallen, my holy of holies has been torn to shreds, and new gods must be enthroned."

6   According to G. Siegmund, op. cit., 266. The illustration of Marx Bound was used as allegory of the prohibition of the *Rheinische Zeitung*, and may be found facing p. 174 of the new (1975) edition of the ET *Collected Works*, vol. I. Cf P.M. John: *Marx on Alienation* (Calcutta: Minerva Associates, 1976), 24 on the Prometheus Bound image.

7   D.W.D. Shaw, *The Dissuaders: Three Explanations of Religion* (Freud, Marx, Durkheim) (London: SCM, 1978), 31.

8   Quoted in Dunayevskaya, op. cit., 3. Cf. Irena Kronska, "An Interpretation of Epicurean Atheism in Marx's Doctoral Dissertation," *Dialectics and Humanism* 4/1 (Winter 1977), 135-150. In *The Holy Family* (1844), Ch. 6, Marx traces the origin of materialism to Epicurus, and the modern development to Descartes and Locke. Duns Scotus (whom he confuses with Ockham) is significant for Great Britain in his history. Cf. Koch, op. cit., 131: the idea of man as self-creator begins "mythologically with Prometheus, historically with Euhemeros, and religio-philosophically with the sophist Protagoras."

9   Ernst Bloch, *On Karl Marx* (New York: Herder and Herder, 1971), 156. Cf. A. van Leeuwen, *Critique of Earth* (New York: Scribner's, 1974), 9f. for Marx's "atomistic" approach to the "an-atomy" of civil society.

10   The word can mean beginning, premise, hypothesis. Cf. D.B. McKown, *The Classical Marxist Critiques of Religion: Marx, Engels, Lenin, Kautsky* (The Hague: Martinus Nijhoff, 1975), 14f for various

interpretations in Marxist literature.

11   *MER*, 42f. Cf. N. Lash, *A Matter of Hope* (University of Notre Dame Press, 1982), Ch. 13 "The Criticism of Religion," 153ff.

12   Engels (*MEGA*, II.428). Quoted in R. Tucker, *Philosophy and Myth in Karl Marx* (Cambridge U.P., 1961), 73; cf. C. Fabro, *God in Exile*, op. cit., 689ff.

13   As noted by J. Thrower in his important study, *Marxist-Leninist "Scientific Atheism,"* op. cit., 335ff. He refers in particular to Gollwitzer as to its "antediluvian" nature, and to J.M. Bochenski "Marxism-Leninism and Religion" in Bochiurkiw and Strong, eds., *Religion and Atheism in the USSR and Eastern Europe* (London: Macmillan, 1975) as to its "antiquarian character" (336f). On current discussion of these topics, cf W. Oxtoby, "Religionswissenschaft Revisited" (*Religions in Antiquity*, Numen XIV Supp., 1968); J. Waardenburg, *Classical Approaches to the Study of Religion*, 2 vols. (The Hague: Mouton, 1973-74), esp. the Introduction, "View of a Hundred Years' Study of Religion" and *Reflections on the Study of Religion* (The Hague: Mouton, 1978), esp. 4, "A Need for Methodology," 52ff.

14   In K. Löwith, op. cit., 108. Cf. K. Clarkson and D. Hawkins, "Marx on Religion: the influence of Bruno Bauer and Ludwig Feuerbach on his thought and its implications for the Christian-Marxist dialogue," *Scot. Journ. of Theol.* 31/4, 533-555.

15   *MER*, 196. Cf. *The Book of Revelation*, 1883: "if we may call Philo the doctrinal father of Christianity, Seneca was her uncle," *MER*, 207.

16   Cf. McLelland, *God the Anonymous*, op. cit., Ch. 1 "Greek Religion and Philosophy" for analysis of the "dichotomy"; cf. McKown, op. cit., 72f for Engels's theory in contrast to Marx's.

17   Cf. Thrower, op. cit., 46ff for Engels on the origin of religion, and use of Tylor; also 358 and 363ff regarding "the motivation behind the religious quest."

18   "Emigrant Literature," *MER*, 142; cf. McKown, op. cit., 70ff for an excellent treatment of Engels on religion.

19   Neil McInnes, "Engels, Friedrich" in *Enc. Phil.* II.518.

20   *MER*, 51; cf. H. Ley, *Geschichte der Aufklärung und des Atheismus* (Berlin: VEB Deutscher Verlag der Wissenschaften, Band I, 1966), 11ff – the class struggle is the key to the Reformation.

21   *MER*, 265 ("Feuerbach and the end of Classical German Philosophy," 1886).

22   *MER*, 300ff.

23   Cf. E. Bloch, *Thomas Münzer als Theologe der Revolution*, 1921; Koch, op. cit., 30ff (Why Münzer and not Luther?); G.W. Forrell, "Thomas

Münzer, Symbol and Reality," *Dialog* 2 (Winter 1963), 12-23.

24   *MER*, 97; cf. Ley, op. cit., 13.

25   Cf. Robert Kingdon, "The Political Thought of Peter Martyr Vermigli" in McLelland, *PMV and Italian Reform*, op. cit., 121ff, and *The Political Thought of Peter Martyr Vermigli* (Genève: Librairie Droz, 1980).

26   *MER*, 147f (Anti-Dühring).

27   Cf. C. Himrichs, *Luther und Müntzer: Ihre ausenandersetzung über Obrigkeit und Widerstandsrecht* (Berlin: Walter de Gruyter, 1962). This careful study contrasts the two in their exegesis of the crucial passage Romans 13, as well as their differing sociological categories relating to Church and society. Cf. 77ff "Revelation im Bunde oder im Kampf mit der Obrigkeit?" See also G.R. Elton, *Reformation Europe 1517-1559* (New York: Harper and Row, 1963) Ch. 4 "The Radicals"; O. Chadwick, *The Reformation* (London: Hodder and Stoughton, 1964), 189: "At the extreme left was the apocalyptic spur with which Thomas Münzer helped to goad the German peasants into their calamitous jacquerie of 1524."

28   Cf. Calvin, *Institutes* III, 6-10; McLelland, *The Other Six Days* (Richmond, Va.: John Knox Press, 1962), 48ff.

29   Bk I, 1 – *MER*, 135.

30   *From Hegel to Nietzsche*, op. cit., 97

31   MS 3 – T.B. Bottomore, ed., *Karl Marx, Early Writings* (New York: McGraw-Hill, 1964), 161.

32   Cf. K. Popper, *The Open Society and its Enemies* (New York: Harper and Row, 1963), 81ff – Ch. 13 Marx's Sociological Dimension.

33   "Die Revolution von 1848 und das Proletariat," quoted in Löwith, op. cit., 154.

34   Conclusion to the *Critique of Hegel's Philosophy of Right*.

35   *Pour Marx* (Paris: F. Maspero, 1967), 49.

36   Ibid., Chs. II and VII – the latter, "Marxisme et Humanisme" is particularly helpful on this point, 225ff. The debate on the question of the development of Marx (Althusser *vs* Lucien Sève, for instance) was anticipated by Lukàcs in 1922 when the famous *History and Class Consciousness* accused a "vulgar Marxism" of reducing Marx's historical materialism to economic determinism – see T. O'Hagan, "Althusser: How to be a Marxist in Philosophy" in G.H.R. Parkinson, ed., *Marx and Marxisms* (Cambridge U.P., 1982), 243-64; Jean-Yves Jolif, "Marxism and Humanism," *Concilium* 6/9: *Humanism and Christianity*, ed. Claude Geffré (New York: Herder and Herder, 1973), 111ff. Cf. also Bottomore, op. cit., 61ff. "The 1850s: the *Grundrisse* Then and Now" for comparison of the 1844 MSS with the Grundrisse of 1857-58; David

McLelland, op. cit., 209ff.; Lash, op. cit., Ch. 2 "Marx: 'Early' and 'Mature'," 10ff. J. Miranda, *Marx against the Marxists: The Christian Humanism of Karl Marx* (Maryknoll, New York: Orbis, 1980), esp. 106ff. "Marx the Humanist."

37   E. Kamenka, op. cit., 10ff.

38   E.g., *Phil. of History* 4.2, *History of Phil.* 2, *Phenomenology of Spirit* 4. For general treatment of the concept of alienation, cf. B. Murchland, *The Age of Alienation* (New York: Random House, 1971); P.M. John, op. cit.; I. Meszaros, *Marx's Theory of Alienation* (London: Merlin, 1970), esp. 99ff "Conceptual Framework"; G. Baum, *Religion and Alienation: A Theological Reading of Sociology* (New York: Paulist, 1975), and n. 43, this chapter.

39   The young Marx specialized in the study of law – the critique of earth is a critique of law. As editor of the *Rheinische Zeitung* in 1842-43 he commented on the legislation against cutting trees when extended to the gathering of wood, advancing the "law of custom" on behalf of the poor. Cf. A. van Leeuwen, op. cit., Ch. 2 "Reprobate Materialism," 33ff.

40   Thrower, op. cit., 357, also 22ff on alienation in Marx, and 345ff, "Religion as Class Ideology."

41   *Religion and the Rise of Capitalism* (London: Penguin Books, 1947), 48.

42   Cf. John, op. cit., 22ff.

43   See Israel, op. cit., 258ff; I. Feuerlicht, *Alienation: From the Past to the Present* (Westport, Conn: Greenwood Press, 1978) for a general survey of the problematics; K.D. Eberhard, *The Alienated Christian: A Theology of Alienation* (Philadelphia: Pilgrim Press, 1971).

44   Cf. M. Buber, *Between Man and Man* (London: Collins, Fontana 1974), 60-108: "The Question to the Single One." The translator, R.G. Smith, renders Buber's *der Einzelne* as "the Single One," as closest to Kierkegaard's own *hiin Enkelte*.

45   *Journals* (Dru edition) No. 831; *On Authority and Revelation* (New York: Harper and Row, 1966), lviiff on politics and religion: the Reformation appeared to be religious but was actually political, whereas the present situation appears to be political but is in reality religious. Cf. Howard Johnston, "Kierkegaard and Politics" and Liselotte Richter, "Kierkegaard's Position in his Religio-Sociological Situation" in *A Kierkegaard Critique*, ed. H.A. Johnston and Niels Thulstrup (Chicago: Henry Regnery Co., 1967). Also John W. Elrod, *Kierkegaard and Christendom* (Princeton U.P., 1981) for the Danish milieu and S.K.'s response in both critique of liberalism ("Christendom") and alternative for authentic social relations based on ethico-religious transformation.

46   T. Molnar, *Utopia: the Perennial Heresy* (New York: Sheed and Ward, 1967), 202.

47   *Contribution to Hegel's Phil. of Right, MER*, 42. See H. Gollwitzer, *The Christian Faith and the Marxist Criticism of Religion* (New York: Charles Scribner's Sons, 1970), pp 15-23: "Excursus on the expression 'Opium of the People'." Gollwitzer cites the researches of Reinhart Seeger (in 1935) who finds Bruno Bauer to be "the creator of the word," with Hess and Marx as "imitators and popularizers." Bauer's 1841 essay *Der Christliche Staat und unsere Zeit* spoke of the "opium-like influence" of theological organization which lulls opposition to sleep. The next year he writes of the "opium haze" of religion, while his brother Edgar in a short story has: "Others drug themselves with religion, they would wish to enter the seventh heaven, and in so doing forget the earth." Moses Hess (1843) links "intoxicants, opium, religion, and brandy"; religion can "make tolerable the unhappy consciousness of servitude . . . just as opium does good service in painful illnesses, faith in the reality of unreality and in the unreality of reality can indeed give the sufferer a passive happiness . . . but it cannot give the manly energy to free oneself from the evil."

      Seeger shows how the comparison of religion with intoxicants was in the air (the Opium War of Britain against China was between 1839 and 1842). "Narcotic sermons" were ridiculed by Goethe, while Engels suggested that brandy and mysticism are alike and allied, not least for the preacher. Moreover, as early as 1840 Heine had characterized religion as "spiritual opium." Gollwitzer notes similar language in 1822 (Gass to Schleiermacher) and d'Holbach's *Le Christianisme dévoile* of 1761: "Religion is the art of making men *drunk* with enthusiasm, in order to hinder them from attending to the evils with which those who rule them overwhelm them here below." Gramsci's hypothesis is that Balzac originated the idea – lotteries are "opium de la misère" (Perhaps with Pascal's wager in mind?) – see Cottier, op. cit., 155n. Finally, Hegel's depiction (*Religionsphilosophie*) of Indian religion as dulling the senses in face of dull and insufferable conditions, like a man with opium creating "a dreaming world and crazy happiness" is considered by Ernst Benz to be the key to the Young Hegelians' transference of the image to Christianity. Cf. O. Chadwick, *The Secularization of the European Mind in the Nineteenth Century* (Cambridge U.P., 1975), 49ff; N. Lash, op. cit., 158ff.

48   Cf. H. Ley, op. cit., Band I, p 11: "Der Doppelcharakter der Religion . . . Protestation (und) Opium." Also Hans Küng, op. cit., 217ff.

49   *Encountering Marx* (Philadelphia: Fortress, 1977 – original 1975), 42.

50   Shaw, op. cit., 49.

51   *On Karl Marx*, op. cit., 64ff.

52   H. de Lubac, *The Drama of Atheist Humanism* (Cleveland: Meridian 1966), 173.

53   *The Brothers Karamazov*, trans. Constance Garnett (New York: Modern Library, n.d.) XI.9, 789; Louis J. Shein, "An Examination of the Kantian Antinomies in *The Brothers Karamazov*," *Germano-Slavica* I.1 (1973), 49-60; "The Concept of the Good in Relation to Justice in Dostoevskii's Ethics," *Canadian-American Slavic Studies* 17.3 (Fall 1983),

422-32. See also Bruce K. Ward, *Dostoevsky's Critique of the West: the Quest for the Earthly Paradise* (Waterloo, On: Wilfrid Laurier U.P., 1986), esp. 117ff., "The Goal of the Final Western Social Formula," and 135ff., "The Silence of Christ."

54   Ibid., VI.1, 350f. On Russian atheism, cf. Siegmund, op. cit., 313-81; Berdyaev, "Russian atheism was born of compassion" – quoted by V. Kesich, "Some Religious Aspects of Dostoyevsky's 'Brothers Karamazov'" (New York: *St Vladimir's Theological Quarterly*, vol. 9 (1965)), 83ff. Kesich notes that "In 1878 Dostyeysky attended Vladimir Solovyov's *Lectures on Godmanhood.*" Also Berdyaev, *The Russian Revolution* (Ann Arbor: University of Michigan, 1961), esp. 38ff: "precisely because Communism is itself a religion it persecutes all religions and will have no religious toleration."

55   Ibid., V.5, 292ff. Cf. Maurice Friedman, *Problematic Rebel* (Chicago: University of Chicago Press, 1970), 149ff on Dostoevsky. "Ivan is a Prometheus without the order that supports Prometheus in his struggle with Zeus, a Job without the trust that enables Job to contend with God and still remain in dialogue with him," 207. For an excellent treatment see S. Sutherland, *Atheism and the Rejection of God. Contemporary Philosophy and The Brothers Karamazov* (Oxford: Basil Blackwell, 1977), esp. Ch. 2 "Ivan Karamazov and Atheism" and Ch. 6 "An Artistic Picture" in which he develops Wittgenstein's concept of "form of life": "Dostoevsky is working on sound philosophical foundations. Book VI, on this view, is an attempt to imagine a form of life in which religion has a part to play, that does have a meaning and sense of its own," 97. This recalls the saying in *The Idiot* that "The atheist is always talking about something else."

56   H. de Lubac, op. cit., 180. Cf. also Matthew Spinka, *Christian Thought from Erasmus to Berdyaev* (Englewood Cliffs, NJ: Prentice-Hall, 1962), 194ff. "Feodor M. Dostoevsky, the Novelist of Good and Evil."

57   Miceli, op. cit., 112ff. Cf. N. Berdyaev, *The Origin of Russian Communism* (London: Geoffrey Bles, 1937), 64ff; Robert Payne, *Lenin* (New York: Simon and Schuster, 1964), 19ff.: "The Forerunner." Kolakowski makes nothing of Nechayev, but notes the impact of Chernyshevsky's novel *What Is To Be Done?* on Lenin (*Currents* II.313ff, 357); cf. Payne, 75ff.

58   Text in *CW* vol 14 (Moscow: Progress Pubs., 1964).

59   Cf. Thrower, op. cit., 137 on Lenin's article; 174f. for the Syllabus (detailed in App. 2, 403-5) and Ch. 5 "The History of Religion" for Tokarev, with trans. of the Conclusion to his major work in App. 3, 407ff.

60   Quoted in H-G. Koch, *The Abolition of God: Materialistic Atheism and Christian Religion* (London: SCM, 1963), 25. In fact, Heraclitus the "riddler" and the "obscure" may equally be invoked on behalf of a Logos concept – see Heidegger, *Early Greek Thinking* (New York: Harper and Row, 1975), Essay 2; McLelland, *God the Anonymous*, op.

cit., 26ff, "Philo and Logos."

61   Arthur Gibson, *The Faith of the Atheist* (New York: Harper and Row, 1968), Ch. 5, 01-30. Fabro, op. cit., 701ff. has a harsher view of Lenin's materialism, while Lash, op. cit., a balanced statement of "Christian Materialism" – Ch. 12, 135ff. See also D.M. MacKinnon, *Explorations in Theology* 5 (London: SCM, 1979), 11ff. "Lenin and Theology."

62   Ibid., 105.

63   *MER* 174. For later developments see L.J. Shein, *Readings in Russian Philosophical Thought*: *Philosophy of History* (Waterloo: Wilfrid Laurier U.P., 1977), III: "Materialist Conception of History," esp. Plekhanov and Mishin.

64   For the contemporary discussion see the "Smart-Malcolm Symposium on Materialism," Part Four of *The Mind-Brain Identity Theory*, ed. C.V. Borst (London: Macmillan, 1973). Unfortunately the J.J.C. Smart lead article "Materialism" locates the problem within the narrow field of linguistic analysis whereas Lenin's philosophy demands metaphysical analysis.

65   Op. cit., 110ff: "The Epistemological Dimension." E.g., "this reality can never be known as a 'what' except with asymptotic approximation" (116).

66   Quoted in E. Voegelin, *From Enlightenment to Revolution* (Durham, NC: Duke U.P., 1975), 237.

67   *Essay on Religion* (Agra: Socialist Lit. Pub. Co., 1939): "'Religion is the opium of the people', said Marx, and his thought is the corner-stone of the whole Marxian philosophy on the question of religion," 1. Berdyaev, *Origin*, op. cit., 195 translates: "Religion is a sort of spiritual brandy in which the slaves of capital drown the image of their humanity and their demand for some sort of worthy human life."

68   Berdyaev, op. cit., 139, 149.

69   Voegelin, *From Enlightenment to Revolution*, op. cit., 226.

70   D.B. McKown, op. cit., 118.

71   Cf. ibid., 119; Althusser, *Lénine et la Philosophie* (Paris: F. Maspero, 1969), 10.

72   *Empirio-Criticism*, op. cit., 81ff, "The Solipsism of Mach and Avenarius," 557.

73   Ibid., 561ff.

9: Re-Visioning Marxism

1   *The God That Failed*: *Six Studies in Communism* by A. Koestler, I. Silone, A. Gide (by C. Starkie), R. Wright, L. Fischer and S. Spender; intro. by R. Crossman (London: Hamish Hamilton, 1950).

2   E.g. E.B. Koenker, *Secular Salvations* (Philadelphia: Fortress, 1965), Ch. 5, 101ff. "The New Rites of Passage" (East Germany is a good example). Koch, op. cit., 137ff notes the rhetoric about Lenin and Stalin, and the socialist baptism and marriage ceremonies.

3   Robert C. Tucker, *Philosophy and Myth in Karl Marx* (Cambridge U.P., 1961), 22, 14.

4   Ibid., 151, 31f, 24. Cf. Gaston Fessard, "The Theological Structure of Marxist Atheism" in J.B. Metz, ed., *Is God Dead?* (New York: Paulist, 1966, *Concilium* 16), 7ff; e.g., "Primitive accumulation plays approximately the same role as original sin in theology" (*Capital* III.33, 153). Fessard emphasizes "the redemptive mission of the proletariat" in Marxism. It should be noted that our interpretation of the "religious dimension" of Marxism is supported by Kolakowski's analysis only obliquely. In *Currents*, vol. II he uses the terms orthodoxy, open orthodoxy, ethical socialism, "Marxism as a Soteriology" (referring to Jean Jaurès), and in vol. III speaks of dogma – both Lukàcs's writings and Lenin's materialism. But of Bloch he is critical if not cynical. He considers Bloch's "futuristic gnosis" confused and vague, less revisionist than unorthodox (although in my own opinion Bloch is close to Lenin on the doctrine of matter as creative). "As a philosopher, Bloch must be termed a preacher of intellectual irresponsibility" (445 – see Ch. 12, "Ernst Bloch: Marxism as a Futuristic Gnosis").

5   S. Bulgakov, *Karl Marx as a Religious Type* (Moscow, 1907), ET by L. Barna (Belmont, Massachusetts: Nordland Pub. Co., 1979).

6   R. Payne, *Lenin* (New York: Simon and Schuster, 1964), 608ff. Cf. the report of Clara Zetkin describing Lenin as bespeaking the image of Grünewald's crucified Christ, 528. The chapter title is "Man of Sorrows." Also Koch, op. cit., 137ff on the apotheosis of Lenin and Stalin. Kolakowski, *Currents* II.381ff. "The Rise of Leninism"; E.P. Thompson, *The Poverty of Theory* (London: Merlin, 1978), 93ff, "An Open Letter to Leszek Kolakowski" – "We both passed from a frontal critique of Stalinism to a stance of Marxist revisionism; we both sought to rehabilitate the utopian energies within the socialist system; we both stood in an ambiguous position, critical and affirmative, to the Marxist tradition" (93).

7   London: Cresset Pub., 1937.

8   *The Abolition of God*, op. cit., 23ff.

9   *A Philosophy of the Future* (New York: Herder and Herder, 1970), 42ff.

10   Ibid., p 62.

11   Cf. *Man On His Own* (New York: Herder and Herder, 1970), 9, from an interview reported by Harvey Cox.

12   Ibid., esp. "Karl Marx, Death and the Apocalypse," 31ff and "Incipit Vita Nova," 73ff.

13   Ibid., "Religious Truth," 115.

14   Ibid., 147ff and 19ff (Moltmann's Introduction on the *homoousios*); *Prinzip* 1412 (quoted in Kolakowski, *Currents* III.438); and Kolakowski's section, "Death as an anti-Utopia. God does not yet exist, but he will," ibid., 436ff.

15   Moltmann, ibid., and "Hope without faith: humanism without God," in Metz, ed., *Concilium* 16, 25ff.

16   Cf. Karl Barth, *K.D.* I.2 (1938) 15.2: "Wahrer Gott und Wahrer Mensch," 145ff.

17   Cf. *Man On His Own*, 142ff. Bloch's estimate is apt, if one considers Gilson's summary of the tradition as a "metaphysics of Exodus," translating Ex. 3:14 as "He Who Is" (like the LXX *ho ōn*) – see McLelland, *God the Anonymous*, op. cit., 32f., 166ff.

18   *Man On His Own*, 144.

19   *Atheism in Christianity* (New York: Herder and Herder, 1972), 61f.

20   Ibid., 27ff., "Prometheus a Myth Too"; *Prinzip* II.1473; Ronald Green, "Ernst Bloch's Revision of Atheism," *Journal of Religion* 49 (April 1969), 128-35.

21   Ibid., 57.

22   Ibid., 117. Cf. Friedman, *Problematic Rebel*, op. cit., 149ff for the Prometheus-Job connection.

23   Ibid., 106; cf. *Prinzip* II.1521.

24   In *The Christian-Marxist Dialogue*, ed. Paul Oestreicher (New York: Macmillan, 1969), 165-169. It had appeared in 1967 in the student journal *Po Prostú;* the article was censored and the journal proscribed. The students posted it on the University noticeboard, and circulated it in manuscript – see Editor's note 165. For a later and substantial work on Christianity see *Geist und Ungeist christlicher Traditionen* (Stuttgart: Kohlhammer Verlag, 1971) in which he presents his "Little Theses on the sacred and the profane," approaching both faith and unfaith in their cultural context while not reducing them *simpliciter*.

25   First published 1959 – see the collection *Der Mensch ohne Alternative* (Munich, 1970), "Der Priester und der Narr: Das theologische Erbe in der heutigen Philosophie"; ET in M. Kuncewicz, ed. *The Modern*

Polish Mind (Boston, 1962), 301ff.

26   Cf. Kolakowski, *Toward a Marxist Humanism* (New York: Grove Press, 1969); A. Esclarin-Perez, *Atheism and Liberation*, trans. J. Drury (Maryknoll, New York: Orbis Books, 1978), 60; Molnar, op. cit., 68ff. Kolakowski's philosophy has been termed "a kind of pseudo-religion" by S.A. Popov (Thrower, op. cit., 371).

27   Cf. G. Kline, "Leszek Kolakowski and the Revision of Marxism" in *European Philosophy Today*, ed. Kline (Chicago: Quadrangle Books, 1965), 113-56, and Bibliography of Kolakowski, 157-63. See K. on "The concept of revisionism" in *Currents*, vol. II, 98ff.

28   *The Alienation of Reason*, op. cit., 41. The history treats more than academic philosophy, dealing also with positivism of law and of literary criticism for instance. But its chief concern is to meet the challenge of dogmatic positivism, e.g., in the form of Logical Empiricism, which he calls "a scientistic defence of threatened civilization" (169).

29   *Doom and Resurrection* (Richmond, Virginia: Madrus House, 1945), 26. Cf. the Journal *Communio Viatorum* which he edited, esp. II.2-3 (Summer 1959) for excerpts from his works.

30   Ibid., 57 (from "The Making of a State" 1927).

31   Ibid., 48.

32   *Evangelium für Atheisten* (with *Nachwort* by Karl Barth) (Berlin, 1958). ET in *Risk*, Spring 1965 (WCC Youth Dept., Geneva).

33   *Church in a Marxist Society, a Czechoslovak View* (New York: Harper and Row, 1970), 114.

34   Ibid., 155.

35   *Encountering Marx* (Philadelphia: Fortress Press, 1977), 94ff.

36   *Christus oder Prometheus? Die Kernfrage des christlich-marxistischen Dialogs und die Christologie* (Marburg: Furche-Verlag, 1972).

37   Ibid., 27ff.

38   Ibid., 32ff. Lochman has in mind the ancient Ophite *Schlengenchristologie*.

39   Ibid., 54ff.

40   "The Place for Prometheus: Theological Lessons from the Christian-Marxist Dialogue," *Interpretation* XXXII (July 1978), 243. Cf. J. Bentley, "Prometheus vs Christ in the Christian-Marxist Dialogue," *JTS* 29 (1978), 483-94.

41   Ibid., 252.

42   H. Martin Rumscheidt, "Religion as Critique: the Atheism of Gardav-
        sky," *Studies in Religion* 6/2 (Autumn 1976-7), 149-57.

43   Münich: Chr. Kaiser Verlag, 1970.

44   Cf. J. Pieper, *Leisure the Basis of Culture* (London: Collins, 1965).

45   Ibid., 65. Cf. H. Rahner, *Man at Play* (New York: Herder and
        Herder, 1967); J. Huizinga, *Homo Ludens* (Boston: Beacon Press,
        1950), McLelland, *The Clown and the Crocodile* (Richmond, Virginia:
        John Knox Press, 1970).

46   *Gott ist nicht ganz tot* (Munich: Chr. Kaiser Verlag, 1968), ET by V.
        Menkes *God is Not Yet Dead* (Penguin Books, 1973). Jan Lochman has
        remarked to me that the original title clearly should be translated "not
        quite dead" (as indeed the German *ganz* does).

47   Ibid., 98.

48   "The realm of reason devised by the Enlightenment philosophers was
        an ideal version of the realm of the bourgeoisie." They merely "mysti-
        fied themselves," generating irrationality and even (as in de Sade) "cyni-
        cal reason." For "Reason as conceived by the Enlightenment is always
        close to terror" (159ff).

49   Ibid., 183.

50   Ibid., 175ff.

51   Ibid., 209.

52   Peter Hebblethwaite, Introduction to *A Marxist Looks at Jesus* (Lon-
        don: Darton, Longman and Todd, 1976), the ET of *Jesus Für Atheisten*
        (Stuttgart: Kreuz Verlag, 1972). The Introduction to the German edi-
        tion is by H. Gollwitzer.

53   Quotations in these two paragraphs are from ibid., 20-37. See also the
        Appendix on "The Life and Thought of Jesus as an Object of
        Research," 205-20.

54   Ibid., 165ff. In this regard, Machoveč has an interesting Vorwort to
        Wieland Zademach's *Marxistiche Atheismus und die biblische Botschaft
        von der Rechtfertigung des Gottlosen* (Dusseldorf: Patmos-Verlag,
        1973).

55   A select bibliography on the dialogue might include: Milan Opočenský,
        "A Christian Existence in Czechoslovakia Today" *Communio Viatorum*
        1964, 3-4; R. Garaudy and Q. Lauer, *A Christian-Communist Dialogue*
        (New York: Doubleday, 1968); F.J. Adelmann, *From Dialogue to Epi-
        logue: Marxism and Catholicism Tomorrow* (The Hague: M. Nijhoff,
        1968); A. MacIntyre, *Marxism and Christianity* (New York: Schocken
        Books, 1968); P. Hebblethwaite, *The Christian-Marxist Dialogue:
        Beginnings, Present Status and Beyond* (New York: Paulist Press, 1977).
        Gregory Baum, "The French Bishops and Euro-Communism"

(*Ecumenism* 16/2 Jan-Feb 1978), 17ff on the significance of "Le marxisme, l'homme et la foi chrétienne," Declaration du Conseil permanent de l'Episcopat français 1977.

10: The Complex of Oedipus – Freud

1   Paul Ricoeur, *Freud and Philosophy*: *An Essay on Interpretation* (New Haven: Yale U.P., 1970); ET by Denis Savage, based on the Terry Lectures given at Yale 1961, 32f; cf. 59: "representatives of reductive and demystifying hermeneutics." Cf. the category advanced by Hartshorne and Reese in *Philosophers Speak of God* (University of Chicago Press, 1953), 467ff. Nietzsche and Freud are best understood in terms of "a skepticism based on motive-torque – on motives repressed and twisted, achieving their satisfaction in another form."

2   Peter Homans, *Theology After Freud* (Indianapolis: Bobbs Merrill Co., 1970), 3ff; Ricoeur, op. cit., 59ff. In his article "Nietzsche, Freud, Marx" (Cahiers de Royaumont, Philosophie No. 6 – Paris: Les Ed. de Minuit, 1967), 183-200, Michel Foucault examines the masters' "techniques d'interprétation," involving "des hiéroglyphes."

3   Cf. Erich Fromm, *Psychoanalysis and Religion* (New York: Bantam Books, 1967), 10ff. "Freud and Jung" in which Fromm offers a "correction of the widely held view that Freud is 'against' and Jung 'for' religion." Gregory Zilboorg, *Freud and Religion* (Westminster, M.: Newman, 1964) remarks: "Freud's atheism is not a *conditio sine qua non* for the practice of good psychoanalysis; Freud's teaching, despite all his passion for atheism, is less dangerous to true religion than Jung's attitude of a sort of utilitarian, pragmatic exploitation, in the service of psychotherapy, of man's belief in God." Also H.L. Philp, *Freud and Religious Belief* (London: Rockliff, 1956), "An Unrepentant Atheist," 1ff. V.P. Gay, *Reading Freud*: *Psychology, Neurosis, and Religion* (Chico, CA: Scholars Press, 1983), 69ff reminds us that Freud's "critique of religion" begins with his analysis of the universal experience of the weird – *unheimlich*, "the Uncanny" (1919).

4   Justin Miller, "Interpretation of Freud's Jewishness," *Journal of the Behavioral Sciences* 17 (1981), 357-74; Ernest Jones, *The Life and Work of Sigmund Freud* (New York: Basic Books, 1953), 3 vols; I.19ff; David Bakan, *Sigmund Freud and the Jewish Mystical Tradition* (Princeton: Van Nostrand, 1958), 47ff.; D.B. Klein, *Jewish Origins of the Psychoanalytic Movement* (New York: Praeger, 1981). Cf. L. Breger, *Freud's Unfinished Journey* (Boston: Routledge and Kegan Paul, 1981).

5   Cf. Philip Merlan, "Brentano and Freud" and "Brentano and Freud – a Sequel," *Journal of the History of Ideas* VI (1945), 375-7 and 451; R.K. Gupta, "Freud and Schopenhauer," Ibid. 722-28.

6   The Freud quotation is from *Totem and Taboo* (Pelican Books, 1940), 196; Ernest Becker, *Angel in Armor*: *A Post-Freudian Perspective on the Nature of Man* (London: Collier-Macmillan, 1969), 39ff, 56, 83.

7   *The Psychology of Unbelief*, op. cit., 74ff. Cf. H. Faber, *Psychology of Religion* (London: SCM, 1976), Ch. 5; *The Future of an Illusion* (1927), III:29ff for the father as "phylogenetic prototype." Cf. *Totem and Taboo* (1912), IV.6. Quotations from *Future* are from the Anchor Book edition, 1964. Cf. *Introductory Lectures on Psychoanalysis*,

Lecture XIII, "The Archaic Features and Infantilism of Dreams"; *Moses and Monotheism*, XVIII.

8   Op. cit., 25. Quotations later are from 35 and 49.

9   *The Individual and His Religion* (New York: Macmillan, 1950) 118. Cf. R.S. Lee, *Freud and Christianity* (London: J. Clarke, 1948), 125ff "God the Father."

10   *Future*, 71.

11   *Interpretation of Dreams* V.D. (246ff), *The Origin and Development of Psychoanalysis*, Fourth Lecture (17), both in "Great Books of the Western World" No. 34 (*Enc. Brit.*, 1952).

12   V.P. Gay, *Freud and Ritual: Reconstruction and Critique* (Missoula MO: Scholars Press, 1979). Hans Küng, *Freud and the Problem of God*, Terry Lectures (New Haven: Yale U.P., 1979), 36, part of *Existiert Gott?* now published in full ET as *Does God Exist?* (New York: Doubleday, 1980). Quotations are from the former. Cf. Alisdair MacIntyre, *Difficulties in Christian Belief* (London: SCM, 1959), 95: "Freud cannot begin without Hume, but Hume is independent of Freud." For the theories in question, noteworthy is Wilhelm Schmidt's hypothesis of Primitive Monotheism (12 vols.): *Der Ursprung des Gottesidee* (Munster 1912-1955). Schmidt was influenced by Andrew Lang's concern with notions of Supreme Beings, and Fritz Graebner's hypothetical reconstruction of religion from an original monotheism. Cf. J. Waardenburg, *Classical Approaches to the Study of Religion* (The Hague: Mouton, 1973), 1:41f, 264ff; L. Honko, ed. *Science of Religion – Studies in Methodology*, *IAHR papers 1973* (The Hague: Mouton, 1979), XXIII on Schmidt's "Methodological Imperialism."

13   R. Otto, *Das Heilige* (ET *The Idea of the Holy*), 1917. The significance of the Uncanny for Surrealism is part of the thesis of Dr. Celia Rabinovich, "The Surreal and the Sacred: Archaic, Occult and Daemonic Elements in Modern Art, 1914-1940" (unpublished Ph.D. thesis, McGill University, 1984). She notes the parapsychological literature existing before Freud (*wissenschaftliche occultisten*) and the charge of Bruno Bettelheim that Freud's English translators "dogmatically" reduced his equation of *psyche* with "soul" to "mind": 31ff, 189ff. Freud's essay "The 'Uncanny'" (1919) is translated by A. Strachey in *On Creativity and the Unconscious* (New York: Harper and Row, 1958).

14   *Introductory Lectures on Psychoanalysis* XXIII, quoted in Sharon MacIsaac, *Freud and Original Sin* (New York: Paulist Press, 1974), 60. Cf. Philip Rieff, *Freud: the Mind of the Moralist* (New York: Doubleday, 1961), 205ff, "The Authority of the Past."

15   Ricoeur, op. cit., 5.

16   Ibid., "The Dream-work and the work of Exegesis," 88ff and "The 'Psychology' of Chapter 7," 102ff. Ricoeur appeals to the Platonic concept of *thumos*, "spiritedness" or "heart" (cf. *Republic* IV) to indicate the ambiguous middle ground of the affective life. In its oscillation

between the sides of reason and desire or Logos and Bios the distinctive *self* is constituted (cf. *Fallible Man*, xxff and *Freud and Philosophy*, 506).

17 Ibid., 159.

18 Küng, op. cit., 14ff. Cf. Ricoeur, 71ff.

19 Op. cit., 18; cf. Zilboorg, op. cit., on Freud as "potential believer."

20 Op. cit., 230.

21 Küng, op. cit., 96.

22 Cf. MacIsaac, op. cit., 78ff: "The Evolution of the Sexual Instinct." Heinz Kohut (*The Analysis of the Self*, 1971 and *The Restoration of the Self*, 1977) describes the Oedipus complex as at most secondary, masking the "nuclear neurosis," a primary narcissistic disorder. He contrasts Guilty Man with Tragic Man, the anxiety of guilt with that of meaninglessness. Kafka's K. is thus the modern Everyman, engaged in an "endless search for meaning."

23 *Interpretation*, 246 (in Ricoeur, 191). Cf. Simone de Beauvoir, *The Second Sex* (New York: A.A. Knopf, 1957, ET by H.M. Parshley) on the destructive nature of interpersonal relations – Self and Other, xvif, 718f; "the castration complex springs from the Oedipus complex. . . . The castration complex and the Electra complex reinforce each other" (40f).

24 J. Jastrow, *Freud, His Dream and Sex Theories* (New York: Pocket Books, 1948), 196ff. Cf. H. Faber, op. cit., 240ff, "The Oedipal Phase"; Gerlad N. Izenberg, *The Existentialist Critique of Freud* (Princeton U.P., 1976): "The Crisis of Autonomy," 35ff and "Determinism and Freedom," 151ff; R. Wollheim and J. Hopkin, eds. *Philosophical Essays on Freud* (Cambridge U.P., 1982), T. Nagel, "Freud's Anthropomorphism," 228ff. and David Pears, "Motivated irrationality, Freudian theory and cognitive dissonance," 264ff.

25 For Augustine see *Conf.* 2.5.10; *De civ. Dei* 8.5ff, Bks 12, 14 passim; *De Nup. et Concup.*, 1.25, 32 and Bks 4,5; Retract. 1.14.2, 2.79 (on the books De Nup.). Cf. J. Burnaby, *Amor Dei: a study of the Religion of St. Augustine* (London: Hodder and Stoughton, 1938), 92ff; E. Gilson, *The Christian Philosophy of Saint Augustine* (London: Victor Gollancz, 1961, ET by L.E.M. Lynch), 143ff, 169f; W. Pannenberg, *Anthropology in Theological perspective*, op. cit., 87ff: "Egoism and the Failure of Selfhood."

26 MacIsaac, op. cit., 107; quotation is from "A Difficulty in the Path of Psycho-Analysis" (SE XVII, 143).

27 E.g., "Leonardo da Vinci and a Memory of his Childhood," "Wit and its Relation to the Unconscious." Cf. *Beyond the Pleasure Principle* (1920): the introduction of economics along with "the *topographical* and *dynamic* . . . deserves to be distinguished by the term

metapsychological" (I). Ricoeur can treat Freud in economic terms (op. cit. 124ff), but with a certain danger, as in "Biblical Hermeneutics" where the structural approach suggests "work of discourse" as in "work of art." "The concept of work must be taken literally. It implies the extension to discourse of categories proper to the world of production and labor" (*Semeia* 4 (1975), 68).

28   Op. cit., 49.

29   Erikson, "The First Psychoanalyst" quoted by Homans, op. cit., 58, cf. 125. I am following Homans' excellent chapter on Niebuhr and Freud here.

30   Cf. *Civilization and Its Discontents*, III and VIII; A. de Waehlens, "Some Aspects of the Psychoanalytical Image of Man," in C. Geffré, ed., *Humanism and Christianity*, op. cit., 55ff on the Oedipal crisis.

31   R. Graves, *The Greek Myths* (Penguin, 1955), 2:105, 12ff.

32   Op. cit., 59.

33   Ibid., 41, 67.

34   Quoted in Ricoeur, op. cit., 291; cf. Part III: Eros, Thanatos, Ananke, 255ff.

35   Küng, op. cit., 121f; cf. MacIsaac, op. cit., 73. See *Psychoanalysis and Faith: the letters of Sigmund Freud and Oskar Pfister*, ed. H. Meng and E.L. Freud (New York: Basic Books, 1963), 35f.

36   N. Frye, *The Secular Scripture: a Study of the Structure of Romance* (Harvard U.P., 1976), 171, 137. His thesis relates to Freud at several points, notably the role of sexuality (including incest) in "kidnapped romance" (57f, 104f). Cf. J.C. McLelland, *The Reformation and its Significance Today* (Philadelphia: Westminster, 1962), 127ff, "Eucharistic Sacrifice" regarding Jungmann, Dix, Casel, etc.

37   *Totem and Taboo*, 198ff. Cf. Erich Neumann, *The Origins and History of Consciousness* (Princeton U.P. – Böllingen XLII, 1970, ET by R.F.C. Hull), 170ff. "The Slaying of the Father," and *Creative Man* (Princeton U.P. – Böllingen LXI-2, 1979), 232ff "Freud and the Father Image."

38   *The Art of Loving* (New York: Harper and Row, 1956), 93ff. Fromm holds that maternal bonds precede and outweigh the Oedipal relationship (*Escape from Freedom*, New York: Holt, Rinehart and Winston, 1941; *The Heart of Man*, New York: Harper and Row, 1964, etc.). A sympathetic theological appraisal is provided by R.S. Lee, *Freud and Christianity*, op. cit., esp. 125ff, "God – the Father." Cf. R.P. Casey, "The Psychoanalytic Study of Religion" in Orlo Strunk, ed., *The Psychology of Religion*, 56-68. "Even Freud can discuss religion in *Die Zukunft einer Illusion* as if it consisted in the main of a single experience, *das oceanische Gefühl*, and a single complex of attitudes, the survival of the ambivalent feelings towards the father" (62).

39   G.W. Allport, *Becoming*: *Basic Considerations for a Psychology of Personality* (New Haven: Yale U.P., 1955), 94ff. Otto Rank, *Beyond Psychology* (New York: Robert Brunner Books, 1941), quoted in Wayne E. Oates, *What Psychology Says About Religion* (New York: Association Press, 1958), 108. Cf. A.J. De Luca, *Freud and Future Religious Experience* (New York: Philosophical Library, 1976). J.C. Flügel, *Men, Morals and Society* (New York: International Universities Press, 1945), 273.

40   Karl Barth, *Church Dogmatics*, III/2, 'The Doctrine of Creation' (Edinburgh: T and T Clark, 1960), 24.

41   Quoted in Miller, op. cit., 370 (letter of 23 July 1882).

42   Bakan, op. cit., 129. For these paragraphs cf. Bakan, 121ff ("The Moses Theme in the Thought of Freud"), Ricoeur, 168f, 243ff and Marthe Robert, *D'Oedipe à Moïse*: *Freud et la conscience Juive* (Paris: Calmann-Lévy, 1974). Freud's essay was published anonymously in *Imago* and relied heavily on the interpretation of Henry Thode's 1908 work. ET by A. Strachey in *On Creativity and the Unconscious*, op. cit., 11-41.

43   Op. cit., 244. Freud once wrote to Lou Salomé that the problem of Moses "has pursued me through my whole life" (Zilboorg, op. cit., 15).

11: The Dance of Dionysus – Nietzsche

1   Various texts of Nietzsche are used, chiefly W. Kaufmann, ed., *Basic Writings of N.* (New York: Modern Library, 1966), including Birth of Tragedy (*BT*), Beyond Good and Evil (*BGE*), On the Genealogy of Morals, (*GM*), Ecce Homo (*EH*) and The Case of Wagner – page numbers cited follow this volume. Also Kaufmann and R.J. Hollingdale, *The Will to Power* (New York: Random House, 1967). In his introduction to this collection of unpublished notes, Kaufmann discusses the "two false views of the *WP*" – the positive of N's sister ("N.'s crowning systematic achievement") and the negative of Schlechta (it "contains nothing new"), xiiiff. A major secondary source has been M. Heidegger's lectures (1936-40) gathered in two volumes, *Nietzsche* (Pfullingen: Neske, 1961); most are translated in four volumes by D.F. Krell (Vol. 4 by F.A. Capuzzi). We refer to these as N-I and N-II for Neske, or H-N1 etc for the ET. See also W. Kaufmann, *Nietzsche: Philosopher, Psychologist, Antichrist* (Cleveland and New York: Meridian Books, 1956), and H. Küng, op. cit., 343ff.

2   See R. Hollinrake, *Nietzsche, Wagner and the Philosophy of Pessimism* (London: Allen and Unwin, 1962), 56f; Paul Valadier, *Nietzsche: l'athée de rigeur* (Paris: Desclée de Brower, 1975), 35ff on "Le laboratoire aux illusions." Paul Tillich observes that the will to power "means neither will nor power" but for both Schopenhauer and N. is "a designation of the dynamic self-affirmation of life" – *Love, Power and Justice* (Oxford University Press, 1954), 36. Heidegger notes N's stimulation and then repulsion by S., and in particular attends to the "misunderstanding" of Kant's aesthetics by both men; S. to his detriment, N. without serious damage (H-N1, 107ff; cf. 34ff, 62ff, 155f).

3   Cf. Kaufmann, op. cit., 111, 130ff, etc. Löwith (op. cit., 179) notes that "in fact, the last aphorism of the *Wille zur Macht* seems to come from the same spirit as Goethe's *Fragment über die Natur.*"

4   Quoted in Löwith, op. cit., 184. Nietzsche's break with Wagner is evident as early as the 1874 *Notes About Wagner*, while the 1888 collection *Nietzsche Contra Wagner* uses previous material from 1877 on. He credited Wagner with inventing "the German spirit as opposed to the Romance" but subsequently called him "decadent" because he was a "child of his time" without knowing it, and hence – unlike N. – unable to "surmount" it.

5   R.C. Solomon, ed., *Nietzsche: A Collection of Critical Essays* (New York: Doubleday Anchor, 1973) on the debate on nihilism: Danto (29ff) vs Schacht (58ff) in particular; Heidegger's 1940 lectures on European Nihilism depict N. as using nihilism to deconstruct modernity, in behalf of a reconstruction of Becoming: the "nichtsein" is not a denial (Verneinung) of Seiende, N-II.25ff.

6   *EH* III on *BT*. Walter Kaufmann has commented on the development of the Dionysus figure in op. cit., 245.

7   *Twilight of the Idols*, "Skirmishes," 49.

8   See J. Duchesne Guillemin, *The Western Response to Zoroaster* (Oxford: Clarendon, 1958), 20ff, "The Indo-Iranian Perspective."

9   *GM*, II.20; cf. *TSZ*, IV:297: "we are all equal, man is but man, before God . . . But now this God has died. And let us not be equal before the mob. . . ."

10   See *WP* II.2 (158-216), Aurora, I.44, 95; also P. Valadier, op. cit. 48ff, and *Nietzsche et la Critique du Christianisme* (Paris: Ed. du Cerf, 1974), 185ff; "The Critique of Religion" in *The Philosophy of Paul Ricoeur*, ed. Reagan and Stewart (Boston: Beacon Press, 1987); A. Nehamas, *Nietzsche: Life as Literature* (Cambridge, MA: Harvard U.P., 1985), 48ff. on Perspectivism, 107ff. on the critique of moral values. In Solomon, op. cit., an excerpt from Danto's book *Nietzsche as Philosopher* (New York: Macmillan, 1965), 68-99, is reprinted as "Nietzsche's Perspectivism," 29ff, while Max Scheler's work on *Ressentiment* (New York: Macmillan, 1961) is excerpted in his article of that title, 243ff.

11   *The Antichrist*, 10. I use Löwith's translation (p 311) as preferable to Hollingdale's in this instance.

12   ET by Hollingdale (Penguin, 1973): quotations 46, 188, 197, 228, 260.

13   Karl Barth, *Church Dogmatics* III/2, 231-242 on Nietzsche. Cf. Henri de Lubac, op. cit., 30f. It may be remarked that N.'s dialectic of "beyond," although related to his solution of the problem of truth, is not the same dialectical movement. He can be quite Hegelian in his use of sublation – e.g., *BGE* 2 ("How *could* something originate in its antithesis?") or *BT* 7 (Wagner says that civilization is *aufgehoben* by music). In *Ecce Homo* speaking of *Birth* he uses Hegelian categories explicitly (*idé, aufgehoben, gegensatz, begriff*) for after all, "it smells offensively Hegelian." Kaufmann (*Nietzsche*, 335ff) is helpful on this point. As to the "problem of the value of truth," it is *power* which ascribes validity to truth-judgments inasmuch as the will to power seeks the highest Value. The "free spirits" (*freien Geister*) of *Beyond* II is contrasted by N. with Plato's "pure spirit" (e.g., Preface) and therefore with Christianity which is merely "Platonism for 'the people'"; it refers chiefly to the freedom *from* dependence and dogmatism, a freedom *for* not easily defined – cf. *BGE* 44, which incidentally makes it clear that they are not "free-thinkers" merely. For Iris Murdoch see *The Philosopher's Pupil* (London: Chatto and Windus, 1983), 130; cf. *The Sovereignty of Good*, op. cit., 7f etc. on the isolated will; existentialism especially attributes to the individual "an empty lonely freedom" (27).

14   Op. cit., 69ff.

15   M. Heidegger, *Holzwege* (1950), 193ff: "Nietzsches Wort 'Gott ist tot'"; cf. N-I, 444 on the Madman passage. J. Derrida, "Différance" in *Speech and Phenomena and Other Essays on Husserl's Theory of Signs*, ET by D.B. Allison (Evanston: Northwestern U.P., 1973), 129-160, esp. 148ff. Also W. Pannenberg, *Basic Questions in Theology*, II:193. Presumably this was clear to Nietzsche in his question, Why truth rather

than untruth? For: "what questions this will to truth has already set before us!" (*BGE* 1).

16   Karl Jaspers, *Einführung in die Philosophie*, 111. C. Fabro, op. cit., 877ff. Cf. Henri de Lubac, op. cit., 18ff: "Nietzsche and the 'Death of God'"; Eugen Biser, *"Gott ist tot"*: *Nietzsches Destruktion des christliches Bewusstseins* (München: Kösel, 1962). Heidegger, N-II, 124ff (Das cogito Descartes' als cogito me cogitare).

17   *Dithyrambs of Dionysus*, ET by R.J. Hollingdale (London: Anvil Press Poetry, 1984).

18   *The Gay Science, with a prelude in rhymes and an appendix of songs*, trans. with commentary by Walter Kaufmann (New York: Vintage Books, 1974. See Intro. 4f on the title. Cf. S.L. Gilman, *Nietzschean Parody: an Introduction to Reading Nietzsche* (Bonn: Grundmann, 1976); M. Paronis, *"Also sprach Zarathustra"*: *Die Ironie N. als Gestaltungsprinzip* (Bonn: Grundmann, 1976).

19   See Hollinrake, op. cit. Ch. 3: "Schopenhauer and Der Ring," 59f for the aria.

20   *Zarathustra*, end of Part I, 104, Penguin ed. This Hollingdale translation puts "Superman" for *Übermensch*.

21   For Heidegger's interpretation see his lectures on "The Will to Power as Art" (H-N1, esp. 92ff, 200ff) and "Wille zum Macht als Erkenntnis" (N-I, esp. 495ff and 616ff: Die Wahrheit und der Unterscheid von "wahrer und scheinbar Welt").

22   R.J. Hollingdale, *Thus Spake Zarathustra*, Penguin ed., 28f. Cf. Kaufmann, *Nietzsche*, 6: "Discovery of the Will to Power," 152ff. While this "discovery" of a monistic principle was supposed to solve his earlier dualities, Kaufmann questions its effectiveness (p. 180): 513.

23   Cf. M. Spinka, op. cit., 192. C.G. Jung considers the Overman "a very Protestant idea"; "You hear this kind of talk in a protestant sermon" – "Comments on a Passage from Nietzsche's *Zarathustra*," 1936, p. 159.

24   Quoted in M. Spinka, op. cit., 193.

25   A. Gibson, *The Faith of the Atheist*, op. cit., 131ff.

26   *Nietzsche, Versuch einer Mythologie* (1919), p. 236, quoted in Gibson, p. 141.

27   *What Nietzsche Means*, 1941 quoted in Kaufmann, *Nietzsche*, p. 83. A famous passage in *Ecce Homo* (*BWN* 692ff) on religion indicates that N. felt himself to have escaped any crisis of faith: "I do not by any means know atheism as a result; even less as an event: it is a matter of course with me, from instinct" (692). Cf. the essays in *Nietzsche and Christianity*, ed. Geffré and Jossua (New York: Seabury, 1981, Concilium 145), esp. Y. Ledure, "The Christian Response to Nietzsche's Critique of Christianity," 42-50.

28   *Nietzsche*, 11: "Overman and Recurrence," 266ff.

29   As A. Schlemmer suggests, "Nietzsche et la Mort de Dieu," *Foi et Vie* Décembre 1973, 8-16.

30   *The Dawn*, quoted in Kaufmann, *Nietzsche* 156. This whole chapter is excellent on the comparison between the two.

31   Cf. Camus, *The Rebel*, 74: "Dionysus, the earth-god, shrieks eternally as he is torn limb from limb. But at the same time he represents the agonized beauty that coincides with suffering. Nietzsche thought that to accept this earth and Dionysus was to accept his own sufferings." One wonders whether Nietzsche was aware of the irony of his choice of a suffering and dismembered god (in the Orphic tradition at least) to replace "the Crucified." It would seem that his typology in his earliest work sufficed to suit his polemical purpose, while blinding him to deeper questions of the meaning of such classical mythology as dying and rising gods. Kerényi is helpful on the significance of Dionysus, but says of N. "his account becomes a fairy tale" – *Dionysos: Archetypal Image of Indestructible Life* (Princeton U.P., Böllingen LXV-2, 1976, ET by R. Manheim), 135; cf. xxiiif, 324ff.

12: The Work of Sisyphus – Camus

1   Quotations are from *The Rebel: An Essay on Man in Revolt*, ET by Anthony Bower (New York: Vintage Books, 1959), 26, 244f. Cf. his comment on the "strange text in Genesis (3:22)" – "It's the story of Zeus and Prometheus all over again. Man had the power of becoming God's equal, and God feared him and kept him in bondage. *Id.* Concerning the divine responsibility" – *Notebooks, 1942-51*, trans. J. O'Brien (New York: A. Knopf, 1966) 57f, Feb. 1943 entry. The 1946 essay "Prometheus aux enfers" (*L'Eté*, Paris: Gallimard, 1954, 81-90) sees Prometheus as "le modèle de l'homme contemporain," but "nous sommes encore sourds au grand cri de la révolte humaine dont il donne le signal solitaire." Myths have no life of their own: "Ils attendent que nous les incarnions."

2   *The Myth of Sisyphus and Other Essays*, ET by Justin O'Brien (New York: Vintage Books, 1955), 144.

3   Ibid., 5.

4   Ibid., 16.

5   R.W.B. Lewis, *The Picaresque Saint* (New York: J.B. Lippincott Co., 1961), 61.

6   Ibid., 71.

7   J. Moltmann, *Theology of Hope* (London: SCM, 1967) 24. But cf. Camus' foreword to the series *Espoir*: "We are in nihilism!" But we may "find the cure in the extremity of the disease. . . . Let us then realize that this is the time of hope" – quoted in Fabro, op. cit., 956.

8   Lewis, op. cit., 86.

9   For a good analysis of the two stages see Maurice Friedman, *To Deny Our Nothingness: Contemporary Images of Man* (New York: Dell Publishing Co., 1967) Chs. 17 and 18.

10   *Sisyphus*, 5f.

11   Ibid., 21.

12   Ibid., 37.

13   G. Marcel, *The Mystery of Being* (Chicago: H. Regnery, 1951, ET by R. Hague), II.68ff.

14   *Rebel*, 137.

15   Ibid., 226ff.

16   Lewis, op. cit., 91.

17   W. Hamilton, "The Christian, the Saint, and the Rebel: Albert Camus" in Nathan A. Scott, Jr., ed., *Forms of Extremity in the Modern Novel* (Richmond, Virginia: John Knox Press, 1965), 55-74. The edition of Camus we are using is *The Plague*, ET by Stuart Gilbert (Penguin Books, 1960).

18   *The Plague*, 106f. For the two sermons see 80ff and 180ff.

19   "The Unbeliever and Christians" in *Resistance, Rebellion and Death*, trans. Justin O'Brien (New York: Alfred A. Knopf, 1961), 69-74. This sentence (69f) poses a problem, in that Jean Onimus, *Albert Camus and Christianity*, trans. E. Parker (University of Alabama, 1970), uses an unidentified source which gives the sense of "I do not part from" (*je ne pars pas*) rather than *je ne partirai jamais* as in *Actuelles I* (see translator's note on p. 36). One may compare the critical approach to the formative years with the more sympathetic treatment, which nevertheless agrees substantially, of Camus' friend Pierre Rubé, "Who Was Albert Camus?" in *Albert Camus – Yale French Studies 25* (Spring 1960), 3-9, as well as the essays in the same volume by Georges Joyaux ("Albert Camus and North Africa") and Henri Peyre ("Camus the Pagan").

20   Op. cit., 96; Hamilton, op. cit., 59. Cf. Onimus, op. cit., 46ff for a more positive assessment of the theology of Paneloux. "A theologian could only approve the terms Paneloux uses right down to the nuances he is anxious to emphasize: neither resignation nor fatalism but crucifying acceptance joined with a will to struggle against Evil" (47).

21   Dietrich Bonhoeffer, *Letters and Papers from Prison* (London: SCM, 1953), 104, 124.

22   Honoré de Balzac, *Le Père Goriot*, 1835.

23   *Resistance, Rebellion and Death*, op. cit., 73.

24   Cf. Padovano, op. cit., 134ff, "Camus and Christianity" for a good statement of this issue. Camus once stated that the "only great Christian mind that *faced* the problem of evil was St. Augustine" (*Notebooks 2* (1942-51), ET J. O'Brien, New York: Alfred A. Knopf, 1965), 140. Cf. J. Woelfel, *Camus, a Theological Perspective* (Nashville: Abingdon, 1975) for a critique of Camus' "Augustinian" idea of divine omnipotence as determinism.

25   From a comment on *The Fall* of September 1956, quoted by Henri Peyre, "Camus the Pagan," in *Yale French Studies*, p. 20. In his final years Camus was concerned to distinguish his position from Existentialism and also from crypto-Catholicism; the latter is especially tempting in regard to his judge-penitent of *The Fall* named Jean-Baptiste.

26   Padovano, op. cit., 101.

27   Gibson, op. cit., 79; Bespaloff's article is "The World of Men Condemned to Death" in *Camus, a Collection of Critical Essays*, ed. Grée, 99f.

28   Quotations in this paragraph are from *Rebel*, 15-25.

29   *The Plague*, 200ff. Cf. *Carnets*, 1942-51 for *Jonas*.

30   Peyre, op. cit., 23f, from *Noces* and the speech to the Dominicans of 1948.

31   Hamilton, op. cit., 69.

32   "The Unbeliever and Christians" in *RRD*, op. cit., 73.

33   *Rebel*, 24.

34   Onimus, op. cit., 45.

35   Cf. Onimus, op. cit., 45f; there is also the novelistic theme in the *Carnets* (213) of a priest whose faith wavers in the presence of suffering.

36   *Carnets*, 206, quoted in Onimus, op. cit., 49.

37   *Sisyphus*, 42.

38   The edition of *The Fall* used is the translation of Justin O'Brien (New York: Vintage Books, 1956). Cf. Lewis, op. cit., 107 for "moral panic"; Padovano, op. cit., 131 for "a movement toward God"; Peyre, "Camus the Pagan" in *Yale French Studies*, 20.

39   Quotations in this paragraph are from 133f and 147.

40   *Sisyphus*, 91.

41   Op. cit., 62.

42   *Carnets* (Paris: Gallimard, 1964) 233.

43   *Essais* (Paris: Gallimard, 1965) 465; thesis in 1224ff: "Héllenisme et Christianisme, Plotin et saint Augustin." I am grateful to Prof. Bruce K. Ward of Laurentian University for his paper "Camus's Critique of the Christian Idea of Hope" presented to the Canadian Society for the Study of Religion, June 1985, based on his research on the Hellenistic orientation of the final cycle.

44   Op. cit., 79.

45   *Rebel*, 31.

13: The Fate of Orestes – Sartre

1   Cf. M. Friedman, *Problematic Rebel*, op. cit., Part IV, "The Modern Promethean"; also his *To Deny Our Nothingness*, op. cit., 250ff.

2   Philip Vellacott, Introduction to *The Oresteian Trilogy* (Penguin Books, 1974), 18. Anne Lebich, *The Oresteia: A Study in Language and Structure* (Washington, D.C.: Center for Hellenic Studies, 1971), 25ff (Suffering's Lesson) and 32ff. (The Symmetry of Justice); also Gilbert Murray, *Aeschylus: The Creator of Tragedy op. cit.*, Ch. 3 "Aeschylus as a Poet of Ideas."

3   *Being and Nothingness, An Essay on Phenomenological Ontology*, translated and with introduction by Hazel E. Barnes (New York: Philosophical Library, 1956), 55ff: "Patterns of Bad Faith."

4   W. Barrett, *Irrational Man: A Study in Existential Philosophy* (New York: Doubleday Anchor, 1962), 241. Barrett reminds us of the situation of occupation and resistance in which the early works were composed. "The Resistance came to Sartre and his generation as a release from disgust into heroism" (241).

5   Theophil Spoerri, "The Structure of Existence: *The Flies*" in *Sartre: A collection of critical essays*, ed. Edith Kern (Englewood Cliffs, NJ: Prentice-Hall, 1962), 54-61.

6   Spoerri, op. cit., 58. "The theme of the flies is marvellously and dreadfully embodied in the idiot at the beginning of the play." The "idiot boy" in the opening scene has flies "pumping away at each of his eyes . . . look at that yellow muck oozing out of them."

7   Gibson, op. cit., Ch. 2: "Faith in Freedom," 17-45.

8   Gibson, op. cit., 17.

9   Cf. *Being and Time*, trans. J. Macquarrie and E. Robinson (London: SCM, 1962) particularly 67ff, 225ff, 279ff.

10   Op. cit., 244 – a view supported by Henri Duméry; see René F. Brabander, "Duméry's Appraisal of Sartre's Position on God and Freedom," 5-21 of *Religion and Human Autonomy: Henry Duméry's Philosophy of Christianity* (The Hague: Martinus Nijhoff, 1972). Cf. W. Barrett, op. cit., 242ff.

11   E.g., *B-N* 77, 221ff. His analysis of "otherness" will concern us later.

12   Cf. Marjorie Grene, *Dreadful Freedom: A Critique of Existentialism* (University of Chicago Press, 1948), 42; also Karl Barth, C.D. III.3.3, "The Knowledge of Nothingness," 334ff on Heidegger and Sartre.

13   Kenneth Douglas develops this theme in his essay "The Self-Inflicted Wound" in Kern, op. cit., 39-46. He takes the woundings as "sterile and childish simulacra of union with another or with oneself or of

self-destruction as self-creation" (46).

14   *Existentialism is a Humanism*, translated by Walter Kaufmann in *Existentialism from Dostoevsky to Sartre* (New York: Meridian Books, 1956), 287-311. (Hereafter *E-H*.)

15   *Search for a Method*, trans. H. Barnes (New York: Random House, 1963), 26f.

16   Cf. F. Jeanson, *Sartre and the Problem of Morality*, ET R.V. Stone; Bloomington IN: Indiana U.P., 1980) Part 3, "Toward the Morality of Ambiguity: the Conditional Realization of the Human," 175ff; J. Kariuki, *The Possibility of Universal Moral Judgement in Existential Ethics* (Berne: European University Studies, Philosophy 87). Iris Murdoch once remarked that Sartre "veers wildly between Kantianism and Surrealism."

17   G. Novack, ed. *Existentialism versus Marxism* (New York: Dell Publishing Co., 1966), Introduction. I owe this and other references to my colleague Dr. Peter Carpenter, whose article "Sartre: a Christian Appraisal" appears in *Scottish Journal of Theology*, 35:243-62.

18   R. Aron, *Marxismes Imaginaires* (Paris: Gallimard, 1970), 48ff. In the Novack symposium noted above, Roger Garaudy treats him under the title "False Prophet: Jean-Paul Sartre."

19   M. Cranston, *The Quintessence of Sartrism* (Montreal: Harvest House, 1969), 43.

20   Cf. for what follows *B-N*, 222ff., 252ff.; Miceli, op. cit., 228ff. "The Social Impossibility and Interpersonal Love"; Robert Champigny, "Comedian and Martyr" in Kern, op. cit., 80-91; Régis Jolivet, *Sartre: The Theology of the Absurd* (Westminster, MD: Newman Press, 1967), 78ff.

21   In *Les Mouches* Jupiter enslaves, even kills. Orestes speaks of his "yeux morts" and Electra says: "Plus elles (les vieilles) ressemblent à des mortes, plus tu les aimes." Cf. Hans Urs von Balthasar, *The God Question and Modern Man* (New York: Seabury, 1967) 136ff on Sartre's "'conversation' with the lost between the lost . . . 'discussion' in the literal sense of the word, that is 'beating asunder'."

22   See particularly *B-N* 3.3, "Concrete Relations with Others," 361ff.

23   Kierkegaard, *The Concept of Dread*, ET by Walter Lowrie (Princeton U.P., 1946), 44; Iris Murdoch, *Sartre* (London: Collins Fontana Library, 1953), 34: the conclusion of Ch. 2 on 'The Labyrinth of Freedom' concerning the tetralogy *Les Chemins de la Liberté*.

24   *The Devil and the Good Lord* trans. Kitty Black, Vintage Books ed. (New York: Random House, 1962), 141:Act 3, scene 10.

25   Padovano, op. cit., 14; Jolivet, op. cit., 31.

26   *The Words*, trans. B. Frechtman (New York: Braziller, 1964), 102. Cf. a relevant statement: "L'athéisme est une enterprise crueller et de longue haleine: je crois l'avoir menée jusqu'au bout" (*Les Mots* 22). Also the tendentious passage: "For the last ten years or so I've been a man who's been waking up, cured of a long, bittersweet madness and who can't get over the fact, a man who can't think of his old ways without laughing and who doesn't know what to do with himself." Cf. the contrasting attitudes of Jolivet (106) and Gibson (35); also Fabro, on Sartre's "patent atheism," 939ff.

27   *Situations* I, 153.

28   Of course there is movement in Sartre's thinking. For instance, in the later work *Between Existentialism and Marxism* (New York: Random House, 1974; original) he himself indicates the shift from the concepts surrounding Being and Nothingness to the critical philosophy (33ff) and the critical existentialism (142ff) of the years beyond *Les Mouches* and *L'Etre et le néant*. Nevertheless, even his exploration of the space and the connection between Marxism and existentialism is not a new departure, nor on the other hand does it materially affect the radical autonomy and isolation of the individual required by his kind of existential project throughout.

29   Karl Barth, *C.D.* III.3, 342 (ET 1960 of *Die Lehre von der Schöpfung*, 3 (1950)).

30   See Cranston, op. cit., 40ff on the pledge, violence and Terror. For Sartre on Genet and Flaubert, see Thomas M. King, *Sartre and the Sacred* (University of Chicago Press, 1974) 87ff, 143ff. The unity of theology and autology is attributed to Coomaraswami, p. 98.

14: Conclusion: Faith Beyond Zeus-Prometheus

1   *Eclipse of God*: *Studies in the Relation Between Religion and Philosophy*
     (New York: Harper and Bros., 1957) esp. 20ff and 65ff.

2   "Aber weh! es wandelt in Nacht, es wohnt, wie im Orkus, Ohne Goett-
     liches unser Geschlecht." Buber, op. cit., 22.

3   Martin Heidegger, *Aus der Erfahrung des Denkens*, in *Basic Writings*,
     ed. D.F. Krell (New York: Harper and Row, 1977) 39.

4   *Hölderlin und das Wesen der Dichtung*, 1936, p 27; ET in *Existence and
     Being*, ed. Werner Brock (Chicago: Henry Regnery Co., 1949). Heid-
     egger remains ambiguous, indeed diffident on the subject of theology.
     To determine human essence in existential terms is not to reach conclu-
     sions about divine existence. "Because we refer to the word of
     Nietzsche on the 'death of God' people regard such a gesture as athe-
     ism. For what is more 'logical' than that whoever has experienced the
     death of God is godless?" *Letter on Humanism* in *Basic Writings* (New
     York: Harper and Row, 1976), 226; cf. 229ff.

5   Langan, op. cit., XIII, "Heidegger's Existential Phenomenology," esp.
     227ff, "The Absence of the Other as Other" (See *Being and Time*, 233f
     on *solus ipse* and 321 on *unheimlichkeit*). Cf. Langan, "Heidegger and
     the Possibility of Authentic Christianity" in G.F. MacLean, *Traces of
     God in a Secular Culture* (New York: Alba House, 1973), 169ff. He
     states in the latter contribution that modern nihilism "has favoured con-
     temporary voluntarism, by leading mankind to interpret itself as will for
     will's sake, for whom God is dead" (171). Also James M. Robinson,
     'The German Discussion of the Later Heidegger' in *The Later Heideg-
     ger and Theology*, ed. J.M. Robinson and J.B. Cobb, Jr. (New York:
     Harper and Row, 1963), 27f on Ernst Hetisch's refutation of the subjec-
     tivist charge of *aletheia*, and 68ff on Jüngel's critique of Ott's "step
     backwards" into metaphysics.

6   R. Musil, *Der Mann ohne Eigenschaften*, 1930-33, 3 vols., unfinished.
     C.S. Lewis, *The Abolition of Man* (New York: Macmillan, 1947).

7   W.H. Masters and Virginia E. Johnson, *Human Sexual Response* and
     Human Sexual Inadequacy (Boston: Little, Brown and Co., 1966,
     1970); Nena and George O'Neill, *Open Marriage*: *a New Lifestyle for
     Couples* (San Francisco: Evans, 1972), *Shifting Gears* (New York:
     Avon, 1975). A new stress on values or purposes appears in *The Pleas-
     ure Bond*: *A New Look at Sexuality and Commitment* (New York: Ban-
     tam Books, 1975), which "confirms their deepest values") Cf. A. Perez-
     Esclarin, *Atheism and Liberation* (Maryknoll, New York: Orbis Books,
     1978) 65ff "The Divinization of Sex."

8   S. Kierkegaard, "Diary of a Seducer," *Either/Or*, vol. I (New York:
     Doubleday Anchor, 1959), 439; cf. *Stages on Life's Way* (Princeton
     U.P., 1940), 105ff for the category of immediacy related to love. In
     Sisyphus Camus comments on Don Juan: "to anyone who seeks quan-
     tity in his joys, the only thing that matters is efficacy" (p. 53).

9   Cf. Helmut Thielicke, "Autarkie des Diesseits," 55ff of *Nihilism* (London: Routledge and Kegan Paul, 1962); Carl Delacato, *The Ultimate Stranger – the Autistic Child* (New York: Doubleday, 1974). On Augustine see G.F. McLean, *Traces of God*, op. cit., 71ff. On the concept of alienation in this context cf. R. Schacht, *Alienation*, with introductory essay by Walter Kaufmann (New York: Doubleday Anchor, 1970); *Temporalitè et Aliénation* (Paris: Aubier, 1975), Actes du Colloque sur le problematique de la demythisation (includes Ricoeur, "Objectivation et Aliénation dans l'Experience Historique," 27ff); G. Morel, *Questions d'Homme: L'Autre* (Paris: Aubier, 1977); M. Scheler, *Ressentiment* (New York: Schocken, 1961), 23ff on sense of impotence facing values secretly desired, and the concept of the victim; W. Lynch, *Christ and Prometheus*, op. cit., 40, 53f on otherness; Colin Wilson's 'Outsider' cycle of 6 volumes, from *The Outsider* (1956) to *Beyond the Outsider* (1965). For a psychological approach see H.C. Rümke, *The Psychology of Unbelief*, op. cit.; R.D. Laing, *The Divided Self* (Penguin, 1965) and *Self and Others* (Penguin, 1971); H. Faber, *Gott in vaterlöser Gesellschaft* (Munich, 1972).

10   C. Lash, *The Culture of Narcissism: American Life in an Age of Diminishing Expectations* (New York: W.W. Norton and Co, 1978). Cf. Peter Main, "The New Narcissism," *Harper's* 251:48 (October 1975) regarding the Human Potential Movement's "autonomy . . . freedom to be me." Rollo May, *Freedom and Destiny* (New York: W.W. Norton, 1981) has an excellent section on 'The New Narcissism' 135ff. M. Foucault, *Histoire de la folie* (Paris: Union Générale d'Ed., 1961) and *Surveiller et Punir* (Paris: Gallimard, 1975).

11   *The Sovereignty of Good* (London: Routledge and Kegan Paul, 1970), 35. Cf. Ayer's *The Concept of a Person* (London: Macmillan, 1963), title essay, 82ff (including debate with Strawson and Hampshire). This represents some advance on his famous position of 1946 in *Language, Truth and Logic* (London: Victor Gollancz) in which the self is a "logical construction" with no reality beyond its "empirical manifestations" – see Ch. VII 'The Self and the Common World.' Cf. Lucien Goldmann, *The Hidden God*, op. cit., 29f on "the Cartesian and Fichtean Ego, doorless and windowless monad of Leibniz, and the 'economic man' of the classical economists."

12   E.J. Pratt, "The Truant," 1943 in *Selected Poems of E.J. Pratt* (Toronto: Macmillan, 1968), 37-42.

13   *A Dubious Heritage: Studies in the Philosophy of Religion After Kant* (New York: Paulist Press, 1977), 3. Cf. Ninian Smart, "Kant and Human Freedom" in *Philosophers and Religious Truth* (London: SCM, 1964), 57ff.

14   Origen, *Contra Cels.* IV especially deals with the doctrine of God in answering the Platonist Celsus. Cf. McLelland, *God the Anonymous*, op. cit., 106ff, "God: Changeless Yet Lively." A good survey of the issue is provided by H.A. Redmond, *The Omnipotence of God* (Philadelphia: Westminster, 1964), esp. Ch. 1 "Theologians speak of Omnipotence."

15   Hartshorne, *The Divine Relativity*: *A Social Conception of God* (New York: Yale U.P., 1948), 51ff, 95; cf. Barth, *C.D.* II.1 (1957), 260ff.

16   Barth, ibid., 329. The dynamism of Patristic thought is lost in this development: e.g., Augustine, *De Trin.* Bk 8, "Ecce tria sunt ergo amans et quod amatur et amor." Mystical theology did not miss the energetics of Spirit, the alterity necessary for Love – e.g., Hugo ("the second Augustine") and Richard of St. Victor. Cf. P. Ricoeur, "The Socius and the Neighbour" and "The Image of God and the Epic of Man" in *Histoire et vérité* (Paris: Ed. du Seuil, 1955).

17   Ibid., 449.

18   Jüngel, ". . . keine Menschenlosigkeit Gottes . . . Zur Theologie Karl Barths zwischen Theismus und Atheismus," *Evangelische Theologie* 31 (1971), 376-90; esp. 4, keine Menschenlosigkeit Gottes, and 5, keine absolute Gottlosigkeit des Menschen. Here is Barth's thesis: "In Jesus Christ there is no isolation of man from God or of God from man. Rather, in Him we encounter the history, the dialogue, in which God and man meet together and are together, the reality of the covenant *mutually* contracted, preserved, and fulfilled by them. Jesus Christ is in His One Person, as true *God, man's* loyal partner, and as true *man, God's*": *The Humanity of God* (Richmond, Virginia: John Knox Press, 1960), 46. Essay 2, 37ff is the title lecture; cf. p. 11 on The-anthropology. Also "The Christian Understanding of Revelation": "to whom man cannot refuse to listen without calling himself into question" – *Against the Stream* (London: SCM, 1954), Brunner, *Divine-Human Encounter* (London: SCM, 1944), 46ff.

19   See Barth, *K.D.* I.2 (1938), Sect. 15.2, "Wahrer Gott und Wahrer Mensch," 145-87. The opposition to monotheletism is clear in Eastern theology as well, from Maximus the Confessor to Gregory Palamas. The latter's distinction between essence and energies allows the weight to fall on active will: "God appears because he acts" – John Meyendorff, *A Study of Gregory Palamas* (New York: St. Vladimir's Seminary, 1974), 211ff.

20   Paul Tillich, *The Protestant Era* (University of Chicago Press, 1948), 46 – see esp. Ch. 3 "Kairos" and 4 "Religion and Secular Culture." The concept was worked out in his *Religionsphilosophie*, and is developed in his *Systematics*, esp. vol I.83ff and 147ff ("Final Revelation Overcoming the Conflict of Autonomy and Heteronomy"); Vol. III.249ff. Cf. Langdon Gilkey, *Naming the Whirlwind* (New York: Seabury, 1976), 40ff: – he cites as "main elements of the secular spirit contingency, relativism, temporality and autonomy"; cf. note on heteronomy, 139. Cf. Jeffrey Stout, *The Flight from Authority*: *Religion, Morality and the Quest for Autonomy* (University of Notre Dame Press, 1981) for analysis of attacks on transcendentalism and foundationalism on the ground of historicism. Karl Barth also uses the same term and concept; e.g., "How can there be any question of a conflict between theonomy and autonomy?" – *C.D.* 2.2 (1957), 178.

21   Mark C. Taylor, *Erring*: *a Postmodern A/theology* (University of Chicago Press, 1984), 22ff.

22   Cf. Barbara Starrett, "The Metaphors of Power" in *The Politics of Women's Spirituality*, ed. Charlene Spretnak (New York: Anchor Press, 1980): even Tillich betrays the coercive model in his *Love, Power and Justice* in her opinion. Now in that work Tillich is careful to define the concept of power ("Being and Power," 35ff) with special attention to compulsion (45ff). Power "needs compulsion," but is legitimate only when "love is united with the compulsory element of power" (50). At the least, this criticism notes an ambiguity remaining in Tillich's analysis of the conceptual relations. For Hartshorne see *Divine Relativity*, op. cit., and esp. *Omnipotence and Other Theological Mistakes* (Albany, New York: University of New York, 1984), 53ff.

23   See T.F. Torrance, *Reality and Scientific Theology* (Edinburgh: Scottish Academic Press, 1985), 3: "The Science of God," 64ff.

24   The debate begins with J.L. Mackie, "Evil and Omnipotence" in *Mind* LXIV (April 1955), 210-12 and "Omnipotence" in *Sophia* I (July 1962), 13-25. The argument is expanded and given wider context in *The Miracle of Theism* (Oxford: Clarendon 1982), esp. 150ff. See the *Proceedings of the Congress* of the Seventh Inter-American Congress of Philosophy, under the auspices of the Canadian Philosophical Association, vol. I (Québec: Les Presses de l'Université Laval, 1967), for Macquarrie on "Divine Omnipotence," 132-37 and P.G. Kuntz on "The Sense and Nonsense of Omnipotence: What does it mean to say 'with God all things are possible'?" 122-31. For Alvin Plantinga, see *God and Other Minds* (Ithaca, New York: Cornell U.P., 1967), Ch. 7 and *The Nature of Necessity* (Oxford: Clarendon Press, 1974). Peter Geach considers theories of omnipotence in "Omnipotence," *Philosophy* 43 (April 1973), 7-20 and *Providence and Evil* (Cambridge U.P., 1977). Cf. S.T. Davis, *Logic and the Nature of God* (Grand Rapids: Eerdmans, 1983), 68ff on the two paradoxes. John C. Moskop, *Divine Omniscience and Human Freedom: Thomas Aquinas and Charles Hartshorne* (Mercer U.P., 1984) stresses Thomist analogy to counter a critique of his argument on future contingencies as if it implies univocal language. Process thinking is on view in D.R. Griffin: *God, Power and Evil: a Theodicy* (Philadelphia: Westminster Press, 1976) 251ff, "Worshipfulness and the Omnipotence Fallacy."

25   W. Pannenberg, *Basic Questions in Theology*, vol. 3 (London: SCM, 1973); Jan Lochman, *Reconciliation and Liberation* (Belfast: Christian Journals, 1980), 123ff "Freedom as a Basic Theme of Biblical Theology: Yahweh is the *'free God'* (126) whose covenant establishes human freedom." Cf. Paul Ricoeur, *Le Volontaire et l'involontaire* (Paris: Aubier Eds. Montaigne, 1950) the first volume of *La Philosophie de la volonté*. In line with modern theories of self-identity, he sees the deliberative process as an act of freedom, reflecting the reciprocity of voluntary and involuntary within subjectivity. E.g., 135ff, "History of Decision: from hesitation to choice" and 341ff, "The Problems of Consent." A.I. Melden, *Free Actions* (London: Routledge and Kegan Paul, 1961) analyzes explanation of actions and concludes that there is a "logical incoherence" in any theory which supposes that action, desire, intention, etc., stand in causal relationships. J.N. Lapsley has edited conference papers on *The Concept of Willing* (Nashville: Abingdon Press, 1967) in terms of Religion and Psychiatry. Eugen Biser tackles the question of

the doctrine of God in an excellent monograph *Theologie und Atheismus: Anstösse zu einer theologischen Aporetik* (München: Kösel-Verlag, 1972), esp. 'Der Aporie der Absolutheit' (70ff) and 'Die Aporie der Vermittlung' (78ff). A good summary of current positions is found in Sidney Hook, ed., *Determinism and Freedom in the Age of Modern Science* (New York: Collier, 1961). Also R. Swinburne, *The Coherence of Theism* (Oxford: Clarendon, 1977) regarding contingency and necessity in God. Ian Ramsey, *Freedom and Immortality* (London: SCM, 1960)) concludes about free will and causation: "We can now see how misleading it is because logically inappropriate, to try to discuss free will in a causal context" (38).

26   W.A. Luijpen, *Phenomenology and Atheism* (Dusquesne U.P., 1964), 145.

27   E.g., *Atheism: The Case Against God*, G.H. Smith (Buffalo, New York: Prometheus Books, 1979); Peter Angeles, ed., *Critiques of God* (Ibid., 1976); Paul Blanshard, ed., *Classics of Free Thought* (Ibid., 1977). On the subject of humanism see also Paul Kurtz, *The Humanist Alternative: some definitions of Humanism* (Ibid., 1973); E. Royce, ed., *The Infidel Tradition from Paine to Bradlaugh* (London: Macmillan, 1976); Paul Kurtz and A. Dondeyne, eds., *A Catholic/Humanist Dialogue: Humanists and Roman Catholics in a Common World* (Ibid., 1972); Claude Geffré, ed., *Humanism and Christianity*, op. cit. – note the thesis of J-M Domenach ("The Attack on Humanism in Contemporary Culture," 17ff) that modern trends in literature, drama and philosophy – Beckett, Foucault and structuralism, etc. – deny the value of humanity. Also H.J. Blackham, ed., *Objections to Humanism* (Penguin, 1965).

28   The Eastern concept of *theōsis* depends on participation (the Platonic *methexis* refined by the Fathers) to avoid mere "divinization" or loss of humanity – cf. V. Lossky, *The Mystical Theology of the Eastern Church* (London: J. Clarke, 1957). For covenant theology, cf. McLelland, 'Covenant Theology – A Re-evaluation,' *Canadian Journal of Theology* (vol. III.3, 1957), 255-71. Cf. Barth's correction of the image of Calvin as merely "rational" in that he related union with Christ to justification and faith (*C.D.* I.1 (1936)), 274. Also *C.D.* III.1 (1958), Sect. 41 on Creation and Covenant, 42ff, and 334ff on Marcion and Schopenhauer (lack of concept of covenant robs creation of its nature as God's "benefit"); 388ff. on Leibniz, close to the Christian thesis that "the world was willed and created good by God its Creator." For Tillich see, e.g., *S.T.* I. Intro., 40ff. ("Experience and Systematic Theology") – "Mystical experience, or experience by participation, is the real problem of experiential theology. It is secretly presupposed by the ontological as well as by the scientific concept of experience." Cf. John H. Randall's "The Ontology of Paul Tillich" in Kegley and Bretall, eds., *The Theology of Paul Tillich* (New York: Macmillan, 1959), 132ff discussing the Augustinian nature of Tillich's ontology. On this see Tillich's important essay "The Two Types of Philosophy of Religion," 10-29 in *Theology of Culture* (New York: Oxford University Press, 1959).

29   E.g., Karl Barth, *C.D.* II.1 (1957), 31.2, "The Constancy and Omnipotence of God," 490ff. – "the constancy of God attested in these

passages of Scripture cannot be an abstract rest. On the contrary, it can only be the rest, the uninterrupted continuity, the unchangeableness, the 'immutability', that belongs to the living God" (493). Cf. C. Hartshorne, *The Divine Relativity*, op. cit.; Walter Stokes, "A Whiteheadian Reflection on God's Relation to the World" in *Process Theology*, ed. Ewert H. Cousin (New York: Newman, 1971), 137ff.

30   K. Kitamori, *Theology of the Pain of God* (Richmond, VA: 1965); J. Moltmann, *The Crucified God* (London: SCM, 1974); McLelland, *God the Anonymous*, op. cit., "Classical Theism and the Crucified God," 157ff.

31   Cf. F. Rosenzweig, *The Star of Redemption* (New York: Holt, Rinehart and Winston, 1971, ET of 1921 edition); E. Rosenstock-Huessy, *Judaism Despite Christianity* (University of Alabama, 1972); H. Stahmer, *Speak That I May See Thee* (New York: Macmillan, 1968); A. Heschel, *God in Search of Man: a Philosophy of Judaism* (New York: Harper Torchbooks, 1955); M. Buber, *I and Thou, Between Man and Man, The Prophetic Faith*, etc.

32   R. Rorty, *Philosophy and the Mirror of Nature* (Princeton U.P., 1979), 13; cf. Ch. 8, "Philosophy without Mirrors"; *Consequences of Pragmatism* (Minneapolis: University of Minnesota, 1980), 163; T.F. Torrance, *Theological Science* (London: Oxford U.P., 1969), 19ff, 180ff, 278ff; *Theology in Reconciliation* (London: Geoffrey Chapman, 1975), Ch. 6, "The Church in the New Era of Scientific and Cosmological Change," 267ff; *Reality and Evangelical Theology* (Philadelphia: Westminster, 1982), 74ff "Questions about the Phonetic Character of Language." Cf. Tillich, *S.T.* I.122f, "The word as a medium of revelation and the question of the inner word." The image of religious knowing as a kind of seeing itself produced a most significant qualification, opening toward the image of hearing. This "third eye" motif is evident in Western mystical theology (as well as Eastern, particularly Buddhism). Richard of St. Victor, for example, notes four types of *visio*, one being understanding by the "eyes of the heart" and related to revelation in the Apocalypse – that modality of contemplation called *alienatio mentis* or *excessus mentis*: *Classics of Western Spirituality* (New York: Paulist Press, 1979), The Mystical Ark 5.2

33   E.g., E. Fackenheim, *God's Presence in History* (New York: New York U.P., 1970), 8ff "Root Experience," 67ff "The Commanding Voice of Auschwitz"; *Encounters Between Judaism and Modern Philosophy* (New York: Basic Books, 1973), 83ff "Abraham and the Kantians" – "While orthodox thinkers argued that the morality of Judaism is revealed but heteronomous, their liberal colleagues have often acted as though it were autonomous but not revealed" (44), and 45ff on "The pristine commanding presence in Judaism." He refers in *God's Presence*, 12f to Buber's *Moses* (New York: Harper, 1958, 75-77) as touchstone for this work: "The real miracle means that in the astonishing experience of the event" cause and effect become transparent.

34   *K.D.* 1.2 (1938), 17.2, "Religion als Unglaube," 324-56, ET by G.T. Thomson and H. Knight (Edinburgh: 1956), 297-325. Cf. E. Fackenheim on "Protestant Concepts of Idolatry," 179ff of *Encounters*, op.

cit., Ch. 4 "Idolatry as a Modern Possibility," 173ff. Barth was influenced by Franz Overbeck's *Christentum und Kultur* (1919) and its thesis that Christianity "has no desire to be a religion" – see Barth's 1920 essay "Unsettled Questions for Theology Today" in *Theology and Church* (New York: Harper and Row, 1962).

35   Ibid., 321. Barth's position is reduced to undialectical argument by W. Pannenberg when he considers Barth's rejection of "natural theology" to be an assumption of Feuerbach's atheism: "Barth's theology assumes the atheism of Feuerbach in the same way as scholastic and orthodox Protestant theology was based upon a natural knowledge of God and a natural theology," op. cit., vol. 3, 100; from "Speaking about God in the Face of Atheist Criticism." Paul Tillich agrees with Barth on this point, that abstract mysticism is essentially negation – cf. *S.T.* II, 87; "The Political Meaning of Utopia," J.L. Adams, ed., *Political Expectation* (New York: Harper and Row, 1971), 75.

36   "Atheismus – pro und contra" in *Zürcher Woche* XV, 24 (1963), ET in Martin Rumscheidt, ed., *Karl Barth: Fragments Grave and Gay* (London: Fontana, 1971), 32ff.

37   Karl Barth, *The Christian Life*: *Church Dogmatics* IV.4, Lecture Fragments, ET G.W. Bromiley (Grand Rapids, Mich: Eerdmans, 1981). The following material is based on "The Gracious God as the Commanding God," esp. 24ff, and more particularly 77.2, "The Known and Unknown God," 115ff.

38   See Steven G. Smith, *The Argument to the Other – Reason Beyond Reason in the thought of Karl Barth and Emmanuel Levinas* (Chico, CA: Scholars Press (AAR) 1983), 80ff, 165ff. A good summary is found in the 1963 article "La Trace de l'autre" in *En Découvrant l'Existence Avec Husserl et Heidegger* (Paris: Vrin, 1982), 187ff. "La philosophie occidentale coïncide avec le dévoilement de l'Autre où l'Autre, en se manifestant comme être, perd son altérité. . . . elle devient philosophie de l'immanence et de l'autonomie, ou athéisme" (188). Derrida, "Differance," op. cit., 152f.

39   H. Merleau-Ponty, *Sens et non-sens* (Paris: Nagel, 1948), 330f, "L'Heros, l'Homme." J. Brun, *Le Retour de Dionysos* (Paris: Les Bergers et Les Mages, 1976), e.g., p. 11 on "le messianisme prométhéen" seeking to eliminate transcendence; after this, Dionysos will lead the new search for ludic meaning.

40   R. Heilbroner, *An Inquiry into the Human Prospect* (New York: Norton, 1974), 142.

41   H. de Lubac, "L'Homme Nouveau," *Affrontements mystiques* Ed. du témoignage Chrétien (Paris: 1950); W. Lynch, *Christ and Prometheus*, op. cit. Cf. John E. Smith, *Religion and Empiricism* (Milwaukee: Marquette U.P., 1967), 65ff: "Zeus, though chief among the gods, is subject to the power of Necessity or Destiny. Beyond Zeus there is a more ultimate reality."

Index

SR SUPPLEMENTS

Note: Nos. 1, 3, 4, 5, 7, 8, 10, and 15 in this series are out of print.

EDITIONS SR

Note: No. 3 in this series is out of print.

8. *Of God and Maxim Guns: Presbyterianism in Nigeria, 1846-1966*
   Geoffrey Johnston
   1988 / iv + 322 pp.
9. *A Victorian Missionary and Canadian Indian Policy:*
   Cultural Synthesis vs Cultural Replacement
   David A. Nock
   1988 / x + 194 pp.
10. *Prometheus Rebound: The Irony of Atheism*
    Joseph C. McLelland
    1988 / xvi + 366 pp.

STUDIES IN CHRISTIANITY AND JUDAISM / ETUDES SUR LE CHRISTIANISME ET LE JUDAISME

1. *A Study in Anti-Gnostic Polemics: Irenaeus, Hippolytus, and Epiphanius*
   Gérard Vallée
   1981 / xii + 114 pp.
2. *Anti-Judaism in Early Christianity*
   Vol. 1, *Paul and the Gospels*
   Edited by Peter Richardson with David Granskou
   1986 / x + 232 pp.
   Vol. 2, *Separation and Polemic*
   Edited by Stephen G. Wilson
   1986 / xii + 185 pp.
3. *Society, the Sacred, and Scripture in Ancient Judaism:*
   A Sociology of Knowledge
   Jack N. Lightstone
   1988 / xiv + 126 pp.

THE STUDY OF RELIGION IN CANADA / SCIENCES RELIGIEUSES AU CANADA

1. *Religious Studies in Alberta: A State-of-the-Art Review*
   Ronald W. Neufeldt
   1983 / xiv + 145 pp.
2. *Les sciences religieuses au Québec depuis 1972*
   Louis Rousseau et Michel Despland
   1988 / 158 p.

COMPARATIVE ETHICS SERIES / COLLECTION D'ETHIQUE COMPAREE

1. *Muslim Ethics and Modernity: A Comparative Study of the Ethical Thought*
   of Sayyid Ahmad Khan and Mawlana Mawdudi
   Sheila McDonough
   1984 / x + 130 pp.
2. *Methodist Education in Peru: Social Gospel, Politics, and American*
   Ideological and Economic Penetration, 1888-1930
   Rosa del Carmen Bruno-Jofré
   1988 / xiv + 223 pp.

Available from / en vente chez:

Wilfrid Laurier University Press
Wilfrid Laurier University
Waterloo, Ontario, Canada   N2L 3C5

Published for the
Canadian Corporation for Studies in Religion/
Corporation Canadienne des Sciences Religieuses
by Wilfrid Laurier University Press